# of Children
An Introduction to
Child Development

of Children
An Introduction to Child Development

Guy R. Lefrancois

University of Alberta

Wadsworth Publishing Company, Inc.
Belmont, California

Designer: Russ Leong

Production Editor: Adrienne Harris

Technical Illustrator: Mark Schroeder

Cover and Interior Cartoons: Tony Hall

ISBN-0-534-00286-2

L. C. Cat. Card No. 72-90581

Printed in the United States of America

2 3 4 5 6 7 8 9 10—77 76 75 74 73

This book has been printed on recycled paper.

Edmonton, Alberta

Dear Reader,

The most important step for an author to take after selecting his topic and before punching the first key on his typewriter is to envision his audience. Since this book was written with you in mind, it's only fair that I let you in on my notions of who you are. I imagine you as a bright and enthusiastic student in psychology, education, nursing, household sciences, or engineering; as a counselor—in training or in practice; as a parent—also in training or in practice; as an interested human; or as a combination of any of the above. The important thing for me to remember while writing this book was that because you are bright and enthusiastic, I should write something other than a compilation of deadly research findings that would clutter your mind with trivia. Also, I tried to remember that I should not give you many things to forget without also giving you something to learn.

I needn't tell you that this book deals with children—how and why they become adults, and what they are like as they change from what they are into something closer to what we are—the title does that. I will simply warn you not to be surprised when, in plowing through the pages of this book, you stumble over a couple of mad psychologists, a worm-racing spinster, Kongor (my friend from Koros), an occasional baboon, one cowboy, a pregnant bitch, and several other nonpsychological things. These deviations from the norm provided me with relief from what could otherwise have been an overly arid and pompous task, and they made my task of writing very enjoyable. I hope they do the same for your reading.

Children don't fit neatly between the covers of a single book. I have therefore been compelled to analyze them and eventually dissect them into the fourteen chapters that comprise the text. The first seven chapters present background information in basic psychological topics: the relative influence of heredity and environment; the role of culture, peer groups, mass media, and schools in development; learning; motivation; and theoretical descriptions and explanations of development—especially those offered by Freud, Piaget, and observational learning theorists. The last seven chapters deal more specifically with the child, beginning with conception and progressing in detail through prenatal development, birth, infancy, childhood, and adolescence. At each stage, the child's social, emotional, physical, and intellectual development is considered along with relevant research in each area.

To aid your study, each chapter is preceded by a one-page outline and terminated with an overview and a main point summary. The outlines indicate where you will go; the summaries are evidence of where you have been. The glossary at the end of the book should be useful for reviewing the entire text; the language employed throughout, English, should also be useful. If you can't read it, you can always look at the pictures.

I hope you enjoy the book and learn about children from it; I suspect that each is necessary for the other.

Yours,

P.S. Sam just tapped me on the shoulder. He says "hi."

Acknowledgments

Among the many people who have directly or indirectly contributed to this book, there is one to whom I owe more than any other—Sam, my untenured and disillusioned friend who continues his lonely vigil in the abandoned coal seams under the very heart of this city. In addition, Richard Greenberg, editor, helped shape the manuscript into something much better than it would otherwise have been. Victoria Pasternack and Adrienne Harris, copy and production editors, worked long and effectively in that same direction. Several reviewers were particularly helpful: Gerald P. Benson, Colorado State University; Carol Millsom, New York University; Donald L. Peters, Pennsylvania State University; and Thomas J. Ryan, Carleton University. Several artists have also contributed their talents: Russ Leong designed the book; Tony Hall created the cover and interior cartoons, and Mark Schroeder provided the technical drawings. A legion of secretaries willingly and expertly devoted many hours to translating the original draft into something that editors and reviewers would and could read: Diane, Gloria, Joan, Judie, Linda, Pat, and Terri. Probably most important of all, Marie provided encouragement, advice, mothering, and loving. To all these people, my very sincere thanks.

CONTENTS

This book is affectionately dedicated to Laurier and Claire, beautiful children, and to all things beautiful.

Part One: The Beginning

The Beginning

In the beginning the earth revolved unconsciously around a cold and distant sun, encased in a solid sheath of ice and frozen snow. No birds and no animals lived upon her for she was a frigid and useless sphere, as incapable of supporting life as of creating it.

Through the long dark void of unmeasured ages this slowly spinning orb moved unceasingly and unerringly along a predetermined path around its sun. Time passed. Days passed as the earth turned upon its axis in a futile effort to be warmed; years passed as the slowly spinning planet completed each new journey about the sun. Years melted into decades, decades into centuries. And the centuries amassed, were sorted and perhaps counted by he who watched the movements of meaningless worlds, the great timekeeper. Perhaps he noticed in passing this galactic system, the sun, and a particular frozen sphere revolving about it, spinning all the while. And he might have stopped and smiled for a brief moment before moving on to other matters, much as you or I might notice small things without realizing their urgency: a young bird in its nest shrieking desperately for the food which it needs to live its brief allotted time; a colony of ants busily pursuing their affairs, trying to maintain a precarious order in an unpredictable world.

Time passed in slowly ascending spirals, in rising planes of decades, in pyramids of centuries. The great timekeeper played geometric games with patterns of time, while the sun's fires slowly warmed the void. And with the mounting efforts of countless millennia the icy case which had bound the earth began to crack. The first crack was a long, wavering line, running east and west at her center for several hundred miles. Finally, a dent was made in the icy armor; it looked as though the earth might eventually burst free like a ripened seed. The timekeeper watched for a moment and saw the earth tilt, exposing a new surface to the sun. Slowly, inexorably, the icy girdle closed and held the earth once more. And the timekeeper moved on.

Perhaps it was ten years later, a hundred, or a million. Eventually the old wound in the ice reopened and in the ever warming rays of sun, increased in length until it completely encircled the globe. Tiny fissures and crevices rapidly appeared along the edges of the big crack, running north and south and reaching closer to the poles with every passing decade. True, there were occasional setbacks, when the icy fingers which stretched from either pole threatened to close and bind the earth once more in their icy grasp. The timekeeper gathered his friends and watched the fierce struggle through several million years until he knew the earth and sun had paired to win.

Yet the earth held no life. Although the melting ice had left water, and although the sun beat relentlessly upon the land, there was no seed—or perhaps there was. Whether the seed was there, frozen for longer than even the great timekeeper knew, or whether the timekeeper himself dropped a small germ in a moment of whimsy, no one knows. The truth is lost in the impenetrable caverns of time past, but the fact remains that there was a seed.

The seed was probably a one-celled body, then two one-celled bodies, then four, then eight, and then perhaps one died, or all died. Then, another seed thawed, or the timekeeper himself dropped another seed and watched again for another million years while the earth cooled, warmed again, cooled again and again warmed; he watched as the source of life struggled through great changes and survived; he watched as the continents heaved and tossed in the restless waters of uncertain oceans, as the earth split and cracked from great painful internal pressures and formed mountains and volcanoes which lived their lives and lost them again to a changing world. As the drama became more interesting and more complex, the timekeeper again gathered his friends. Together they observed the million mutations and evolutionary changes which created the earliest fishes and plants and they were there when the first of man's immediate forerunners reared his head above the ocean, looked at the land, and decided that he wanted to live there. This pathetic creature crawled among the ferns in the swampy jungles of an ancient ocean coast and promptly died.

But other creatures followed, and some lived, reproduced, adapted, mutated, and died; then tried again, lived, changed once more, adapted, or died. It was always a struggle for survival, and the battle always went to the strongest, the fastest, the fiercest, and the most cunning. Meanwhile, the centuries continued to build in ceaseless, restless geometric forms until they stood side by side in patterns of millions, and the life forms became more complicated, more differentiated, and better adapted. The animals and the fish ate, drank, slept, fought, and procreated. Some died, some survived, and new ones were born. They established their territories and their patterns of living. And one day the great timekeeper saw one of the earliest proto-apes, perhaps of the species Pliopithecus, *pause as he sat in the branches of a large tree munching on a piece of fruit. The timekeeper's attention was drawn to this creature, because he did not pause merely to rest or to look for enemies; he seemed to have paused in order to amuse himself. He placed the fruit on the edge of a limb, watched as it began to roll off, and caught it as it dropped. He repeated this activity over and over again, and the timekeeper summoned his friends. Together they watched the clever animal become so engrossed in his game that he fell easy prey to a prowling cat. Other proto-apes, and eventually numerous primitive gibbonlike creatures, began to play games. Perhaps it was partly for this reason that they sorted themselves into tribes where more than one could play while others watched for enemies, and still others gathered food.*

The crystal shapes of million-year patterns continued to accumulate until 25 stood edge to edge: 25 million years between the first of the proto-apes and the appearance of a creature so intelligent that he would eventually be able to wonder at his own intelligence. Homo sapiens, *the self-named* wise man, *had made his humble appearance.*

Early man was a crude, unskilled, ignorant, and foul-smelling creature. With considerable amusement the great timekeeper watched his fumbling attempts to adapt to his environment. And as the timekeeper watched, he noticed the general progression of human adaptation. He *observed that during the early period man's survival depended on his ability to amplify his motor capabilities:* he discovered how to propel missiles and eventually to invent tools and machines. As years passed he amplified his sensory capacities by inventing microscopes, telescopes, telephones, television, and countless other instruments to aid his limited sense perception. And now man has become interested in amplifying his intellectual abilities, which he attempts through the use of computers, through a scientific study of himself which he calls* psychology, *and through the invention of such powerful aids to thought as theoretical systems, languages, and other symbolic means of representing the world. He continues to invent and discover better, easier, and faster ways of adapting to his environment. And as a result of his ingenuity, man is now in imminent danger of destroying both his environment and himself through various rather final ways.*

The Question

The earth continues its endless journey about the sun, spinning slowly and wobbling slightly as it goes. But it is no longer the ice-encased, frozen, lifeless sphere that the timekeeper first observed eons ago. Now more than 3 billion humans wander over its surface like tiny ants, many struggling desperately to survive—others struggling not so desperately. Time is no longer measured in crystal shapes of a million years, or even in pyramids of one hundred years. Now small round dots of seconds roll from a million mechanical timepieces into groups of 60, and turn into hours. Hours curl into days, days into weeks, weeks into months, and months slide slowly into years. We are all timekeepers, and time is precious.

Unlike the great timekeeper whose game it was to watch the epic panorama of **phylogenetic development**† through the eons of change which were its preface, we watch a smaller drama—one with a shorter preface and an end about which we know little. This text is a record of that small action, a play which deals with the human child. The story begins at **conception** and ends at death. It asks one primary question: *What forms a child into an adult?*

The Answer

It might appear presumptuous to attempt to answer *The Question* in this brief section since this entire **text** is devoted to answering the very same question. Indeed it is probably presumptuous to attempt to answer the question at all, since most psychologists readily admit that no one knows with complete certainty what it is that makes a child into an adult. This is not to say that we know nothing; rather it is an admission that much of our information is speculative and incomplete. Nevertheless,

---

* This idea is credited to an article by Jerome Bruner, *The Course of Cognitive Growth* (1964).

† Boldface terms are defined in the glossary at the end of this text.

a brief answer is available. It is a relatively simple answer; its explanation, however, requires the remainder of this text.

Here is the beginning of an answer: whatever a **child** becomes is a combined function of his **genetic endowment** and of his experiences as he develops. Obviously, there are several crucial questions whose answers are not evident from this statement. For example, to say that **heredity** and **environment** determine development fails to explain what the relative contribution of each is, or how the effects of each are manifested in the behavior of a growing child. Chapters 2 through 7 describe what is known about the relative contributions of heredity and environment, and include discussions of motivation and learning; the following chapters provide some theoretical explanations of development and descriptions of developing children.

The Discipline   The discipline which concerns itself with the growing child, his heredity and environment, is **psychology**, or more specifically **developmental psychology**. Whereas psychology is a general term referring to the science that studies the behavior of man (and lower organisms as well), developmental psychology is concerned with those aspects of human behavior that change from childhood to adulthood, and with the processes that account for these changes.

To develop is to grow, to mature, and to learn. Each of these terms is defined below.

Growth ordinarily refers to physical changes, which are primarily quantitative since they involve *addition* rather than transformation. Such changes as increasing height or enlargement of the nose are clear examples of growth.

Maturation is a more nebulous term which is employed most often to describe changes that are relatively independent of the child's environment. These changes are frequently attributed to genetic predispositions. In virtually all aspects of human development, however, there is an interaction between maturation and learning. Learning to walk, for example, requires not only that the child's physical strength and muscular coordination be sufficiently developed, but also that he have the opportunity to practice the various skills involved.

Learning is defined as the result of experience rather than as a maturational process. All changes in behavior resulting from experience are examples of learning, provided these changes are not simply the temporary effects of drugs or fatigue (Walker, 1968).

Development, then, is the total process whereby an individual adapts to his environment. Obviously, since growth, maturation, and learning are processes that account for adaptive changes, they are all aspects of development. The central difference between learning and development is simply that the former is concerned with immediate, short-term adaptation, whereas the latter refers to gradual adaptation over a period of years (Lefrancois, 1972a). Learning theorists have traditionally been concerned with discovering the underlying principles of learning. Seldom have they been concerned particularly with describing differences between the learning processes of children and adults. Developmental theorists, on the other hand, have been largely preoccupied with child-adult differences in learning and behavior, and with how a child's learning processes develop as he matures. Developmental psychology, then, has as its subject the human child from conception to adolescence. It undertakes two essential tasks: (1) observation of the child and his progress in adapting to his world; and (2) formulation of an explanation of that adaptation.

Although creating children is a very ancient art, the scientific study of children is relatively recent. Indeed, for many years such phylogenetically inferior animals as dogs and horses were much more likely to be the subjects of detailed observation than were children. And early "teaching" books usually dealt with animal training rather than with child rearing. One probable reason for this lack of information is that dogs and other animals are considered simpler to understand than children. A second reason for the long neglect of child study is rooted in the naïve but appealing notion that children and adults are identical, that children are, in effect, miniature adults who differ from normal adults only quantitatively. Perhaps a third reason why the child has just recently become a subject for psychological investigation is his place in the affection of adults. For those imbued with the **culture** and **values** of contemporary affluent Western societies, it is difficult to imagine a time and place when children were neither loved nor wanted by their parents, or when they were wanted but not because they were loved. And yet that time is not long past.

In the crowded and diseased slums of eighteenth-century European cities, thousands of parents, ignorant of all but the most difficult birth-control practice, bore children whom they promptly abandoned in the streets or on the doorsteps of churches and orphanages. Foundling homes sprang up all over Europe in an almost futile attempt to care for these children, the majority of whom died in infancy. Kessen (1965, p. 8) reports that of 10,272 infants who were admitted to one foundling home in Dublin in the last quarter of the eighteenth century, only 45 survived. Indeed, until the turn of that century, even if a child were not abandoned his chances of surviving till the age of 5 were less than one in two (Kessen, 1965, p. 8). In the face of this tragic mortality rate, it is small wonder that parents were reluctant to become **emotionally** attached to their children — so reluctant that they could quite callously leave them on an open door-step, probably to die if they were not rescued before long, though probably to die in any case. The high mortality rate of abandoned children was not restricted solely to eighteenth-century Europe, but was characteristic of nineteenth-century America as well. Bakwin (1949) cites evidence which indicates that with few exceptions children in infant homes (asylums) in the United States prior to 1915 almost invariably died before the age of two. This well-documented inability of infants to survive in children's homes or in hospitals was labeled **hospitalism,** and was identified by symptoms of listlessness, inability to gain weight, unresponsiveness to stimuli, pallor, and eventual death. The cause of death

The History of
Child Development

may well have been the lack of **love** between parent and child (Bowlby, 1940; 1953; see Chapter 9).

The nineteenth century appeared to herald some improvement in the status of children in Europe, for the incidence of abandonments decreased drastically. Unfortunately this proved not to be an index of increasing love and concern for children, but only of their economic value. In nineteenth-century Europe children became highly prized, not as objects of love, but as useful chattel. In thousands of factories and mines throughout Europe child labor flourished. The Seventh Earl of Shaftesbury described in moving detail the plight of children as young as 5 or 6 years, male or female, who worked 10 hours a day or more at grueling labor in conditions so hazardous that many became ill and died (Kessen, 1965).

It is difficult to imagine that age from our present perspective, child centered as we are. Yet, the shocking pictures of starvation we see on our television sets feature many more children than adults, because there are more children than adults starving. It appears that unless man's very basic physiological needs are satisfied, he cannot concern himself with such higher level tendencies as parental love and **humanitarianism** (Maslow, 1954). But medicine and law have saved the child, not only from death, but also from abandonment and excessive abuse, usually. Now, in the wisdom and kindness of a wealthier age, children can be loved and studied, for they are less often an economic burden or an economic necessity. Indeed there appears to be little reason to have them except to love them (Johnson and Medinnus, 1969).

Child psychology as a science began with the first reported systematic observations of children made by such men as Preyer (Dennis, 1949), Darwin (1877), and G. Stanley Hall (1891). Whereas both Darwin and Preyer had simply written **subjective** accounts of the early development of their own children, Hall pioneered the use of the objective questionnaire as a tool for studying the child. Interestingly, the questionnaires were presented to parents and teachers rather than to children. Typically they asked adults to try to remember what they felt and thought when they were children. Among other significant figures in the early development of this science was Alfred Binet, who devised the first practical intelligence scale for children (Binet and Simon, 1905), a scale which has survived through numerous revisions and which remains one of the most highly respected individual intelligence tests in current use (Terman and Merrill, 1960). John B. Watson is also acknowledged as an early pioneer in the study of children because of his introduction of experimental approaches to child study and his documentation of the emotional development of young children (see Chapter 4). More than anyone else, Freud is responsible for drawing the attention of both parents and professionals to the importance of the early years of a child's life.

Methods of Studying Children

It is unfortunate but true that when humans have reached the point where they would presumably be able to make sense of the thoughts and emotions of infants, they can no longer remember what it is like to be an infant. It is equally unfortunate that very young children cannot speak. All that we know of the private life of a preverbal child is based on inferences which relate to his behavior or to the absence thereof.

The child's behavior, however, is not always the **overt** variety which grandmothers have become accustomed to interpreting as behavior, but is frequently very subtle and almost imperceptible. One such behavior has played a significant role in the development of experimental child psychology. It is labeled the **orientation reaction** and refers to the tendency of humans and lower animal forms to respond to all novel stimulation in a similar "orienting" manner. The orienting response in such animals as dogs and cats is highly evident: upon hearing a new sound, for example, a dog will pause, his ears may perk up and turn slightly toward the sound, and other aspects of his attitude may communicate to an observer that he is attending. The human infant will not respond in identical fashion, since the control that humans have over the external parts of their **ears** is rather limited and unimpressive in most cases. But other distinct and measurable changes will take place, and these in combination define the human orientation response. Components of this reaction include changes in pupil size, **cardiac** acceleration or deceleration, changes in the conductivity of the skin to electricity (galvanic skin response, or GSR), and various other physiological changes that are observable only through the mediation of sensitive instruments. The value of the orientation response to the child psychologist is that it can be used as an indication of attention, since by definition it occurs only in response to novel stimulation to which the individual is then attending. In the same way its disappearance can be employed as an index of learning since once the stimulus is no longer novel (has been learned), the individual will cease to orient. Reese and Lipsitt (1970) describe numerous recent investigations of the orientation response in infants.

Contemporary psychologists, many of whom pride themselves on being impeccably **objective**, have developed a number of methods for studying children. All of these methods involve observation either of the overt physical behavior of children, or of their verbal responses. Child observers may focus on natural events, such as children playing on a playground, or they may collect observational data on less naturally occurring events, such as a child being interviewed, or they may collect experimental observations.*

In an **experiment**, the observer manipulates some aspects of a situation in order to study the effect of an **independent variable** on another variable which is termed **dependent**. A **variable** may be a measurement, an outcome, or some way of classifying people or events. For example, an investigator who is interested in the relationship between social class and verbal ability might simply compare the scores on a test of language skills of two groups of children, one from a low socioeconomic background and

Experimental Methods

---

* A number of other classifications of ways to study children are also available, most of them more complex and more complete than this list.

one from a higher socioeconomic level. In this experiment social class is an independent variable, and the test score is a dependent variable.

Other experimental procedures involve the use of **experimental groups** and **control groups**. The former is ordinarily composed of subjects who are treated in some special way. The object of the experiment is, in this case, to discover whether the treatment (independent variable) affects some outcome (dependent variable). In order to ensure that any changes in the dependent variable are due to the treatment, it is necessary to employ a second group, the control or "no-treatment" group, which is identical to the experimental group in all possible relevant ways. The effect of the treatment is then assessed by comparing the results of the experimental group to those of the control group, rather than by comparing scores made by members of the experimental group after treatment to scores made before treatment. This is only one of a large variety of experimental designs (arrangements) which are employed in psychological research (Campbell and Stanley, 1963).

Nonexperimental Methods

Nonexperimental approaches to the study of children are particularly useful when the object is to describe the typical behavior of children and to arrive at some understanding of behavioral differences between children of different ages, and to examine changes that occur in the course of development. Usually it is neither desirable nor possible to intervene experimentally in this type of research.

There are two approaches to a descriptive study of children: the **longitudinal study** and the **cross-sectional** study. A longitudinal study is based on observation of the same subjects over a long period of time, whereas a cross-sectional study is based on the comparison of different subjects of different developmental levels, hence *cross-sectional*. There are two ways, for example, of arriving at some notion about the different rules employed in games played by 2-year-old children and 6-year-old children. One method is to observe a group of 2-year-old children at play, and 4 years later, repeat the same procedure with the same children. This is the longitudinal approach, which, for this purpose, is more time-consuming than necessary. The same results could be obtained by observing several 2- and 6-year-old children at only one point, and comparing them directly. There are occasions, however, when a longitudinal approach is necessary despite the fact that it is time-consuming. If an investigator wishes to discover whether intelligence test scores change with age or whether they remain stable, he could best do this by observing the same child (or children) at different periods in his life. He could not answer the same question by employing a cross-sectional approach.

Methods of Observation

The simplest and most obvious way of observing children is simply to look at them, but the simple and obvious is not always the most accurate or the most scientific. In fact, there appear to be three distinct techniques for observing children (Rosenzweig, 1949): the objective approach, in which the investigator simply notes the child's behavior; the subjective approach, in which the child reports his own ideas about his behavior to the investigator; and the **projective technique**, in which the child is encouraged to respond in his own way when faced with a structured situation or problem, while the investigator interprets the child's response. The well-known Rorschach Ink Blot examination is a projective testing device. The assumption underlying its use is that the subject unconsciously projects his feelings and preoccupations when interpreting the ink blots.

Wright has presented a detailed classification and description of various objective methods of observing children (Table 1.1). His classification is based on six possible experimental methods, which he explains as follows (Wright, 1960):

> Diary description traces developmental changes as these occur at biographically sampled intervals. Specimen description covers intensively and continuously the behavior and situation of the child during more or less extended behavior sequences. Time-sampling records selected aspects of behavior if and as they happen within precisely limited time spans. Event sampling singles out naturally segregated behavioral events of one or another class and records these events as they arise and unfold. Field-unit analysis divides the behavior stream into consecutive units as they occur and describes each unit in turn while the iron is still hot. Trait rating selects dimensions of behavior and bases judgments about them on observations during extended sequences of behavior. Recording techniques and analysis procedures, noted in the table, are made to suit these different sampling plans (pp. 73, 75).

The additional distinction between open and closed methods simply refers to the fact that some of these methods (diary and specimen descriptions) are open to a wide variety of behaviors as they occur, whereas other methods are limited to predetermined time periods or behaviors.

The Book and Its Subject

A word of caution is appropriate at this point. This book deals with the "average" child, with the "normal" processes of conception, **fetal growth**, **birth**, **infancy**, **childhood**, and **adolescence**. It describes the "typical" behavior of this normal child as he develops, and it discusses theoretical explanations of normal patterns of development. *But there is no average child!* He is a convenient invention, a necessary creation if one is to speak coherently of those aspects of human development that are generally characteristic of children. The reader should bear in mind, however, that each child is a unique individual, that each will differ from the "average," and that no one theory will account for all behavior. A human child is incredibly more complex than even the most extensive theoretical description of him. A theory can deal only with the objective details of human behavior, not with its essence.

Main Points

1. The child's development from birth to death (*ontogeny*) may be viewed from the perspective of the evolution of the human species (*phylogeny*). The former is the subject of this book.

Table 1.1 A Digest of Methods in Observational Child Study

| Methods | Sampling Plan | | Recording Technique | Analysis Procedure |
	Continuum Coverage	Material Coverage		
Open				
Diary description	More or less regular day to day intervals	Successive steps in behavioral growth and associated life episodes	Itemization of growth changes and summary narration	Classification and interpretive study
Specimen description	Continuous behavior sequences	"Everything" of ongoing behavior and situation	Detailed sequential narration	Interpretive study or coding, scoring, and statistical analysis
Closed				
Time sampling	Intermittent short and uniform time units	Selected variables of behavior or situation or both	On-the-spot coding or narration or both	Scoring and statistical analysis
Event sampling	Event time spans	Behavioral events of a given class (as arguments)	On-the-spot coding or narration or both	Scoring and statistical analysis
Trait rating	Continuous behavior sequences	Selected dimensions of behavior	Rating based on cumulative direct observation	Scoring and statistical analysis
Field unit analysis	Successive behavior units	Selected variables of behavior or situation or both	On-the-spot coding	Scoring and statistical analysis

From "Observational Child Study" by Herbert F. Wright in *Handbook of Research Methods in Child Development*, edited by Paul A. Mussen. Copyright 1960 by John Wiley and Sons. Inc. Used by permission of John Wiley and Sons. Inc.

2. The question central to this book is, What forms a child into an adult?

3. The answer is heredity and environment.

4. Both the question and the answer are the province of developmental psychology.

5. Development is the total process whereby a child adapts to his environment. It includes the processes defined by maturation and learning.

6. History is replete with evidence of child neglect and abuse. Children have only recently become subjects for psychological study.

7. Methods for studying children may be experimental or may simply involve naturalistic observation. In either case the observations may be objective (made directly by the investigator), subjective (reported by the child), or projective (based on the child's imaginative responses to structured situations).

8. Longitudinal observation involves the study of one or more children at different periods in their lives. Cross-sectional studies employ comparisons of children selected from different developmental periods.

9. The "average" child is a conceptually useful invention. He does not exist.

A moving description of changes in the status of children throughout history is provided by: **Further Readings**

Kessen, William. *The Child.* New York: John Wiley, 1965.

In the following article Bruner compares the development of the child's representation of reality to the evolution of man. He describes an intriguing parallel between the appearance of the child's ways of representing the world and the history of man's inventions.

Bruner, J. S. The course of cognitive growth. *American Psychologist,* 1964, **19,** 1–15.

Wright provides a useful, clear-cut, and detailed discussion of ways of observing children in:

Wright, H. F. Observational child study. In P. H. Mussen (Ed.), *Handbook of research methods in child development.* New York: John Wiley, 1960. Pp. 71–139.

Part Two: Shapers of Development

Of Chickens and Children: Genetics

The tragic tale of Robert Edward Cuttingham—"Chicken," as he came to be known—is not a well-known story; it is told here for the first time. It is not because the story was previously unavailable that it was not related; it is because those responsible deliberately hid the facts for as long as they could. And when the facts did become common knowledge, they were whispered quickly and quietly in the dark. Indeed it is a terrible and tragic story.

I first met Chicken on one of those long, lazy days of early fall. The leaves had already crisped and curled; they lay in shallow carpets among the poplars, or floated slowly down the autumn current of the little river along which I walked. I was a young lad of 11 years. I knew little of the world except what I had seen as I wandered through the lonely valley where I was born. He came shuffling toward me, crouched and bent over, his arms hanging by his sides, and his hands slightly curled backwards. As he approached he twisted his head from side to side, looking at me with a beady, darting glance, and making small clucking noises deep in his throat. When he was about three feet away he stopped, cocked his head to one side, and stared at me with one eye. I stared back, stunned.

"What's your name?" I finally managed to ask. He cocked his head a bit more. I repeated the question. "Cluck," he answered. I realized then that he was the chicken-boy, Robert Edward Cuttingham, the boy whose feebleminded parents had left him too long and too often with the chickens. The rumor was that he always slept in the chicken coop during the long summer and that he retreated indoors only when the nights became so cold that the water froze on the river. They said also that he slept perched on a railing, and that when he awoke in the morning he filled the air with a crowing noise, adding to the cacophony of the other birds. To my knowledge no one had ever seen or heard him do these things, but many claimed to have observed him scurrying around the farmyard, pecking at little pieces of grain scattered on the ground.

The early life of Robert Edward Cuttingham was a source of great amusement for the local wits who gathered at the lake in the evening and ran about flapping their arms and crowing like demented roosters. And it gave parents a useful threat to encourage obedience in their misbehaving children. No child was very anxious to be given to the chickens and become a chicken-boy.

The seriousness of the problem did not come to light until the local school teacher suddenly realized that Robert Edward Cuttingham had reached school age, but had not yet begun school. Eventually the superintendent of schools himself visited the Cuttinghams to advise them of their duty. He discovered (as we all knew) that the parents both were so feebleminded that they readily agreed to whatever he suggested—as a result, he returned to school with Chicken in tow. Chicken was not exactly in tow; he was actually scurrying along behind the dignified superintendent, occasionally stopping to peck at something, and then dashing frantically to catch up, all the while clucking, peeping, and chirping, much like a chick darting about behind its mother.

In time, his teacher discovered that clucks, chirps, peeps, and a peculiar eerie crowing were the extent of Chicken's vocabulary; while he was not afraid of people, he had neither the desire nor the ability to socialize, and he was not likely to learn much in school, particularly since he refused to stay indoors. He had soon learned that there was nothing to eat on the classroom floor.

"Cluck"

Eventually Chicken was taken away, and his parents disappeared into the hills, never to be seen or heard from again. As for Chicken, legend has it that after his capture, he soon languished and died, although no one knows for sure—perhaps he still scurries about the hills, crowing in the eerie space between the cold end of night and sunrise.

Wild Children

Most of us have learned from our grandmothers to assume that we know a great deal about the relative effects of heredity and environment, and indeed, we do know a great deal. It takes little scientific knowledge to realize that the result of **amorous consorting** (a delicate expression for an indelicate activity) between two English Setters will be a number of baby English Setters, and that similar activity between two chihuahuas will *not* result in little English Setters. Nor does it require a person of massive **intelligence** to reason that those animals that are kept out of contact with people will probably be less sociable than those that are raised as house pets. Similarly, it is generally expected that the babies produced by a Chinese couple will be noticeably different from those produced by an African or Anglo-Saxon couple. But these are simply the gross and obvious facts of heredity; the scientific **phenomenon** is frequently more subtle than this.

Accounts of **wild children**, such as the tale of Robert Edward Cuttingham, hold a peculiar kind of fascination for most people. Such stories have appeared widely in popular journals, frequently exaggerated for the sake of sensationalism, and occasionally reported in psychological and anthropological literature as well. Typically the stories are of children who have allegedly been abandoned by their parents and who appear to have been adopted by such wild animals as chickens, wolves, bears, or tigers. When recaptured, the children behave in much the same way as their adoptive parents. Among the better known of these stories is one reported by Singh and Zingg (1942), a story of two children, Amala and Kamala, who reportedly were dug out of a wolf's den. Subsequent attempts to socialize the children and to teach them to speak were unsuccessful. They languished in captivity, continued to growl at people, and preferred uncooked meat. None of the thirty cases of wild children reported by Singh and Zingg (1942) fared better. Some learned to walk and laugh, a few learned to eat vegetables in addition to meat, an even smaller number learned to socialize with other children and with adults, but none learned to speak.

It might appear at first glance that reports of wild children would support the notion that it is a human environment which is conducive to the development of certain abilities and traits that are conspicuously absent in children who have been reared by animals. Not surprisingly, this view has received relatively wide support in psychological literature (Gesell, 1940; Zingg, 1941). In other words, it is widely accepted that these children are **retarded** because they have not had contact with humans during their formative years.

There is also an alternative **hypothesis** that might well be as valid as the first, but that is a contradiction of it. Proponents of this hypothesis maintain that evidence surrounding the reports of feral children is highly circumstantial—that, in fact, there is not a single documented case of a child actually having been raised by a wild animal. The supposed evidence is drawn from reports of children being found with animals, or in animal lairs. The identity of these children usually has been unknown, so that the length of time which they spent in isolation can only be conjectured, and, of course, no one has actually observed them with their alleged adoptive parents. This second hypothesis asserts that, given this flimsy evidence, it is as likely that the so-called wild children were initially **brain** damaged or otherwise retarded, which would explain why they were abandoned by their parents in the first place. Dennis (1941, 1951) asserted strongly that most of the wild children have traits in common with mental defectives and idiots as well as with wild animals, and that they were likely mentally defective to begin with and would have continued to be mentally defective, whether with animals or with men.

Heredity   I have just returned from a short sojourn into the wilderness; it is
a tonic of which I avail myself whenever I can. This time I spent a week
wandering about the rolling hills and around the forbidding muskegs that
cover the isolated domain of the grizzly bear. It was early spring and the
arctic grayling had begun its feverish journey down the little streams to
the lakes and ponds. For a week I spent long days fishing in these streams
or wandering about looking lazily for signs of bears. The transition from
that idyllic world to this prosaic one was indeed abrupt.

But heredity is a prosaic subject only in the most academic sense,
and while this book is an academic book, it need not deal solely with
the frequently arid domains of the academician. Hence, I shall speak not
only of the mechanics of heredity, but also of its marvels and its mysteries.

The Marvel   As I wandered through the spring fresh hills during my lazy hunt, it
occurred to me that all around were the marvels of heredity, for all
around me were the living things which nature fashions so carefully and
yet so abundantly that they appear to have sprung up in haphazard and
indeterminate fashion everywhere; all of nature's products seem to be
precisely patterned according to a blueprint which determines the
smallest detail of the living organism. The marvel of heredity is that
every spruce tree began as a small seed that could not become anything
but a spruce; every willow-bush started as a willow seed; the poplars
came from seeds which fell from parent trees some warm July; and the
little grayling hastens to deposit his seed in fertile waters because of his
insurmountable urge to produce offspring in his likeness. Such activity is
the marvel of heredity, but it is also its mystery, for no one knows precisely how a small germ ordains the characteristics of its progeny.

The Mechanics   The mechanics of heredity are both impressive and little understood.
We know that human life begins with the physical union of the mother's
egg cell (*ovum*) and the father's **sperm cell**. For life to occur, a physical
union between the ovum and the sperm is necessary—and since two
people of opposite sexes are involved, it ordinarily* requires a physical
union between a male and female as well. The mechanics of this union
are not sufficiently academic (nor prosaic enough, I might add) to be
appropriate for a textbook of this nature. They are therefore left to your
imagination.

Enough imagining. A single ovum is produced by a mature and
healthy woman usually once every 28 days (somewhere between the
tenth and the eighteenth day of her menstrual cycle). Some women
occasionally produce two or more eggs, or a single fertilized egg sometimes divides, thus making possible multiple births. A mature and
healthy male produces several billion sperm cells over the period of a
month.

---

* "Ordinarily" since conception is possible with **artificial insemination**, a procedure
which eliminates the need for sexual union.

The ovum is the largest cell in the human body. It is approximately 0.15 millimeter in diameter—about half the size of each period (.) on this page. The sperm cell, on the other hand, is one of the smallest cells in the body, 0.005 millimeter in diameter. What the sperm cell lacks in size is made up by the length of its tail, impressive in terms of its relative length—fully twelve times longer than the main part of the cell to which it is attached (see Figure 2.1). It is this long tail that enables the sperm to swim toward the ovum. Arey (1965) makes the interesting observation that all of the sperm needed to produce the next generation in North America could be contained in an area no larger than the head of a pin.

The egg cell and the sperm cell, as the origins of human life, also carry the determiners of heredity. Each sex cell, whether it be ovum or spermatozoon (sperm cell), initially possesses 23 pairs of **chromosomes,** one member of each pair inherited from the male parent and the other from the female parent. These pairs are separated during the special

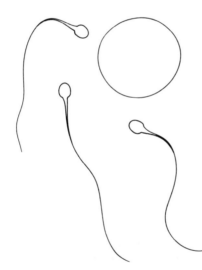

A diagram of three sperm cells surrounding and laying siege to the much less mobile   Figure 2.1
ovum. Note their relative sizes and the long tails on the spermatozoa.

series of cell divisions that give rise to gametes, so that the sperm and egg receive only one member of each pair. The end result is that each sperm and egg contain 23 single chromosomes rather than 23 pairs of chromosomes. These chromosomes are the carriers of heredity.

Of the 23 chromosomes contained in each sperm and each ovum, one is particularly important for determining sex: it has been labeled the **sex chromosome,** since it determines whether the resultant offspring will be male or female. As shown in Figure 2.2, the father produces two types

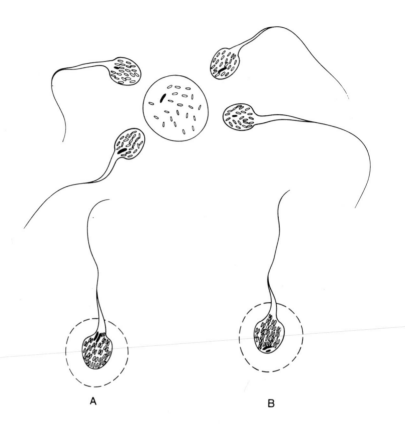

Figure 2.2   The top part of the figure represents four spermatozoa, two with the large (X) sex chromosome, and two with the smaller (Y) sex chromosome. The ovum always contains only the X sex chromosome. In (A) the zygote (fertilized egg) contains an X spermatozoon and will result in a girl. In (B) the zygote contains a Y spermatozoon, and will therefore be a boy.

of sperm, one type with a larger sex chromosome labeled X, and one type with a smaller chromosome labeled Y. If the sperm that fertilizes the ovum contains an X chromosome, the offspring will be a girl; if the sperm cell contains a Y chromosome, the result will be a boy. Since the mother produces only X chromosomes, it is accurate to say that only the father's sperm can determine the **sex** of the offspring (a fact of which Henry VIII was probably ignorant as he beheaded his wives for failing to give him sons). It is interesting to note that the X chromosome which is contributed by the mother to her son is sometimes the carrier of such sex-linked, predominantly male defects and illnesses as color blindness, hereditary baldness, and hemophilia.

The units of heredity carried by the chromosomes are called *genes*; each chromosome carries thousands of genes. Scientists know that since the 23 pairs of chromosomes which comprise the fertilized egg (**zygote**) consist of 23 chromosomes from each of the immediate parents, and since each preceding generation has received a "patchwork" of chromosomes from their parents, the fertilized egg contains mixed subparts of chromo-

It's too bad Henry VIII didn't learn about genetics.

somes from a large number of ancestors. It is also estimated that each sex cell contains between 40,000 and 60,000 genes, each of which is responsible for determining some characteristic of the offspring (Schein-feld, 1956).

If the characteristics of an individual were simply determined by the presence or absence of a corresponding gene, heredity would still be a complex and mysterious process. The concept of heredity is made doubly complex by the fact that a child may acquire different forms of the genes from each of his parents, and that the outcome of this inheritance may be a function of the relative *recessiveness* or *dominance* of these genes (or several genes acting in combination to further complicate the matter). For example, one can greatly oversimplify by stating that there is a gene which is responsible for the length of an individual's legs: a long gene determines long legs, and a short gene determines short legs (in reality, the "length" of genes is irrelevant). For the sake of simplicity let us assume further that the gene for long legs is dominant and that the one that determines short legs is recessive. There are clearly three possibilities: two long genes, two short genes, or one of each. Given two long genes, the individual will have long legs; given two short genes, he will have short legs; and given one of each, he will not have one of each—that is, he will not have one long leg and one short leg. Since the gene for long legs is dominant, the individual will have long legs. (See Figure 2.3 for a less fictitious illustration.)

It was stated at the outset that this discussion of the genetic basis of human characteristics would be an oversimplification, and as it ap-

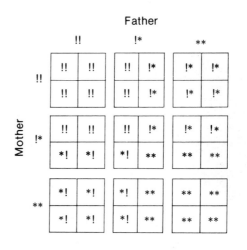

Figure 2.3   **Major gene** rather than **polygenetic inheritance. Huntington's chorea** (!), a disorder involving mental deterioration and eventual death usually after the age of 20, is caused by a dominant gene. Hence only where at least one of the parents suffers from the disorder can the offspring be affected. The matrix illustrates the possible results of matings between parents who are **homozygous** with respect to Huntington's chorea (!!), **heterozygous** with respect to the disorder (!*—these individuals will also suffer from the disease since the gene is dominant), and those who are homozygous with respect to normality (**).

pears here, it is. A more current, complete, accurate, and more complex discussion of the mechanisms of heredity would discuss the function of various combinations of **deoxyribonucleic** acid molecules (DNA) in indeterminate interaction with ribonucleic acid molecules (RNA) (Crick, 1962, 1963; Gall, 1958; Watson, 1963; Watson and Crick, 1953). Among the principal reasons for believing that the DNA molecule is the carrier of hereditary information is the fact that the nucleus of a sex cell is 40 percent DNA molecules, and researchers know that the nucleus of the cell is involved in heredity. DNA is a long, chainlike molecule consisting of different sequences of four chemical subunits. Munsinger (1971, p. 14) indicates that all possible combinations of these four chemical subunits in a chromosome could code for fifty times more information than the *Encyclopaedia Brittanica*. Pikunas (1969) concludes from these studies that differences in heredity probably result "from (1) variations within chromosomes and their genetic structures of DNA, RNA, and other substances, and (2) the almost unlimited combination possibilities in the process of fertilization" (pp. 51–52).

Recent Findings
and Speculation

  The **DNA** that forms the genes is arranged in the shape of a double helix (a double spiral arrangement). These molecules are capable of reproducing and rearranging themselves. It is in the particular arrangement of the four chemical subunits of the DNA molecule that genetic information is coded. It is not yet possible to alter the sequences of subunits with favorable results through artificial means, although the effect of those substances that cause mutations is presumably to alter the arrangement of DNA molecules in the genes.

It appears that most human traits are not transmitted in as simple a manner as in the earlier example of long and short genes. There appear to be relatively few characteristics of human beings that are determined by the presence or absence of a single specific gene. Similarly, there are few traits that are determined simply by the recessiveness or dominance of the genes transmitted from parents to offspring, although such characteristics as eye color in humans, and the presence or absence of wrinkles on peas appear to result from the presence of a single dominant gene, or from the presence of two recessive genes. (See Figure 2.3.) It is probably true, however, that almost all human characteristics determined by heredity are determined polygenetically (the **transmission** of a trait involving the necessary presence of several specific genes, rather than simply the presence of dominant or recessive genes), making it considerably more difficult to investigate the processes of inheritance.

The effects of single pairs of genes is almost negligible for most human qualities. It is not at all clear, however, which pairs of genes in what particular combinations account for the qualitative and quantitative differences that exist among individuals. Studies of human genetics are typically concerned with attempting to discover (1) whether or not (or to what degree) various characteristics may be attributed to the effects of heredity, (2) which characteristics are more likely due to environmental influence, and (3) which traits result from a combination of heredity and environment. Since this approach to the study of genetics is almost necessarily limited to examinations of the behavioral and physical similarities of individuals with greater or lesser degrees of genetic similarity, the term *behavior genetics* has evolved. Most investigations have studied sets of twins for the obvious reason that identical (**monozygotic**) twins are genetically identical, whereas fraternal (**dyzygotic**) twins are no more alike than ordinary **siblings**, except in the similarity of their **intrauterine** and **postnatal** environments. A number of such studies are reported later in this chapter and in the following chapter.

Recent discoveries about the structure of DNA and its relation to human genetics suggest the intriguing possibility that man can, possibly in the near future, engineer the outcome of human conception. It is already possible to identify individuals whose offspring are likely to suffer from certain defects (see, for example, **Huntington's chorea**, Figure 2.3), and, of course, there are simple and effective means of ensuring that these individuals will not have children. Should mentally defective children be sterilized? Should individuals suffering from genetically based functional psychoses (schizophrenia) be sterilized? The answer is a moral and ethical one, rather than purely scientific. More optimistically, it may be possible eventually to detect and perhaps to alter dangerous chromosomal abnormalities by artificial means.

Cloning, the process of reproducing identical individuals from various cells of the body, has now become a fascinating and somewhat frightening possibility, since (barring mutation) all cells in a single individual possess identical genetic messages, excluding mature sex cells. Body cells (somatoplasm or somatic cells), each of which contains the same genetic complement, reproduce by means of *mitosis*: the division of a single "parent" nucleus into two "daughter" nuclei that are genetically identical to each other and to the parent nucleus. The division of the nuclei is usually accompanied by division of the whole cell, so that two complete daughter cells are formed. Growth of all tissues of an organism is accomplished in this manner, except for the sperm and eggs. Sex cells (germ plasm) divide from 23 pairs of chromosomes to 23 single chromosomes by a process called *meiosis*—a special form of mitosis in which the chromosome number is reduced to one half. The products of this division, the sperm and eggs, are not genetically identical to the parent nucleus.

Current genetic speculation admits that it may eventually be possible to induce mitotic division of an individual's cells to produce another individual exactly like him, and if one can produce one identical individual, there is no reason why a scientist (or perhaps a technician) could not produce thousands of identical individuals. There remain a number of unanswered questions, however, not the least of which is how to determine what ordains a particular cell to become part of the brain and not part of the kidney. But this, and other problems may eventually be solved, and cloning may become a reality. Cloning has already been partly accomplished with amphibians, and may be possible with humans by removing the nucleus of an ovum and replacing it with the nucleus of a cell from the individual who is being cloned.

Would it be ethical or desirable to create a million people exactly alike?

The Mystery

But to isolate and localize the carriers of heredity is not to explain them completely. An unexplained and most significant part of heredity, which we shall approach slowly and circumspectly, concerns a very old question: what is the relationship of heredity to environment in determining the characteristics of living organisms? We have no real hope of answering this question, but some hope of clarifying it.

Although we assume that heredity accounts for most of the physical characteristics of human beings, its effect is not necessarily simple and obvious. It is true that such traits as hair or eye color, length of nose, or size of the head appear to be clearly hereditary. While **obesity,** height, complexion, and numerous other physical characteristics may be largely determined by genetic endowment, they are also clearly susceptible to the effects of environment, particularly if the environment does not provide sufficient nourishment for the physical development of the individual. The former is no less true, but not quite so obvious in the case of intellectual or personality development. A somewhat superficial analysis of the relative contributions of nature (genetic endowment) and nurture (learning, environment) might lead to the conclusion that nature determines the possibilities, whereas nurture makes them either probable or improbable.

Literature examining the contributions of heredity and environment to child development is extensive and dates back at least as far as the recognized beginning of psychology as a scientific study. Among the first well-known names in the controversy that still surrounds the hereditary-environment question is Francis Galton, Charles Darwin's cousin, who became concerned that the supply of gifted men in England seemed to be diminishing relative to the number of people who were less gifted. He also noted that most of England's outstanding men were either related to each other or came from a very small number of families (Galton, 1869). Galton theorized that genius is hereditary and became convinced that parents should be carefully selected for favorable genetic characteristics, a practice termed **eugenics**. Johnson and Medinnus (1969) report a number of attempts to select parents to produce a particular type of individual. Among these was the attempt by Frederick the Great to produce tall soldiers to serve as honor guards for Prussia's noble families. He wished to accomplish this by mating the tallest and strongest of his soldiers with robust peasant girls. Unfortunately (or fortunately) it is not always possible to control the activities of tall soldiers and robust, red-cheeked peasant girls. Nor was there any scientific documentation of whatever progeny might have resulted from these relatively uncontrolled activities, so that Frederick the Great actually added very little to our knowledge of human genetics.

A somewhat more successful attempt to employ *eugenics* was undertaken by Alfred Noyes (1937) at Oneida, New York, in a communal-religious society. The community flourished for two generations during which Noyes and other leaders of the group determined which pairs of adults would produce children. The group practiced what they called multiple marriage. Since this practice appeared to be nothing more than "free love" to outsiders, the movement succumbed when the federal government prosecuted Mormon polygamy in the 1880s. Noyes (1937) later claimed that he had succeeded in producing a group of people who were intellectually and physically superior to the normal population, although his evidence is principally unverified opinion.

About the time that Noyes and his followers were attempting to produce a race of genetically superior Americans (see Holbrook, 1957), another group was producing large numbers of apparently intellectually and morally inferior Americans. These notorious families, the Jukes and the Kallikaks, were distinguished by criminal records, immorality, poverty, and a notable lack of intelligence. This family produced more than 2,000 people in 130 years, over half of whom spent time in state institutions for the feebleminded, prisons, and penitentiaries—a fact interpreted by many as further evidence of the inheritability of intelligence, or its lack, and of personality predispositions.

Goddard (1914) studied the Kallikaks and their descendants in some depth. His study is particularly noteworthy for the almost experimental nature of the observations, although the situations occurred spontaneously and were not contrived. The Kallikak family had two main branches, both originating from the same father, but each having strik-

Phenomena due to Heredity—or Environment?

Family Studies

ingly different maternal origins. One branch allegedly stemmed from an illicit affair between a soldier and a feebleminded tavern girl. The other began when the young soldier returned from the war and "married into a good family." The progeny from the first branch were not exactly exemplary citizens; indeed, they were reported to have "excelled only in dereliction and stupidity" (Harlow, McGaugh, and Thompson, 1971); the descendants from the second branch, on the other hand, were normal, reputable people who lived normal reputable lives.

Although these studies of the Jukes and the Kallikaks can be interpreted as evidence that heredity is largely responsible for intelligence, and perhaps even for such remote personality characteristics as criminality and slothfulness, each can also be interpreted as evidence that the environment is the predominant developmental influence. It is likely that the environments of the Jukes and the earlier branch of the Kallikak family were culturally and economically impoverished more than that of the later branch of the Kallikaks—a possibility which might account for their apparent inferiority. In addition, both of these early studies are severely criticized on methodological grounds: no clearly reliable instrument had yet been devised to measure intelligence, making it difficult to ascertain whether there was in fact as marked a difference between the two branches of the Kallikaks as Goddard (1914) believed. Also, descriptions of various members of these families were based on the reports provided by a field worker who frequently relied on accounts provided for him by acquaintances of the Kallikaks, and not the family members themselves. Finally there remains the haunting possibility that Martin Kallikak, the young soldier, was not really the father of the tavern maid's child. Its paternity was established solely on the basis of the mother's testimony—and the mother was supposedly feebleminded.

Animal Studies   While the breeding activities of people cannot easily be controlled or directed for social, practical, and ethical reasons, those of animals can. At least partly for this reason, a large proportion of the evidence gathered in support of the belief that heredity is an important factor in development is based on conclusions derived from studies of animal breeding. Clearly all these studies suffer from the inherent difficulty in comparing humans and animals. Nevertheless, these findings lead to generalizations with important implications for understanding human development.

First, it has been observed that it is possible to breed animals to determine their personality characteristics as well as more obvious physical traits: the animal called a Black Labrador necessarily results from the mating of two parent Black Labradors. Not so obvious, but no less true, the animal which has the temperament of the Black Labrador is not likely to result from the mating of any two parent animals other than two Black Labradors.

Among the best known of the controlled investigations of the inheritance of learning ability in animals is Tryon's (1940) experiment at the University of California. Tryon attempted to produce a strain of bright rats and one of dull rats through a process of selective breeding. He started with a parent generation of 142 rats, half male, and half female, interestingly enough. Each rat was run through a 17-unit maze for a total of 19 trials. Tryon counted the total number of errors made by each rat as it learned to run the maze. The count ranged from 14 errors for the brightest rat to 174 for the dullest. Next he paired the bright rats with each other and mated the dull ones with each other. The progeny from these artificial marital arrangements were then introduced to the same 17-unit maze, and their error scores were tabulated. Now the brightest offspring of the bright rats were mated with each other, while the dullest offspring of the dull rats were paired. The duller rats produced by bright parents (possible even in the best of families) and the brighter rats produced by the dull parents (also possible) were eliminated. This procedure was continued through a total of 18 generations, with the brightest of the bright and the dullest of the dull being paired and all others being sacrificed in the interests of science. The striking result of this experiment was that the dullest rats among the bright group were brighter than the brightest rats from the dull group; conversely, the brightest rats from the dull group were duller than the dullest ones from the bright group. Indeed, after 8 generations there was no longer any overlap between the groups (see Figure 2.4).

The experiment was carefully controlled. The offspring from dull parents were occasionally exchanged with those from bright parents, allowing the mother rats to raise offspring which they themselves had not produced. This was designed to eliminate the possibility that early maternal attention was responsible for the apparent difference in brightness, assuming that brighter female rats would be likely to give their offspring the kind of attention particularly beneficial for stimulating their infants' intellectual growth. In addition, errors were scored electronically to eliminate the biases of the experimenter from the final results.

Searle (1949) later tested the same strains of rats on a variety of other learning tasks and found that the **maze-bright** rats were not necessarily bright for all tasks. Similarly, the **maze-dull** rats were not found to be universally dull. Tryon's earlier conclusions regarding maze-learning differences between the two strains were not invalidated, however. Indeed, his conclusions were reaffirmed by a different experimental procedure 27 years later. A biochemical analysis of the cerebral cortexes of Tryon's two strains of rats performed by Krech and his associates (1954) revealed marked chemical differences in favor of the maze-bright strain. The conclusion that some aspects of learning ability can be inherited, at least in rats, seems fully warranted (Krech, Crutchfield, and Livson, 1969). There is little reason to suppose that the conclusion is not also valid when applied to man.

Since control of matings among humans is not ordinarily feasible, investigators have had to rely on naturally occurring situations to study the effects of nature and nurture. For a number of reasons, twins have provided psychologists with a rich source of information about the effects   **Twin Studies**

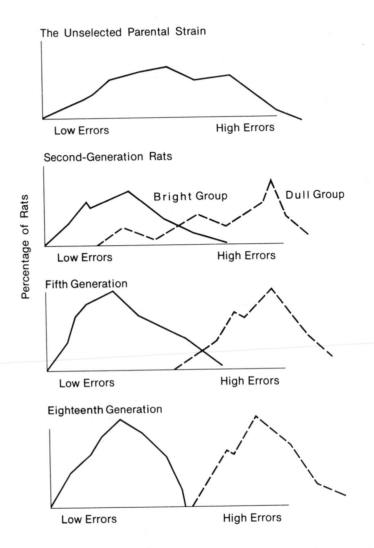

Figure 2.4   An approximate representation of Tryon's successful attempt to produce maze-bright (the solid line) and maze-dull rats (the broken line) through selective breeding. (From *Yearbook of the National Society for the Study of Education.* Copyright, 1940, by Guy Montrose Whipple, Secretary of the Society. Used by permission.)

of environmental and genetic factors on various aspects of development. To begin with, identical twins are the only genetically identical individuals that it is possible for two humans to produce. They are genetically identical since they result from the segmentation of a zygote, a fertilized ovum, which has already obtained its full complement of chromosomes from the sperm and from the ovum. This segmentation results in two fertilized eggs, each with an identical genetic makeup, producing identical (**monozygotic**) twins. The other type of twins, **dyzygotic**, results from the fertilization of two different egg cells by two different spermatozoa. This is possible only when the mother produces more than one egg, and will obviously result in twins who are no more alike genetically than ordinary siblings. In comparing the effects of heredity and environment, however, it is customary to assume that fraternal twins have environments which are probably more similar than those of siblings, if only because they share the same womb at the same time, and because they are of the same age as they develop. Identical twins are likewise assumed to have highly similar environments, at least as similar as those of fraternal twins.

It follows that any greater similarity between identical twins than between fraternal twins will be due to the influence of heredity. By the same token, if fraternal twins are more alike than ordinary siblings it would not be due to their greater genetic similarity, but due to their more nearly identical environments, both prenatally and postnatally. Unfortunately for research, the incidence of twins is relatively low — approximately 1 case in every 86 births. Furthermore, identical twins are much rarer than fraternal twins. The precise causes of twin births are not known, although it appears that there is a hereditary factor since twins are found relatively frequently in some families and not at all in others. In addition, the age of the parents seems to have some bearing on the probability of giving birth to twins: Krech et al. (1969) report that women between the ages of 30 and 38 are more likely to have twins; similarly, regardless of the age of the mother, older fathers are more likely to sire twins than are younger men.

There have been a large number of twin studies conducted: Wingfield, 1928; Newman, Freeman, and Holzinger, 1937; Conrad and Jones, 1940. Hunt (1961) has summarized some of the findings of these studies as follows: the average correlation coefficient of intelligence test scores for identical twins is approximately .90 while that for fraternal twins is .65. If members of identical and fraternal twin pairs have had similar environments, the correlations cited above may be interpreted as evidence that measured intelligence is at least partly determined by heredity. Related to these studies is the observation that with decreasing genetic similarity, there is a corresponding decrease in similarity between intelligence scores. Table 2.1 is a summary of a number of correlations for intelligence test scores (based on data provided by Hunt, 1961, p. 18). Not surprisingly, the lowest correlation (.00) obtains with respect to genetically unrelated children whereas the highest correspondence (+.90) is found in the case of identical twins. These data clearly support a

Correlations between Intelligence Test Scores for Persons with Varying Degrees of Genetic Similarity | Table 2.1

Identical twins	.90
Fraternal twins	.65
Siblings	.50
Parents and their children	.50
Cousins	.25
Grandparent-grandchild	.15
Unrelated children	.00

genetic explanation. As the astute reader will note, they can also support an environmental position (see Chapter 3).

Twin studies have also compared attributes other than intelligence. For example, Vandenberg (1967) found that a large number of personality traits describable as active, vigorous, impulsive, and sociable are inheritable, whereas more stable and reflective personalities are less so. Perhaps more striking is Gottesman's (1962) finding that various types of neuroses appear to have a genetic basis. Gottesman and Shields (1966) discovered a significantly higher concordance for schizophrenia between members of identical twin pairs than for members of fraternal twin pairs. Specifically, Gottesman and Shields found that of 28 pairs of identical twins, there was 42 percent concordance with respect to schizophrenia. The procedure was to identify members of twin pairs from among a population of schizophrenic patients, and then to determine how many of these individuals had a twin who was also schizophrenic (of all members of twin pairs who were schizophrenic, 42 percent had a schizophrenic twin). The concordance between members of fraternal twin pairs was only 9 percent, from a sample of 34 pairs.

Heredity and Intelligence

The twin studies cited in this chapter support the belief that intelligence has a strong genetic basis. (Chapter 3 shows that the evidence supporting this contention is by no means unequivocal, and that the belief is not nearly universal.) A number of relatively recent reports summarize the data on the inheritance of intelligence. Thompson (1954), in his review of the literature available prior to 1950, concludes that there appears to be a strong hereditary factor involved in intellectual *performance* (on intelligence tests). He is careful to point out, however, that heredity is only one of the factors that determines intellectual functioning. Erlenmeyer and Jarvik (1963) arrived at a similar conclusion on the basis of more than 30,000 correlations which they gleaned from early studies. These studies, with few exceptions, demonstrate an increasing degree of correlation between scores on intelligence tests and the subjects' genetic relatedness.

Among the strongest proponents of the theory that heredity accounts for most of the variation in intelligence test scores is Burt (1966), who believes that heredity and environment interact; but he goes further than most psychologists by stating that the contribution of environment to intelligence is minimal. Recently Jensen (1968, 1969) advanced a similar point of view. **Jensen's hypothesis** is derived from comparisons between the performance of different racial groups on selected measures of intellectual ability. On these measures, the American Negroes tested frequently performed less well than the American whites. And, Oriental groups appeared to perform better than Caucasian groups, a finding which has often been overlooked. Jensen argues that *prenatal* environmental factors are most influential with respect to intelligence, but that racial and social class differences in intelligence test scores cannot be accounted for in terms of environment alone. Thus, some of the observed differences in intelligence are due to genetic factors. It follows from

Jensen's argument that American Negroes may be less well endowed genetically for intellectual potential than American whites.

It should be stressed that Jensen's point of view is simply a hypothesis — he does not advance it categorically as a logical conclusion. Despite this, however, his argument has been interpreted by many as "racist" and has been summarily discarded. Less emotional critics of Jensen's hypothesis have pointed out that none of his evidence is sufficient proof of his theory (see *Harvard Educational Review*, Reprint Series No. 2, 1969). It must be acknowledged, however, that there is as yet no evidence to disprove the hypothesis, either, and that the possibility that different races have different gene pools (ancestral contributions of genes) with respect to intelligence is not altogether improbable.

A relatively widely accepted point of view in this nature-nurture controversy is implicit in the following "rubber-band" hypothesis from Stern (1956):

The Stern Hypothesis

> The genetic endowment in respect to any one trait has been compared to a rubber band and the trait itself to the length which the rubber band assumes when it is stretched by outside forces. Different people initially may have been given different lengths of unstretched endowment, but the natural forces of the environment may have stretched their expression to equal length, or led to differences in attained length sometimes corresponding to their innate differences and at other times in reverse of the relation (p.53).

Certainly only one side of a many-sided question has been given in this chapter. The next chapter examines the environmental side of the nature-nurture question.

This chapter began with a description of Robert Edward Cuttingham — "Chicken," we called him. It was neither implied nor stated that heredity was the sole cause of Chicken's problem, but it was admitted that he did have a problem of some seriousness. Nor did it seem clear that environment was the cause of his problem, although it might have been. The problem remains unsolved. The chapter discussed the mechanics, the marvels, and the mysteries of heredity. Having dispensed with these, the chapter examined some of the phenomena which have been attributed to heredity rather than to environment, with special emphasis on the development of intelligence, not only because it is an interesting and important subject, but also because a great deal of energy and ink have already been devoted to it. We moved from the Jukes and the Kallikaks through countless pairs of twins, normal, dull, intelligent, or schizophrenic, and finally concluded with two strong spokesmen for the belief that heredity is the most important factor in intellectual performance, Burt and Jensen.

Summary

1. Stories of bear-children, chicken-kids, tiger-infants, and wolf-children have frequently been used as evidence that the environment is a potent force in determining the course of development. Opponents of this theory do not

Main Points

necessarily deny the conclusion but question the validity and the significance of the evidence.

2. The manner in which genetic information is coded in a DNA molecule is known, but the precise interaction between heredity and environment remains a mystery.

3. The hereditary basis of life resides in the egg cell (ovum) and in the sperm cell (spermatozoon), each of which contains one half the number of chromosomes found in ordinary human body cells. In the chromosomes are the carriers of heredity, the genes.

4. Two chromosomes of special importance are the sex chromosomes, X and Y. Only the father can produce a Y chromosome, while both mother and father produce X chromosomes. The presence of a Y chromosome in the fertilized egg determines that the offspring will be male; two X chromosomes determine a female.

5. The fertilized egg (zygote) contains thousands of genes which, singly or in combination, have the potential to determine particular characteristics of the individual. The genes may be present in varied forms in the egg and the sperm. A simplified but not inaccurate view of the mechanics of heredity states that it is the recessiveness or dominance of a gene which determines whether the characteristic(s) that it represents will be manifest in the individual.

6. Galton was one of the first proponents of the theory that intelligence is genetically determined. Highly circumstantial evidence in the form of studies of two families, the Jukes and the Kallikaks, has frequently been employed to support this belief.

7. Tryon's study of rats supports the contention that heredity is of primary importance in the development of intellectual capabilities. Through selective breeding he succeeded in producing two strains of rats (maze-bright and maze-dull) which were so different that the dullest rats among the bright group were brighter than the brightest rats among the dull group.

8. Studies of twins have also been invoked as evidence that intelligence as well as physical characteristics, some personality traits, and even mental disorders seem to have a genetic basis. The most striking supportive evidence is that the correlation between intelligence test scores for identical twins is approximately .90, whereas for fraternal twins it is .65.

9. Among current exponents of the view that intelligence has a more significant genetic than environmental basis are Burt and Jensen.

10. The Stern hypothesis presents a summary of the evidence relating to the nature-nurture controversy by stating that genetic endowment is like a rubber band which assumes its final length (the actual performance of an individual) as it interacts with the environment. Implicit in this summary is the notion that it is easier to stretch a long band than one that was short to begin with.

Further Readings   The classical account of a number of reported cases of wild children is found in:

Singh, J. A., and R. N. Zingg. *Wolf-children and feral-man.* New York: Harper, 1942.

The Singh and Zingg book should be followed by Dennis' rebuttals:

Dennis, W. The significance of feral-man. *American Journal of Psychology,* 1941, **54,** 425–432.

Dennis, W. A further analysis of reports of wild children. *Child Development,* 1951, **22,** 153–158.

For a more detailed and complete explanation of human genetics than is provided in this chapter, you are referred to:

Fuller, J. L., and W. R. Thompson. *Behavior genetics.* New York: John Wiley, 1960.

Manosevitz, M., F. Lindzey, and D. D. Thiessen (Eds.). *Behavioral genetics: Method and research.* New York: Appleton-Century-Crofts, 1969.

Moody, P. A. *Genetics of man.* New York: W. W. Norton and Co., 1967.

Schienfeld, A. *Your heredity and environment.* Phila.: Lippincott, 1965.

Those interested in a current and widely cited expression of the controversy between those who believe that intelligence is determined mostly by the environment, and those who believe that it is primarily genetically determined, are referred to the following reprints from the *Harvard Educational Review.* This reprint series includes an article by Arthur Jensen that gave rise to a great deal of popular reaction. In the article Jensen argues that environmental factors are not nearly as important in determining intelligence as are genetic factors. The reprint series includes replies to Jensen's position by Kagan, Hunt, Crow, Bereiter, Elkind, Cronbach, and Brazziel.

Environment, heredity, and intelligence. *Harvard Educational Review,* Reprint Series No. 2, 1969.

The classical account of the study of twins to determine the relative influence of heredity and environment on the development of intelligence and personality is the following book:

Newman, H. H., F. N. Freeman, and K. J. Holzinger. *Twins: A study of heredity and environment.* Chicago: University of Chicago Press, 1937.

A more recent book that deals with the same topic is:

Koch, H. L. *Twins and twin relations.* Chicago: The University of Chicago Press, 1966.

Of Rats and Children: Environment

I am the sole acquaintance of a mad psychologist—not angry, but insane (although both varieties are quite common). His insanity has not affected his work, but has severely limited his social life. He has been engaged in a series of experiments which, while rather bizarre, have led to conclusions that might well cause an intellectual revolution for those sane psychologists who still dabble in the art of thinking.

For reasons that will become clear to you shortly, I shall call my demented colleague Sam. Sam has been living in a long-abandoned coal mine whose tortuous shafts wind their dark and forbidding way deep into the bowels of this city. The entrance to this humble abode is by way of a manhole cover directly behind one of the city's fine hotels. There are several alternate entrances at lower levels, hidden behind the thick brambles of rosebushes and small shrubs which grow along the steep banks of the river that courses through the city. Sam has lived within the coal seams since he was denied tenure at the university where he taught. This rejection occurred 3,356 days ago, according to Sam's reckoning. I just returned from visiting him; I brought him a cake. Although he was overjoyed, I fear that he will probably feed it to his rats.

Sam took his ignominious leave from the university some 9 years ago with a large number of rats of the species rattus norvegicus albinus. *Since then he has been engaged in a lengthy and complex research program, the results of which are of tremendous importance for the substance of the present chapter.* The project may be described as longitudinal research of a most intensive nature.*

You may recall the famous experiment Tryon conducted with rats in the early 1940s. (If not, you are advised to return to the previous chapter and read it with a little more attention.) Tryon succeeded in producing strains of maze-bright and maze-dull rats solely through a process of selective breeding; these rats appeared to be markedly different in their ability to learn how to run through a maze. Sam's achievement is no less brilliant. He too has succeeded in producing maze-bright and maze-dull rats, but his effort required merely one generation. Sam's success shows that environment can be as powerful an influence as genetics in determining brightness in rats. His brightest rat is named Samuel.

It is unfortunate for Sam that his research has been replicated elsewhere by other psychologists who live more public lives. Since others have replicated and published Sam's research, his ideas have lost their original impact. Still, I shall report for him an experiment that replicates what he has repeatedly demonstrated for himself and for me during long years of research. His findings are remarkable, despite his dementia.

The Issue

A cursory examination of the contents of this chapter and the preceding one may make it appear that the central issue is whether environment or heredity is more potent in determining the course of human develop-

---

* Sam's findings are reported here with his permission.

ment. Secondary issues focus on whether specific aspects of human development come under the control of genes or are more influenced by environmental factors. Although this analysis is valid, there is a more basic issue implicit in these discussions — the modifiability of man. Indeed one might say that the **nature-nurture controversy** is not really a controversy at all, but is simply an attempt to answer questions concerning the extent to which human behavior is modifiable. The two hypothetical camps historically aligned on either side of the controversy represent the two extreme responses to the question: that development is entirely genetically ordained and therefore completely unmodifiable (subject to nature), or that development is completely modifiable (nurture). Both answers are clearly untenable. Neither an exclusive belief in the power of genetics nor the conviction that the environment alone determines human development is acceptable.

It should be pointed out that the genetic determination of human traits does not necessarily imply that these tracts are unmodifiable. Indeed, the genetic endowment of an individual may be modified through exposure to mustard gas, cosmic rays, irradiation, and certain drugs (such as thalidomide). Although one could say that these modifications are the effects of environmental influences, they are nonetheless transmitted through physiological rather than through psychological means. They do not fall into the same category as ordinary environmental forces, but are known instead as *mutations*.

A striking example of the environmental modification of a genetically determined characteristic is provided by **phenylketonuria** (PKU). PKU is an easily detectable metabolic defect that is genetically transmitted, and that manifests itself in the body's inability to oxidize the amino acid phenylalanine. The result is severe **mental retardation** appearing in infancy. Fortunately, however, it is now possible to detect the presence of PKU through a routine examination immediately after birth. Fortunately also, the presence of PKU can be controlled through dietary means, permitting the children affected to lead normal lives. Here, then, is a dramatic example of the extent to which the environment (in this case something as simple as the child's diet) can determine the course of development *in spite of* the genetic forces that act in opposition.

The basic issue in this chapter, then, is the extent to which individual characteristics can be modified by the environment — an issue fraught with philosophical questions. To believe that the developmental process is entirely determined by the environment is tantamount to denying a prevalent notion borrowed from the literary humanism of another age. This notion maintains that man is the master of his own destiny, that where there is a will, there is a way. It follows from this belief in free will that no environment, however depraved, can ruin a good man; conversely, no environment, however good, can reform an evil man. The philosophical issue has simply been exposed; it will not be discussed further, but it is yours to think about if you like such activities. However, this chapter is more concerned with describing scientific evidence that illustrates the influence of the environment on the behavior of men.

Among those who have been successful in replicating Sam's experiments are David Krech and his associates (1960; 1962; 1966), who, like Sam, were assisted in their research by the lowly white Norway rat. It might seem strange to make frequent use of rats in an attempt to understand human behavior. However, there are many things that can be done with social impunity to a rat; the same antics with a human child would be wholly unacceptable. In addition, rats lead relatively uncomplicated lives, reproduce very rapidly, and are simple and economical to look after. Children, on the other hand, lead very complex lives, are quite expensive and difficult to look after, and are usually incapable of reproducing. Hence there are both practical and ethical reasons why the rat is sometimes a preferred subject.

Krech and his associates reared groups of rats in either enriched environments or in deprived environments. The environment of a laboratory rat is assumed to be enriched when it contains a wide variety of rat toys, such as marbles, exercise wheels, posts to gnaw on, and when the cage in which he is confined is airy and well lighted. A more deprived environment is produced by lining the rat's cage with tin to obscure his view, keeping it dimly lit, preventing him from associating with humans or other rats, and by keeping all toys out of his cage. It has been demonstrated repeatedly that rats raised in enriched environments are intellectually superior to their less fortunate confrères, at least when intellectual superiority is measured in terms of their ability to learn quickly the pattern of a maze (Hebb, 1949). It has also been discovered (as mentioned earlier) that the chemical composition of the brain of a rat which has been raised in an enriched environment is measurably different from that of a rat reared in a deprived environment (Krech et al., 1966). The difference is marked by an increase in cholinesterase and acetylcholinesterase in the brains of rats from enriched environments. These substances are thought to be involved in the transmission of impulses from one neuron to another, thereby facilitating learning. Even as gross a measure as the brain weights of enriched and deprived rats indicates a significant difference in favor of the rat who has been favored by his environment.

These objective data argue strongly for varied and plentiful environmental stimulation in the early stages of a child's life (a topic treated in more detail in a later chapter). Further they suggest that a rat can be drastically affected by his environment. By extrapolation the same conclusion may be applied to man. Fortunately, the evidence supporting this conclusion is not restricted to studies of the behavior of *rattus norvegicus albinus;* there are studies and naturalistic observations of human children which lead to the same conclusion. However, even in the interests of science it is not considered proper to decapitate children to examine the chemical structure of their brains. Most of the studies of humans have obviously lacked the experimental controls possible when employing rats; they have also lacked the precision of measurement sometimes possible with the **rat**. What studies of human children offer that no rat study can offer is the chance to observe and to measure processes con-

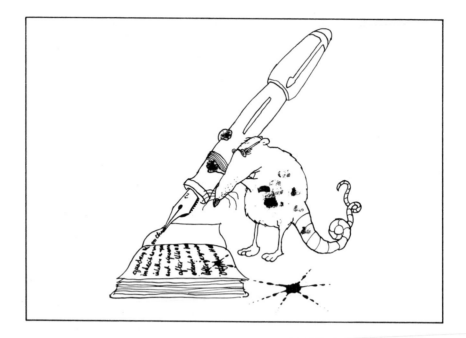

Rats that are raised in enriched environments are intellectually superior to their less fortunate confrères.

sidered to be uniquely human, or at least unavailable to such phylogenetically unfortunate animals as rats.

A number of studies of human children brought up in conditions of varying deprivation, not by experimental design, but as a result of the cruel whims of chance, are described in the following section. These studies measure language learning and such motor abilities as walking and human intelligence. The rat is ordinarily incapable of communicating by means of language, his intelligence is assumed to be quite different from man's, and his ability to walk does not occur at the end of a long period of maturation and/or learning. Hence these findings are uniquely human.

The Children

The Hollow Children

The Krech studies indicate that enriched environments can be beneficial to rats and that impoverished environments can be detrimental to their development. Although it is probably acceptable to assume that the same is true for humans, there is a scarcity of reliable supportive evidence. As noted before, it is not usually possible to deliberately restrict the environmental stimulation of young children to observe what the effect will be on their intellectual development (as well as on the development of personality). Those studies which address the problem are usually the result of natural rather than contrived circumstances, and often lack the necessary experimental controls. For example, children from isolated areas who have not had the same degree or quality of environmental stimulation as their more fortunate counterparts in less isolated regions may also have lacked a normal genetic endowment. It is not altogether unreasonable to assume that frequently those parents who are forced by economic or social conditions to isolate themselves are of inferior intelligence in the first place, and that their children might also be of inferior intelligence regardless of where their parents lived. Thus, it is difficult to determine whether deprivation of environmental stimulation or heredity was responsible for inferior development. A well-known study that provides controls for this possibility is the study of intelligence test scores of isolated mountain children, known as the Hollow Children, reported by Sherman (1933), and by Sherman and Key (1932).

The Hollow Children were so named because they lived in various isolated hollows rimmed by the Blue Ridge Mountains some 100 miles west of Washington, D.C. The Hollows were settled by English and Scotch-Irish immigrants who had been forced to retreat into the mountains when the land on which they lived was granted to German immigrants. There they remained, some more deprived of contact with the external world than others who dwelt closer to civilization. Since the ancestry of each hollow region was the same, we might validly assume that the genetic pool of the area was highly similar.

Four Hollows in the Blue Ridge range were selected by Sherman and Key (1932), each characterized by a different degree of isolation. Colvin, the innermost Hollow, appeared to be the most isolated. During the previous 12 years (from 1918 to 1930) there had been a school in session for a total of 16 months. Only three of the adults who lived there were literate, and physical contact with the outside world was virtually impossible and consequently nonexistent. As the researchers proceeded outward through Needles Hollow, Oakton Hollow, and finally to Rigby Hollow toward civilization, schools were in progress for an increasingly longer period of time. In Rigby Hollow, for example, a school had been open for a total of 66.5 months in the preceding 12 years (see Table 3.1), many of the adults were literate, there was a road which linked the Hollow to the outside, there was a post office which provided residents with literary contact with the world, and many subscribed to magazines or newspapers. A small village, Briarsville, of the same ancestry as the Hollows, but situated at the foot of the Blue Ridge Mountains rather than in the isolation which existed beyond the range, was employed as a control group.

The experimenters administered 386 intelligence tests to the Hollow Children and 198 tests in Briarsville. These tests included different

	Total Time in Months School Was Open in the Hollows From 1918 to 1930	Table 3.1
Colvin	16	
Needles	30	
Rigby	66	
Oakton	66.5	
Briarsville	108	

Table 3.2 Comparisons between Mountain
Children and Contrast Groups
on Some Measure of Intelligence

	Mountain Children	Briarsville Children
National Intelligence Test	61.2	96.1
Pinter Cunningham	75.9	87.6
Year Scale Performance Test	83.9	118.6

measures ranging from the time-consuming but highly reliable Stanford Binet, to the Goodenough Draw-A-Man test, requiring only that the subject draw the "very best" picture he can of a man. Not all tests were given to each child.

Two aspects of this study are of particular importance here. First and not surprisingly, as the experimenters moved from the most isolated to the least isolated of the Hollows, the performance of the children on the various intelligence tests increased markedly (see Table 3.2). Second, a striking relationship was found between the age of the children at the time of testing and their measured intelligence (Figure 3.1): the older the children, the more retarded they became. Indeed, the very young children were not significantly below the test norms, but the 14- and 15-year-old

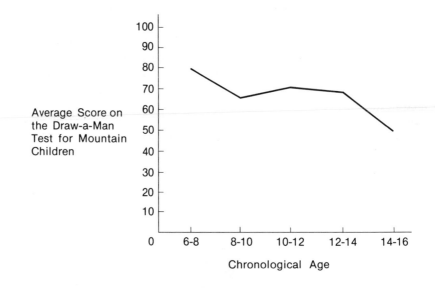

Figure 3.1 One example of increasing retardation with increasing age.

children were markedly disadvantaged. Both of these observations seem to provide additional evidence that the environment is a potent force in determining the intelligence test scores of individuals. This is somewhat different from saying that their intelligence is itself affected since it may simply be their ability to take the tests which is affected. However, given the inexact and uncertain definitions which are current for the term "intelligence," it is accurate to conclude that to the extent that intelligence is "that which intelligence tests measure" (Boring, 1923), the impoverished environment in which these children were raised had a detrimental effect on their intelligence. Sherman and Key (1932) contend that "the only plausible explanation of the increasing difference with increasing age is that children develop only as the environment demands development" (p. 289).

The Sherman and Key (1932) study provides evidence that intellectual performance may be detrimentally affected by the environment. A corollary study which demonstrates the effect of impoverished environments on the motor development of young children was conducted by Dennis (1960). The subjects for his study were very young children who lived in three orphanages in Tehran, the capital of Iran. Two of the orphanages (Institutions I and II) afforded their charges very similar treatment; the third (Institution III) was somewhat different. The principal difference between Institutions I and II is that the latter accepts children after the age of 3, most of whom have spent their first three years in Institution I. Over 90 percent of the children in Institution I were admitted prior to the age of 1 month and remained until they were between 2 and 3 years of age.

Institutionalized Children

Among the most salient features of the children's environment during their first three years in Institution I is the abject poverty. Infants spend almost all of their time lying in their cribs, *on their backs*. They are seldom, if ever, placed prone—a fact believed to have considerable significance in explaining their early motor development. The infants are fed by means of a bottle propped up on a small pillow, while they are lying in their cribs; later, when solid foods are introduced, they are either held for short periods by one of the attendants while being fed, or are fed sitting up in their cribs. During these first years, the child is in his crib continually except when bathed, changed, or occasionally, fed. When he learns to sit up or to pull himself to a standing position, he might be occasionally removed from the crib and placed on a piece of linoleum on the stone floor. The author (Dennis, 1960) reports that in two of the rooms there were benches along one wall. Children who had learned to sit were often placed on these benches, across the front of which was a railing to prevent them from falling. Apart from the cribs and these benches in two of the rooms, none of the rooms had toys or any other children's furniture. The walls were painted white and were devoid of pictures.

The preceding description makes it clear that the amount of human contact for the children in Institution I was minimal. Part of this is due to the extremely high staff–child ratio—one attendant to 8 or more children.

These attendants were responsible not only for feeding the children, but also for bathing and changing them, for changing their beds, and for cleaning the rooms. Conditions in Institution II were similar except that the children were older, since they usually came from the first orphanage to the second. Institution III, established mainly to demonstrate better methods of child care, was characterized by a more normal kind of physical and social environment. The ratio of attendants to children was 1 to 3 or 4; most of the children also came from Institution I, but had been moved to the new orphanage in the early months of their lives. Institution III provided toys and ample opportunity for the children to play. Attendants held the children while feeding them, frequently placed them prone in their cribs, and allowed infants over 4 months old to spend time each day in playpens on the floor.

Dennis' study (1960) of these three institutions primarily involved testing motor development and comparing the results among the different institutions. Table 3.3 summarizes his findings, which clearly demonstrate motor retardation in Institutions I and II. Consider, for example, that in Institution I only 8 percent of the children could walk alone by the age of nearly 3 years, whereas 94 percent of the children of the same age in Institution III could do so. According to Dennis' data, the pattern is the same for all other aspects of motor development. Interestingly, of

Table 3.3   Percent of Each Group Passing Each Test

Institutions	I	I	II	III	III
N	50	40	33	20	31
Age in Years	1.0–1.99	2.0–2.99	3.0–3.99	1.0–1.99	2.0–2.99
Sit alone	42	95	97	90	100
Creep or Scoot	14	75	97	75	100
Stand Holding	4	45	90	70	100
Walk Holding	2	40	63	60	100
Walk Alone	0	8	15	15	94

From "Causes of retardation among institutional children: Iran" by Wayne Dennis in *The Journal of Genetic Psychology*, 1960, 96, pp. 47–59. Used by permission of The Journal Press and the author.

those children in Institutions I and II who were capable of locomotion by some means other than walking, only 10 did so by creeping; the remaining 57 propelled themselves with their arms and legs while in a sitting position — most of the children scooted rather than crept. In contrast, in Institution III, all the children who were capable of locomotion but incapable of walking did so by creeping. The same general trend has been observed in children who are reared in private homes rather than in orphanages. In explaining the scooting behavior of children in the first two institutions Dennis maintains that it is necessary for children to have some opportunity to *learn* the abilities involved in creeping — and it is apparent that this learning can be fostered or impeded by the environment. Given Dennis' data, the most logical conclusion is that it must be essential for young children to lie prone as well as supine if they are to learn to creep.

The more general conclusion supported by the Dennis experiment is that locomotor skills involved in sitting, standing, and walking, are not solely the result of genetically predetermined maturational processes, but may be severely retarded by experiential factors; it is reasonable to suppose that they can be accelerated by experiential factors as well.

Lee (1951) provided additional evidence relating environmental factors to human development. Lee's study consisted of following several groups of Negro children through grades 1 to 9, and administering intelligence tests to them at various intervals. All subjects were born in the southern part of the United States and had moved to Philadelphia later, or had been born in Philadelphia and had remained there. He identified four distinct groups of subjects: those born in Philadelphia, and those who had moved there while in grade 1, grade 4, or grade 6. To understand the results of the study, it is necessary to accept Lee's assumption that the intellectual stimulation provided for Negro children in the South during the 1940s was generally inferior to that provided for the same children in Philadelphia schools (this assumption seems reasonable in view of the significant differences in intelligence test scores of comparable groups of Negro children born in the South and those born in Philadelphia). The data presented in Figure 3.2 indicate the magnitude of these initial differences and the changes in scores on tests administered after the children had spent some time in Philadelphia. Two aspects of the findings presented in this table are of special note: first, the markedly inferior scores of all groups comprising children who had moved from the South in grade 1 or later; secondly, the increased performance of children who had moved at a younger age. As Bloom (1964) notes, "The

The Effect of Changes in the Environment

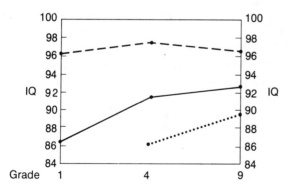

Grade 1   4   9

Changes in intelligence test scores on measures obtained in grades 1, 4, and 9 for Negro students born and raised in Philadelphia (dashed line), those born in the South and moving to Philadelphia in grade 4 (solid line), and those who did not move to Philadelphia until grade 9 (dotted line). (Adapted from Lee, *American Sociological Review,* 1951, p. 231. Copyright 1951 by The American Sociological Association. Used by permission of the American Sociological Association and the author.)

Figure 3.2

point of the Lee study is the decreasing effect of an improved environment with increasing age" (p. 76). Bloom contends that the environment will have the greatest effect on a trait during that trait's period of fastest growth.

Twins   Studies of various traits of twins have frequently demonstrated the importance of heredity in development (see Chapter 2). Mentioned earlier were the greater similarities between **identical twins** than between **fraternal twins**, and the lower correlations of intelligence test scores between fraternal twins (Table 2.1). The inconclusiveness of this data, however, stems from the simple observation that increasing genetic similarity frequently implies greater similarity in environments. It is logical, for example, to assume that most sets of identical twins have more similar environments than do cousins, or siblings. One may argue, therefore, that the higher correlation between various intelligence measures for identical twins is due at least in part to their more identical environments. The problem is somewhat complicated by the counterargument that many parents of fraternal twins do not realize that their offspring are not identical until their formative years have passed, and that many parents would treat fraternal twins just as they would identical twins, particularly if the twins were the same sex. The observed differences between identical twins and fraternal twins, if one assumes that the environments of each are probably highly similar, must then be due to genetic rather than to environmental factors. Employing the same data, an environmentalist could point to the difference between fraternal twins and siblings as additional evidence that environment influences development. Table 2.1, for example, reports correlations of .65 and .50 for intelligence test scores of fraternal twins and siblings, respectively. Since fraternal twins are no more alike genetically than siblings, environmentalists assume that this observed difference is a result of environment rather than genetic factors.

    Newman, Freeman, and Holzinger (1937) studied twins reared together and twins reared apart. It is obvious that identical twins reared apart would be unlikely to have very similar environments; certainly those reared together would have more nearly identical environments. Interestingly, the data from this study (reported in Table 3.4) provide

Table 3.4   Correlations for Intelligence, Weight, and Height for Identical Twins Reared Together and Apart*

	Intelligence (Group Test)	Height	Weight
Identical twins reared together	.92	.98	.97
Identical twins reared apart	.73	.97	.89

*Data from Newman, Freeman, and Holzinger, *Twins: A Study of Heredity and Environment*, p. 347. The University of Chicago Press, 1937. Used by permission.

clear evidence that intelligence, height, and weight are at least partly determined genetically. The power of heredity is implicit in the high correlations between members of twin pairs for each of these measures, whether they were reared together or apart. On the other hand, the much lower correlation for intelligence test scores for twins reared apart in comparison to those reared together (.73 as opposed to .92) is strong evidence that environment is also a powerful factor in determining measurable intelligence. The environment's influence on height and weight is apparently much less pronounced since the correlations are quite close for twins reared together and for those reared apart.

In 1938, at a time when most psychologists throughout the world were convinced that intelligence was a predetermined and unchanging quality, a man by the name of Harold Skeels resolved to bring a group of retarded children to normalcy. The results of this longitudinal project first reported by Skeels et al. (1938), continued by Skeels and Skodak (1965), and finally concluded by Skeels (1966), provide one of the most dramatic illustrations yet available of the reversibility of mental retardation. Subjects for the study were 10 girls and 3 boys, all under three years of age and not physically handicapped, but who had been tested and found to be sufficiently mentally retarded to warrant their transfer from an orphanage for normal children to an institution for the mentally retarded. When these children were transferred, their intelligence test scores ranged from 35 to 89, with a mean of 64.3. All were considered unadoptable because of their apparent mental retardation. Another group of children from the orphanage was selected as a contrast group. The intelligence test scores for this group ranged from 81 to 103, except for two children with IQ scores of 50 and 71. The mean chronological age of the experimental group was 19.4 months compared to a mean age of 16.6 months for the contrast group. Children in the contrast group were to remain in the orphanage until they were placed for adoption; those in the experimental group had already been transferred to an institution for the mentally retarded, from which they were about to be rescued by the exigencies of psychological research.

The experimental procedure employed with these children is interesting and unorthodox. The children were transferred from the orphanage to an institution for the mentally retarded and placed in wards that had previously been reserved for the older and brighter females who were inmates of the institution. Each of the wards contained approximately 30 women who ranged in chronological age from 18 to 50 years and from 7 to 12 years in mental age, and each ward had one matron in charge and one attendant. The experimental program required that no more than one or two children be placed in each of the wards. Almost immediately, the inmates and the attendants became very fond of the children in their ward and began to compete with other wards in the achievements of their children. Each ward wanted their child to be the first to walk, the first to talk, and the first to learn how to read and write. The children received constant attention and were subject to an overwhelming variety of stimulation. As soon as they learned to walk, they began to attend a kinder-

The Skeels Study

garten, to go to school programs, and to take part in singing and dancing exercises. Probably of considerable significance in the children's later development is that an older woman usually formed a very close attachment to each child—in effect, each child was "adopted" by a mother-figure early in his stay at the institution. In Skeels' (1966) words, "The contrast between the richly stimulating, individually oriented experience of the children in the experimental group and the depersonalizing, mass handling, and affectionless existence in the children's home can hardly be emphasized enough" (p. 17).

Eventually each child was judged to have benefited from his experience in the home as much as he would, and was at that point considered ready for adoption. Of the experimental subjects only one was returned to the orphanage and later committed to an institution for the retarded; six children spent brief periods in the orphanage prior to being adopted; five went directly into adoptive homes from the institution; and one remained in the institution until adulthood. Although Skeels (1966) reports in detail the progress made by each of these children as they grew toward adulthood, I will report only the final description of this group and its comparison with the contrast group. It should be noted, however, that the experimental group *gained* an average of 28.5 IQ points per child in the first 2½ years of the study, whereas the contrast group *lost* an average of 26.2 IQ points per child.

Twenty-one years later each member of both groups was located, interviewed, and tested. The results of this final follow-up are indeed impressive. All thirteen members of the experimental group were self-supporting; they had completed a median of grade 12 (four had gone to college and one had received a B.A. degree and had taken some graduate work); eleven of them were married and nine of them had children, and their incomes compared favorably with the national average.

In light of the accomplishments of the experimental group, the outcome for members of the contrast group appears tragic. Of the original group of twelve, one died in adolescence in a public institution for the mentally retarded, three were still wards of institutions for the mentally retarded, and one was a patient in a mental hospital. Only two of the subjects had married, one had had a child who was mentally retarded, and the other had four normal children. The median educational achievement of the control group was third grade.

The implications of the Skeels study argue strongly for the importance of love and cognitive stimulation in infancy and early childhood and demonstrate the deleterious effects that the absence of these experiences can have in the child's later life. The study does not deal with the relative contributions of heredity and environment in human development, but it does provide additional evidence for the importance of environmental stimulation for a child's successful development.

Sam   I have spoken of this with Sam. He was sitting on an empty crate and nudging Samuel with his foot. The rat has become so tame and so intelligent that he and Sam are virtually inseparable. They eat together at the same table, sometimes from the same dish; they sleep together, they play together, and whenever Sam must venture out into the world to scrounge his meals from the rich garbage cans behind the big hotel above him, Samuel sits below the manhole cover and whimpers until his master returns. We spoke of the importance of early environmental stimulation, and Sam listened with great interest. After all, he was among the first to demonstrate how the intelligence of the white rat can be affected by altering his environment. After I finished describing for him the results of the research that I have reported in this chapter, he replied that he too was familiar with each of these studies, that he had given them much thought, and that he had some advice to give me.

> About this book of yours, [he said in his characteristic way] let me give you some advice. Of course it is important for students to have some feeling for the particular contributions of heredity and environment in the development of human abilities, but this understanding need not be acquired through repetition of the old nature-nurture controversy. It is just too obvious that both environment and heredity interact in determining the outcome of the developmental process. And the extent to which each is responsible for the determination of such abilities as are measured by tests of intelligence need not concern them here, although it is a question which appears to be of some concern to contemporary psychologists. The student should develop—as a result of reading the two chapters of your book that deal with genetics and heredity on the one hand, and with the influence of environmental factors on the other—an appreciation of the fact that neither can be considered in isolation, and that each is of considerable importance. Having arrived at this appreciation, he should be made aware of the fact that because of social, moral, or ethical restrictions, or perhaps because of the practical impossibility of the whole thing, it is extremely difficult to control the genetic pool of a group of people. All attempts at eugenics with human society have been abortive; only the rat has remained a docile, cooperative, and uncomplaining subject, and perhaps he has now served his major purpose since he has demonstrated what we cannot demonstrate with people, and any further demonstration would probably be in vain. Therefore, since it is not possible to control heredity, psychologists must emphasize the study of environment rather than heredity. Once the genetic code is broken, then it may be possible to alter man genetically in ways that will be beneficial to him, and at that point the question can be re-examined. If the student understands this after finishing your chapter on the environment, then he is ready to move on to a consideration of the specific agents and agencies in the child's environment that are primarily responsible for the direction which development takes. Throughout this, however, he should occasionally be reminded that although such factors as the family, peer groups, and the school are very powerful forces, both the potential and the limits for development have been predetermined to some unknown degree by the genetic endowment of the individual.

Sam cleared his throat, petted Samuel absentmindedly, and prepared to continue. Unfortunately one of the big sewers broke at just this moment. We could hear its contents splashing against the cement walls, and Sam, instantly afraid of flooding, mobilized both of us: we spent the next half hour frantically rushing crate after crate of squealing rats, some labeled "BRIGHT" and others "DULL," to the safety of a seam above the broken sewer.

Summary

This chapter has presented a small selection of many studies purporting to demonstrate the influence of environmental factors on the development of some human characteristics. It began with a description of Sam, the untenured university professor who lives and conducts research in the damp, dark recess of the coal seams under this city. The reports of Krech's success, in producing superior groups of rats simply by enriching their environments should have given the reader some idea of the nature of Sam's research.

The Sherman and Key study of the Hollow Children in the Blue Ridge Mountains west of Washington, D.C., provided dramatic and tragic examples of the effect of impoverished environment on development. Dennis' account of the Tehran orphans also examined impoverished environments. A brief glimpse was offered of the possibility of overcoming the effects of early deprivation by means of a more normal environment (the Lee study), and then the studies of twins were reconsidered to demonstrate that data employed to support the contention that heredity is the most powerful influence in development can also serve the opposite function. Finally the chapter began to end with the story of the Skeels children who would have almost certainly been mentally retarded and institutionalized all their lives had there been no intervention in their early years. In the end we came again to Sam, listened to his advice, and lost him in the gloom of his lonely world.

Main Points

1. Studies of the effects of enriched and impoverished environments on the albino Norway rat have led to the conclusion that it is possible to alter the "intelligence" of lower animals by altering their experiences; and by inference, the same must be possible with man.

2. Studies of children living in isolated mountain regions (the Hollow Children) provide dramatic evidence of the deleterious effect that deprived and un-stimulating environments have on children.

3. The environment's influence on the development of motor potential such as the ability to walk is evident in the case of the institutionalized children, reared in an unstimulating and undemanding environment, who were markedly retarded in their motor development by the age of 2 or 3 years.

4. Apparently the damaging effects of early deprivation can sometimes be partially overcome by exposure to a more stimulating environment. In general, a stimulating environment will be more effective when provided during the earlier, rather than during the later, years of childhood.

5. The correlations between various physical and psychological measures for twins frequently indicate that fraternal twins are more closely related than siblings—that is, their scores for various traits tend to be closer than those for siblings. Since fraternal twins are no more alike genetically than siblings, and since their environments are in most cases more similar, this greater similarity may be evidence of the environment's influence in determining these traits.

6. Probably the most dramatic illustration of the reversibility of severe retardation in children is provided by the Skeels study, which involved enriching the social and intellectual environments of 13 mentally retarded children, all under the age of 3. By the time they reached adulthood all were self-supporting and for all purposes indistinguishable from any other normal individual. A comparable group did not fare as well.

7. Sam suggests that although it is important to recognize the influence of heredity in the development of human characteristics, it is more important for students and psychologists to concentrate on the role of the environment. We can control the environment to some extent; genetics still remains beyond our control.

Articles by Krech, Rosenzweig, and Bennett provide intriguing evidence of physical changes in the brain of the lowly white rat resulting from environmental enrichment.

Further Readings

Krech, D., M. Rosenzweig, and E. Bennett. Relations between brain chemistry and problem-solving among rats raised in enriched and impoverished environments. *Journal of Comparative and Physiological Psychology,* 1962, **55,** 801–807.

Krech, D., M. Rosenzweig, and E. Bennett. Environmental impoverishment, social-isolation, and changes in brain chemistry and anatomy. *Physiology and Behavior,* 1966, **1,** 99–104.

Hunt provides a convincing argument for the importance of the environment in the development of intelligence in the following work:

Hunt, J. McV. *Intelligence and experience.* New York: The Ronald Press, 1961.

The effects of environmental deprivation on children are dramatically revealed in an article by Dennis:

Dennis, W. Causes of retardation among institutional children: Iran. *Journal of Genetic Psychology,* 1960, **96,** 47–59.

Of special interest to those involved in the education of disadvantaged children from preschool to college is the following book, which describes a variety of programs that provide more enriched environments for students:

Gordon, E. W., and D. A. Wilkerson. *Compensatory education for the disadvantaged: Programs and practices: Preschool through college.* New York: College Entrance Examination Board, 1966.

Of Baboon Groups and Monkey Troops: Socialization

Hunters have often said that the greatest game animal of all must surely be man—to pursue a creature of such intelligence would be more exhilarating than any other chase, and success in capturing him would be the most coveted trophy. The second greatest game animal must surely be the Great Ape that dwells in the dense jungle forests of the hilly country in East Africa. He is not only a creature of singular intelligence, but he is also remarkably unafraid of man, and quite capable of killing him as quickly, and perhaps more horribly, than either the much feared grizzly bear of the American Rockies, or the African lion.

Hunting the Great Ape requires a great deal of courage (perhaps foolishness is a better word), and it requires a native guide who is also extremely courageous or foolish. In addition it demands some considerable good fortune. The scene usually opens with the hunter and guide sitting around a small table in the oppressive heat of some dismal, fly-infested **bar** *in a large African city, and eventually leads to the oppressive heat of some dusty and desolate African road. In time the hunter and his guide invade the forbidding tangles of jungle growth at the foot of the hilly country and work their way up toward the summit. Here the air is cooler and darker; the sun penetrates the thick canopy of the rain forest only briefly, if at all. If the hunter has been lucky in his choice of a guide, he will soon find himself crouching inside one of the tunnels constructed by the Great Apes; if the hunter has not been lucky, he will find himself sitting again at a table in the same small bar, drinking the same tepid beer in a dejected attempt to rid himself of the oppression that Africa bestows upon those who are strangers to her, and trying as well to drown*

Hunting the Great Ape

the hollow fear which arose when he first seriously considered going after the Great Ape. If he is a man, he will return again to the lair of the ape, and if not, he will return to the safety of his well organized and domesticated world.

But the man who does find himself crouching in the tunnel constructed by tribes of apes to facilitate their comings and goings in the otherwise impenetrable jungle growth has to live with his fear. The hunt progresses with the guide crouched low to avoid scraping his head on the overhanging and loosely interwoven branches which form the ceiling of the tunnel. And as he scurries through the labyrinth of tunnels, his behavior seems strange; each time he reaches an intersection in the tunnel he stops and sniffs the air, drawing in deep breaths, for skilled guides know that the Great Ape has a pungent odor and can be detected by his smell long before he is even close.

The odor now guides the guide, who in turn guides the hunter, and slowly, with their hearts pounding wildly, they approach the tribe of Great Apes. It is early afternoon, although it is impossible to see the sun for the gloom which pervades these rank tunnels. The guide has told the hunter that now the tribe of apes will be feeding in one of the small clearings, found in even the densest jungle growth. If the hunt proceeds smoothly the apes will not be aware of the hunters until they burst into the clearing where the animals are feeding. At that same instant the dominant ape, the leader of this tribe, is expected to charge. The hunter has been warned. The guide, who insisted on being paid in advance, will disappear into the underbrush at the first sign of ape, leaving the hunter alone.

As the ape charges he will rend the air with blood-curdling screams, and beat his chest so violently that an unwary listener might consider that he was hearing the sounds of a massacre of women and children, replete with cannonade. The hunter has a pistol in his hand; a rifle is too difficult to maneuver in the confined space of an ape tunnel. It is a heavy calibre handgun, but not very accurate. A bullet in the heart would kill the ape instantly, but to attempt shooting a hurtling ape in the heart is nearly as foolish as pursuing him in the first place. The hunter must wait until the ape is almost upon him; then, if the ape behaves according to plan, for one brief moment he will come to an abrupt and complete halt. In that short space of time the hunter must shoot and he must shoot absolutely accurately, for a wounded ape will almost certainly kill his attacker with one powerful blow of his huge arms or his great jaws. What will happen if the hunter freezes and cannot shoot? No one knows for sure. Perhaps the charge of the Great Ape is all bluster and bravado; perhaps his heart is beating even more wildly than the hunter's. On the other hand, the beast might indeed continue his charge and eliminate the rude intruder.

Such is the hunt for the Great Ape from the hunter's point of view, but what is the ape's view of all this? How does he perceive himself, his role in his troop, and his role in the hunt? Many studies of monkeys and apes have begun to answer such questions (for example, Southwick, 1963; DeVore, 1965; Schaller, 1963). Basic to the answer is the fact that a relatively clear-cut social hierarchy has been observed in virtually all of the troops of monkeys or apes that have been studied. Zuckerman (1932) was among the first to report this hierarchy for various types of subprimates; Carpenter (1942) asserted that **dominant behavior** appeared to be a conspicuous characteristic of all societies of monkeys and apes. He defined a dominant individual as one that "has priority in feeding, sexual and locomotor behavior and . . . is superior in aggressiveness and in group control to another or other individuals" (p. 39). The dominant animal in a troop is almost invariably male, and he not only has the privileges attendant upon being the leader but also has the responsibility of looking after the immediate society. And so perhaps it is with a deep sense of duty that the dominant Great Ape charges toward the hunter.

The hierarchical arrangement observed in subhuman primate groups suggests that a kind of group culture exists. This chapter deals with specific agents of socialization, and among the most important of these is culture.

The Child's Environment

The child does not develop simply as a function of the two mysterious forces which have been discussed earlier: heredity and environment. True, much of heredity remains a mystery, and will continue to be a mystery throughout this book. The environment is less mysterious, but no less complicated. This chapter will continue the discussion of environmental influence on child development but will go one step farther than preceding chapters by attempting to describe the child's environment. Among other things, this environment includes the *culture* in which the child finds himself, such powerful influences on the child as his immediate *family* and his **peer groups**, and those objects and activities which consume the greatest amount of his time: watching **television**, reading **books**, and attending **school**. The uncertain, complicated, and interactive relationship of these influences to the child is illustrated in Figure 4.1. The diagram represents the child, complete with all of the penchants, predispositions, abilities, and peculiarities implicit in his genetic endowment, and the influence of his world upon him. This world, as experienced from his unique perspective, is the child's environment. It is important to keep in mind that were the central figure in the illustration a real child, and not the abstract "child-in-general," his environment might be described quite differently. The culture, as a general term encompassing family and peer group relationships, would remain important, but in addition one could now include such specifics as the members of his peer group who are most important to him, his pet dog Ishmael, his model airplanes, and his strong feelings against spinach. All these variables play a significant role in determining what he will eventually be like. Unfortunately, the illustration can deal only with some of the more obvious aspects of the so-called "normal" child, who does not really exist. He is simply a convenient invention for the sake of discussion.

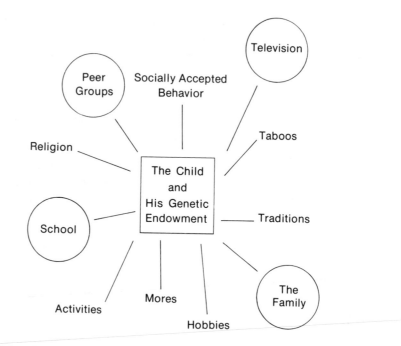

Figure 4.1   The child's culture interacts with his genetic endowment to determine the sort of adult he will become. The circled entries are dealt with in this chapter.

Culture

Culture is an inclusive term not easily defined. It is not inaccurate, for example, to say that a culture is the sum of all the mores, traditions, beliefs, values, customary ways of behaving, and implicit and explicit rules that characterize a group of people. Nor is it inaccurate to say that the trappings of a culture are its schools, its religions, and its laws. More specific definitions of culture might include child-rearing practices, chief occupations, principal leisure activities, taboos, and modes of behavior considered especially worthwhile.

Understandably, those aspects of man most clearly determined by genetic factors are the least variable across cultures. Although there are some very obvious differences among people of different races (and presumably of different cultures), there are certainly more similarities than differences. People ordinarily have two legs, two arms, a single head, and a single navel. These and related similarities are more significant for humans as a species than the fact that skin pigmentation, hair texture, and shape of the facial features may differ among races or cultures.

Since genetically determined characteristics appear to be relatively invariant across cultures or races, it is more interesting to consider those human qualities that appear to be most variable, and to speculate about the influences of heredity and environment in determining these qualities. Consider, for example, the fact that languages are often wholly unrelated in different parts of the world. Few would argue that the ability to speak a specific language is genetically predetermined. Social customs also vary widely from one culture to another, and these too are not the result of genetic, but of environmental factors. Indeed, it is almost axiomatic that those characteristics of human behavior which are most variable from one culture to another, or from one subculture to another within a larger cultural group, result more from the environment than any genetic predetermination. The central problem has little to do with whether or not culture represents a significant environmental force; we are concerned here with examining the *extent* to which culture affects human behavior, and determining precisely which aspects of behavior are most affected. Any answers will inevitably be incomplete and somewhat speculative.

Any consideration of the role of culture in development necessarily   Cultural Relativity
includes Benedict's (1934) term **"cultural relativity"**—the belief that a person's behavior can only be understood and evaluated within the context of his cultural environment. Clearly, socially acceptable behavior is not universal. Secluded tribes of Amazon natives still may occasionally eat a missionary; such behavior would be somewhat less acceptable in American society.

Every culture determines which behaviors will be considered right and which behaviors will be considered evil by its members. Of more interest to psychologists is the fact that culture also plays a large role in determining personality characteristics. Considerable anecdotal evidence supports this hypothesis in our society; much more dramatic evidence of its validity is provided by Margaret Mead's (1935) often quoted studies of three New Guinea tribes. Mead studied the Arapesh, the Mundugumor, and the Tchambuli tribes, each of which was characterized by sex roles that appear strange from the perspective of our cultural backgrounds, and that were dramatically different from each other. Of principal interest to Mead were the dominant personality traits of each of these tribes, particularly as they were reflected in male-female differences.

Mead described the Arapesh as a culture in which both sexes were "placid and contented, unaggressive and noninitiatory, noncompetitive and responsive, warm, docile, and trusting" (Mead, 1935, p. 39). On the other hand, among the Mundugumor both men and women "developed as ruthless, aggressive, positively sexed individuals, with the maternal cherishing aspects of personality at a minimum" (Mead, 1935, p. 190). Finally there were the Tchambuli, who lived principally for art, and where Mead found a "genuine reversal of the sex attitudes of our own culture" (Mead, 1935, p. 190). The approved personality characteristics in each of these tribes varied greatly, ranging from a society where "feminine" behavior is the norm for both sexes, to a society where "masculine" behavior is the norm for each, and finally to a group where the males are "feminine" and the females are "masculine." It is interesting to note that the predominantly feminine Arapesh were an agricultural tribe that lived in the inhospitable and infertile mountain regions some distance off the coast of New Guinea. The Mundugumor were a cannibalistic tribe, most of whom lived along the banks of the Sepik, a fast-flowing jungle river that they feared passionately, but that they occasionally employed as a means of approach to the hamlets they raided periodically in search of victuals. The Tchambuli were an artistic and an agricultural people. The men spent most of their time practicing elaborate dances that they sometimes performed for the women, devising new ceremonies, or experimenting with various art forms. The Tchambuli women spent most of their time gathering food for themselves and for the men.

Mead (1935) contends that such personality traits as masculinity and femininity are culturally determined, that since the qualities ordinarily associated with each are so clearly influenced by the cultural environment, there is no justification for believing them sex linked. Although the categorical nature of Mead's conclusions have been questioned (Piddington, 1957), particularly because of the relatively undocumented and subjective nature of her evidence, in view of the evident disparities in behavior and personality characteristics among different cultural groups, her conclusions cannot be discounted summarily. At the same time, however, caution should be exercised in interpreting and generalizing from evidence such as Mead's. The personality characteristics which she defines as the norm for each of the tribes are simply norms. It is almost inevitable that brief summaries of her work should make it seem that all Arapesh natives were feminine, that all Mundugumors were masculine, and that all Tchambulis had reversals of sex roles (employing our roles as standards). Indeed, even a careful examination of Mead's (1935) writings reveals that these are personality characteristics "approved" by the culture, and not necessarily possessed by all its members. In any culture, however small and cohesive, there are individuals who vary considerably from the established norms. These expressions of individuality may be manifestations of different genetic endowments within relatively **homogenous** cultures, as Piddington (1957) suggests, or they may be the result of different individual environments within cultures which are only superficially homogenous. These general data can only illustrate that, through socialization, people who are brought up in the same culture will probably resemble each other more than they will resemble those who come from different cultures. Culture, then, as part of the child's environment, is a potent force in determining the outcome of the developmental process.

The ways in which culture is transmitted from one generation to another are of central importance to a study of child development. A complete examination of the topic requires an account of the ways in which children learn, since culture is transmitted through learning rather than through maturation or other genetically based processes. But a complete treatment of this topic is well beyond the scope of the present discussion.* This section focuses on two related processes which account for social learning: group pressure and imitation. These two processes are related in that social pressure has been offered as one explanation for the effects of imitation. For convenience and clarity, however, each topic will be treated separately.

---

*A more complete discussion of human learning can be found in two other works by the author (Lefrancois, 1972a; 1972b).

Group Pressure

The effect that the opinions, the feelings, the exhortations, or the behavior of groups can have on the behavior of an individual is more difficult to illustrate in the complex, impersonal societies which have produced you and I, than in the simple and highly personal cultures which produced a Tchambuli or an Arapesh. In a small and personal society all members are intimately aware of the behavior of every individual in the group; the transgressions as well as the good acts of each can have serious repercussions on everybody. Accordingly, the pressure to conform to accepted and desirable codes of conduct is immediate and strong. Thus it is that *most* of the Arapesh are gentle and feminine, and *most* of the Mundugumor are competitive, hostile, and otherwise masculine.

There is less pressure to conform in our society for two reasons: there is no single code of approved conduct as clearly delineated as in a more primitive culture; the pressure that the group can bring to bear on an individual is much more remote, and consequently of less moment.

Group Pressure

The feelings of abandonment and alienation assumed to affect increasing numbers of people in our culture (Maslow, 1954; Rogers, 1951, 1969) are partly the result of the anonymity that results from living in societies in which the community has become so broad that the individual is lost. While this anonymity provides respite from the demands of social groups, it also complicates an examination of the role of social pressure in development. Nevertheless, there are numerous instances of clearly discernible effects of social pressure on the beliefs and the behavior of individuals; for example, advertising techniques which appeal to the consumer on the grounds that all his peers are using a particular brand have proved effective. There are illustrations of social pressure provided by Asch's (1955) study of conformity in group situations. In a series of studies he demonstrated repeatedly that individuals can be made to behave in direct contradiction to their beliefs as a result of group pressure. The typical situation involves 6 or 7 confederates who have been instructed to answer incorrectly a number of simple perceptual problems. For example, subjects are shown three lines of different lengths which they are asked to compare to a standard (Figure 4.2). The task requires simply that they select the line equal in length to the standard—a task which is simple enough for almost any subject to answer correctly when not subjected to any contradictory pressures. Then a single uninitiated subject is introduced among the confederates, who are seated in such a way that he will be the last to answer. For the first several items the confederates answer correctly; afterward they consistently answer incor-

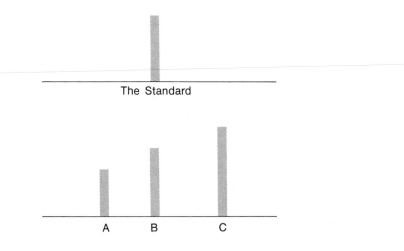

Figure 4.2   An illustration of Asch's investigation of the effects of social pressure. Subjects are required to indicate whether A, B, or C is equal in length to the standard.

rectly, and they *agree* on the incorrect answer. Presumably, this situation is stressful for the subject. He is being subjected to considerable social pressure: he knows what the correct answer is—or at least he thinks he knows—but he also wonders at the answers of his fellow subjects. Approximately one-third of the time during the study, the pressure was great enough for the subject to agree with the confederates and answer incorrectly.

For the developing child, social pressure includes the parents' influence, the influence of the school, the pressure applied through various peer groups, and possibly the pressure from religious standards. Unfortunately there is little research that elucidates the role of social pressure in childhood. Nevertheless it is important to bear in mind its significance as an environmental influence. Social pressure is treated elsewhere in this text under the heading of social learning, and again in this chapter in the discussion of peer groups.

Numerous theoretical explanations for social learning are based on the belief that culture is transmitted through a process of **imitation** (Miller and Dollard, 1941; Bandura and Walters, 1963). Again this is more apparent in primitive societies than in complex technological societies, partly because a society at a low level of technical development can usually provide its children with miniature *working* replicas of the tools it uses. In addition, the parents, who are the chief agents for transmitting cultural information, demonstrate adult activities in the presence of children. Bandura and Walters (1963) describe child-rearing practices among the Cantalense people, a Guatemalan subculture. In this culture parents provide their young children with the tools which are employed daily (for example, a miniature broom or a corn-grinding stone), and are also constantly with the children. From the child's earliest years he is exposed to a model of the behavior that he will engage in once he has matured. In this culture there is little direct tuition—that is, the parents do not tell the child "This is how you must hold a broom, and this is how you must move it to sweep the cockroaches out of the house." There is obviously no need for such tuition since the learning demanded of the child is elemental enough that it will occur completely and solely through observation.

Social Imitation

Another instance of social imitation is the Canadian Ojibwa Indian whose livelihood consists mainly of hunting and trapping, and who transmits his culture from one generation to the next simply through observational learning. From the time he can walk well enough to keep up with his father, the young Ojibwa boy follows him around his trapline to the lakes and streams where the father fishes, and simply watches him. Very early he is given his own traps, which he sets as he has seen his father set traps, in the manner of the grandfather, and of his great-grandfather. Similarly the young Ojibwa girl learns how to prepare cooking fires and to make meals and clothing from the provisions of the woods and streams simply by observing her mother engage daily in these activities.

Observational learning, while not as evident in our culture, is no less prevalent. A **model** need not be a particular person whose behavior is copied by another, as in the case of the illustrations described above. Anything which serves as a pattern for behavior may be considered a model: literature, movies, television programs, verbal and written instructions, religious tenets, or folk heroes. Frequently models are **symbolic** rather than living people, and these are the most prevalent models in a technological society. Their effects are manifested in a variety of ways in the behavior of adults as well as children. Chapter 7 gives a detailed description of the influence of models on the growing child.

The Arapesh, the Tchambuli, and the Mundugumor are dramatically different as a result of the differences in the cultures in which they were born and reared. It is not as obvious that a child from a **minority group**

Minority Groups

in the American culture is also frequently very different from other children of the "majority" group. Yet this is as clear an illustration of the effects of environmental forces on development as Mead's account of the three New Guinea tribes, and is a much more pertinent illustration for this discussion.

American and Canadian minority groups are typically identified in ethnic terms: black, Puerto Rican, Mexican, North American Indian, perhaps even a French-Canadian minority. Minority groups can also be identified in economic terms: the affluent minority and the poor majority, or perhaps, the affluent majority and the poor minority. Minority groups may also be religious or social (sororities or the Masons, for example). Frequently they are defined in terms of a combination of dimensions: the average American black is less well educated, poorer than the average American white, and belongs to a different race.

Currently there is considerable interest in the plight of minority groups, directed toward the realization of social, political, economic, and educational equality, and perhaps a tacit admission of responsibility and guilt on the part of the majority. Several recent studies examining the characteristics of children from minority groups are reviewed in this text (see, for example, Chapter 10 for a discussion of the language of the lower class child and Chapter 12 for a discussion of the effects of teacher expectations on his behavior). A recent Ford Foundation Report (Crossland, 1971) demonstrates graphically how many fewer members of minority groups attend college than do members of white middle class American society. Among the explanations for this situation is the fact that college entrance examinations are highly verbal and that American Negroes, because of cultural differences, typically score approximately one standard deviation below the mean for white groups; in addition, minority group primary and secondary schools appear to have lower quality teachers and insufficient facilities (such as libraries); the areas in which minority groups live are often farther removed physically from college campuses than middle class suburbs; probably for cultural reasons, minority groups' intellectual motivation is lower than middle class whites'; and finally, there is racial discrimination among entrance examiners.

In light of what is known about the influence of environment on human development, consider for a moment how different the life of an Eskimo child might have been had he been born in your home—and how different your life might be had you been born in his.

The Family   The family is widely acknowledged as among the most powerful socializing agents in a young child's development (Sears et al., 1957), but peer groups, school, social clubs, church groups, and scout troops gradually replace the family as the child matures. In the early years the child's immediate family is essential for his physical survival and is his primary source of love and affection; it satisfies most, if not all, of his physiological and his psychological needs. From the family the child will acquire most of his important early learning. If it is true, as Bloom suggests (1964), that by the time the child has reached the age of 6, fully two-thirds of his intellectual capacity will have been developed, then the importance of the family in the child's early life can hardly be over-estimated.

It is interesting to speculate about the origins of the family, particularly since few of our phylogenetic precursors seem to have developed a **nuclear family** (mother, father, and children) of the type that characterizes most of the world's contemporary cultures. Even the apes and monkeys that have been studied extensively ordinarily live in groups consisting of unrelated members. In addition, their sexual conduct (which, incidentally, is much more restrained than is commonly believed), gives no evidence of any permanent attachment between a male and a female or between a male and a group of females (or vice versa in a hypothetical world of liberated female monkeys or apes). Much less have they developed the **extended families** (parents, children, grandparents, uncles, and so on) which are characteristic of many contemporary societies (Murdock, 1949). Early sociologists such as Lloyd Morgan (1894, 1896) assumed that the social organization of early man was parallel to that of the apes and monkeys described above. Morgan believed that bands of men and women lived apart, and that the men visited the women only when the urge to rape them became overpowering. Engels (1902) also thought that primitive man did not live in family groups, but in a communistic tribe where sexual relations were indiscriminate and matter of fact.* Whatever the origins of the family, it is generally true that in societies such as ours, people live in relatively cohesive nuclear family groups, ordinarily consisting of parents and their immediate young children. These nuclear groups occasionally extend to include other relatives — an act which does not ordinarily strengthen the cohesiveness of the group, especially when the other relative is a **mother-in-law**.

The child's immediate family is not only largely responsible for the satisfaction of his needs, but it is also instrumental in determining the type of person that the child will become — notwithstanding the fact that his genetic inheritance has already set certain limitations and is responsible for a variety of predispositions. Many of the family's influences on the growing child are implicit in this text. The remainder of this section deals with the apparent effects on the child of his relationship with his parents, the size of his family, and his ordinal position in the family.

Parent-Child Relations

The effects of the parent-child relationship on the development of the child's personality is of considerable practical interest; while much research has been devoted to examining this question, it still remains unanswered. Researchers have found it difficult to describe the relations that exist between parents and children, and to ascertain precisely what the personality of the child is. It is particularly difficult to determine, for example, whether a permissive approach to child rearing develops

---

*There are indications that contemporary American society may be reaching the beginning of the cycle again.

independent or dependent children, when the nature of parental permissiveness is no easier to define than the dependent or independent child is to identify. To further confuse the issue, parents' and children's behavior is inconsistent in different situations. For example, Hatfield et al. (1967) observed mothers and their children in a playroom setting and found their behavior highly inconsistent from one session to another. Under such circumstances, the nature of the mother-child relationship is puzzling at best.

Despite these difficulties, there are a number of general conclusions about parent-child relations extant in psychological literature. These conclusions deal primarily with the effect of such qualities as parental permissiveness, dominance, warmth, and rejection, on the child's independence, self-control, masculinity-feminity, assertiveness, and so on. One especially representative study (Baumrind, 1967) investigated preschool children who were identified as belonging to one of three personality groups: the first group consisted of children described as buoyant, friendly, self-controlled and self-reliant; the second group contained discontented and withdrawn children; the third group consisted of children who lacked self-reliance and self-control. Parents of the children in the first group were significantly more controlling, demanding, and loving than parents of either of the other groups. Interestingly, parents of the discontented and withdrawn children also exercised much control, but were detached rather than warm and loving, whereas parents of the children who lacked self-reliance (had low self-esteem) were warm but highly permissive. This study is representative of a number of other studies that have also purported to demonstrate that children of relatively demanding but loving parents tend to be better adjusted, more independent, and more self-reliant. Interestingly, Getzels and Jackson's (1962) investigation of creative children revealed that the more highly creative children in their sample had parents who expected more of them at an earlier age (controlling and demanding), but who were nevertheless warm and loving.

Despite the fact that research has indicated a tendency for some parental traits to result in certain characteristics in their children, the inference that children's personalities are *caused* by these parental traits is not warranted on the basis of the evidence. Furthermore, the results of research in this area are neither definitive nor in complete agreement with one another.

Birth Order

Among the intriguing observations in connection with studies of the family and its role in child development are those relating to birth order. Galton (1896) was among the first to note the effects of birth order when he observed that among the great scientists that Britain had produced there was a preponderance of firstborn children. Koch (1955) studied 360 5- and 6-year-old children extensively and concluded that firstborn children have an advantage in several areas of development. Koch found, for example, that firstborn children spoke more articulately than those who were born second, that they scored higher on measures of intellectual performance, and that they were more responsible and better planners. These findings concur with Wright's observation (1969) that firstborn children are more **reflective** than their siblings, whereas those born later are frequently more **impulsive**. These measures are based on the work of Kagan (1965a; 1965b; 1966a; 1966b). Reflection is defined as the child's tendency to evaluate alternatives and to delay his decision to avoid errors. Impulsive children, on the other hand, make more errors since they are more concerned with rapidly solving a problem than with its correct solution.

In comparison to their younger siblings, firstborns have a higher **need to achieve** (Sampson, 1962) in academic or scholastic performance (Altus, 1965, 1967; Schacter, 1963), are more curious (Altus, 1967; Brim, 1958), are more competitive (Koch, 1955), and are more likely to prefer the novel or complex (Eisenman, 1967). The probability that a firstborn will attend college is usually higher than that of other siblings (Bayer, 1966), although it is interesting to note that in Bayer's nationwide sample of 50,000 subjects, last-borns were as likely to go to college as firstborns. *Newsweek* (1969) recently reported that of the seven original astronauts, two were only children, and the remaining five were firstborns; of the first twenty-three astronauts to travel in space, twenty-one were either only children or firstborns. Of the remaining men, one had an older brother who died as an infant; the second was 13 years younger than his older brother.

The meaning of birth-order data is not completely clear, despite the rather impressive agreement among the conclusions derived from various studies. The most redundant and most often investigated finding is that firstborn children appear to excel in scholastic achievements. It is also generally agreed that firstborn children develop language more rapidly, as do only children. Interestingly, twins and triplets show retarded language development, not only in comparison to firstborns, but also in comparison to children who have no twin (Davis, 1937). Blatz (1937), for example, found that the Dionne quintuplets were much slower in language development than the average child.

These last observations offer some possible explanations for the observed effects of birth order. Generally, these effects are not simply due to being firstborn or last-born, but to the type of social interaction most characteristic for firstborn as opposed to later born children. It is not surprising that children from multiple births develop at a slower rate than children from single birth, since they are almost necessarily in much closer contact with their twin, and at the same time, have less individual interaction with the parents. Similarly, it is reasonable to attribute most of the observed differences between firstborn and later born children to the more intensive and stimulating interaction which firstborn children enjoy with their parents prior to the advent of succeeding children. Certainly, birth order alone explains little, although, as the evidence shows, it may be of value in predicting some of the child's characteristics. There is also the possibility that some of these observed differences may have physiological bases: for example, the intrauterine environment of firstborn children may be different from that of later born children. In light of the plausible social explanations that have been advanced, however, it is unlikely that physiological explanations will contribute much to the intriguing phenomena associated with the order of birth.

Family Size The smallest family interesting to a developmental psychologist is one with only one child—a condition which a number of old wives and grandmothers fear can be injurious to the healthy development of that child. Strangely, research does not support this venerable belief. Davis (1937), for example, reports that only children consistently develop more rapidly than children with siblings, particularly in language development. Faris (1940), McCurdy (1957), and West (1960) provide evidence of superior intellectual achievement and greater eminence among only children. In addition, there is no conclusive evidence that being an only child has any ill effects on the child's personality. These results clearly agree with the findings about birth order. The superior achievement of only children may be explained in the same way as the attainments of firstborns: each firstborn is an only child for some period of time; consequently, each is favored with a greater degree of parent-child interaction in his formative years.

The effect of belonging to a large family has not been investigated as thoroughly as the effect of ordinal position within the family, partly because the topic is at least superficially more sociological than psychological. Therefore much of the research is sociological, consisting more of descriptions of life in large and small families than of reports of measured

The effect of belonging to a large family has not been investigated as thoroughly . . .

differences among the children produced by each. Bossard and Sanger (1952) and Bossard and Boll (1956) report that larger families seem to be more authoritarian than smaller families and also less overprotective, less overindulgent, and less intrusive. Bossard and Boll's (1956) interviews with members of 100 families of 6 or more children each have led them to a variety of generalizations concerning the authority structure, the discipline, and the typical personality types of large families. Although their data is interesting and provocative, it is not designed to elucidate the different effects that family size might have on children. In addition, researchers cannot easily separate the effect of family size from social class, religion, or rural vs. urban environment.

A peer group is a group of equals. Most individuals in our society have a peer group, excluding Sam and other hermits whose peers, by definition, are also isolated and therefore of little consequence to their development. Actually most people have a number of peer groups: individuals whose occupations bring them into frequent contact with one another, individuals who are related by virtue of common causes, similar ambitions, identical avocations, geographic accident, or the whims of Fortune. Each of these groups elicits specific behavior from its members more or less different from that elicited by other groups, and each is somehow influential in determining a person's values, beliefs, goals, and ideals.

Peer Groups

A very young child does not ordinarily have a peer group that is of great psychological moment to him, since he remains dependent upon his immediate family during most of his formative years, and since he is not ordinarily brought into extensive or prolonged contact with other children until later in life. Piaget (1951) has observed that prior to the age of 3 or 4, children do not interact with other young children except in a very transitory and superficial manner. The play behavior of several 3-year-olds, even in the same room and with similar toys, is almost invariably egocentric rather than social. Sears et al. (1957) maintain that until the age of 5 or 6, the child's family is the primary influence in his life—the source of positive reinforcement for his behavior, or the source of punishment. After this first stage, however, the child turns gradually to peer groups, whose influence eventually supersedes that of his parents in importance. The influence of peers, then, is of paramount importance in the middle and later years of childhood, a fact which is integral to the remainder of this book.

In connection with the influence of peer groups on the child, studies have shown the deleterious effects that absence of contact with peers appears to have on the young of infrahuman species. Harlow and Zimmermann (1959) report that infant monkeys reared in isolation are frequently unable to achieve mature social relations when finally brought into contact with their peers. Such monkeys, particularly males isolated for a prolonged period, are typically incapable of normal sexual activities. The females fare better since their sexual role is passive rather than active; consequently, they occasionally become pregnant and bear young.

But it is both striking and potentially significant that these monkey mothers are unable to display the maternal attachment typical of mothers reared under more normal conditions.

Despite the research cited above, relatively little is known about the peer group's role in developing an individual's ability to interact socially with others. While it is possible to isolate young monkeys to observe the effects of this isolation on their later behavior, most of the research reported has necessarily involved maternal isolation, and the possibility that the mother is more closely connected with the development of affectional systems than peer groups is more than likely (Harlow, McGaugh, and Thompson, 1971). Additional information relating to peer groups is included in Chapters 12 and 13.

Other Environmental Forces

A child's environment consists of more than the culture in which he finds himself and the family and peers that surround him; it includes as well the physical environment and the activities the child engages in. Obviously such variables as climate and geographic location have a profound influence on the activities, and perhaps on the personality and intellectual characteristics of children, although it is frequently difficult to separate these from cultural influences. Furthermore, environment includes the nurseries, kindergartens, and schools which the child attends, for these institutions expose him to atmospheres sometimes dramatically different from his home. The school's influence on the child's social and cognitive development is difficult to assess since there are now very few children who do not attend school. It is probable that the absence of schools would affect not only the literacy, but also the development of the child's intellectual capacities—for example, the children of the Hollows (Sherman and Keys, 1932). It is also likely that their social and emotional growth would suffer.

Television, Comic Books, and Violence

There is a fear in the hearts of grandmothers that the mass media of communication will taint their still tender and highly corruptible young. First they feared **fairy tales**, few of which have happy endings, and even fewer of which are without violence. But the force of attacks on the Brothers Grimm and on Hans Christian Andersen never reached the passionate intensity with which the finger waggers went after the **comic book**, whose primary characteristics have been described as "violence in content, ugliness in form and deception in presentation" (Wertham, 1954, p. 90). In a stinging indictment documented with numerous case studies, Wertham ascribes many of the ills that beset young children to their addiction to comics, which, he maintains, are replete with unexplained, unjustified, and often unpunished violence, sadism, and other forms of criminal perversion. He claims that comics qualify neither as art nor literature, that they are antieducational, and that they demonstrate that the greatest evil is not crime, but the stupidity that allows the criminal to be apprehended. His book is aptly titled *Seduction of the Innocent.*

Arnold (1969) presents an equally scathing indictment of comic books, objecting to the models of violence that they present to young readers. But comics are only one of the mass exponents (and proponents) of violence; there are also books, toys, and television — the latter being the most widespread and the most powerful.

Federal Communications Commissioner Nicholas Johnson reported that of the 60 million homes in the United States in 1969, over 95 percent had television sets (Johnson, 1969). Moreover, the average male viewer between the ages of 2 and 65 will watch television for almost 9 full years of his life (each year consisting of 365 24-hour days). Before they reach the age of 18, children spend approximately 22,000 hours watching television. Given these inordinate amounts of time spent in front of television sets, it is important to consider the influence of television on a child's development.

For some time now, prophets of doom have been decrying the influence of television on children. Their primary claims, based on personal opinion rather than experimental data, are that television is producing a generation of passive people; or, alternately, that the violence that pervades many television programs will produce a generation of violent people. Critics ordinarily adopt one or the other stance, since the two are essentially antithetical. Furthermore, claim the critics, television has a deleterious effect on family relationships, on the social development of children, and on sports, reading, and playing bingo. Although the evidence is incomplete, there is sufficient research to provide a partial response to these criticisms and to present a more balanced impression of the actual influence of television on the lives of children.

First, it cannot be denied that many television programs contain violence in one form or another: sometimes verbal, frequently physical, and occasionally symbolic. It is not as clear that such violence has a discernible effect on the attitudes or the behavior of children. Himmelweit, Oppenheim, and Vince (1958) found that approximately one-fourth of the boys and one-third of the girls in a sample of 1000 young television viewers reported that they were frightened by violence on television. The same study, however, failed to find any higher frequency of maladjustment, delinquent behavior, or aggression among television viewers than among nonviewers. In contrast to these findings, Bandura, Ross, and Ross (1963), Bandura and Walters (1963), and Bandura (1969) consistently show an increase in aggressive behavior as a result of exposure to aggressive models. This behavior appears to be independent of whether the model was a live person, or whether a film depicted either cartoon characters or real people. The typical experiment involves having children view models (live or filmed) who engage in aggressive acts with inanimate objects such as inflated rubber clowns. The child is then presented with the objects against which the aggressive acts were directed, and his play is observed, usually through a one-way mirror. Young children typically respond aggressively when placed in this situation *after* viewing an aggressive model; children who have not been exposed to an aggressive model, or who have been exposed to a model who sits quietly or interacts with the toy in a nonaggressive manner, typically respond nonaggressively.

It is probably unrealistic to generalize from studies such as these to real-life situations. There is an apparent contradiction between the findings of Himmelweit et al. (1958) and those of Bandura and his associates, but the contradiction is largely resolved when the differences between the situations are considered. First, the aggression presented in an ordinary television program is directed against people rather than inanimate objects, and children learn early in life, through socialization, that aggression against people is normally punished. Next, the experimental situation generally requires that the child be exposed to the *same* objects as were employed by the model *immediately* after he has observed the model, or very shortly afterward. A child who watches a violent scene on television is rarely presented immediately with an object (or person) similar to the one upon whom the televised violence was inflicted. Finally, to assume that striking a rubber clown with a mallet, kicking it, or punching it is evidence of aggression is to suggest a redefinition of the term as it is ordinarily employed by those who condemn television because of its violence. After all, inflated rubber clowns are designed to be punched, kicked, and otherwise aggressed upon; the object in the experiment was provided for that purpose.

The findings of Himmelweit et al. (1958) are also relevant to the passivity which television is expected to produce in children; they indicate that television viewers have a wider range of interests than nonviewers. In a related study, Schramm, Lyle, and Parker (1961) found that American children who watch television read as many books as nonviewers; on the other hand, they read fewer comic books. Commercial

The Influence of Television

television is reputed to accelerate the development of language skills, although this effect is most pronounced among children of deprived backgrounds (Himmelweit et al., 1958; Schramm et al., 1961). Similarly, the amount of general information to which the child is exposed prior to coming to school has increased dramatically with television. Still, television's cumulative effects are only beginning to be felt. The generation of television-reared children has not yet come fully into its own.

The Great Apes

This chapter has only glimpsed complex forces that comprise the child's environment and in large part determine his future personality. The child's relationship to these forces (Figure 4.1) was labeled an *interactive* model, implying that family, culture, peer groups, and other environmental factors interact in complex, though little understood, ways. But the forces that shape the behavior of the mountain gorilla are less complex: he belongs to a troop, and his mother is his only family; his culture is simple, consisting neither of language, nor religion and other ceremonial tradition, nor schools—and he very infrequently, if ever, has access to a television set.

While the infant gorilla lives with a troop, he spends most of his first 3 years with his mother. During this time he sleeps with her in beds which she and other gorillas have constructed by interlacing branches to form low cradles above the ground. Although he is weaned at 8 months, he continues to demonstrate a strong attachment to his mother for at least 4 years. He is a playful little thing, spending much of his time following the leader in and out of jungle thickets, up into trees, or across the open terrain of the high mountain country, and sliding down its treacherous slopes.

Will the infant gorilla grow up to be aggressive, or gentle and tender, artistic and creative, or bold and cunning? If you or I had to answer this question, should we investigate the nature of the early mother-child interaction; would we need to understand his peer group; or would we simply observe several adult gorillas of the same sex? Similarly, will a human infant grow up to be aggressive, or gentle and tender, artistic and creative, or bold and cunning? Should one observe the like-sexed adults of his cultural group? Or, should one ask further about the quality of the mother-child interaction, his peer groups, the significant events in his life, and about his television set? The question is worth thinking about.

Summary

We opened this chapter with a description of the hunt for the Great Ape, one of the great game animals of the world. It was not clear whether the hunter remained in the oppressive heat of his fly-infested bar, or whether he was still standing uncertainly in the heat of the jungle listening to the bloodcurdling roar of an angry gorilla. But the outcome of the hunt is not as important to this book as it would be for a novel, for we stopped only briefly with the Great Ape to show that he, like the human child that concerns us in this text, is not an animal whose behavior can be considered in isolation. Like most children he belongs to a group constituted of parents, siblings, and peers, and his behavior within this group, together with the behaviors expected of him (and which he later expects of himself), derive from the position he occupies. Next we studied the human child, in whose development culture, family, and peers play a significant role, and we considered the influence of these factors on the developing child, beginning with differences among cultures that may logically be attributed to environmental forces. We examined the effects of their families on children, their birth order in these families, and the size of the family. Finally, we discussed briefly the role of peer groups and television in a child's development. In the end we returned to the Great Ape, not only because he is interesting in his own right, but because he is my relative.

Main Points

1. The greatest game animal is probably man; the second greatest is the mountain gorilla. The lives of both are determined mainly by their cultures.

2. Culture, family, peer groups, and activities such as attending school and watching television constitute powerful influences on the child's behavior and development.

3. Culture may be defined as the sum of the mores, beliefs, customs, traditions, accepted behaviors, and implicit and explicit rules which characterize a people. The trappings of a culture are its language, its religion, and its schools (where some exist).

4. The concept of cultural relativity (attributed to Ruth Benedict) holds that the behavior of an individual cannot be understood in isolation from the group of which he is a member.

5. Among the most dramatic examples of culture-linked differences in personality are those provided by Margaret Mead's study of three New Guinea tribes, in which men and women both showed feminine characteristics (Arapesh), both showed masculine traits (Mundugumor), or had reversed masculine-feminine roles (Tchambuli).

6. The pressure to conform, which appears to be less powerful in our society than in the intensely personal groups that typify primitive societies, can nevertheless be potent enough to lead people to believe (and say or do) things which are at variance with their rational inclinations or beliefs.

7. Socialization is the process whereby culture is transmitted from one generation to the next. A widely accepted theory of socialization is premised on the notion that a great deal of social learning takes place through imitation.

8. The family is possibly the most powerful socializing agent in a child's development. In our society the nuclear family structure (parents and their offspring) is most common; in most other societies extended families (parents, children, grandparents, uncles, aunts, first cousins, second cousins, great-grandparents, bastards, or any combination of these) are much more common.

9. Firstborn children are often more reflective than their siblings; in addition, they are also more likely to go to college, to achieve eminence, to score more highly on tests of intellectual performance, and to develop language facility sooner. Children from multiple births (twins, triplets, quadruplets, quintuplets, sextuplets) frequently exhibit retarded development, particularly in their acquisition of language. Only children appear to have advantages similar to those of firstborns.

10. Peer groups have relatively little influence in the infant's development, but become increasingly important as the child develops, until the peer group

eventually replaces the family in importance as a source of reinforcement and advice.

11. There is little conclusive evidence that television leads to passivity, withdrawn behavior, or violence, as its critics have predicted. There is evidence, however, that television increases vocabulary (particularly in deprived children), and that television viewers are more curious and have wider ranging interests than nonviewers.

12. Infant gorillas live in troops, love their mothers, and like to slide down slopes on their hind quarters.

Further Readings

The following two references are intriguing descriptions of possible behavioral relationships between man and infra-human primates. The first is a book-length description of Gua, an ape who is reared with Donald, a human child. The similarities in the early developmental patterns of the two are remarkable. The second is a more technical discussion of nonhuman primates in research.

Kellogg, W. N., and L. A. Kellogg. *The ape and the child: A study of environmental influence upon early behavior.* New York: McGraw-Hill, 1933.

Schrier, A. M., H. S. Harlow, and F. Stollnitz (Eds.). *Behavior of non-human primates: Modern research trends.* Vol. 1. New York: Academic Press, 1965.

A relatively clear and simple description of human socialization is provided by:

McNeil, E. D. *Human socialization.* Belmont, Calif.: Brooks/Cole, 1969.

The classical and highly readable description of the three New Guinea tribes where men and women either exchange or reverse sex roles is contained in:

Mead, Margaret. *Sex and temperament in three primitive societies.* New York: New American Library, 1935.

Bossard and Boll's investigation of over 100 families, each consisting of more than six children, provides some insight into life in large families.

Bossard, J. H. and E. S. Bolls. *The large family system.* Philadelphia: University of Pennsylvania Press, 1956.

Current reports of minority group children's educational achievement and opportunity is contained in the following study:

Crossland, F. E. *Minority access to college: A Ford Foundation report.* New York: Schocken Books, 1971.

A current description of ghetto and minority group schools, and of poverty in America, is contained in:

Henderson, G. (Ed.). *America's other children: Public schools outside suburbia.* Norman, Oklahoma: University of Oklahoma Press, 1971.

A large-scale American and Canadian investigation of the effects of television on children is reported by:

Schramm, W., J. Lyle, and E. G. Parker. *Television in the lives of our children.* Stanford, Calif.: Stanford University Press, 1961.

In the following book Arnold presents an impassioned indictment of violence in children's literature, comic books, and television:

Arnold, A. *Violence and your child.* Chicago: Henry Regnery Co., 1969.

Of Korons: Learning

Imagine that you are a Koron just arrived from Koros in the Androneas system. I use "Koron" because it is more meaningful than to say "imagine that you are a Venutian" or "imagine that you are a Martian," for I have known a Koron, but have yet to meet either a Venutian or a Martian. Quite frankly I doubt that the latter two exist although I know for a fact that Korons are real since one of them lived with me for almost a year.* Imagining, then, that you are a Koron, imagine now that you find yourself looking at the human race from the perspective that a newly arrived Koron might have. You know almost nothing about humans, but you see some 3 billion of them scurrying about on the face of the earth (you might use the word "head" instead of "face" since you are from Koros). You desire information about these humans so that you can report the results of your observations to your superiors on Koros; therefore, you begin by noting the physical characteristics of the species, and you make a series of relatively platitudinous statements about sizes and weights of various members of the species. Consequently, you are chastised and instructed to proceed to an investigation of the psychological characteristics of the species. Indeed, these were your initial instructions. To save time you begin by reading the first four chapters of this book. It is an interesting exercise because you will eventually find yourself at this precise point in the text.

What have you learned about human development from your lazy stroll through these initial four chapters? And if the text were not continuing, but you as a Koron needed desperately to proceed with your investigation of human development, where would you go from here? The first question you may answer for yourself; as for the second, I will facilitate your work by providing an answer. You will recall that this part of our study is concerned with the environmental forces that are responsible for the outcome of development. A simplified summary of the substance of this section is that the child becomes whatever he is observed to be as an adult as a result of his genetic endowment in interaction with his environment. Furthermore, environment is not a global and nebulous force but consists of a number of identifiable influences, such as culture, family, peer groups, and other activities that consume much of the developing child's time. Although these terms are still somewhat nebulous, they are conceptually simpler to deal with than the global term *environment*. Finally, the evidence with which we support our belief that various environmental forces in combination with the individual's genetic complement determine his development, is dependent upon observations that we make about *changes in the behavior of individuals* with the passage of time, and presumably, with the accumulation of experience. From here we are led directly to the present chapter, since changes in behavior that result from experience are those changes that define learning.

---

*Those of you who do not believe this are referred to Lefrancois (1972b)—a book actually written by a Koron.

Learning and Development

It is quite impossible to attempt to explain or describe human development without considering learning, since learning accounts for a great many of the differences that exist between children and adults, or between children of different ages. Development is defined in Chapter 1 as including both growth and learning, since it is concerned with changes that occur in the capacities and in the behavior of individuals, and since such changes result from growth (a natural process) and/or learning (an environmental process). Learning may be defined as all changes in behavior that result from experience, provided that these changes are not the effects of drugs or fatigue (which cause temporary changes in behavior). It implies a relatively permanent change in behavior; such changes are implicit in development. Among the changes in behavior that appear as an infant develops are the ability to stand, to walk, to climb stairs, to speak words, to solve problems, and to play bingo. Quite simply, a growing child *learns* to do these things; they do not appear spontaneously. If a child is not provided with the appropriate experiences, he will not acquire the abilities described above.

Types of Learning

A hungry psychologist does not approach the task of studying learning by contenting himself with the observations made in the preceding paragraph; he goes beyond those preliminary observations, searching for explanations that will enable him to account for the widest variety of learned behaviors, that will enable him to predict behavior, and that perhaps will enable him to control it. Astute and clever scientist that he is, he finds it wise to begin with observations of the simpler behavior of lower animal forms. Animal behavior can be controlled much more precisely than that of the most phylogenetically advanced of all creatures — the one who is asking the questions.

The first eminent contributor to modern knowledge about human learning was the Russian psychologist Ivan Pavlov. In the course of research that he was doing with dogs, Pavlov (1927) observed that the older and more experienced animals in his laboratory began to salivate when they saw their keeper approaching. Since none of the dogs had ever tasted the keeper, Pavlov reasoned that they were not salivating because they expected to eat him now, but probably because they had formed some sort of **association** between the sight of the keeper and the presentation of food. The observation does not seem particularly novel or striking to us since many people have noticed that their pets anticipate food when they see a refrigerator door opening or when they hear the sound of a can opener. When I was a lad, we had a cat who hid whenever he heard the alarm clock being wound since he knew it meant that he would be put into the cellar for the night. I did not pursue my observation as Pavlov did; it was probably just as well since he had already published the results of his work. Pavlov's early observations are significant in that they lead to explanations for learning. Initially a dog will salivate only when he smells food or when it is actually in his mouth. This is simple, unlearned behavior called **reflexive** behavior, because a **stimulus** (in this case, the food) leads immediately to a **response** (salivation) without any learning taking place. A reflex is an unlearned stimulus-response connection. The fact that the sight of the keeper eventually came to lead to salivation in Pavlov's dogs (as did bells and buzzers in later experiments), although it did not originally do so, is an empirical illustration of learning—a change in behavior has occurred as a result of experience. This is the first and simplest of the two types of learning that are both referred to as **conditioning**. It is called **classical conditioning**.

Learning through classical conditioning is sometimes referred to as learning through stimulus substitution, since a stimulus that is originally neutral (one that does not elicit a response) comes to be associated with a stimulus that does occasion a response. The two stimuli are now equivalent since they elicit similar responses; one can be substituted for the other.. In the case of Pavlov's dogs the keeper is substituted for the food; both stimuli elicit salivation.

Classical Conditioning

The psychology of learning has its own language for the stimuli and responses involved in classical conditioning. The stimulus that is part of the original stimulus-response link (the reflex) is termed the **unconditioned stimulus**; the stimulus that is originally neutral but comes to be effective through repeated pairing with the unconditioned stimulus is called the *conditioned* or conditioning stimulus; the corresponding responses are termed the *conditioned response* or the **unconditioned response**, depending on whether they occur in response to the unconditioned or the conditioned stimulus. The process involved in classical conditioning is illustrated in Table 5.1.

Classical Conditioning   Table 5.1

1. UCS (food) ————————→	UCR	(salivation)
2. CS (buzzer) ————————→		(no salivation)
3. UCS + CS (food and buzzer)→	UCR	(salivation)
4. CS (buzzer) ————————→	CR	(salivation)

In (1) an unconditioned stimulus leads to an unconditioned response, whereas in (2) a conditioning stimulus does not lead to the same response. In (3) the unconditioned stimulus is paired with the conditioning stimulus a number of times so that eventually the conditioning stimulus elicits the original response (4).

The relevance of classical conditioning to human learning is not as apparent as its relevance to the behavior of lower animals, since a great deal of our behavior consists of complex verbal interactions rather than of simple, overt physical responses. Nevertheless, a relatively large number of human behaviors may be attributed to classical conditioning. Emotional responses, particularly, often appear to be reflexive and unlearned, but eventually are controlled by various external stimuli, presumably as a function of having been frequently paired with these stimuli.

For example, Watson (1930) observed that infants react with fear to loud noises, and he deduced that it should therefore be possible to make a child fear any other distinctive stimulus simply by pairing it frequently enough with a loud noise. In this case the noise is an unconditioned stimulus, since it elicits a fear response without any learning having taken place, and the responses associated with fear are therefore unconditioned responses. The neutral stimulus that Watson chose was a white rabbit, an inoffensive stimulus that does not ordinarily produce any fearful responses in young children. The unwitting subject was an unfortunate 8-month-old infant named Albert. To demonstrate the effectiveness of classical conditioning in producing emotional reactions, each time Watson presented little Albert with the rabbit he made a loud noise behind Albert. The poor infant reacted with a great deal of fear, as Watson had expected. After repeating the procedure several times, Watson ceased making the noise, but simply presented the rabbit to Albert. Much to Watson's delight, as soon as the child saw the rabbit he was terrified and began to whimper, attempting desperately to crawl away.*

Although Watson's experiment with little Albert is probably more systematic and deliberate than most situations in which children acquire their emotional responses, the results can be expanded to child development in general. There are many instances when a child will react with fear, with love, with anger, with joy, or with any other emotion he is capable of feeling; and whenever the emotion arises, it is unlikely to occur only in response to the specific stimulus that gave rise to it. Consider, for example, what would have happened if Watson had not produced a rabbit every time he made a loud noise behind Albert. Imagine, if you can, that you are little Albert, sitting on the porch of your grandfather's house (your grandfather is an inspired psychologist whom other people call "Watson," but whom you call "Grandpa Watson" when you are forced to address him). Your grandpa has borrowed you from your unsuspecting mother so that he and his pretty assistant Rosalie Rayner (Watson and Rayner, 1920) can experiment with you. You wonder whether the rabbit you saw in the cage as you came in will be brought out for you to play with. Suddenly there is a terrifying clamor behind you—your eminent grandfather is beating gongs, screaming, whistling, jumping up and down on the old boards, and kicking an inverted washtub. Meanwhile, Miss Rayner, who is probably as inspired as your grandfather, is screeching and hitting the wall with a long plank. You tremble in fear, as you sit there on the green steps. Eventually they allow you to go home, without once letting you pet the white rabbit.

The following day, your grandfather and Miss Rayner return for you and your loving but misguided mother grants permission. They repeat the procedure again, and again the following day, and perhaps once more the following week, and twice each year for the next 3 years. At the age of 5 you go fishing with your father, and as you prepare to step into the boat you suddenly begin to tremble and perspire; fear wells

---

* It should also be noted that Watson eventually cured little Albert of his great fear of white furry animals by exposing him to rabbits when the boy was eating. The effect of this procedure was to **countercondition** a pleasant response in place of the fear.

up in your heart; you shudder; finally you can no longer contain yourself and you run screaming into the lake. The seat of the boat was painted the same dull green as the porch of your grandfather's house.

While somewhat extreme, the illustration is not unreasonable. There is considerable anecdotal evidence that emotional reactions do generalize from one situation to another, or that aspects of particular situations become strongly associated with the emotional reactions that those situations have occasioned. The person who reacts with fear to the sound of a dentist's drill is not trembling because the *sound* of the drill has been responsible for any pain that he has felt in the past. But, the sound of the drill has always been associated with pain and has thus acquired the capability of eliciting reactions that are associated with pain. Similarly, a child who dislikes his teacher and who reacts negatively to the presence of that teacher may eventually react negatively to the classroom itself, or perhaps to school related activities, or to adults who resemble his teacher, or to children who resemble other students in his class, or to pencils.

Among the various explanations advanced for an object's acquiring meaning is one based on a classical conditioning procedure (Osgood, 1957; Staats and Staats, 1963). This explanation essentially maintains that the meaning of an object is derived from all of the associations that it has had in the past. For example, a white rabbit meant fear and unpleasantness for little Albert at one point in his life. That was not because the animal incorporates fear as part of its *logical* meaning, but because its *psychological* meaning for a specific individual was derived from associations with fear-producing situations. Obviously meaning is much more complex than this example implies, but the process by which individuals acquire **affective** (connotative or emotional) meanings may be accurately described by the model of classical conditioning presented in the foregoing section.

Operant Conditioning

While people like Watson (1930), Guthrie (1935), and other American psychologists tried to determine how much human learning they could explain through classical conditioning, B. F. Skinner (1951, 1957, 1961) later suggested that a great deal of human behavior falls outside the confining limits of this explanation — a fact which now appears obvious. He observed that there are indeed many behaviors that occur in direct response to stimuli, and that for these behaviors it is not inappropriate to employ a simple model of classical conditioning. In addition, he asserted that most significant human behaviors are not **elicited** by any obvious stimuli, but appear instead to be **emitted** by the organism, for whatever reason. Skinner labeled such behaviors **operants**; responses that are elicited by stimuli he labeled **respondents**.

Having described these two major classes of behavior, Skinner undertook the work for which he has now become famous — explaining how operant behavior is learned. He eventually developed a model of **operant conditioning** (also called instrumental learning). Together with *classical conditioning*, these are the two types of learning that are basic to understanding human behavior.

The simplest explanation of operant conditioning is that a response followed by **reinforcement** will be more likely to reoccur when the organism finds itself in a similar situation to that which surrounded the behavior's first occurrence. In other words, the consequence of a response determines whether it is learned or not learned—a statement that is fundamentally different from saying that learning will occur as a function of the stimuli to which it has been conditioned, regardless of the consequences of a response. Clearly, when little Albert reacted with fear to the rabbit, it was not because his fear responses led to pleasant consequences, but because the rabbit was paired with some other fear-producing situation. The principal differences between operant and classical conditioning are illustrated in Table 5.2.

Table 5.2

Classical	Operant
Deals with *Respondents,* which are *elicited* by *stimuli.*	Deals with *Operants,* which are *emitted* as *instrumental* acts
Type S (stimuli) Pavlov	*Type R* (reinforcement) Skinner

Operant Learning Model
1. Response$_x$ ⟶ Reward and discriminated stimuli (S_D)
2. S_D ⟶ Response$_x$

As an illustration of operant conditioning, consider the case of a used-car salesman who once worked in an area in which poor people bought used cars and now works in an area in which rich people buy used cars. His selling technique, perfected through many years of experience in the used-car business, involves telling people how easy it is to pay a small sum of money every month for the next 28 years when one can own the car "this very day, my friend. This very afternoon, as sure as I'm standing here in front of you, you can get behind the wheel of that car and drive away with it. Yes sir! I tell you, here are the keys, and you just give me $12.34 down and a few cents a day for the next 28 years, and off you go." This technique is not likely to be successful in the new environment in which the salesman finds himself, but it is quite likely that within a short period of time he will have so few reinforcements for his efforts that he will begin to emit a new range of operant behavior. After a time he will find himself reinforced more and more frequently, without actually realizing how his behavior has changed. An observer listening to him might notice a different technique, which, like the first, was acquired as a result of reinforcement.

I want to show you something special here that we just received, Doctor Lefrancois. By the way, how's the dog? And the wife and kids? Great, great. Now here is a car that will serve you well. Suits you to a T. Just came in — very special. Got a real deal on it. Volume you know. Now if you want to pay cash, and I know that a man in your position will surely want to pay cash and avoid all that interest. You know, some people get taken on payments something fierce. Me, I wouldn't sell a guy a car on terms — not with those outrageous interest rates. Ah, here it is. It's just 10 years old, it has just a little over 100,000 miles on it, but you can have it for $25 cash, right now.

Rats.   Most of Skinner's work has investigated the conditions under which operant behavior becomes learned or *extinguished* (a term that means something like forgetting; it is defined more precisely later). His investigation required that he define and examine the various kinds of reinforcement that are available, and that he experiment with the manner in which reinforcement may be given to the subject. The work is relatively simple, and its results are clearly applicable to much of the learning that children engage in as they develop. Most of Skinner's subjects have been rats (of the celebrated *rattus norvegicus albinus* variety) although he has also used some chickens, pigeons, and children. A typical Skinnerian experiment employing a rat easily illustrates most of his major findings.

The experiment takes place in a cagelike structure that is not inappropriately labeled a **Skinner box** (see Figure 5.1). Its floor consists of a wire grid through which a low amperage electric current may flow. At

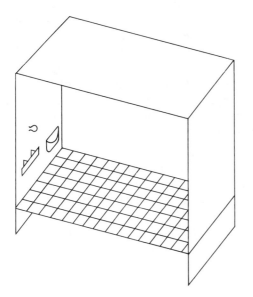

A Skinner Box   Figure 5.1

one end of the cage is a bar or lever that the subject can depress. This lever is connected to a food-dispensing mechanism so that whenever the lever is depressed, a food pellet drops into a tray that is also located at that end of the cage. Above the bar is a light that may be connected to the lever so that it will shine whenever a food pellet drops into the tray. The experimenter may also disconnect either the light or the food mechanism and operate either of these manually.

The simplest experiment that can be performed with this device and a hungry rat is to teach the rat to depress the lever. Actually no teaching need be done since the rat is capable of learning this complicated response all by himself, provided that the food mechanism is connected to the bar. (Besides, rats are extremely inattentive whenever scientists attempt to talk to them.) Indeed, he will learn to depress the lever in a remarkably short period of time, simply as a result of being reinforced with food for doing so. All the elements necessary to explain operant learning are present; the bar-pressing behavior of the rat is an operant, since it does not occur in response to any specific or known stimulus, and the food reinforces this behavior. Repeating the procedure demonstrates the increased probability of the response occurring again, whenever the rat finds himself in the same situation. Most reasonably intelligent rats whose brains have not been excessively damaged with electrodes inexpertly implanted in them will go directly to the lever.

I mention brain-damaged rats since it was once my embarrassing misfortune to find myself in the company of a rat whose brain had been extensively damaged by an overzealous undergraduate. I had intended to demonstrate to a large group of students how simple and easy it is to condition a rat to depress a lever. I attempted to do this while I delivered a brilliant and scintillating lecture. I placed the Skinner Box on a table at the front of the room so that the students could observe the rat as they listened to the wisdom which was mine to offer them that day. For some reason that was not immediately apparent to me, but that became painfully clear later, the usual number of students fell asleep. I had not expected this behavior on that day since I thought that the rat at least would keep their interest focused on the front of the room, rather than on the inside of their eyelids; but the rat had also gone to sleep. It was only later that I discovered him to be a severely brain-damaged example of *rattus norvegicus albinus.*

Reinforcement. One of Skinner's first tasks was to define the nature of reinforcement. Since he was determined to be objective, and since he did not intend to formulate elaborate theoretical explanations for the phenomena that he observed, he advanced a simple and objective definition for the term: whatever increases the probability of a response occurring is reinforcing. A **reinforcer** is the stimulus that reinforces; reinforcement is the *effect* of a reinforcer. It is important to note that reinforcement is defined by its effect, since this eliminates a great deal of the confusion that still exists around the difference between such things as negative reinforcement and punishment. **Negative reinforcement** is one kind of reinforcement; the other is **positive reinforcement**. Both positive and negative reinforcement increase the probability of a response occurring. The difference between the two is that positive reinforcement is effective as a result of a reward being added to a situation after the behavior has occurred, whereas negative reinforcement is effective through the removal of an unpleasant stimulus. If, for example, the rat is fed every time he depresses the lever, and the effect of the food is an observable increase in the probability that the response will occur again, this is positive reinforcement; the rat is rewarded by an addition. If, on the other hand, a sadistic psychologist has turned on the current in the grid on which the rat is standing, and will shut off the current only when the rat depresses the lever, the effect of this will also be an increase in the probability of the lever's being depressed again. In this case, however, the reinforcement of the rat's depressing the lever is the removal of the stimulus, rather than presentation of a reward, and is therefore an example of negative reinforcement.

Punishment. **Punishment** is distinguished from reinforcement by its effects. Whereas reinforcement, whether positive or negative, serves to make a response more likely, punishment does not. There is general agreement, however, that it does not have a directly opposite effect; that is, punishment does not necessarily decrease the probability of a response occurring, but may simply lead to its temporary suppression. In addition, punishment can have undesirable side effects, not the least of which are the negative emotional reactions that frequently appear, and sometimes become associated with the punisher rather than with the offense. Distinctions among the various kinds of reinforcement and punishment are illustrated in Figure 5.2. The illustration makes it clear that both may involve pleasant or unpleasant stimuli, but that whether these stimuli are added to or removed from the situation determines their effect. Reinforcement and punishment are defined primarily by their effects.

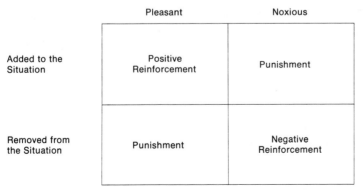

The four alternatives that define punishment and reinforcement.   Figure 5.2

Illustrations of positive and negative reinforcement were provided earlier; the illustration that follows describes the two types of punishment. Consider the case of a young lad whose nefarious daily activities recently included dropping cigarette butts into the goldfish bowl, thereby poisoning and killing all of its occupants. As a consequence of his behavior the boy's mother isolated him in his room, thus depriving him of social contact and food. This type of punishment specifically involves removing a pleasant stimulus. If, when the boy's father comes home, he proceeds to apply the hickory stick to his unfortunate progeny's rump, he will have served to illustrate the second type of punishment, that which involves presenting a noxious or unpleasant stimulus.

Other Kinds of Reinforcement. Skinner further distinguishes among three types of reinforcers, each of which can be either positive or negative. First, there are those stimuli that are reinforcing in the absence of learning. That is, there are stimuli that an organism does not have to learn about. Animals and people know that food, drink, and sex are pleasant (although perhaps the latter is not recognized as pleasant without some learning or maturation). These stimuli are referred to as **primary reinforcers** since they are related to primary (unlearned) drives. Second, there are stimuli that are not reinforcing to begin with but that become reinforcing when paired frequently enough with primary reinforcers — the process is obviously classical conditioning. The rat in his Skinner box can demonstrate *secondary reinforcement*. The light is clearly a neutral or nonreinforcing stimulus initially. The rat would be very unlikely to learn bar-pressing behavior if the light went on but no food dropped into his tray. If, on the other hand, a food pellet is released into the tray whenever the rat depresses the lever, and in addition, the light goes on, the light will eventually acquire secondary reinforcing properties. Thus, if he has been well conditioned he will continue to press the lever simply to see the light go on.

There are in addition those stimuli that have been paired with primary reinforcers or secondary reinforcers so often that they have become reinforcing in a number of situations, and for a variety of different behaviors. These are called **generalized reinforcers**. It is not certain that there are generalized reinforcers for rats, but examples are plentiful for humans. Praise, social prestige, money, power, and many other behavioral consequences are reinforcing in almost any situation and for nearly any behavior. Recently it has become customary to refer to all nonprimary reinforcement as *secondary;* generalized reinforcement is simply one example of secondary reinforcement.

Schedules of Reinforcement. Learning operant behavior is dependent not only on the presence or absence of reinforcement or punishment, but also on the manner in which they are presented (the **reinforcement schedule**). In an experimental situation the psychologist has two basic choices: he can decide that reinforcement should occur for every correct trial (response), or that it should occur only part of the time. The first schedule of reinforcement is labeled **continuous**; the second is *intermittent.* If the experimenter opts for the first choice, he has no further decisions to make since reinforcement will occur for every correct response. If he decides to reinforce intermittently (also called partial reinforcement), he can make one of two further choices. He can decide that the reinforcement will be based on the passage of time (**interval reinforcement**) or that it will be based on a proportion of trials (**ratio reinforcement**). In either case, he has still another decision to make. The reinforcement can occur at **random** (*variable*) times, or it can be **fixed**. That is, he can decide that every fifth response will be reinforced (fixed-ratio reinforcement) or that one of every five responses will be reinforced but that it will be done on a random basis (variable-ratio reinforcement). Similarly, he can decide to reinforce every 30 seconds on the average, but at random times, or precisely on the thirtieth, the sixtieth, and the ninetieth second (and on, and on). All of this might sound complicated, but it is simplified in Figure 5.3.

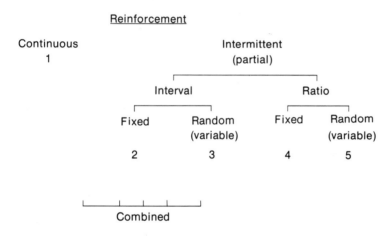

The five basic schedules of reinforcement: continuous, fixed interval, random interval, fixed ratio, and random ratio. These may be combined in a variety of ways.   Figure 5.3

Effects of Different Schedules.   Schedules of reinforcement directly affect the rate with which a response is acquired and the length of time or the number of trials that are required before the response is extinguished once the reinforcement has been withdrawn. Both these variables (acquisition and extinction rate) are considered measures of learning. Extinction is defined as the cessation of a response resulting from the withdrawal of reinforcement. Extinction differs from forgetting since it requires that a response occur in the absence of reinforcement. Forgetting is the cessation of a response as a function of the passage of time, rather than as a function of the withdrawal of reinforcement. Extinction is a relatively rapid process, depending on the schedule of reinforcement that was used in the conditioning process; forgetting occurs more slowly.

In general, continuous schedules of reinforcement lead to more rapid acquisition of a response, both for animals and for children; they also lead, however, to more rapid extinction when withdrawn. The behavior of an organism generally reflects expectations that it develops as a result of reinforcement. For example, under a fixed-interval schedule of reinforcement (the reinforcement occurs after the first correct response following a fixed period of time), the rate at which a rat will emit bar-pressing responses decreases immediately after the reinforcement, but increases dramatically just prior to the next reinforcement. Under variable schedules of reinforcement, the rate of response remains relatively high and uniform, presumably because the animal has not been able to develop expectations about reinforcement (see Figure 5.4).

Schedules of reinforcement appear to have similar effects on humans as they have on rats, pigeons, and other creatures. As I have noted elsewhere (Lefrancois, 1972a), the fisherman who has caught fish in the same stream every time he fished in it will probably cease to go to that stream after several outings during which he catches no fish (rapid extinction following continuous reinforcement). Conversely, a fisherman who only occasionally catches fish in a stream will probably continue to go to the stream even after catching no fish for many consecutive trips (slow extinction following intermittent reinforcement).

Shaping.   Most significant human behaviors are operant behaviors. Not only are they not elicited as responses to any known stimuli, but they appear to be learned primarily as a function of their consequences. Most of these behaviors are highly complex, however, so that

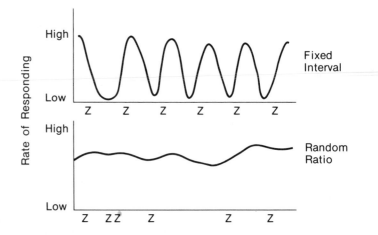

Figure 5.4   An approximate representation of bar-pressing behavior under two different schedules of reinforcement with reinforcement occurring at Z.

it is difficult to describe learning as simply the emission of an operant followed by reinforcement. Ordinary human behavior frequently involves sequences of more or less complex responses, rather than simple responses such as the bar-pressing behavior of a rat. And even the rats bar-pressing behavior is sufficiently complex that an experimenter does not usually wait for it to appear and be reinforced, if his intention is to condition the rat. Instead he employs the technique called shaping, developed by Skinner to teach animals behaviors that are not included in their comman repertoire of activities.

Shaping involves reinforcing any response emitted by the organism that brings it closer to the desired behavior. For example, a rat who is being conditioned to depress a lever is first trained to become accustomed to eating from the food tray in the Skinner box and to the noise made by the mechanism when it releases food into the tray. Through a process of classical conditioning the sound of the mechanism comes to be associated with food and may be used as a signal to the rat that food is being provided. Next, it is relatively simple to get him to depress the lever by reinforcing every move that brings him closer to the bar and by not reinforcing any other move. For obvious reasons the procedure is also referred to as the *differential reinforcement of successive approximations.*

We can increase our understanding of complex human behaviors by studying Skinnerian shaping techniques. Refined motor activities probably require eliminating ineffective responses and modifying effective responses. The reinforcement (for example, applause) that a performer receives concerning the quality of his behavior may signal him to modify his behavior to elicit the greatest amount of reinforcement. This reinforcement gradually *shapes* the performer's behavior. Verbal behavior is particularly susceptible to the effects of positive or negative reinforcement. Only the most insensitive person will continue to talk after most of his audience shows signs of falling asleep. Frequently, however, the lack of reinforcement is more subtle than this, but no less effective. Greenspoon (1955), and Verplanck (1955) have shown that a subject's language behavior can be altered dramatically without his being aware of it. The typical experimental procedure is to have a subject say words. The experimenter has decided beforehand what variety of expression he wishes to reinforce—nouns, verbs, expressions of feelings, and so on. The reinforcement includes making some subtle sign of approval whenever the subject responds in the desired way. The experimenter may reinforce the subject by smiling, nodding almost imperceptibly, saying "hmhm," or simply looking attentive. Almost invariably the subject significantly increases the frequency of the words or expressions that are being reinforced.

The experiments with verbal conditioning demonstrate the tremendous susceptibility of human behavior to reinforcement. They also help explain why conversations can be so easily manipulated by people who intuitively or consciously realize that they can control much of the content of a person's speech by simply withholding or presenting reinforcement.

Operant
Conditioning
and Children

Reese and Lipsitt (1970) recently reviewed a large number of studies exploring operant conditioning in children. Many of these studies were concerned with verifying conclusions about children from experiments that were originally conducted with animals. In general these conclusions have been found to be valid. For example, children, like animals, are more resistant to extinction following intermittent reinforcement, than following continuous reinforcement. Siqueland (1968) found that newly born infants can be conditioned to turn their heads, and that this behavior is more resistant to extinction if it has been reinforced on an intermittent schedule. Similar patterns apply to an infant's smiling response (Etzel and Gewirtz, 1967), vocalization (Weisberg, 1963), kicking (Lindsley, 1963), and numerous other behaviors.

We do not rear our children in experimental situations, however. We seldom enclose them in Skinner boxes (although Skinner himself did) to observe or control their learning. Nor do most of us have access to the elaborate and expensive equipment required to measure the intensity and frequency of such responses as head turning, visual fixation on an object, kicking, smiling, sucking, or salivating. Consequently, many people (among whom are a number of otherwise normal psychologists) have summarily dismissed Skinner's work and related theory and research. It is currently fashionable (and has been for at least 30 years) to claim that a child is not a rat. This observation has added little to our understanding of human behavior and development. Humanists argue further that a child is much more than simply an organism; his behavior cannot be reduced solely to such simplistic notions as stimulus and response. Nevertheless, we can derive a much better understanding of human behavior and learning by analyzing the elements in the process. To do so is not necessarily to dehumanize the child, although it may not consider all facets of his humanity. But humanism is the subject of the final chapter, which is yet some distance.

In the meantime, pretend again that you are a Koron and that you are serious about wanting to discover how relevant operant conditioning is for explaining, predicting, and controlling human behavior. To facilitate your interpretation, imagine that the world is an enormous Skinner box (as Gardiner [1970, p. 77] has), and that it is filled with smaller Skinner boxes. The people who inhabit these smaller boxes emit a variety of operants, some of which have been reinforced in the past, and some of which are being emitted for the first time. These new behaviors will be learned if they are reinforced—they will result in relatively permanent changes in behavior if their consequences are pleasant. The obvious question, if this analogy holds for human behavior, is what is the source of reinforcement for human operant behavior.

Sources of
Reinforcement

There are three different types of reinforcement: primary, secondary and generalized, each of which can be either positive or negative. Generalized reinforcers are most important in determining human behavior. There are other ways of classifying reinforcement. Reese and Lipsitt (1971) refer to appetitional reinforcers (food and water), social reinforcers (physical contact such as caresses) and auditory and visual reinforcers (sounds or pictorial stimuli). Bijou and Sturges (1959) have identified the following five classes of reinforcement that may be instrumental in affecting the child's behavior.

First there are *consumables*—meat and potatoes, milk, water, and rum. Their effectiveness in influencing behavior is not as obvious for well-fed children as for indigent children who lack consumables. Most of our children are sufficiently nourished that they do not engage in many behaviors that are designed to get them food, particularly after they have passed through their infancy. However, it is no secret that a baby who cries when he is hungry, thereby awakening his mother and alerting her to his desperate need, will soon learn to cry whenever he is hungry. Nor is it a secret that a child's behavior can frequently be modified in desirable directions by rewarding him with candies and other consumables.

A second class of reinforcers that have been used in experimental situations (but that also occur frequently in a child's daily activities) are called *manipulatables*. These include all the objects that a child finds pleasant to play with; chief among these are his toys.

There is a third class of reinforcers, comprising *visual and auditory* stimuli, that is more relevant to experimental situations than to real life. That is, most visual or auditory stimuli that are reinforcing are social stimuli as well and are therefore more properly classified with the next groups of reinforcers. Nevertheless, visual or auditory stimuli—such as a bell that signifies an accomplishment or a display of lights that signals success with a one-arm bandit—may be employed occasionally with children.

The fourth category of reinforcers is *social* stimuli: smiles, verbal praise, physical contact such as a pat on the back or a handshake. These are probably among the most powerful reinforcers for humans.

Fifth, there are reinforcers called *token* reinforcers. This category includes chips, disks, counters, or anything that can be exchanged for some more meaningful reinforcer. This procedure has been successful in numerous experiments particularly with mentally retarded children (educable retarded, slow learner, or disadvantaged child are all more euphemistic but essentially synonymous expressions). Birnbauer, Wolf, Kidder, and Tague (1965) report successful attempts to increase the academic achievement of retarded students by employing a token reinforcement system consisting of check marks that can be exchanged for some more desirable reinforcer. The check marks were entered on a student's sheet only when he performed correctly on programmed material. When the reinforcement was discontinued there was a marked drop in his level of academic performance. A similar experiment was reported by Perline and Levinsky (1968) in which token reinforcement was used to eliminate disruptive behavior.

Another method of reinforcement is called the Premack (1965) principle. It is based on the fact that behaviors which occur frequently and spontaneously can be employed to reinforce other behavior. An obvious application of this principle is a teacher who allows his students to read their favorite books when they complete their assignments. In this case, reading occurs frequently and spontaneously and is assumed to be pleasant; therefore, it can be reinforcing.

Other Views of Learning

The preceding sections of this chapter have described two basic types of learning: classical and operant conditioning. The discussion has been simplified to avoid the confusion that may result from a more detailed examination of some of the concepts discussed. The definitions and explanations of learning presented thus far are based mainly on the work of Pavlov (1927), Thorndike (1949), Skinner, (1953), and Watson (1930). Hill (1963), Hilgard and Bower (1966), Kimble (1961), and Lefrancois (1972a, 1972b) present more detailed treatments of related topics. An examination of the references cited above should make it clear that the relatively simple concepts discussed in this chapter are summaries of much more complex formulations.

The account of learning presented in the discussion of classical and operant conditioning is sometimes referred to as **behavioristic theory**, or as S-R (stimulus-response) theory. Behavioristic theory is concerned solely with those aspects of behavior that are objective (observable). Objective behavior is limited to stimuli and responses. There are two predominant alternative orientations regarding learning: the **neobehavioristic** and the cognitive. Neobehavioristic theories are behavioristic insofar as they are concerned with the role of stimuli and responses in human behavior and learning. They are labeled *neo* because, unlike early behaviorists such as Watson and Guthrie, modern behaviorists are also concerned with what happens to the organism between the presentation of a stimulus and the occurrence of a response; they deal with *intervening* or **mediating** events, as well as objective stimulus–response events.

Cognitivism refers to the theory that is more concerned with *cognition*—that is, with such things as knowing, perceiving, problem solving, decision making, awareness, and related intellectual activities—than with stimuli and responses. Some contemporary theorists who are neobehaviorists are Osgood (1957a, 1957b), Hebb (1949, 1966), Berlyne (1960, 1965, 1966), and Staats and Staats (1963); Ausubel, (1963, 1968), Bruner (1957a, 1957b, 1968), Piaget (1952, 1957, 1968), and the Gestaltists are cognitivists.

These classifications are crude, and none of the researchers mentioned above is involved purely with one orientation to the complete exclusion of the other. No responsible theorist will explicitly deny the validity of an operant or a classical conditioning explanation for some aspects of human learning, though not all have explicitly accepted such explanations either. Each cognitivist is potentially a little behavioristic.

Since psychology became a science (assumed to coincide with Wundt's introduction of scientific methodology to psychology in Leipzig in 1879), learning theories have been a source of incessant controversy. Succeeding theoretical positions sought to establish themselves on the bones of those that had come before—a procedure that ordinarily required the destruction of the older position first. Learning theorists continually destroyed older theories and built new ones on their remains. Throughout their struggles, theorists were trying to arrive at the learning theory that would account for *all* human behavior. None has yet been found; indeed, more skeptical researchers have abandoned the great struggle for an all-encompassing answer. They now quest for explanations of smaller aspects of learning. It is a quest that is premised on the assumption that there is no unitary theory that will explain all learning, but that there are different models that might explain different phenomena in learning. There have been attempts to integrate knowledge about learning (for example, Melton, 1964; Gagné, 1970; Bandura, 1969). One attempt at integration, Bandura (1969), is discussed below. Aspects of Bandura's theory form a recurrent theme in the description of the developing child that comprises the final part of this narrative.

Bandura contends that human behavior is a product of three related control systems, each distinguishable from the others by its particular behavior. First, there is behavior directly controlled by external stimuli; second, there is behavior controlled by its consequences; and third, there is behavior that is controlled by internal (symbolic) processes. Consider an illustration of these behavior control systems stolen from a facetious but not inappropriate passage from Lefrancois (1972b):

Behavior
Control Systems

> For example, a man who pursues a buck-toothed, cross-eyed, knock-kneed, pigeon-toed, skinny, red-headed woman may well be directed by stimuli, outcomes, and symbolization. In the first place, the pursued redhead is a woman, and because of stimulus generalization the pursuer reacts to this woman as he would to any other. His pursuing behavior is under the direct control of the stimulus *woman,* because *woman* is the stimulus that has been present at the time of many previous reinforcements. But human behavior is not this simple. The pursuer does not just respond to this signal in the blind manner expected of an unsophisticated rat, but he responds in a manner directed by its immediate outcomes. If his initial approach is met by strong resistance, he may modify it; if it is rewarded, he may intensify it; if the intensification leads to more reward, it may be reintensified; if it leads to a cessation of reinforcement, it may be deintensified. Quite simply, the human male is capable of changing his behavior in accordance with its outcomes. But the direction of activity is not this simple either. Man does not react solely to stimuli or to the consequences of his behavior, although it is obviously necessary that he do so to some extent. Also, his actions are guided by symbolic processes. For example, the human male pursues an unattractive redhead because he can represent imaginally the consequences of being successful in his attempt to capture her. He can clearly visualize that such an ugly woman must possess hidden talents to offset her lack of obvious qualities — she must certainly be an excellent cook.

Each of these behavior control systems can also be differentiated by its theoretical implications. For example, behavior directly controlled by stimuli includes numerous responses with which early behaviorists, who based their theories on models of classical conditioning, have been concerned. All reflexes such as sneezing, coughing, the startle reaction, and salivation, are obviously controlled by the stimuli that inspired them. Furthermore, all stimuli that become associated with behavior through classical conditioning acquire control over that behavior. For example, blowing a puff of air into a person's eyes can cause him to blink. If the puff of air is paired with some other distinctive stimulus such as the sound of a bell, the second stimulus will also (through classical conditioning) elicit the eye-blink response. A great many of our behaviors are controlled by stimuli that have become meaningful through classical conditioning.

Responses elicited by a stimulus which was frequently present at the time of reinforcement or of punishment form another class of behaviors controlled by stimuli. After being reinforced for certain behavior in one situation and perhaps punished for the same behavior in another situation, a child learns when certain behaviors are appropriate. This behavior comes to be controlled by the stimulus complex that defines the situation. More specifically, a child who invariably shrieks in glee and runs about madly whenever he is taken to the park, but who walks slowly and sits quietly in church, is demonstrating behavior that is directly controlled by the immediate situation.

The second behavior control system includes behaviors that are controlled by their outcomes rather than by stimuli that exist independent of the behavior. Operant conditioning explains this form of response. The outcome of behavior is not simply the reinforcement or the lack of it to which we referred earlier. All the feedback that an organism receives from his environment about the appropriateness of his behavior, unless the individual is totally unresponsive, will direct his future behavior. It is true that such environmental feedback is a type of reinforcement, since knowledge that one is performing correctly is reinforcing, just as knowledge that one is not performing adequately is not reinforcing, or even punishing. Furthermore, many behaviors that may be initiated by external stimulation may eventually be directed by its outcomes. Similar to our earlier example, the child who runs screaming through the park was responding directly to the situation. If, however, a funeral is being conducted in the park as the boy comes whooping through, his behavior is likely to be influenced almost immediately by the severe social disapproval which he will meet.

Behavior that is controlled by symbolic processes defines the third behavior control system. Simply, man is able to represent to himself _internally_ both the probable outcomes of his actions and their long-range consequences. Were it not for our ability to anticipate long-range reinforcement (outcomes), we would not undertake a great many behaviors in which we engage. Most of the goals toward which we strive are distant; indeed, there are those who work toward goals which they do not expect to obtain in their lifetimes. Thus much of our behavior may be controlled by our _imagining_ its consequences.

Symbolic processes also determine behavior through the internal verbalizing of rules. Bandura (1969) cites an experiment by Miller (1951) in which subjects were conditioned to react negatively to the letter "T" and positively to the number "4" by means of electric shocks. Next they were instructed to think *T* or *4* alternately as a series of dots were presented to them: they were asked to think *T* for the first dot, *4* for the second, *T* for the third, and so on. Although the electric shocks were discontinued following the first part of the experiment, subjects still experienced an autonomic reaction (increased heartbeat, for example) coincident with the dots that were associated with the letter *T*. This can be interpreted as the effect of internal (symbolic) processes on behavior.

The majority of Bandura's work has attempted to explain social learning through processes of imitation (covered in more detail in Chapter 7). Nevertheless, his classification of human behavior based on whether it is controlled by stimuli, controlled by its outcome, or controlled through symbolic processes is conceptually simple, concise, and potentially valuable for increasing our understanding of the child's progressive adaptation to his world.* **Child Learning**

While an understanding of the principles of classical and operant conditioning is essential to an examination of human development, the processes underlying much of the behavior of children are still much more complex than the theories presented in this chapter would suggest. Many of the principles of operant conditioning apply to the behavior of young children, and relatively simplistic explanations of emotional responses may occasionally make use of the psychologist's knowledge of classical conditioning. However, the fundamental point, which was mentioned but not emphasized, is that the child is infinitely more complex than is the rat. One aspect of the child's complexity that renders simple S-R explanations of human behavior somewhat less than adequate is the fact that the child can speak. (Sam, troublemaker that he is, claims that his rat can understand Russian, however.) It has been reported, however, that most children cannot speak when they are first born; they usually acquire the ability to speak sometime during the first year or two of their lives. If one of the principal differences between man and animal is language, it should follow that the very young child's behavior (or perhaps a very old man's) is more like an animal than yours or mine. Psychological research supports this hypothesis.

In addition to the studies cited earlier demonstrating the principles of operant conditioning in the behavior of young children, consider the following study reported by Lipsitt, Kaye, and Bosack (1966). Twenty infants (35 to 94 hours old) were divided into control and experimental groups. All subjects had short tubes placed in their mouths and a record was kept of the number of sucking movements made by the infants. After 15 seconds, the tube was removed for a short period, and then reinserted for another 15 seconds. The difference between the experimental and the

*See Chapter 7 for a discussion of two related topics: social learning theory, and behavior modification.

control group was that the former was given a water-dextrose (sugar) solution during the last 5 seconds of the 15 second period; the control group received the dextrose solution by spoon 30 seconds after the tube had been removed. As expected, the experimental group increased their rate of sucking prior to the tube's removal; the control group showed no increase.

The Kendler Research   In contrast, the bulk of the Kendler studies (Kendler and Kendler, 1959, 1962; Kendler, Gluckberg and Keston, 1961; T. S. Kendler, 1963) illustrate through experiments in discrimination learning that simple learning theory is far from adequate as an explanation of child behavior. The typical discrimination-learning experiment requires the subject to learn to select between two stimuli, both of which vary in at least two ways. For example, one stimulus might be square and black, and the other round and red. The possibilities are black squares, black circles, red squares, and red circles. With reinforcement, both children and animals (rats, pigeons, pigs) can learn to discriminate among the relevant choices. Suppose that red is the relevant variable; then both red squares and red circles are reinforced and the subject soon learns that the *form* of the stimulus object is irrelevant. Following this initial learning, there appears to be little difference between the performance of human subjects and animal subjects, particularly if the humans in question are relatively young. However, if one or two further variables are introduced into the situation, there is a remarkable change. The first variation requires the subject to respond to the opposite of the relevant dimension. That is, if red were selected, he would be required to respond to all black stimuli (either by selecting them or by depressing a key). This type of learning is considered a **reversal shift**. Another variation requires the subject to respond to the previously irrelevant dimension: here he would select the stimulus by its shape rather than its color. This second variation is labeled a **nonreversal shift** (see Figure 5.5).

Investigations comparing the relative difficulty of these two response shifts for children and for rats indicate that a nonreversal shift is the simpler of the two types of learning for the rat, but that the reversal shift is simpler for human children and adults (Kendler and D'Amato, 1955). The analysis of this finding reveals both the relevance and the inadequacy of S-R theory as an explanation of learning.

If a discrimination problem is solved through simple stimulus-response (by associating one stimulus dimension with reinforcement, and by associating all other stimulus dimensions with nonreinforcement), it follows that learning a reversal shift would be relatively difficult. The subject would not only have to learn to respond to a dimension of the stimulus for which he had never been reinforced, but he would also have to learn *not* to respond to the previously reinforced dimension. A nonreversal shift, on the other hand, would require that the subject discriminate between two dimensions of the stimulus that had been rewarded or not rewarded an approximately equal numbers of times. If, on the other hand, the solution to the discrimination problem were arrived at through some sort of rule mediating in the subject's attempts to solve the problem, and not solely or not primarily through simple association, a reversal shift should be simpler since it would require only slight modification of that rule. The rule in our example is concerned with identifying the relevant dimension of the stimulus. In a reversal shift, that dimension does not change – hence there remains only one response (the black rather than the red). Since a nonreversal shift involves a change in the relevant dimension (shape rather than color), two alternatives are possible (round or square).

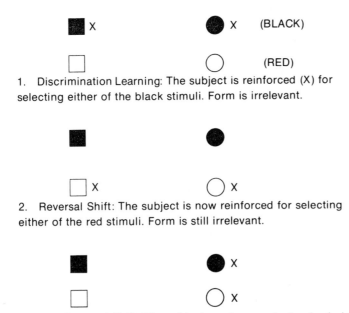

1. Discrimination Learning: The subject is reinforced (X) for selecting either of the black stimuli. Form is irrelevant.

2. Reversal Shift: The subject is now reinforced for selecting either of the red stimuli. Form is still irrelevant.

3. Non-Reversal Shift: The subject must now select only circles. Color has become irrelevant.

Discrimination learning, reversal shifts, and nonreversal shifts.   Figure 5.5

If your mind is not completely **boggled** by now, recall that the rat finds a nonreversal shift easier than a reversal shift. To clear your confusion, reread the preceding section – it is tremendously important. We have ascertained quite definitely what both you and your grandmother have probably suspected for some time – rats and children are fundamentally different. These experiments also illustrate that the child learns in a manner basically different from the rat's because something called *mediation* assists him. Mediation is the formulation of rules, which may take the form of verbal responses. The child's ability to verbalize and to use rules (to mediate) is integral to his ability to learn. (See Part Four of this text, particularly Chapter 11.)

Summary   At the beginning of this chapter you were asked to imagine that you were a Koron from the Androneas system, not so much to discover what it feels like to be a Koron – for Kongor (Lefrancois, 1972b) always maintained that Korons do not feel, they simply think – but so that you would gain a fresh perspective in your commendable attempt to achieve a better understanding of the human child. It was hoped that from this new perspective, looking down at the human race as it were, you would see that the child's progress in struggling to adapt to the world is evident in the behaviors he exhibits. Further, the process of development can be defined as sequential changes in these behaviors or in the capabilities that give rise to them. Since learning is concerned with changes in behavior that result from experience, it became obvious that a discussion of learning was in order. Thus, the chapter then proceeded to a discussion of two fundamental types of learning – classical and operant conditioning. The major features of each and the behaviors they explain were discussed in some detail. It was pointed out that there are numerous other theoretical approaches to human learning, but that these could not be dealt with in this chapter. Bandura's description of the systems that control human behavior integrated the theories of human learning. Finally, children were distinguished from rats through the conceptual process of mediation. The learning theories in this chapter are recurrent themes in the third part of this book.

Main Points   1. Development includes growth and learning. Learning is a relatively permanent change in the behavior of an individual resulting from experience.

2. The two basic types of learning are classical conditioning and operant conditioning. Classical conditioning involves pairing two stimuli repeatedly so that they eventually become functionally equivalent. Operant conditioning results in an increased probability of a response occurring following reinforcement.

3. Pavlov, Watson, and Guthrie are frequently associated with classical conditioning; Skinner and Thorndike are connected with operant conditioning (instrumental learning).

4. Skinner investigated schedules of reinforcement and their effect on rate of learning, rate of response, and rate of extinction. Schedules of reinforcement are basically continuous or intermittent. Intermittent reinforcement may be interval or ratio; each of these may be either random or fixed. To complicate the matter further, any combination of these is possible.

5. In general, continuous schedules of reinforcement are most effective in the early stages of learning, although extinction occurs more quickly. On the other hand, intermittent schedules lead to slower extinction.

6. Extinction is the cessation of a response with removal of the reinforcement. Forgetting is the cessation of a response with the passage of time. A response may be forgotten when it is not emitted for a long time; it may be extinguished if it occurs frequently but is not reinforced.

7. Shaping is a technique employed by Skinner to teach an animal to perform tasks that are ordinarily beyond its repertoire. It involves the differential reinforcement of successive approximations (rewarding activity which approximates the desired response).

8. A reinforcer is a stimulus that increases the probability of a response occurring. The most important reinforcers for humans are generalized social re-

inforcers. Other reinforcers include consumables, manipulatables, visual and auditory stimuli, and tokens. In addition a pleasant activity may be employed to reinforce an unpleasant activity (the Premack principle).

9. Two approaches to learning, in addition to the behaviorism of Watson and Skinner, are neobehaviorism and cognitivism. Neobehaviorism denotes concern with stimuli and responses and with intervening processes; cognitivism deals with such topics as awareness, insight, perception, problem solving, knowing, and decision making.

10. Bandura's discussion of the three systems that control human behavior integrates some of the current information about learning. He distinguishes among behavior directly controlled by external stimulation, behavior controlled by its outcome, and behavior controlled by symbolic processes. In practice most human behavior incorporates all three systems.

The following three references provide clear and sometimes interesting accounts of various theoretical approaches to learning: Further Readings

Hilgard, E. R., and G. H. Bower. *Theories of learning* (3rd Ed.). New York: Appleton-Century-Crofts, 1966.

Hill, W. F. *Learning: A survey of psychological interpretations.* San Francisco: Chandler Publishing, 1963.

Lefrancois, G. R. *Psychological theories and human learning: Kongor's report.* Belmont, Calif.: Brooks/Cole, 1972.

A very clear and simple explanation of operant conditioning is contained in:

Keller, F. S. *Learning: Reinforcement theory* (2nd Ed.). New York: Random House, 1969.

The theory of observational learning described in this chapter is presented in the following two references. The first is simpler but less comprehensive.

Bandura, A., and R. Walters. *Social learning and personality development.* New York: Holt, Rinehart & Winston, 1963.

Bandura, A. *Principles of behavior modification.* New York: Holt, Rinehart & Winston, 1969.

An advanced and detailed description of current experimental approaches to the study of children, together with recent findings in this field, is contained in:

Reese, H. W., and L. O. Lipsitt. *Experimental child psychology.* New York: Academic Press, 1970.

Of Dr. Barss and Green Grass: Motivation

They phoned very early that morning—too early.* My head was throbbing as I went to pick up the phone, and the inside of my mouth did not taste very good. It was not a good morning. However, the night had not been bad, and a rotten morning is not a bad price to pay for a good night (Lefrancois' Second Law).

"Hello!" It was a hearty, booming, wide-awake-it's-morning voice— the kind of voice that I detest with unbridled passion in the early morning. "Are you Guy Lefrancois?" He pronounced it atrociously. I grumbled that I indeed was that person, and who the hell was he and what the hell did he want at this time of the morning.

"I am Dr. Barss, your psychology instructor," he said. "Yes sir, indeed sir, what can I do for you sir, and how are you this morning, sir?" I rejoined very politely. Then he took the opportunity to inform me that I had been fortunate enough to be selected as one of the participants in a psychological investigation of considerable importance. I cringed inwardly as he continued. I was to go to one of the newer buildings on campus the following day, providing I was free for the weekend, and if I was, they would pay me $38.33 a day for helping them. But of course I would help them and what did I need to do, I asked in my usual cooperative manner as I pinched my lean billfold and drooled a little into the mouthpiece.

"Nothing. You don't have to do anything at all. We'll ask you a few questions, give you one or two very short tests, and put you to bed." I knew, of course that there must be a catch. "There is absolutely no catch," he continued. "All you need do is take those few tests and then we'll let you go to bed and you can stay there just as long as you like. And we'll pay you $38.33 for each day you help us. Heh, heh, heh."

Okay. Thirty-eight dollars and thirty-three cents a day is a lot of bread, and, of course, a little wine too. I was on campus at 6 o'clock the following morning. My head felt fine, I had brushed my teeth, and I had smiled profusely and shouted good morning to a dozen people already. What a great day. The tests were simple, almost stupid, really. I had to count backward by twos from 30. I closed my eyes and said, "30, 28, 26, 24, . . . , 2." The other tests included a short intelligence test, something that looked like a perception test, and a questionnaire that asked whether or not I believed in ghosts, which I didn't.

After the tests, I was taken to a small room that contained a cot and a toilet. That's all—just one cot and one toilet, both in working order, as far as I could tell. My instructions were simple. I was to lie down and amuse myself however I wanted, provided I remained lying down. I could go to the toilet, of course, and I could sit on the edge of my bed when they fed me—they assured me that I would indeed be fed in a normal manner with normal everyday foods. No drugs to expand my mind, shrink it, put it to sleep, keep it awake, or otherwise tamper with its ordinary functioning. $38.33 a day for doing absolutely nothing. I couldn't believe it. I

---

*The following fictionalized introduction is based on an actual experiment reported by Heron (1957).

lay down and relaxed. Old Barss' assistant placed a visor over my eyes; it was translucent, but I couldn't see a thing through it. Then they slipped some soft gloves on my hands, put cardboard cuffs over these and up my arms, turned on a noisy fan, and left.

I must have fallen asleep, because I eventually woke up. I couldn't tell how long I had been out; they had taken my watch from me when they dressed me in the hospital gown. Anyway, I couldn't have looked at my watch — I couldn't look at anything except the insides of my eyelids, and there wasn't much to see at the time. I did have a term paper to prepare, however, so I lay there and tried to organize it in my mind, but I suddenly developed a terrible itch. Scratching with cardboard-covered cotton-gloved hands is not very satisfying, and I couldn't quite reach the spot with either my right foot or its companion. Consequently, I suffered for a few seconds before the itch disappeared.

After a while I used the toilet. It was a major occasion. An indeterminate length of time later a soft-soled (and hard-hearted) attendant brought in a tray of food. I smelled it coming, and sprang up to get it, flinging off my visor in the process. Even in the interests of psychological research I would have refused to eat with a visor on. I like to see what I'm putting into my mouth before it gets there. I ate; the attendant returned, motioned for me to put my visor back on and get into bed, and left. He was not exactly sociable. Throughout that long afternoon I lay there, imagining that I was some great, courageous, famous, wealthy, wise, lovable, intelligent, gentle, and otherwise admirable fellow engaging in all sorts of exciting and rewarding activities. It was probably the longest and the dullest afternoon I have ever spent.

Supper came and went, and with it the attendant, unfriendly fellow that he was. During the course of the evening I managed to convince myself that I needed to use the toilet on at least five separate occasions. I couldn't sleep; I couldn't think; I couldn't even scratch myself — but I needed that $38.33. Sometime that night, or early in the morning, they played a recording for me. I was extremely grateful and listened to it very carefully. It had been taped by Professor Barss, and it was a logical argument for the existence of supernatural beings.

"After all," Professor Barss pleaded, "We cannot completely discount the late Dr. Maxwell Scheinfolderingburn's evidence. He spent a lifetime pursuing the elusive poltergeists that dwell in those remote regions. In his memoirs he has described in detail the circumstances of that search. Once he came upon one of those caves that you sometimes read about — a small opening in a large cavern high in the mountains. And in that cave there dwelt a coven of poltergeists. He has photographs to prove his claim. . . ."

Morning came. The attendant floated in. "Hey, tell me . . ." He floated out, leaving an unappetizing tray. I ate; the attendant returned, and I began again to ask him whether he could . . . and he motioned for me to put on my visor and return to my bed, and left. I was beginning to dislike him.

It was a few hours later that they started. I had been lying on my back, listening to the humming of the fan, and watching the insides of my eyelids when I thought I saw something moving across my field of vision. I looked more closely: it was a chicken, an ordinary yellow chicken. He walked across the inside of my right eyelid from right to left, disappeared for a second, then entered my left eyelid from the tear duct, walking at the same pace as when he crossed my right eyelid. No sooner was his tail out of sight than another appeared in the right corner of the inside of my right eyelid—another yellow chicken walking at the same pace. This one got half way across my right eyelid, stopped, turned toward my pupil and said "awk." I had momentary visions of Robert Edward Cuttingham. No sooner had this second chicken disappeared than another appeared to replace him. It was becoming a little confusing, since there were often as many as four or five yellow chickens marching across the insides of my eyelids saying "awk" quite softly and very politely.

Awk!

I discovered I could make the chickens disappear simply by opening my eyes, but I found it amusing to keep them closed and examine the parade. Soon I tired of this and decided to lose them for good. They wouldn't go away! Whether my eyes were open or closed, the chickens kept walking across my eyelids. I couldn't control them. Chicken after yellow chicken, they kept parading and "awking." When the attendant finally came with my midday tray I had had it. I said so. "I have had it," I said, as I walked past him toward the door. For some strange reason the door seemed farther away than it apparently was, since I ran into it with my nose. I prepared to vent my frustrations on the hapless attendant when Professor Barss entered. He had been observing me through a hidden viewer and had come to the same conclusion as I — that I had indeed had it.

Human Motivation

Why did I accept Professor Barss' invitation and why did I remain? What caused the hallucinations? Why do children behave as they do, learn the things they must know to exist in our complicated society? Why does my 2-year-old daughter persist in throwing her dinner on the floor every evening and then telling me how much she loves her daddy?

These are the questions that motivation theory attempts to answer, and although they will not be answered completely to my satisfaction, or to yours, this chapter should provide enough information about the causes of human behavior and development to enable you to achieve a better understanding of the subject of this book — the human child.

Motivation accounts for human behavior; it is the force that initiates behavior, that maintains it, and that explains its termination. But what is it?

Some Older Views

Psychological Hedonism

Ask a grandmother why people behave the way they do and she is likely to say that they do the things they like, and don't do the things they don't like. Grandmothers are like that — wise and to the point. An ancient philosopher sifting through records of the ramblings of grandmothers' minds would label their philosophy *hedonism* — the belief that people act in order to obtain pleasure and avoid pain. A psychologist would agree, although he might choose to call it **psychological hedonism**. The appeal of this explanation derives from direct observation: indeed people do appear to behave hedonistically. Few people deliberately seek pain and few deliberately avoid pleasure. It should be noted, however, that some grandmothers slip and say nonhedonistic things like "Of course, occasionally we have to do things we don't like because we have to do them, that's all, and because they're our duty." Indeed, when people engage in unpleasant activities, they usually do it because the consequence of avoiding the activity is worse than the act itself, or because the anticipated outcome of the activity is sufficiently pleasurable to compensate for its distastefulness. Such considerations were the basis for Jeremy Bentham's (1789) *hedonistic calculus,* a socio-philosophical theory that man considers the pleasurable and the painful consequences of an act and weighs their relative values in his mind prior to acting. This explanation of human motivation, that man acts in order to obtain pleasure and avoid pain, is useless unless pleasure and pain can be defined specifically. It is largely for this reason that later attempts to account for behavior have abandoned the pleasure-pain principle in favor of more specific formulations.

Instincts

When Darwin proposed that man was descended from less complex animal forms, that he was simply another animal at a more advantageous position in the phylogenetic order of things, and when this view of man gained acceptance, it was inevitable that explanations for animal behavior would be extended to man. From animal behavior, psychologists inferred that the driving force for human motivation also was a complex, unlearned, and unmodifiable urge to act that we call **instinct**. William James (1890), the spokesman for this movement in psychology, included among human instincts such *natural* propensities as locomotion, fear, sympathy, vocalization, and cleanliness, in addition to the more obvious reproductive and survival instincts. McDougall (1908) and Bernard (1924) made significant additions to lists of human instincts. McDougall included tendencies for self-improvement, self-abasement, self-assertion, and for parenthood, among a long list of other alleged human propensities. Perkins (1969) reports that Bernard pushed the whole process to its extreme by publishing a list of 6000 instincts, including "the instinct to avoid eating apples that grow in one's own orchard." Subsequent attempts to explain human motivation through instinct were abandoned, primarily because of the arguments' circularity and its failure to explain motivation. Naming an instinct does not explain the behavior that it underlies. Lefrancois (1972a) illustrates the circularity* of the instinct argument as follows:

> If man makes love, it is obvious that he has an instinct for mating (or perhaps for making love—the point is never quite clear). Why, then, does one make love? Well, because one has this instinct, you see. How do we know about this instinct? Well, because people make love. Why is there an instinct for making love? For survival—propagation of the species and all that. Well, then, there must be an instinct for survival too. Of course. *Ad Infinitum* (p. 20).

Have you ever wondered why a chick follows its mother? Ducklings follow mother ducks, goslings follow mother geese, and skunks follow mama skunks. Is there a following instinct? Konrad Lorenz, Tinbergen, and a host of ethologists (people concerned with the behavior of lower animals) and psychologists have observed this phenomenon and labeled it **imprinting**. Imprinting denotes the acquisition of relatively complex, species specific behavior as a result of exposure to appropriate stimulation at the right time. Quite simply, when a newly hatched chick sees its mother moving about it begins to follow her and will continue to follow her for some time: it has *imprinted* on the mother. Interestingly, it needn't be the mother hen that the chicks imprint upon; they are quite unselective. They will imprint on the first moving thing they see during this **critical period**, whether it be an object, an animal, or a person. Lorenz (1952) attempted to imprint greylag geese on himself so successfully that the geese continued to follow him around when they matured. Much to his embarrassment one fully grown greylag goose persisted desperately in foisting her amorous intentions upon Lorenz.

Imprinting

---

* More recent explanations of human behavior are often equally circular.

One fully grown greylag goose persisted in foisting her amorous attentions upon Lorenz.

The relevance of imprinting to human behavior is not clear since humans do not engage in the type of behavior that is typically investigated in studies of imprinting. Young children do not follow their mother around as do little chickens. Nevertheless, one of the findings from this research may be important for an understanding of human behavior. If a young precocial bird is not exposed to a moving stimulus early enough in life, it will not imprint on any object (it will not learn to follow). Similarly, if a mother sheep is not allowed contact with her offspring (or any other young lamb) soon enough after it has given birth, it will be quite incapable of developing any degree of maternal attachment for that lamb. (Collias, 1956). In fact, it may spend considerable time running at and butting the unfortunate lamb that has been presented too late. This finding that there is a critical period within which certain behaviors apparently can be learned effortlessly, and that exposure to the same stimulus (called a *releaser*) before or after this critical period will result in the organism's inability to learn the response, may be of considerable significance.

Most of the work with potential relevance to human behavior has been conducted with infrahuman species. For example, Harlow (1958) has found that monkeys isolated from normal social contact with peers are frequently incapable of mature sexual relations later. From these findings the hypothesis has developed that humans have a critical period for developing certain capabilities (Scott, 1962). Similarly, Schneirla and Rosenblatt (1960) argue that early learning is critical for whatever learning follows, both for humans and for some lower animals. No critical periods with age boundaries as definite as those found in lower animals and with behaviors as specific have actually been discovered in man. The relevance of imprinting to human motivation is still based on provocative speculation.

Need theory is included in this section on *Older Views,* not because this theory is now as defunct as psychological hedonism or instinct theory, but because it was among the earliest formal psychological attempts to understand human motivation as distinct from animal motivation. However, animal behavior can be explained much more adequately by needs than human behavior, since animals apparently have much simpler needs than humans do.   Needs

A need is defined as a deficit or lack that motivates behavior. If man has needs, and if behavior is designed to satisfy these needs, then it is possible to arrive at understanding motivation via man's needs. We know that man requires certain things for his physical survival: food, air, drink, and the maintenance of normal body temperature. Unfortunately for psychology, these needs are of almost no importance whatsoever in explaining modern man's daily activities, since most of us are adequately fed, sheltered, and watered, and we have yet to realize physiologically how unsatisfying the air of our cities is, although we sometimes claim to having realized it psychologically.

On the other hand, most undomesticated lower animals spend nearly all their time engaged in survival activities. They sleep, awaken, look for enemies, feed, look for enemies, feed, hide, rest, drink, look for enemies, become frightened and flee, pause, look for enemies, eat, drink, hide, and sleep. All of these activities are undertaken in direct response to the basic needs that the animal has. However, our hypothetically civilized Western man, paragon that he is, behaves quite differently. Harlow (1953) has noted:

> . . . man is a strange, if not bizarre, creature: he is the only known organism to arise in the morning before he is awake, work all day without resting, continue his activities after the diurnal and even the crepuscular organisms have retired to rest, and then take narcotics to induce an inadequate period of troubled sleep (p. 4).

If man is driven by his needs, it is not by the basic biological needs that are of such importance to lower animals (which is clearly not to say that physiological needs are nonexistent in man). Since biological needs are ordinarily satisfied with little effort, and since man continues to engage in all sorts of difficult and strenuous activities that appear unrelated to any primary need that he might have, considering these basic needs does not significantly help explain human behavior. Nevertheless, psychologists still attempt to apply a concept of needs to man by elaborating the concept and making it more abstract: they have invented *psychological needs,* and have listed these in the manner of Bernard's (1924) compendium of 6000 instincts.

Raths and Burrell (1963), for example, present a list that includes the need to belong, to achieve, to acquire economic security, to avoid fear, to love and be affectionate, to be free from feelings of guilt, to achieve self-respect, and to understand. Murray (1938) identified 12 physiological (viscerogenic) needs and 28 psychological (psychogenic) needs, among which are the need to avoid humiliation, the need for autonomy, for deference, for dominance, for exhibition, for achievement, for abasement, and so on. By now it is clear that listing needs explains behavior no better than listing instincts did; to say that a person engages in self-abasing behavior because he has a need for self-abasement is no more meaningful than to say that he abases himself because of a natural instinct for self-abasement. Man does indeed behave as though he had certain needs, and although naming the need explains nothing, information about how the need is acquired and how it is manifested in an individual's behavior may help to further our understanding.

Some Newer Views

The experiments and explanations discussed in this section are included as "newer views" not necessarily because they are chronologically younger than other alternatives, but because they appear to have wider contemporary currency than the theories discussed in the previous section. Some derive from earlier theories that sought to explain behavior through the satisfaction of needs; others are based implicitly if not explicitly on Hull's (1943, 1951, 1952) theory of human behavior, which was premised on the assumption that needs initiate drives, and that drives instigate and maintain behavior. Subsequent satisfaction of the need reduces the drive and the particular behavior ceases. The theory that all behavior is based on the need to reduce drive has been abandoned in the face of considerable contradictory evidence, although the notion that the satisfaction of needs reinforces behavior continues to play a significant part in many contemporary theories.

Need for Achievement

Achievement motivation, also called the need for achievement (abbreviated nAch), is currently receiving a great deal of attention. Achievement motivation is a psychological need expressed in an individual's desire to attain a certain standard of excellence. Therefore, the need should be more powerful among competitive, achievement-oriented individuals, and perhaps also among competitive and achievement-oriented cultures. McClelland (1951, 1955, 1958) found both of these predictions correct. One index of achievement motivation that he employed in comparing various countries was the number of achievement-related expressions in the children's literature of that nation. Not surprisingly, he found a high correlation between national productivity and the imagery related to achievement in the elementary school texts employed when the country's present producers were children. The study raises the possibility of predicting or controlling economic growth (or decline) through the influence exerted by literature. DeCharms and Moeller

(1962), who plotted the incidence of achievement and affiliation imagery as well as moral teachings in children's readers from 1800 to 1950, corroborate McClelland's early findings. They hypothesized that such basic cultural trends as the movement from the "protestant ethic," emphasizing hard work and rigid ethical values, to the "social ethic" (Whyte, 1956), emphasizing "belongingness" (conforming), would be reflected in children's readers. They discovered a significant decline in the amount of moral teachings in elementary readers during the period studied, substantiating their hypothesis. In addition they found an increase in achievement imagery until 1900, but a steady decline after 1900. Interestingly, the number of patents issued during this period paralleled the quantity of achievement imagery in readers. The implications for parents, writers, educators, and politicians are clear.

More commonly used measures of the need for achievement are derived by analyzing children's stories for achievement-related themes and imagery. Subjects are presented with four pictures from the Thematic Apperception Test (TAT) and are asked to write stories about each picture. McClelland found that children with high scores on this test are more likely to complete tasks, particularly if they think these are measures of intellectual ability. They also tend to get higher grades in school, and have higher levels of aspiration.

Need for achievement is assumed to be a learned rather than an innate need. Evidence is provided by research showing a high relationship between parental attitudes and their child rearing practices, and their children's achievement motivation. Winterbottom (1958) asked the mothers of 29 boys several questions about their expectations for their sons: At what age did they expect their children to know their way around the city? When did they expect them to try new things for themselves? to do well in competition? to make their own friends? Not surprisingly, Winterbottom found that the mothers of the children with a greater need for achievement expected more of them at an earlier age. The most striking difference between mothers of boys with a low need for achievement and those with a high need was related to their demands that their sons try new things. Evidently achievement motivation is fostered by parental emphasis on independence.

Another study reported by Rosen and D'Andrade (1959) also shows a relationship between parental attitudes and level of need achievement in children. The subjects were 40 boys, 20 of whom scored low in nAch, and 20 of whom scored high. The purpose of the study was to discover whether there would be some relationship between the level of aspiration of the *parents for their children* and the need for achievement scores obtained *by the children*. Parental attitudes toward their children's performance were also examined. Each boy was *blindfolded* and required to build a tower with blocks. The parents were asked how many blocks they expected their son to pile up; then they were allowed to observe the son's performance and give him directions if they wished, providing they did not assist him physically. Several findings from this study are especially important. First, the parents of boys with high scores on

Fathers of those who scored low on need achievement were typically authoritarian and excessively demanding.

measures of nAch had significantly higher levels of aspiration for their sons. Mothers of boys who had high nAch scores tended to be warm and supportive. Interestingly, fathers of those who had low nAch scores typically were **authoritarian** and excessively demanding.

Atkinson (1964, 1965, 1966) proposed more recently that there are two factors involved in need for achievement—the motive to achieve and the motive to avoid failure. In combination these yield a desire for achievement which may be either positive or negative: if the desire to achieve is stronger than the fear of failure there is a tendency to approach a challenge; when the desire to avoid failure is stronger than the urge to achieve there is a tendency to avoid. Atkinson's measure for need achievement is based on the McClelland procedure employing TAT (thematic apperception) pictures and stories containing themes and imagery of achievement. Subjects also take an anxiety test (Sarason et al., 1960), the scores of which are subtracted from nAch scores to indicate the strength of the need to achieve. Atkinson (1964) demonstrates a high correlation between scores on his measures of nAch and actual achievement-oriented behavior.

Smith (1959) summarizes some of the research and theory that is most relevant to the origins of achievement motivation in children (particularly in boys, since most studies have been concerned with them) by concluding that one may expect a high need for achievement as a result of early parental demands for accomplishment, intense positive emotional rewards for achievement, high goals set for children by their parents, high parental regard for their children's competence and interest in the child's achievement endeavors (p. 109).

Considering the ability to modify achievement-oriented behavior in adults (McClelland and Winter, 1969) through training, it is reasonable to assume that such behavior is highly susceptible to other environmental influences. There is the unresolved dilemma, however, of reconciling the increasing cultural pressures to meet and surpass external standards of excellence with the implicit belief in the right of every individual to determine his own goals and aspirations. In addition, a great stress on achievement may be incompatible with some more *human* values that parents and society in general at least pay lip service to. Furthermore, well-intended attempts to increase the desire for achievement in economically depressed peoples (see for example, McClelland and Winters, 1969) almost invariably involves drastic modifications of traditional ways of doing things, and a concomitant destruction of at least part of the culture of the people involved. There are ethical considerations here as well. One should not glibly assume that an increased need for achievement is necessarily a good thing. The question bears careful examination.

The intuitive wisdom of grandmothers has informed us that the grass is always greener on the other side of the fence. In other words, those things which we do not possess or which are unattainable, are allegedly more attractive than what we have. Interestingly, a number of psychologists have contradicted this pearl of ancient wisdom. Festinger (1957, 1962) and Brehm and Cohen (1962) have proposed an explanation for some human behaviors that deny that the grass is greener—it usually isn't.

Cognitive dissonance, the label for Festinger's theory, may be defined as conflict between pieces of information, beliefs, or between behavior and belief. According to this theory, whenever cognitive dissonance exists, the individual engages in behavior designed to reduce the dissonance. Cognitive dissonance, then, is motivating since it instigates behavior. It follows that knowledge of cognitive dissonance theory may be useful in predicting the behavior in which an individual will engage. The child who is placed in a situation where he must make a choice, but whose choice will effectively prevent him from obtaining something else that he clearly finds attractive, is experiencing cognitive dissonance. Once he has chosen there will be some conflict, however minor, between the choice he has made and the other choice that he could have made. According to the theory, the child will then engage in some activity that will reduce the dissonance. Festinger (1957) demonstrates the validity of this analysis in the following experiment. A number of girls ranked record albums in order of attractiveness. Once each girl completed the ranking she was offered a choice of two records, each of which she had ranked as being moderately attractive. The girls were led to believe that there was a slight possibility they might receive both records (and some did). Others were given only the record they had chosen; a third group received neither of their choices. One might expect that those girls who received both records, and those who received none, would not experi-

Cognitive Dissonance

ence any dissonance since there would be no conflict between the outcome of their decision and their desires; a conflict results only from having to choose. On the other hand, those girls who received only the record they had chosen could be expected to feel some dissonance, since they could just as easily have chosen the other record, and since both were equally attractive. If the grass is indeed greener, once the girl has made her choice, and once she has in her possession the object that she has chosen, the other should become more attractive. In fact, however, the record chosen is almost invariably perceived as the more desirable when the subjects are asked again to rank the records. In contrast, the girls who received either both records or neither showed no change in their rankings.

Festinger and Carlsmith (1959) provide a second experimental illustration of cognitive dissonance. A number of college students were asked to participate in an experiment involving motor performance. Once they had volunteered, all subjects were directed to engage in an extremely boring and apparently pointless task: placing 12 spools on a tray using only one hand, emptying the tray, then placing another 12 spools on the same tray, removing these, replacing them, removing them again, replacing them, and so on. Next, the subjects were required to turn all 48 pegs in a pegboard one quarter turn (again employing only one hand) and to repeat the procedure for an hour. Then the entire group of subjects was divided into three subgroups, all of whom were asked to judge the interest and usefulness of the experiment. One group that did so without further instructions or treatment served as a control group for perceived degree of interest and scientific usefulness of the spool-and-tray routine.

The other two groups were asked to serve as confederates in the experiment. They were told that the experiment was designed to investigate the role of "attitude" in the performance of simple motor tasks, and therefore it was important for the other subjects to believe that the experiment was an exciting and useful piece of work. Accordingly, members of these two groups were asked to talk individually to one of the upcoming subjects to give him the appropriate mental attitude toward the experiment. In recognition of their services, each subject would be paid — members of one group would each receive $1.00; members of the second group would be paid $20.00. Neither group was aware that the other group was being paid at a different rate. Subjects were then interviewed by a supposedly neutral party to unmask their real feelings about the hour-long experiment, an experiment clearly as boring and as scientifically useless as the experimenters could devise. The experimenters' prediction based on cognitive dissonance theory was that the subjects who had agreed to lie about the experiment would experience conflict between their behavior and their beliefs, and that they would probably seek to reduce this conflict in a variety of ways. Possibly they might refuse to tell the lie. Given the nature of the relationship that ordinarily exists between professors (the experimenters) and their students, and perhaps also because of the interest that students frequently have in scientific investigations, none of the subjects was likely to refuse. The subjects could also reduce the dissonance by changing their opinions of the experiment. If they believed the experiment neither boring nor scientifically useless, they would suffer no dissonance. In fact, this was the course many of the subjects followed—a finding that corroborates the predictions of cognitive dissonance theory.

The differences in the behavior of the two groups provides additional confirmation for the validity of cognitive dissonance theory. Those who were paid $1.00 for their participation consistently perceived the experiment as interesting and useful; those who received $20.00 for their time considered the experiment useless (see Figure 6.1). The strength of the tendency to align beliefs with behavior was not dependent on the magnitude of the reward, but was inversely proportional to it (for similar investigations, see Festinger, 1962).

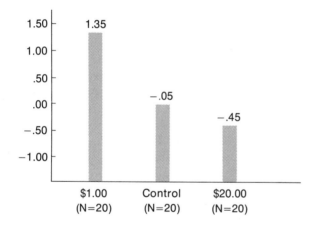

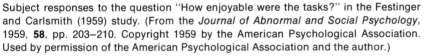

Subject responses to the question "How enjoyable were the tasks?" in the Festinger and Carlsmith (1959) study. (From the *Journal of Abnormal and Social Psychology,* 1959, **58**, pp. 203–210. Copyright 1959 by the American Psychological Association. Used by permission of the American Psychological Association and the author.)   Figure 6.1

The explanation for the behavior described above is relatively simple. Those who were paid the larger amount of money also had greater justification for their participation and consequently had less need to justify their behavior by calling the experiment useful. Those who received simply token payment understandably felt a great deal more dissonance, and the magnitude of this dissonance (guilt is an appropriate term in this case) is reflected in the magnitude of their attitude change.

A slightly different illustration of cognitive dissonance is reported by Festinger (1962). He cites an experiment by Aronson and Carlsmith in which children were exposed to temptation to observe what effect resisting temptation would have on their attitudes toward the desired objects. Subjects were 4-year-old children who were permitted to play briefly with five toys, and were then asked to rank the toys in order of attractiveness. The toy that each child ranked second in attractiveness was removed or placed on a table in the room. The experimenter left the child alone with the toys, but forbade him to play with the toy that was on the table (or that was taken out of the room). Those children for whom the toy was left on the table were subjected to one of two experimental conditions: in one the experimenter threatened severe punishment if the child disobeyed; in the second the threat was milder punishment.

All subjects resisted temptation—a result that, according to dissonance theory, would cause conflict between actual behavior and desire and would presumably be reflected in attitude changes. The less attractive the forbidden toy, the less the dissonance. Hence, the change in attitude should be toward lowering the toy's attractiveness in subsequent rankings. In fact, this was what happened when the toy was left in the room with the child. When the toy was removed, the subjects did not change their attitudes. The physical absence of the toy apparently removed all temptation and consequently any dissonance associated with resisting it.

The difference between subjects threatened with severe punishment and those who were given only mild threats is interesting. The situation is analogous to the experiment in which subjects were paid different sums for telling the same lie. Subjects threatened with severe consequences if they succumbed to temptation had ample justification for being obedient and would consequently be expected to feel little dissonance. Those subjects threatened with less harsh consequences could be expected to suffer greater dissonance as a result of resisting temptation. The magnitude of opinion change manifested by the two groups corroborates these theories. The first group (the severely threatened group) still perceived the toy as highly attractive; the second group now considered it much less attractive (see Figure 6.2).

The above-mentioned experiments illustrate dissonance in decision-making situations, in circumstances that force subjects to tell lies, and in conditions in which temptation is resisted. Each of these situations has obvious parallels in everyday life wherein there are vast quantities of cognitive dissonance. The person who has decided to smoke (or who is unable to stop smoking) in the face of evidence pointing to the dangers of smoking is subjected to dissonance that he has probably long since reduced in one of several ways, for example, by denying that smoking is dangerous. Children are frequently subjected to dissonance as a result of observing their parents engaging in behavior that is forbidden to them. There is a conflict here between the child's expectations of his parents and the behavior he sees them engaging in, or between the awareness of a behavior both forbidden to him and appropriate for his parents. Festinger (1957) contends that whenever the expectations one has about appropriate things and forbidden things are not fulfilled, dissonance results. It is in this sense that dissonance is a fact of life.

People reduce dissonance in several ways. Whenever the dissonance involves a conflict between a person's behavior and his self-expectations, he can reduce the dissonance by ceasing the behavior. It is theoretically

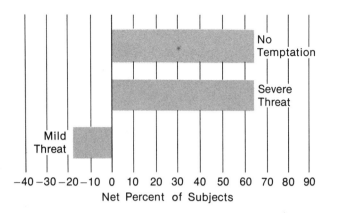

The consequences of resisting temptation when children are threatened with punishment of varying severity, and when the object of temptation is removed. The graph shows the difference in the percentage of children who found the toy more attractive after the experiment minus the percentage who found it less attractive. Those threatened with mild punishment experienced considerable dissonance which they reduced by lowering the toy's attractiveness. (From Leon Festinger, "Cognitive dissonance," in *Scientific American,* October 1962, p. 100. Copyright © 1962 by Scientific American, Inc. All rights reserved. Used by permission.)

Figure 6.2

simple, for example, to remove the dissonance associated with smoking by ceasing to smoke. In practice, however, it is frequently more difficult. A second way to reduce dissonance — one that is frequently less demanding — involves altering one's attitudes or opinions, as subjects in several of the dissonance experiments did. Once the conflicting attitude has been aligned with the behavior there is no longer any dissonance.

Distorting information or perceptions is a third common way to reduce dissonance. To believe that one's wife is more attractive than the neighbor's wife, it is useful to perceive her as more attractive, nor is it very difficult since beauty is highly subjective in any case. Through a similar process, a man who has chosen a cornflower blue car comes to believe that his car is the most beautiful blue he has ever seen, despite the fact that he was equally tempted by other shades of blue prior to making his decision. In line with this method of reducing dissonance is the tendency to overlook information that is not consonant with one's beliefs, while perceiving and remembering information that agrees with one's preconceived notions. Information distorted by the prejudices that we all carry with us is often less a conscious distortion than simply a process of noting and remembering consonant information and overlooking or forgetting dissonant information.

But dissonance theory explains only some aspects of human behavior: those in which there is a conflict of a particular kind. Kurt Lewin's theory (1935, 1936, 1947, 1951) also attempts to account for human behavior through an examination of the resolution of conflicts. Lewin defined **conflict** as the state in which an individual cannot make an easy decision about the course of action he should engage in; either he is

Conflicts

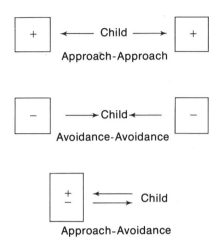

Figure 6.3   The three types of conflict that beset the child. The boxes represent goals that are attractive (+) or unattractive (−) or both (+ and −). The arrows indicate the direction of and child's tendency to behave.

equally attracted to two goals but must make a choice between them, or he may wish to avoid two unpleasant outcomes, but avoiding one means that he must suffer the other. Finally, an individual can have conflict about a goal that has positive and negative features that cause him uncertainty. Figure 6.3 illustrates these three situations graphically.

The approach-approach conflict arises when one is confronted by two goals of equal attractiveness. For example, my son wants to stay home to play in his new swimming pool; at the same time he wants to accompany me on my motorcycle. He is simultaneously drawn in two directions by two different activities, each of which is attractive to him. The resolution of the conflict involves choosing between the alternatives. But knowing that a decision must be made is not a solution to the problem, since any decision will have some undesirable aspect.

The approach-avoidance conflict involves simultaneous attraction toward and repulsion from a single goal object having both positive and negative characteristics. Consider, for example, a child who dearly loves strawberries, but who suffers a severe allergic reaction whenever he eats them. Setting a bowl of juicy red strawberries in front of this child is not only a cruel temptation, but also a clear example of an approach-avoidance conflict. To say that the solution involves deciding whether or not to eat the strawberries is tantamount to saying that a decision must be made, but the decision does not really eliminate the problem—in either case the reasons for one behavior are weakened by the awareness of another possible decision.

The avoidance-avoidance conflict involves two different goal objects, both negative. In this case, avoiding one of the negative goals assures the other goal, also negative. Children frequently find themselves engaged in this conflict when they are in pain. Pain is something to avoid; unfor-

An Approach-Approach Conflict.

tunately, the cure for pain is also something to avoid. A toothache is indeed unpleasant; but the ministerings of even a tender dentist are not exactly pleasant. A child who has cut a finger would surely like to have the pain removed. If, however, he knows that his grandmother's treatment involves pouring iodine on the open wound, and if he has learned through painful experience the effects of iodine on an open wound, he finds himself faced with an avoidance-avoidance conflict, whose resolution will be most unpleasant, no matter what decision he makes.

It should be relatively clear to the reader by now that although it is interesting to analyze human decision making in terms of the conflicts that arise from the attractiveness or unattractiveness of alternatives, we are still left with only an interesting description of the human condition unless we can achieve a clearer understanding of the mechanisms that underlie an individual's decision making. Of course, it is more than a mere academic exercise, since describing the human condition is one of the principle functions of psychology.

Among the aspects of this "human condition" that fall beyond the scope of traditional theories of motivation is the curiosity of man. The most phylogenetically advanced species tends to spend a great deal of time in exploratory or curiosity-based activities — activities that have no obvious connection with survival, with the alleviation of unpleasant conditions, or with the resolution of conflicts (Berlyne, 1960, 1963; Fowler, 1965). Traditional attempts to account for this type of behavior have generally been unsuccessful, primarily because exploratory behavior

Exploratory Behavior

is not goal directed in the ordinary sense – that is, it is defined as behavior with the changing of stimuli as its sole purpose (Berlyne, 1963).

Even rats engage in **exploratory behavior** when they are presented with the opportunity (Kivy, Earl, and Walker, 1956; Fowler, 1958; Woods and Jennings, 1959; Williams and Kuchta, 1957). Experiments that demonstrate this behavior typically employ a T or Y maze (shaped like the letter after which it is named), the arms of which may be the same color and brightness, may be different colors, or may vary in their complexity. The inquisitive rat is allowed to explore the maze visually through glass barriers at the entrance; thus, he can look into either arm of the maze to his content, but he is effectively prevented from entering. After he has become familiar with the maze the barriers are removed and his behavior is observed (see Figure 6.4). Employing this procedure it has been demonstrated that the rat reacts positively to change (Fowler, 1958), to novelty (Dember, 1956), and to complexity (Williams and Kuchta, 1957). Altering one of the arms of the maze after the rat's initial visual exploration, introducing a new arm, or making one more complex stimulates the rat's curiosity. His responsiveness to the changes is calculated by the time he spends in either arm after the barriers are removed. Significantly, rats usually spend more time in the changed (or more complex) arm of the maze.

Similar experiments have been performed with humans. Berlyne (1958a) has shown that 3-month-old infants prefer patterns with more complex contours to simpler patterns. In addition, both children and adults react positively to complexity, novelty, incongruity, uncertainty, intensity, surprise, and conflict (Berlyne, 1957a, 1957b, 1958a, 1958b,

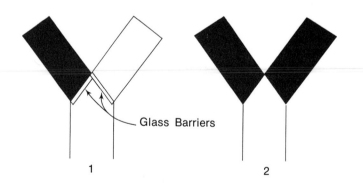

Figure 6.4   A procedure for demonstrating the rat's responsiveness to change. In (1) the rat is permitted to explore the arms of a Y maze visually; one arm is black and the other is white. In (2) the barriers have been removed and the white arm is exchanged for a black one. The rat consistently spends more time in the changed arm than in the one remaining unchanged, despite the fact that both are the same color and brightness.

1960, 1961). The human propensity for exploring the environment is frequently called curiosity.

Berlyne has investigated extensively stimuli called **collative variables** — so called because their effectiveness requires collating information and comparing it to other information. Novelty and surprise do not exist in isolation: an object is novel if it does not resemble other objects—it is novel in *comparison* to other objects. Incongruity, surprise, complexity, intensity, and conflict, are all properties which are relative to other stimuli; more importantly, all are properties that derive from a conflict between expectation and the actual stimulation. Berlyne's explanation for the effects of the collative properties of stimuli is similar to his explanation for the effects of conflict on human behavior, discussed later in this chapter.

Much of the child's behavior is exploratory. Assuming that his basic biological needs are well satisfied and his psychological needs are met adequately by his immediate family, much of his activity not directed toward reducing need-related drives takes the form of play behavior—and most of a child's early play behavior involves games that are essentially exploratory. According to Piaget, by the time a child is a little more than a year old he engages in a great deal of deliberate exploration of his environment. The motive behind this behavior is important for understanding the young child.

While it is practically impossible to understand completely the reasons behind human behavior (given the incredible complexity of that behavior and the highly idiosyncratic nature of human decision making), it is possible to begin to understand a child's behavior by integrating the varied explanations that psychology makes available. The three integrations presented here are based on behaviorism, humanism, and arousal theory. The final integration of these three integrations is left to you.

A Behavioristic Integration

Contemporary behavioristic interpretations of human behavior (as discussed in Chapter 5) are based on the hypothesis that much behavior is determined by its consequences. Therefore, a behavioristic view of motivation says quite simply that the motive for behaving (or not behaving) is the reinforcement or the lack of reinforcement the individual expects or that he has received in the past. The reinforcement of the outcome of behavior is referred to as the *incentive* value of the outcome; consequently, this explanation of human behavior is called **incentive motivation**. A description of incentive motivation depends on sources of secondary reinforcement. It is assumed that stimuli acquire the capacity to reinforce, thereby becoming sources of incentive motivation, as a function of their association with primary reinforcement or with other sources of secondary reinforcement. Behavior may be explained through reinforcement, whether primary or secondary, assuming that the reinforcement has incentive value. The expectations that guide many behaviors have incentive value insofar as the individual perceives the results of his behavior as reinforcing.

While this simplified behavioristic interpretation of human motivation may account for some human behaviors, it does not apply to curiosity or exploratory behavior, nor to behavior that is explicable through cognitive dissonance theory. The second integration, based on arousal theory, may have wider application.

An
Arousal-Based
Integration

The introduction to this chapter described an experimental situation in which a subject was deprived of changes in sensory stimulation for a prolonged period of time (based on Heron, 1957). Hallucinations, impaired mental functioning, some distorted perception, altered emotional states, and increased subjectivity resulted from this deprivation. Other replications of the same experiment, some employing much more rigorous procedures, others employing more severe sensory restrictions, have generally supported the findings of the original experiment (see Zubek, 1969). It appears that humans need not only sensory stimulation, but also changes in the nature of that stimulation. The individual lying on a cot with cardboard cuffs over his arms, cotton gloves on his hands, a plastic visor over his eyes, and the constant monotonous hum of an air conditioner echoing in his ears, is not deprived of stimulation. Indeed, he is subjected to as much stimulation as he would ordinarily experience. He can feel the cotton of the gloves if he pays attention to them; light strikes his retinas through the translucent visor when his eyes are open; he hears the constant sound of the fan; he can taste the inside of his mouth, and he can probably smell various odors if he attempts to. The important difference between his condition and that of a man who is sitting in his living room watching television, reading a newspaper, or arguing with his wife, is that the stimulation in the experimental situation is unchanging. Explaining why this condition has such a profound effect on human functioning may be relevant for understanding man's behaviors.

The most common explanation centers on what is known or suspected about **arousal** and human behavior. "Arousal" is employed either as a physiological or a psychological concept; both are relevant. Physiologically, arousal refers to the degree of activation of the organism, measured in changes in respiration rate, in the skin's conductivity to electricity (galvanic skin response or GSR), in heart rate, and changes in electrical patterns of brain waves (**EEG**). Arousal varies from sleep (or related states such as coma) at its lowest level short of death, to high excitement, frenzy, or panic at the highest level. As a psychological concept arousal refers to the individual's degree of alertness. With increasing physiological arousal there is a corresponding increase in psychological arousal, since the two are defined by the same kinds of changes.

The relevance of arousal for human behavior is shown in Figure 6.5, which depicts how effectiveness of response changes with alterations in level of arousal. At the lowest level of arousal, behavior is least effective. Obviously, a sleeping person is quite incapable of responding to the simplest stimulus. As arousal increases behavior also increases in effectiveness until an optimal level of arousal and effectiveness is reached. Past this optimal level of arousal further increases are accompanied by a decrease in the effectiveness of behavior. For example, under conditions

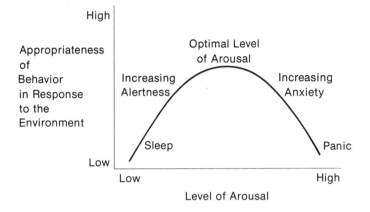

The relationship of level of arousal to effective behavior. With increasing arousal, behavior becomes more appropriate until an optimal level is reached. Beyond this point, further increases in arousal result in decreased effectiveness.   Figure 6.5

of panic, behavior frequently deteriorates. The immediate response to the announcement that a public place is on fire is a notorious example. Schultz (1964) describes several major fires in which hundreds of people died needlessly. In one case, they piled into both sides of a revolving door simultaneously; in another, they fell upon one another in their haste to climb down a stairway. In both instances the fires were relatively minor, were easily extinguished and damaged little of the contents of the buildings. Ironically, few of the dead were actually burned; most had been trampled to death or had succumbed to fear or suffocation in the mad throng that pressed in on them.

Arousal and motivation are related by two assumptions. First, there is an optimal level of arousal for different tasks that varies, depending on the individual and the nature of the task. Intense, concentrated activities require higher levels of arousal than habitual behaviors. The second assumption is that people behave in order to maintain their level of arousal at or near the optimal level. This second assumption is crucial for understanding the relevance of arousal theory to human motivation: if correct, it may prove a more efficient explanation for human behavior than all traditional explanations combined.

The theory of an optimal level of arousal has several implications. If arousal level is too low, the individual should engage in activity designed to raise it; similarly, if arousal is too high, the individual should attempt to reduce it. What increases or lowers arousal? Arousal increases with the intensity, complexity, novelty, and surprise value of all the stimulation that impinges on the organism at one time. Level of arousal, then, is a function of stimulation. Further, not only stimulation emanating from the external world affects an individual's level of activation, but also stimulation from internal sources — from his stomach if he is hungry, from an area of pain if he is sore, and from his mind if he is thinking or experiencing. It follows that attempts to increase arousal will take the form of a search for stimulation, and that stimulation characterized by collative properties (as described above) will be most effective in raising and maintaining arousal. Similarly, attempts to lower arousal will involve withdrawal from stimulation. Consider the power of these concepts as explanations for what you and I do. We become hungry; if we don't eat, we become restless, agitated, uneasy. If we suspect that we will not be able to eat, perhaps we become panicky; quite simply, we become aroused. Reducing this arousal depends on whether or not we can obtain food. Therefore, even those behaviors that appear adequately explained by need theory are also amenable to explanations employing arousal theory.

Arousal theory explains other behaviors as well. Indeed, it is probably the most plausible explanation for a child's exploratory behavior, since the result of exploration is to constantly change the stimulus field, and changing stimulation is among the most important determinants of level of arousal. When people are bored they look for things to do; activity increases arousal.

Our reaction to fear can also be explained by arousal theory. The intense stimulation accompanying danger may be assumed to increase arousal. This assumption can be verified easily by checking heart rate, brain wave patterns, and other physiological changes that accompany fear. The behavior of a frightened person is either "flight or fight." In either case, the result will be a reduction of arousal by removing or changing the stimulation that caused the reaction. Flight removes the individual physically from the frightening stimulus. Fight, on the other hand, changes the stimulus so that it is no longer frightening, or changes the person who is frightened so that he is no longer capable of feeling fear.

Berlyne (1965) includes **epistemic** behaviors, those designed to acquire information, in the class of human behaviors explicable through arousal theory. In this case, the premise is that conflicts resulting from awareness of a problem, or from a lack of knowledge, are arousing; solving the problem or acquiring the missing information reduces arousal. Hence epistemic (knowledge oriented) behavior results from attempts to reduce the arousal that accompanies a problem.

Finally (in this chapter, but not in an exhaustive sense), arousal theory may explain an individual's behavior under conditions of **sensory deprivation**. With prolonged monotony in the sensory environment the subject finds it increasingly difficult to maintain an optimal level of arousal. He attempts to arouse himself by daydreaming, or concentrating on intellectual activities such as preparing term papers. This method for increasing arousal soon becomes ineffective. Subjects frequently whistle to themselves, talk out loud, recite poetry, or attempt to engage the experimenters in conversation (Heron, 1957). They make frequent use of toilet facilities; they toss and turn; they listen attentively to recordings, and in the end they invariably discover that these relatively monotonous and limited activities are still not sufficient to maintain arousal at a normal level. Perhaps for this reason many subjects begin to hallucinate. When conscious activity is clearly insufficient to arouse an individual, the cortex seems to wrest control and provide stimulation that is beyond conscious control — hallucinations.

In summary, children are curious, they engage in considerable exploratory behavior, and they react to changes in stimulation; their needs, while intimately involved in much of their behavior, are of relatively little value in explaining it. Hence arousal theory may provide a clearer understanding of the child's behavior.

Humanistic psychologists concern themselves with the uniqueness of the individual child. A prevalent humanistic notion is that it is impossible to describe the environment in a meaningful way, much less a child, since the salient features of the environment are relative to each individual. To understand an individual's behavior, one must attempt to perceive the world as he sees it from the perspective of his knowledge, his experiences, and his goals and aspirations. Such an orientation does not imply that one cannot understand human nature or human behavior generally, although it renders the task more difficult. It does imply, however, that the value of understanding human behavior in a general sense may be relatively limited for attempting to understand the behavior of one child, for he is himself; he is not the average child. The average child does not exist. And that is important.

Maslow (1954) has proposed one of the best known humanistic integrations of motivation. Essentially, his is a need theory, although it differs significantly from the older conceptualizations of needs. Maslow has described five general systems of needs that vary in their importance to the individual, and thus can be arranged in hierarchical order (see Figure 6.6); once the lower level needs are satisfied, higher level needs are freed to motivate behavior. *Physiological needs* are at the lowest level

A Humanistic
Integration

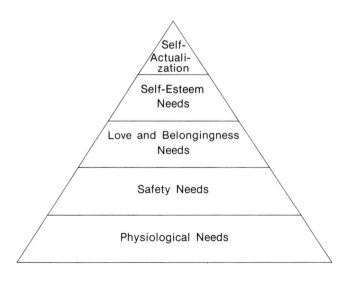

Maslow's hierarchy of human needs. The needs at the lowest level of the hierarchy must be satisfied first. Once these are satisfied, higher level needs can be tended to.

Figure 6.6

of the hierarchy. These are basic biological needs long recognized as the most important for lower animal forms, but less important for man, providing they are relatively well satisfied with little effort. The need for food, water, shelter, temperature regulation, and oxygen, are included among these physiological needs.

The next level of Maslow's need hierarchy consists of **safety needs**: people have a need to maintain an orderly and predictable environment, not threatening in either a physical or a psychological sense. The importance of this need for young children is reflected in their early efforts to achieve stable relationships with their environment. Psychoanalytic theory (Erickson, 1968) has long recognized the child's need to develop a sense of trust in the people and the things that surround him — with this trust he achieves psychological safety.

Once the basic physiological needs of the organism are satisfied, and once the environment is orderly, predictable, and stable, thus meeting the individual's safety needs, the next level of needs can influence his behavior. These are the *love and belongingness needs,* the need for human relationships in which there is a mutual exchange of affection, the need to feel loved and wanted, to feel accepted by a group. It is difficult to overestimate the importance of these needs in a growing child's life. Much of his early activity is directed toward achieving reassurance of love between himself, his parents, and his siblings. Later his peers become increasingly important, and much of his behavior will demonstrate his need to be accepted and loved by his peers.

Next come **self-esteem needs**, which are reflected in an individual's desire to have others hold him in high esteem and to hold a high opinion of himself, as well. Included in this category are the achievement needs discussed earlier in this chapter.

The highest level needs and clearly the most humanistic are those related to **self-actualization**. To actualize oneself is to become whatever one is capable of, to develop one's identity through self-fulfillment. Self-actualization is among the chief concerns of the humanistic psychologist, since he is primarily concerned with human uniqueness and individuality and since self-actualization is by definition the expression of that uniqueness and individuality. The eminent position occupied by this system of needs not only marks its importance for fulfilling the humanity of man, but it also indicates that man will not be driven by the need to actualize himself until all the other lower level needs are satisfied.

And so you are reminded again, gently to be sure, that the child is more than a subject, a concept, or even an organism, about whom psychologists and grandmothers make wise or less wise comments in more or less vain attempts to understand and explain his behavior. You were once a child. Remembering how it felt is a potentially useful exercise. You might attempt it tonight, or tomorrow if you prefer.

Summary   This chapter began with a description of a striking experiment designed to provide some understanding of the forces that account for human behavior. In the experiment individuals are placed in conditions of monotonous sensory stimulation for prolonged periods of time. Among the most striking effects of this isolation is the appearance of hallucinations in some of the subjects.

Next, the chapter considered some of the prevalent explanations for human motivation. The importance of motivation in the development of children is obvious. To understand the behavior and development of children we must ask why they behave as they do. Some of the answers provided are old, some are newer; none is clearly the only right answer. The older answers often consider the role of instincts and of imprinting in behavior. Unfortunately, those answers appear to be more appropriate for lower animal forms than for human offspring. A larger group of motivational theories are categorized as need theories. They attempt to explain behavior by describing the needs that man appears to be satisfying through his behavior. This approach is not always completely futile, although it fails to clarify our understanding of children to the extent that its proponents had hoped. As with instincts, naming a need does not explain the behavior it is alleged to cause. On the other hand, identifying and investigating a need might contribute to our knowledge of behavior. The chapter stopped only long enough to assert that biological needs, although they must be satisfied for our continued survival, are ordinarily of secondary interest to psychologists. Since our biological needs are usually well satisfied, man ordinarily tends to pursue his psychological needs rather than his physiological ones. Here the chapter turned to some of the newer views on motivation: need achievement, cognitive dissonance, the resolution of conflicts, exploratory behavior. Finally it attempted to integrate these various topics through behavioristic, arousal-based and humanistic theories. It is significant that the chapter concludes on a humanistic note—there is danger of forgetting that we are concerned with a human child and not the arid and abstract concepts of the hungry academic psychologist seeking to explain behavior.

1. Theories of motivation attempt to explain why people behave as they do.   **Main Points**

2. *Psychological hedonism* is the belief that people behave in order to achieve pleasure and avoid pain.

3. Instincts are complex, species specific, relatively unmodifiable behavior patterns that are genetically determined. They appear to be of minor importance in the behavior of children.

4. Imprinting describes the process whereby instinctlike behaviors are learned during a critical period of time through exposure to the appropriate stimulus (releaser). The "following" behavior of young chicks is one example of imprinting.

5. A need is a state of deficiency or lack in an organism. It may be physiological (the need for food or water) or psychological (the need for affection or achievement).

6. The need to achieve is considered an acquired need that motivates a great deal of human behavior. Evidence suggests that parents who are warm and supportive, but who expect their children to achieve independence at an early age, are likely to produce children with a high need to achieve.

7. Cognitive dissonance is a state of emotional conflict between two items of information relating to beliefs, behavior, or observations. It motivates behavior designed to reduce the dissonance.

8. In situations in which a subject feels justified for behaving counter to his

beliefs, there will be little dissonance and no need for behavior designed to reduce the dissonance. On the other hand, when there is little justification for engaging in dissonant behavior, the individual frequently modifies his beliefs to make them more consonant with his behavior.

9. Three types of conflicts require a decision that cannot be completely satisfactory (that is, they produce cognitive dissonance). A person can have competing tendencies to approach two desirable goals (approach-approach); or the motivation to avoid an unpleasant goal, when doing so means suffering another equally unpleasant alternative (avoidance-avoidance); or he may have a tendency to approach and avoid a goal that has both positive and negative characteristics (approach-avoidance).

10. Humans and some infrahuman species frequently engage in behavior that is unrelated to satisfying needs, to resolving conflicts, to social pressure, or cognitive dissonance. This other behavior has as its apparent purpose changing the stimulus field and is known as exploratory behavior.

11. A behavioristic integration of motivation theory refers to the incentive value of outcomes which have acquired secondary reinforcing characteristics. It explains behavior in terms of reinforcement.

12. An arousal-based integration of motivation considers the relationship between arousal and behavior and is premised on the assumption that there is an optimal level of arousal for maximally effective behavior, and that people behave in an effort to maintain arousal at the optimal level.

13. A humanistic integration of motivation can be based on Maslow's hierarchical model of needs. This hierarchy expresses Maslow's belief that basic physiological needs are of primary importance until they are satisfied; then higher level needs become preponderant. The ultimate need is self-actualization—the need to fulfill oneself by using one's capabilities to the fullest.

Further Readings

Two short paperbacks that present surveys of motivational positions are:

Birch, D., and J. Veroff. *Motivation: A study of action.* Belmont, Calif.: Brooks/-Cole, 1968.

Murray, E. J. *Motivation and emotion.* Englewood Cliffs, New Jersey: Prentice-Hall, 1964.

A fascinating and very popular description of instinct and imprinting in animals, particularly in geese, is contained in:

Lorenz, K. *King Solomon's Ring.* London: Methuen, 1952.

The application of achievement motivation to problems of economic development, an area of tremendous potential importance, is described in:

McClelland, D. C., and D. G. Winter. *Motivating economic achievement.* New York: The Free Press, 1969.

The following two references present a clear and detailed description of cognitive dissonance theory. The first is a book explaining the theory and relevant research in detail. The second is a highly readable and entertaining article summarizing the major points of the book:

Festinger, L. *A theory of cognitive dissonance.* Stanford: Stanford University Press, 1957.

Festinger, L. Cognitive dissonance. *Scientific American,* October 1962.

An excellent description of curiosity and arousal-based approaches to motivation is provided in the first part of the following book by Fowler. The second part of the book contains reprints of classical articles in motivation:

Fowler, H. *Curiosity and exploratory behavior.* New York: The Macmillan Co., 1965.

Part Three: Some Theoretical Views of Development

Of the Ihalmiuts, Ootek and Howmik: Theories

Childhood* for the typical Eskimo child is a period of unrestricted joy. His parents realize that after the first few carefree years, the child will face long and difficult times, if he is lucky. If he is not lucky, he will be defeated by the depths of a hungry winter when the deer have been too long in coming, and all the dogs have been eaten. There is enough suffering in the world of the older child and of the adult, the old ones say. Let the little ones amuse themselves while they are still unaware of what is to come. And if a little boy decides that he will be a great hunter, he is not to be laughed at, for he will indeed be a hunter when he is grown. If he wishes to go hunting this very moment, his father will arise from beneath the caribou robes and fashion a small bow for his son. It is a real bow— not a toy—and it is fashioned with all of the seriousness with which the father would fashion his own bow. When the bow is done, the son may dress, take his bow, and go out into the barrens with the elders' traditional words of encouragement for the departing hunter echoing faintly in his ears. If he returns with a bird, he will be praised as the mightiest of hunters; if he comes back with nothing, he can expect the teasing and ridicule that an adult hunter would face in like circumstances. For when the Eskimo child decides to be like his father, he is allowed to be like his father in his own eyes as well as in the eyes of the adults in his world.

Childhood for the typical American child is also a relatively carefree and pleasant interlude between birth and maturity, although it is not always the period of unrestricted joy experienced by the Eskimo child. It is true that he has few responsibilities, few demands made of him, and he can frequently indulge in the egotistical activities that advancing years make more difficult. However, the child's wishes are not his parents' commands; indeed, his wishes are influential only when they do not discomfort his parents or his older siblings. In addition, it is often with amusement or faintly disguised condescension that parents accept the feeble attempts of their child to be like his father or his mother. And from the earliest years, behavior transgressing implicit or explicit family rules is likely to be punished.

Mowat (1952) once asked an Eskimo father why he never spanked his children, even when they behaved in the most exasperating manner. The Eskimo was dumbfounded; such punishment was so far removed from the realm of possibility that he was unable to understand the question until it had been repeated and rephrased several times. When at last he understood the substance of the question he became fiercely angry. His answer is revealing and instructive:
"...Who but a madman would raise his hand against blood of his blood?...Who but a madman would, in his man's strength, stoop to strike against the weakness of a child? Be sure that I am not mad, nor yet is Howmik [his wife] afflicted with madness" (p. 141).

---

* Based on a description by Farley Mowat in his novel *People of the Deer* (Boston: Little, Brown and Company, 1952).

Theory and
Description

Developmental psychology not only describes how it is to be an infant, a child, or an adolescent, but also attempts to explain how and why an infant becomes a child, and eventually an adult. Although it is possible to describe some characteristics of childhood (as in the first few paragraphs of this chapter and much of the next part of this text), in all cases the descriptions are necessarily of a nonexistent average child. Not that such descriptions are not useful for understanding individual children, but they simply can never be entirely complete. It is also possible to describe some of the processes that account for child development, or at least some of the currently held beliefs about these processes; whereas the first task is purely descriptive, the second is theoretical. This chapter is concerned with the second approach. It presents brief accounts of three different ways of looking at the process of development.

The three theories described in this chapter are not intended to represent all theoretical approaches to development, but were chosen because of their value for explaining particular features of development. Freud's theories deal convincingly with personality; Jean Piaget's work organizes and interprets knowledge about the child's intellectual development; and Bandura and Walters provide a basis for understanding social behavior through social learning theory. These theories are presented here not simply because it is considered appropriate to deal with a few theories of development in a text allegedly devoted to that subject; rather they are presented to provide some structure, clarity, and meaning for the next part of this text — a part consisting of descriptions of children as they are developing.

Sigmund Freud

The name Freud conjures visions of a bespectacled psychiatrist sitting on a chair beside a deeply padded reclining couch with ornate French Provincial legs and a seductive curve at one end. On the couch lies an unhappy female, probably suffering from some mild neurosis that is highly psychosomatic in origin. The patient is wealthy, and the psychiatrist is expensive. People helping people. It is a beautiful scene. While Sigmund Freud's theories provide a language and set of concepts for discussing mental disturbances, they are also appropriate for describing some features of development. Indeed they are among the earliest systematic theories of development and are among the most intriguing and the richest in sheer wealth of detail. The picture presented of them here is necessarily highly simplified and somewhat selective, but it is a fascinating one.

It is useful to understand from the outset that Freud's account of the development of personality (Brill, 1938; Brown, 1961) encompasses several parallel analyses. On the one hand, he provides a description of the cognitive aspects of development; on the other, he describes the parallel stages through which an individual progresses in his **psychosexual development**. Both of these descriptions are premised on some common ideas about the human condition.

Basic Ideas

Among the most fundamental Freudian ideas is the notion that human behavior, and consequently the direction that personality development takes, derive from two powerful tendencies: man's urge to survive and his urge to procreate. The survival instinct is of secondary importance since it is not usually impeded by the environment (a more precise Freudian term for environment is *reality*). The urge to procreate, however, is constantly being thwarted by reality; this notion accounts for the overriding importance of sexuality in Freud's account of human development.

Sexuality, however, is a relatively broad term in Freud's writings, signifying not only those activities that are clearly associated with sex, but all other activities that may be linked with sexual behavior, however remotely (for example, such behaviors as thumbsucking or smoking). Sexual urges are sufficiently important in this system to warrant a special term — **libido**. The libido is the source of energy for the urge; accordingly, the urges themselves are referred to as *libidinal urges*.

In later writings, Freud introduced two new concepts to explain the source of the energy or drives that motivate human activity. These are referred to as *instincts* in Freudian terminology and are known as **Eros** and **Thanatos** (Greek words meaning love and death). Freud's postulation of these instincts suggests that man possesses two competing urges: one relating to death and called the death wish or death instinct (*Thanatos*); the other relating to the desire to live — the life instinct (*Eros*). Eros includes the libidinal urges, since the urge to live is associated with survival and procreation.

Eros includes the most important instinctual urges that characterize human behavior. Accordingly, these urges are the most intimately involved in a child's development. Accepting the central position that Freud assigns to Eros lessens the difficulty of understanding the larger system he develops.

The General Developmental Process

The newborn infant has a simple, undeveloped, primitive personality, consisting solely of the libidinal urges (*Eros* and *Thanatos*) that will be his lifetime source of psychic energy. Freud's label for the child's earliest personality is **Id**. Very simply, Id encompasses the instinctual urges that man is heir to; Id is the level of personality that contains all of man's motives.

The Freudian infant is a seething mass of instincts and reflexes, a bundle of unbridled psychic energy seeking, almost desperately, to satisfy his urges that are predicated upon his desire to survive and to procreate, as well as his desire to die. He has no concept of what is possible or impossible, no sense of reality. An infant has no conscience, no implicit ethical or moral rules that govern his conduct. He seeks immediate gratification of his impulses. If he is hungry, he cries; he reaches for a nipple and sucks noisily and greedily. He is like a little beast — a lovable little beast, but a little beast nevertheless.

Almost from birth the child's instinctual urges come into abrupt collision with reality. The hunger urge (linked with survival, and hence with Eros) cannot always be satisfied immediately. The *reality* of the situation is that the mother is frequently occupied elsewhere and the infant's gratification must often be delayed or occasionally denied. This constant conflict between the Id and reality develops the second level of personality, the **Ego**. The Ego is the rational level of human personality, oriented towards reality. The Ego grows out of a realization of what is possible and what is not. It also comes to include the awareness that delaying gratification is frequently a desirable thing, that long-term goals often require the abnegation of short-term goals. While the Id desires immediate gratification, the Ego channels these desires in the most profitable direction for the individual. Note that the levels of personality represented by the Id and the Ego are not in opposition. They work together toward the same goal—satisfying the needs of the individual.

The third level of personality—labeled the **Superego**—sets itself up in opposition to the first two. The term *Superego* designates the moral and ethical aspects of personality. Like the Ego, it derives from contact with reality, though it is more concerned with social reality than physical reality. The differentiation of Ego and Superego does not occur until early childhood, through a process of socialization. Superego frequently involves religious and cultural prescripts. It is interesting that most religious prescripts, as well as many implicit and explicit social and cultural rules, oppose the urges assumed to exist in the Id. Hence, the Superego and the Id are necessarily in frequent conflict—a fact presumed by Freud to account for much deviant behavior.

In summary, Freud's theory establishes three levels of personality: the Id, the Ego, and the Superego (see Figure 7.1). The first is the source of psychic energy, deriving from both life and death instincts. The Ego is reality oriented and mediates between the Id and the Superego to maintain a balance between the Id's urges and the Superego's prescripts.

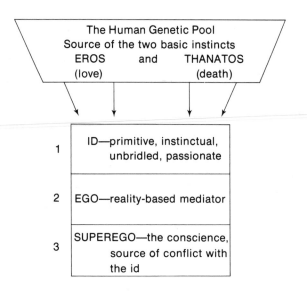

Figure 7.1   The Freudian conception of the three levels of human personality in order of development.

It is as though the Id were continually saying, "I want to eat; I want to be caressed; I want to possess that lovely blonde; I want to kill that sow," while the Superego chides (in a grating confessional voice to be sure) "Don't you dare; deny your desires; Thou shalt not rape, or otherwise molest; hands off that sow." And the Ego, seated between these warring factions, attempts calmly to reconcile them. "Have you considered eating only at mealtime, and with some moderation? Smoke a cigarette instead. Perhaps you should think of marrying that blonde. As for that sow, let the farmer kill it. You can watch. How would that be?"

Freud's account of the development of the three levels of personality may be interpreted as a description of cognitive development. His ideas are also relevant to an understanding of the motivational changes that occur as an individual develops. Freud divides changes in motivation into a sequence of stages that are distinguishable by the objects or activities necessary for the individual's gratification during that stage (see Table 7.1).

Psychosexual Stages

The sequence of stages he describes is relatively easy to remember if one keeps in mind that Freud was primarily concerned with the sexual components of personality development and believed that Eros, or sexual urges, is the primary motivation for behavior throughout life. The labels for each stage reflect changes in the areas of sexual gratification of the child's body as he matures, beginning with the **oral phase** and progressing through the **anal phase**, the **phallic phase**, a **latency period**, and finally the **genital phase**.

The oral phase lasts through infancy (approximately to the age of

Table 7.1   Freud's Stages of Psychosexual Development

Stage	Approximate Age	Characteristics
Oral	0–8 months	Sources of pleasure include sucking, biting, swallowing, playing with lips.
		Preoccupation with immediate gratification of impulses.
		Id is dominant.
Anal	8–18 months	Sources of sexual gratification include expelling feces and urination, as well as retaining feces.
		Id and Ego.
Phallic	18 months to 6 years	Child becomes concerned with his genitals. Source of sexual pleasure involves manipulating genitals. Period of Oedipus or Electra complex.
		Id, Ego, and Superego.
Latency	6–11 years	Loss of interest in sexual gratification. Identification with like-sexed parent.
		Id, Ego, and Superego.
Genital	11–18 years	Concern with adult modes of sexual pleasure, barring fixations or regressions.

8 months). It is characterized by the infant's preoccupation with his mouth and the gratification he experiences from activities associated with his oral region. Obviously, some of the pleasure derived from sucking is intimately linked with the appeasement of hunger or with the mother or some other person who is responsible for nourishing the infant. It is interesting to note, however, that oral stimulation is often sought by children at times when they are apparently sated. A child may suck his thumb, his lips, tongue, or any object with which his mouth comes in contact. Freud assumes that in the early part of this developmental phase the child is primarily satisfying his erotic urges, although there is an undertone of the death wish implicit in the fact that he destroys what he consumes. In the later parts of this period, additional evidence of *Thanatos* appears when the child bites the objects that he recently employed for gratification, even though he continues to suck as well.

During this first phase, the child's personality consists mainly of Id. He seeks constantly to satisfy his urges, is incapable of delaying gratification, and has little contact with reality. Toward the end of the first year, the area of sexual gratification shifts gradually from the oral to anal region. According to Freud, in the early part of this period the child derives pleasure from his bowel movements. It may even be pleasurable for him to be spanked, since any stimulation of the anal region may be a source of libidinal gratification for the child. This stage also involves continual conflict between parents and child. The child who has just discovered the pleasures associated with defecation insists on expelling feces whenever he can. Mothers, for a variety of reasons, may object to this practice. Later in this phase the child acquires control of his sphincter muscles and then may derive considerable pleasure from withholding bowel movements to enhance his anal sensation. This behavior also opposes his mother's wishes. As a result of these conflicts, he begins to develop an Ego — a sense of reality, an awareness that some things are possible while others are not, coupled with the ability to delay gratification to some extent. For example, toward the end of this phase (around 18 months) the child can accede to his mother's wishes and retain his bowel movements until the moment when expelling them is more appropriate.

Eventually the constant interplay between the child's Id (his instinctual urge to gratify his impulses) and the parental and environmental restrictions of reality, the Ego, becomes more differentiated. And in time the source of sexual gratification shifts from the anal to the genital areas. This third phase, which lasts roughly from ages 2 to 6, is labeled *phallic,* not only because the zone of sexuality has shifted from the anal to the genital region, but because the phallus (the male genital) is of primary importance in the sexuality of girls as well as boys. Young children overtly manifest their sexual urges by frequent masturbation during this period. While gratification had been obtained earlier by sucking, or expelling or withholding feces, the child now obtains erotic gratification from manipulating his genitalia.

The Freudian concept of normal development next takes the male child (*between 18 months and 6 years*) through the troubled stage known as the **Oedipus complex**, when his increasing awareness of the sexual connotations of his genital area has led him to desire his mother. Not only does he desire his mother in a literal and physical sense (ostensibly subconsciously, however), but he also wishes to replace his father as the object of his mother's love, like King Oedipus in the Greek legend, who had unwittingly slain his father and married his mother, fulfilling a prophecy made at his birth.

The male child is torn between love and hatred for his father. The love is a continuation of his earlier affection for his father; the hatred stems from his jealous love and carnal desire for his mother. The **castration complex**, develops as a consequence of the child's fear that his father will retaliate and defend his position in the family by castrating him or cutting off his penis—a thought sufficient to make any boy shudder, even though it is presumably subconscious.

The conflict is eventually solved when the child finally renounces all claim to the sexual attentions of his mother, *repressing* all remaining sexual cravings for her, and **identifies** with his father. The resolution of the Oedipus complex marks the transition between the genital phase and the period of latent sexuality that follows.

Although the girl (between 18 months and 6 years) does not suffer the trauma of the Oedipus complex, she has a related difficulty. For her also the phallus is of primary importance, obviously not because she possesses one, but precisely because she does not. Her nightmare is not a fear of castration, but the agony of realizing that her penis has already been removed. She suffers **penis envy** in the most literal sense; the accompanying complex is called the **Electra complex**. It begins with the young girl innocently assuming that she does have a penis, and, like a male child, competing with her father for her mother's affections. As soon as she fears she has lost her penis, she identifies with her mother and competes for her father's affections. Freud assumes that she desires to have a child by him to compensate for the penis that she has lost. Gradually both the boy and the girl overcome these initial complexes and come to identify with their like-sexed parent. Freud interprets the observation that people sometimes select spouses who resemble their opposite-sexed parent as a manifestation of latent tendencies from the phallic phase of development.

Following the resolution of the phallic phase complexes, the child enters a period of latency (from age 6 to 11) marked by a loss of sexual interest and a continued identification with the like-sexed parent. The process of identification is important in Freud's system. It not only involves attempts to behave like the parent with whom the child is identifying, but also implies attempting to be like the object of identification. The boy who identifies with his father not only puts his hands in his pants pockets like his dad and spits nonchalantly against the fence post, but also incorporates his father's beliefs, as he interprets them. During this stage the Superego that began to form in the late anal phase and in the phallic stage becomes more clearly differentiated from the Ego, and more characteristic of the culture in which the child finds himself, since his sense of his culture derives from immediate associations with parents, teachers, and peers.

With the loss of sexual interest following resolution of the complexes of the phallic phase, boys become increasingly interested in other boys and actively avoid contact with girls. Similarly, girls show a marked preference for female playmates and actively avoid boys. These apparently natural tendencies imply that neither boys nor girls in elementary school are likely to be very upset if they are denied contact with children of the opposite sex.

Following this lengthy period of sexual neutrality the child (between 11 and 18 years) enters the stage of adult sexuality, the *genital* phase. At the inception of the genital phase there is a revival of infantile modes of gratification expressed in renewed pleasure in the eliminatory functions and in **masturbation**, which is apparently universal at this stage (see Chapter 13). In addition, the child frequently forms relatively strong attachments to others of the same sex. These homosexual attachments are gradually superseded by heterosexual attachments that characterize normal adult sexual relationships. Also during this last developmental phase, the Superego (**conscience**) becomes somewhat more flexible. During its early stages, the Superego is rigid and almost tyrannical, but normally becomes progressively more flexible and less rigid with increasing maturity.

Fixation and Regression

In a simplified sense there are three alternative routes that the development of personality can take. It can follow the normal route described above, in which the child progresses through each stage, developing Ego and Superego as he matures, so that he becomes a socially well-adjusted individual. According to Freud, whether or not an individual attains the desired end depends on the amount of sexual gratification he receives during each of the phases of development, and if the amount of sexual gratification is too little or too great, one of two possibilities may occur. First, an individual might develop a **fixation**, in which development ceases at a certain stage, and no further development of personality ensues. This is assumed to occur primarily from excessive gratification of sexual impulses at a particular stage. On the other hand, when sexual impulses are insufficiently gratified the individual may *regress* to a previous stage in which he was happier. **Regression** and fixation are the alternatives to normal, healthy development.

Fixation implies preoccupation with the activities that resulted in sexual gratification while in the fixated stage. An adult partially fixated at the oral phase (the oral character) is described as dependent, demanding, and preoccupied with oral gratification. He chews his nails, sucks his thumb, smokes, drinks, talks a great deal, and otherwise exercises his mouth and oral regions. The anally fixated character is compulsive, stingy, hoarding, and perhaps aggressive. Hoarding compulsions are apparently related to the pleasure an infant derives from withholding feces during the anal phase of development. Similarly, the phallic character is primarily concerned with satisfying his sexual urges, without regard for the objects of his sexual gratification. He is the sadist or rapist.

Mention of Freud's theories is incomplete without a consideration of **defense mechanisms** — the irrational and sometimes unhealthy methods some employ to compensate for their inability to satisfy the demands of the Id and to overcome the anxiety that accompanies the continual struggle between the Id and the Superego (A. Freud, 1946). Defense mechanisms are invented by the Ego in its role as mediator between the Id and the Superego; they are the Ego's attempt to establish peace between the two factions so that the personality can continue to operate in an apparently healthy manner. While defense mechanisms are integral to an understanding of the disturbed personality, they are less important for explaining the development of the normal child, and will be reviewed only briefly here.

Some Defense Mechanisms

The first and most important defense mechanism is *repression,* whereby the individual buries anxiety-provoking memories in his subconscious mind; **displacement** is the appearance of previously repressed behavior in a more acceptable guise. **Reaction formation** is behavior in opposition to the individual's actual inclination; **intellectualization** emphasizes the content of the behavior and excludes any emotional concomitants of that behavior. An individual **projects** when he attributes anxieties that are really his own to someone else; and finally, **denial** involves a distorted, subjective perception of the world — the world as the individual would like it to be, rather than as it is objectively.

These defense mechanisms can be illustrated by the behavior of one of my patients, a neurotic in Freud's terms. Since defense mechanisms result from attempts by the Ego to reconcile the ever-present differences between the Id and the Superego, it follows that the Ego that has not been successful in creating defenses may find itself mediating a disturbed personality. Neurotic disorders, however, may frequently take the form of an overreliance on defense mechanisms.

My patient — I shall call him Bill — was a young man who came to my office over a period of several years. When he first came to my office Bill was a very troubled individual. I used a standard opener: "What the hell is the matter with you?" Bill didn't know, but had been ridiculed by his friends for sleeping with a rag doll named Nora (his mother's name, incidentally). He developed such acute anxiety that he had voluntarily decided to approach me for help. "Aha," I thought, "here is a classical case of *displacement.* Bill feels anxious about his attraction to his mother, and has displaced this attraction to the rag doll."

But that was not the only way in which Bill was a textbook example. For example, he claimed vehemently that he disliked his mother. It was clear to me that he had ambivalent feelings toward his father who had died when Bill was 2 years old, but it was also clear that he did *not* hate his mother — in fact, he loved her with a warmth that a mother would find touching in a son. It is likely that she had indeed found it touching when Bill was very much younger, and that her response was the root of the anxiety-provoking attachment that he still felt for mama — hence, the strong *reaction formation.* It was interesting to me that Bill had succeeded in *repressing* all memories of the tender moments he had shared with his mother. (I uncovered this through hypnosis, feeling very much like a young Freud, for Freud also began his eminent career using hypnosis.)

Eventually, I wondered aloud at Bill's solicitous behavior toward his mother, despite his professed hostility. He constantly sent her flowers, cards, and gifts, and brought her meals which he had carefully prepared in his apartment next door. Invariably he spent Saturday evenings watching television with her and Sundays playing Bingo with her in the church basement. He also drove her to the Women's Auxiliary every Tuesday evening and frequently took time off work to drive her to her appointments, of which she had a great many since she was a hypochondriac. He explained to me that his behavior was traditional between a son and his ancient mother. He was quite convinced that there were no emotional overtones to his touching filial behavior. A textbook example of *intellectualization*.

During another session, Bill provided me with an overt illustration of *projection,* when he spoke at great length of the highly reprehensible behavior of his neighbor, a 40-year-old man who still lived with his mother, and who always held her arm when they walked through the park. Bill could see them through his binoculars if he climbed atop his roof and stood on an inverted apple box; he watched them every morning and was convinced that the son was in love with his mother. "How shameful," Bill assured me with very real horror. Bill was clearly projecting his illicit desires for his mother onto his neighbor.

Finally we returned to Bill's sleeping habit. I intended eventually to explain to him that his rag doll was a substitute for his mother — and that is not as easy to explain as one might think. Bill, however, absolutely refused to admit that his behavior was unusual or to understand that the rag doll was symbolic of his anxiety. "No sir," Bill informed me with customary respect. "No sir. Why should I feel guilty or anxious about it? Don't you know that all kinds of people — both men and women — between the ages of 1 and 74 sleep with dolls or teddy bears? I'm no different than most." This, of course, is an example of *denial*. Bill perceived the world as he wanted it to be in an effort to reduce the anxiety that he felt about his behavior. At last I referred Bill to a psychiatrist. When last I heard, Bill and his mother had rented a small cottage in southern France. I am told that the old lady speaks beautiful French.

Freud in Review   Freud provides an immensely rich basis for understanding psychic life. Unfortunately for our purposes, his theory is more suitable for an understanding of pathological behavior than ordinary development. Nevertheless, knowledge of Freudian theory is still valuable for providing an insight into normal development. The contemporary image of the human child is less a seething bundle of Id, as described by Freud, than an alert, active, responsive individual, as described by psychologists like Piaget. In his preoccupation with describing abnormal behavior and development, Freud has perhaps overemphasized those aspects of the human condition that are most likely to lead to pathological behavior. One need not deny primitive, instinctual urge to gratify sexual impulses, to survive, and perhaps even to die, but must still admit that there is only one aspect of the human condition, and perhaps less important than Freud suspected.

Jean Piaget, too, has provided psychology with one of its most in- Jean Piaget
formative systems, and new research and theorizing continue to flow
from the center in Geneva where Piaget has spent most of his long and
productive career. Barbel Inhelder deserves more than honorable mention as Piaget's closest associate and constant collaborator throughout
his career. Their work has been primarily concerned with cognitive development. Since we have considered the child's personality development through Freud's work, the child's intellectual achievement deserve
further study.

The questions a man asks when he arrives somewhere unfamiliar to Orientation
him, or when he begins work in an area previously unknown, are necessarily colored by the information, the prejudices, and the habits that he
brings with him. Since Piaget's early training was in biology, when he
became interested in children it was almost inevitable that he would apply
the questions of biology to his study of development. The biologist is
concerned with the **adaptation** of species. Accordingly, there are two
questions of overriding concern to him: first, he asks about the mechanisms or procedures that have allowed some organisms to survive while
others have passed into oblivion; second, he is concerned with developing
taxonomies of species — with ordering them in **phylogenetic** order from the
simplest to the most complex, or chronologically from the first to the
most recent.

Several implications of these questions are especially relevant when
considering the human child. First, ranking species in chronological order
is, in effect, the same thing as ranking them from the simplest to the most
complex. Thus, in both cases the hierarchy begins with simple single-
celled plant/animals and culminates with man — the species that is both
the most recent and the most complex. It is doubly interesting that the
progress of development can also be considered chronologically — that is,
from birth or conception to maturity — or in terms of the increasing complexity of the child's abilities at different stages. Thus, as in biology, if one
develops a hierarchy of child development either on the basis of the progressive complexity of the child's behavior or in terms of the chronology
of development, the same general picture will emerge.

Piaget therefore asked two questions about human development that
parallel the biological questions cited above. His first question focused on
the mechanisms of adaptation: What is it in the child's makeup that allows him to adapt to this incredibly complex world in a remarkably efficient manner — although over a rather long period of time? Second, he
attempted to develop some method for classifying the progressive adaptation of the child, in much the same way that biology developed taxonomies of species. Quite simply, then, Piaget applied questions of phylogeny
to the ontogeny of man. The summary provided in this chapter focuses on
his answers to these questions. Further details of his research can be
found in Part 4 of this text.

The story of development is a story of adaptation. A child is not born Mechanisms of
knowing how to cope with the world; indeed, he doesn't know that the Adaptation

world exists as an external reality until late in the first year of his life or even in the second. His simple, innate behaviors are limited to a finite number of reflexes, some of which are of almost no practical importance whatsoever, but several are very crucial for development. Among the most important of these reflexive behaviors are sucking, looking, reaching, and grasping. These primitive behaviors are called **schemes** (used interchangeably with *schema* or *schemata*). They exist at birth, but are imperfectly suited for the tasks that face the child. From the very first moment, survival demands that he begin to adapt. Adaptation, according to Piaget, occurs through the interplay of two related processes, **assimilation** and **accommodation**, which together comprise the only two ways that children, as well as adults, interact with the world.

How do people interact with the world? Quite simply, they perform the things of which they are capable and that are appropriate for the circumstances. If those behaviors of which an individual is capable are not appropriate, he must learn new behaviors. First, he uses various parts of his environment for activities he has already mastered; next the environment modifies previously learned activities. The first behavior defines *assimilation;* the second defines *accommodation.* By means of these two processes, the young child will adapt to his world. A more complete description of adaptation derives from the following discussion of Piaget's notions of human intelligence. It also provides a basis for understanding Piaget's answer for the second question of how to order and classify developmental phenomena.

Intelligence   For Piaget, intelligence is not a nebulous quality that people possess in greater or lesser quantities, as it appears in much psychological literature. Instead, intelligence is a way of behaving that is reflected in an individual's adaptation. Since adaptation is accomplished through the interaction of the twin processes of assimilation and accommodation, intelligence is defined in terms of these twin processes. Simply, intelligence is manifested in behavior appropriate to the demands of a situation. In Piaget's terminology, intelligent behavior requires a balance between assimilation and accommodation such that there is not a preponderance of one or the other. The technical term given to this balance is **equilibrium**. It is therefore correct to say that intelligence is a tendency toward equilibrium manifested in the assimilatory and accommodating behavior of an individual.

Lest this discussion become too complex, too jargonistic, and too remote from common experience, I shall illustrate intelligent behavior in a young child (also in Lefrancois, 1967). An infant is born with the capacity to suck. Almost any object that is placed in his mouth will elicit sucking responses, as will tactile stimulation of the lips and surrounding areas of the mouth. Piaget (1952) has observed that the primitive sucking motions made by a young child are unsophisticated. The infant is unsure of just how to hold his mouth and how to accommodate his sucking to the particular size and shape of the object presented. He will starve to death unless he assumes the correct posture. Thus, an act as simple as sucking a nipple requires more than assimilation; the child must also accommodate. The environment demands a balance between these two processes, since aspects of the child's reflexive sucking behavior are clearly appropriate and should be retained; other aspects of that behavior are unsuitable for obtaining milk from the nipple and must be modified. The result is a simple adaptation—a manifestation of intelligence.

In describing intelligence, Piaget refers not only to the processes of assimilation and accommodation, but also he refers to the cognitive or intellectual aspects of behavior. *Schemes,* the reflexive behavior the child is born with, also have neurological and structural connotations. Piaget says, in effect, that since there is a behavior (sucking, for example), and since it is this particular behavior and not any other, there must be something in the child that determines this sort of behavior from the specific stimulation. A scheme therefore denotes more than the simple behavior after which it is named; it also includes the intellectual components of that behavior.

Figure 7.2 represents Piaget's conception of intelligence diagrammatically. The "intelligence-in-action" that he discusses is the interaction of the individual with his environment through the **functional invariants** (so called because they do not change as the child develops) of assimilation and accommodation. The specific nature of that interaction is determined by structure (the schemes that the child has in his repertoire). The interaction with the environment modifies these schemes, thereby changing and adding to structure. Evidence that structure exists and that functioning has occurred is manifested in the child's behavior, labeled **content**.

Knowledge of the way children interact with their environment and what is meant by **structure** is essential for understanding the cognitive development of children. This understanding is necessary since structure

Structure and Stages

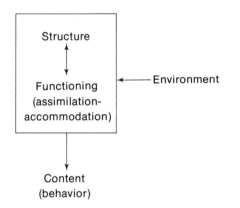

Piaget's view of intelligence-in-action. The individual (represented by the box) interacts (functions) with the environment as a result of activities in his repertoire (structure). The result of this interaction is behavior (content).

Figure 7.2

is what changes through the course of development; hence, an account of the child's cognitive structure at different ages forms the basis for Piaget's description of children. Development consists of a series of qualitatively different **stages** through which each child passes. Each stage is marked by strikingly different perceptions of the world and adaptations to it; each is the product of learning that occurred during the previous stage and a preparation for the stage that follows. These stages and their major characteristics are discussed briefly below and summarized in Table 7.2.

Table 7.2   Piaget's Stages of Cognitive Development

Stage	Approximate Age	Some Major Characteristics*
Sensorimotor	0–2 years	Motoric intelligence. World of the here and now. No language, no thought in early stages. No notion of objective reality.

Preoperational
  Preconceptual
  Intuitive
	2–7 years
	2–4 years
	4–7 years
		Egocentric thought.
		Reason dominated by perception.
		Intuitive rather than logical solutions.
		Inability to conserve.

Concrete Operations	7–11 or 12 years	Ability to conserve. Logic of classes and relations. Understanding of number. Thinking bound to concrete. Development of reversibility in thought.
Formal Operations	11 or 12 to 14 or 15 years	Complete generality of thought. Propositional thinking. Ability to deal with the hypothetical. Development of strong idealism.

*Each of these characteristics is detailed in appropriate sections of Chapters 10, 11, 12, and 13.

During the first two years of life the child is in the **sensorimotor period,** Piaget's label for the period during which the child understands his world largely through the activities he performs upon it and through his immediate and direct sensation of it. His intelligence, therefore, is sensorimotor. He has not yet begun to abstract the properties of objects or to reason generally about these objects from memory or without their physical presence. Only toward the end of the second year does the child finally realize that objects have a permanence and an identity that exist apart from his actual perception of them. Prior to this realization, the world is literally a world of the here and now; it ceases to exist when he does not perceive it. With normal stimulation the child begins to acquire language during this period and progresses slowly from a sensorimotor to a symbolic intelligence.

Following this transition, the child enters a lengthy period of development that Piaget calls the **preoperational period**. This stage spans the ages from 2 to 7 and is frequently considered in two shorter subperiods: the **preconceptual** lasts from the age of 2 to 4; the period of **intuitive thinking** lasts from 4 to 7. Both subperiods are preoperational since the child has not yet acquired the ability to think in the logical manner required for **operational** thought. An operation is a mental act (a thought) that can be reversed — and from this reversal follow some logical consequences that are entitled *reversibility*. For example, a 4-year-old child who is presented with a plasticene ball and who then observes a clever psychologist stretching this ball into a long, snakelike object, will usually believe that there is more plasticene in the snake than there was in the ball, since the snake is so much longer. He will continue to maintain this belief even though he realizes that the snake could be rolled back into a ball identical to the original ball. This potential **reversibility** has no logical consequences for him; it is what Piaget and Inhelder (1941) term *empirical*, as opposed to *operational*, reversibility. Thus, the child is aware of the possibility of reversing an action in the real world (empirically), but cannot think (operationalize) about the logical consequences of doing so.

The major acquisition of the following period of development is the ability to think operationally. The period is labeled **concrete operations** and lasts from the age of 7 or 8 to 11 or 12. The child's thinking is now dominated by logic rather than by simple perception or intuition (characteristics of the preceding stage). However, he restricts application of the rules and procedures of logic to real, concrete objects, or to objects or situations that he can conceive of. He is still unable to reason logically about hypothetical situations or events; he cannot go from the real to the merely possible or from the possible to the actual. His thinking is bound to the real world, the *concrete*. When the child finally liberates himself from the restrictions that have bound him to the concrete world, he enters the last stage of cognitive development — **formal operations**, beginning around the age of 11 or 12 and ending at 14 or 15. During this stage the child's thought becomes as logical as it will ever be; it is the culmination of a decade spent in preparation for it.

Child development, in Piaget's view, is best described as the emergence of progressively more logical forms of thought — that is, as the development of ways of thinking that become increasingly effective in helping the individual adapt to the demands of his environment. It is interesting that the major characteristics of behavior in each of the four developmental stages seem to pervade all aspects of the child's intelligence — his notion of space, time, number, reality, causality, and so on. Piaget and his collaborators have sought confirmation of the general pattern of development outlined in this chapter in all of these areas of functioning. They have generally found that confirmation, and despite several studies to the contrary, most attempted replications of Piaget's work have yielded results similar to his.

Piaget in Review

There is no doubt that Piaget is largely responsible for the tremendous recent upsurge of interest in the intellectual development of children. Like Freud, he stands as a great system builder in the recent history of psychological thought. The impact of his work, published in more than 200 articles and several dozen books, is reflected everywhere in the contents of contemporary journals in psychology, child psychology, and developmental psychology, as well as in the thousands of Piaget-oriented dissertations written by sheepskin-hungry scholars. Many of the more detailed findings of that work are described in the sections on cognitive development in Part 4.

Social Learning Theory

A child is neither produced in a vacuum, nor does he live in one. His environment is not as antiseptic as the theories advanced to account for development might suggest. Thus, since you are so forgetful, it is once more necessary to remind you of two things: there is no average child; each child has a very personal environment. Piaget's conceptual child and the Freudian child are convenient inventions of theoreticians who were concerned with systematizing and unifying their theories and who wished to avoid contradictions in doing so. For example, it is clear that they could not easily speak with authority of Robert Edward Cuttingham or of Sam the psychologist in the same breath, for their worlds have been so different, and the influence of these environments on people is also quite different. The portrait of the child painted by Freud or Piaget is restricted and static; it lacks the dynamism of the living, growing child.

Bandura and Walters (1963; Bandura, 1969) supplement the two positions just described in this chapter. Their theory is one of several that have attempted to explain **social learning** in children, and to fill in the picture of development begun by Freud's theories of personality and Piaget's theory of cognitive development. The theory is premised on the assumption that much significant social learning occurs as a result of imitation (see Chapter 4), and that one can explain the effects of imitation with the principles of operant conditioning. Children imitate; imitative behavior may be considered an operant; and reinforcement frequently follows imitation. Each of these statements is examined below.

First, children do in fact imitate. I recently observed my 4-year-old son standing in front of the hall mirror, looking at himself and raising his **eyebrows** so as to give him a definitely quizzical expression. He seemed so pleased with himself that I called his mother (my wife, incidentally) to see this great display of histrionic ability. She, not altogether kindly, reminded me that I had indulged in a great deal of eyebrow raising after watching a movie in which the hero had displayed some impressive eyebrow dexterity.

Second, imitative behavior can be considered operant despite the fact that a model is ordinarily involved. The model does not usually serve as a direct stimulus for the imitative behavior since it is frequently absent at the time of the imitation. Hence, whatever learning occurs in the absence of the model-as-stimulus. The model seems to provide a pattern for behavior, rather than eliciting the behavior itself. In most cases, the behavior will not be learned unless some sort of reinforcement follows.

Third, reinforcement does frequently follow imitation. It can take a variety of forms. The behavior itself may often be reinforcing, particularly if it is socially approved. For example, a child who learns to say "milk" from hearing his mother say "milk" may be rewarded with a drink of that precious liquid if he says the proper word at the right time. In that case the consequences of the imitative behavior are clearly reinforcing. In addition, adults often reinforce their children directly for imitation. A father whose son stands just like his daddy, with his feet apart and well braced, and with his hands in his hip pockets, may draw attention to his son's admirable posture, reinforcing the child's act. Other adults who reinforce the child for imitating his father, are a second source of reinforcement, separate from the model. **Vicarious reinforcement** is a third source of reinforcement that is important in observational learning (synonymous with learning through imitation). People will frequently imitate the behavior of others and continue to do so, even when they are receiving no reinforcement whatsoever. It is assumed that this type of behavior is related to the imitator's unconscious expectation that if another person is behaving in a specific way and is reinforced for it, then the same manner of behaving will be reinforcing for him, too. That the observer does indeed derive some reinforcement, however minor, from the imitated behavior is clear if he persists in the behavior despite lack of any external reinforcement. It seems that he must be enjoying reinforcement *vicariously* — hence the label.

Imitation frequently involves more than an observer's simply copying a model's behavior. Indeed, the effects of imitation can take a number of different forms. Further, a model is not necessarily a person; it can be anything that serves as a pattern for behavior — books, manuals, folk heroes, television heroes, religious heroes, and a host of real or imaginary villains as well. Such models are referred to as *symbolic models;* they are probably of greater significance than real-life models in highly technological and relatively impersonal societies.

> Manifestations of Observational Learning

Bandura and Walters (1963) describe three different effects of imitation on social learning in children. Acquiring novel behavior, the **modeling effect**, is well illustrated by a child who suddenly begins to say all manner of surprising words in the presence of his grandmother — not because he heard these words at home, of course, but because the neighbor's children do not have such well-behaved parents. Such precisely imitative responses demonstrate the modeling effect on behavior. This effect was also illustrated by the Bandura, Ross, and Ross experiments cited earlier. Not only were children exposed to aggressive behavior more likely to play aggressively with the plastic clowns, but they were also observed to engage in many precisely imitative responses. For example, if the model had employed a rubber mallet to strike the clown, the child was likely to employ the same mallet to strike the clown in the same way; if the model had kicked and punched the clown, the child was likely to do the same.

Another important manifestation of the modeling effect is the acquisition of language. The statement that imitation is involved in learning language seems almost platitudinous. At the risk of being platitudinous,

then, let me point out that an Eskimo child learns to speak Eskimo and not French, and a French child, when he learns to speak, ordinarily says his first words in French.

My hypothesis (arrived at after consultation with my grandmother) is that a child is likely to learn to speak the language that is spoken around him, in much the same way that a parrot learns to mimic the words in his environment.

The effects of imitation are also found in the phenomena labeled the **inhibitory effect** (the suppression of deviant behavior) and the **disinhibitory effect** (the appearance of previously suppressed deviant behavior). These effects are usually the result of punishment or reward to the model for engaging in deviant behavior. Consider the hypothetical case of a teen-ager from an upstanding, conservative, middle-class family whose friends have recently discovered the joys of losing themselves in the unreal world of marijuana. The behavior is clearly deviant by the child's own standards, but the amount of reinforcement (in terms of social prestige, acceptance by the group, and other expressions, real or feigned, of drug-related joy) that others appear to derive from smoking pot may well *disinhibit* this behavior in the child. There is really no new learning involved, as in modeling, but merely the disinhibition of previously suppressed behavior. If this teen-ager later observes members of her peer group punished by law, parents, or school authorities, or experiencing ill effects of the drug, she might suddenly cease engaging in this behavior. Again, there is no new learning involved, although there is a change in behavior resulting from the influence of models; thus, this change illustrates the *inhibitory effect*.

Teachers generally seem to have a good intuitive understanding of the inhibitory effect. Consider the teacher who singles out a wrongdoer from a class filled to the brim with wrongdoers. The implicit (and sometimes explicit) hope of the teacher is that the effect of the punishment will generalize to all other potential wrongdoers and will serve to inhibit all future expressions of similar behavior. In practice, however, the inhibitory effect appears to be relatively weak. People have an interesting propensity, whenever they witness tragedy or pain that might have befallen them, to assume quite irrationally but with great conviction that these unpleasant things happen to other people but never to themselves. Similarly, the apparent ineffectiveness of our penal system is due in part to the weakness of the inhibitory effect. When a criminal is hanged, electrocuted, guillotined, or otherwise sent back to where he came from, we, the civilized and rational, justify our behavior by pointing to the effect his punishment will have. "It will serve as an example to all other criminals, and we will have fewer of them to hang, or guillotine, or whatever." In other words, we appeal to the power of the disinhibitory effect in the face of evidence that suggests its ineffectiveness.

A striking experiment illustrating the disinhibitory effect is provided by a variation of the Milgram (1963) experiments performed by Walters and Thomas (1963), and by Walters, Thomas, and Acker (1962). The subjects in the Milgram study (1963) were told that they would participate in the experiment as confederates of the experimenters. They were asked to help the experimenters examine the effects of punishment on learning by administering electric shocks to a subject whenever he made an error. In reality, however, the person described to them as a "subject" was the real confederate in the experiment who had instructions to make a predetermined number of errors. The "confederate" sat in front of a panel with a series of toggle switches labeled from 15 to 450 volts in 15-volt increments. The object of the Milgram experiment was to see how far he would go when instructed to begin with the 15 volt-shock and progress upward one switch for every subsequent error. The distance between the person administering the shock and the "subject" was important. In one case the shocker could see, hear, and even touch the "subject," who had been instructed to vocalize the agony of the electric shocks and eventually to scream, "I refuse to continue!" In other variations the "subject" was farther removed physically, but still within sight and hearing distance, or behind a curtain so that he could not be seen but could still be heard, or he was removed completely so that he could neither be seen nor heard. There are two particularly striking findings. First, all the "confederates" (the real subjects) did comply with the experimenters' instructions and administered shocks to the others, even when the "subjects" refused to continue. Secondly, the average intensity of the shocks administered prior to discontinuing the experiment varied directly with the distance between the real subject and the person he was shocking (as shown in Figure 7.3): the greater the distance between them, the greater the shocks.

In the Walters et al. (1962, 1963) variation of this experiment, subjects were told that they were participating in a study of memory. This

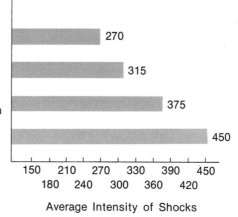

1 Subject can hear, see, and touch stooge — 270

2 Subject can hear and see the stooge — 315

3 Subject can hear the stooge but cannot see him — 375

4 Subject can neither hear nor see the stooge — 450

Average Intensity of Shocks

Figure 7.3   Average intensity of shocks administered by subject to a stooge as a function of the distance between them. (Adapted from Milgram, "Some conditions of obedience and disobedience to authority," *Human Relations*, 1965, 18, pp. 57–76. Used by permission of Plenum Publishing Corp. and the author.)

ploy was to justify having each subject view one of two film sequences, either a very violent scene from the film *Rebel Without a Cause,* or a peaceful scene of adolescents engaged in art work from an educational film. Next, subjects were asked individually to help the experimenter with another study concerned with the effects of punishment on learning. From then on the procedure was similar to that just described for the Milgram experiment. Again, the results were rather striking. Subjects in both groups were initially very cooperative. However, the effect on the subjects of the violent film sequence as opposed to the peaceful sequence was manifested in significant increases in the intensity of the shocks administered by members of the group who had seen the violent film: violent models apparently have the power to disinhibit violent behavior in subjects; peaceful models may have the opposite effect. Both this experiment and the Milgram experiment illustrate the disinhibitory power of models. In the first case, the experimenter's instructions serve as a model; in the second, both his instructions and the film are models.

A third effect of imitation is known as the **eliciting effect**: the behavior engaged in by the learner as a result of observing a model is neither identical to the model's behavior, nor deviant, nor novel for him, but is simply related to it. In other words, it is as though the model's behavior suggests some response to the observer and therefore *elicits* that response. For example, if a child "acts up" in school and a number of his classmates also misbehave, it is clear that his behavior has occasioned the related behavior in other children, but it is also clear that they are imitating a type of behavior rather than a specific behavior.

It is likely that much of the behavior that children and adults engage in daily is a manifestation of the eliciting effect. People around us are examples of success, achievement, intelligence, happiness, or whatever else turns us on at the time. We may not necessarily try to do exactly what they have done, but we are likely to attempt in our own way to emulate their behavior. If we assume, for example, that those who are wealthy are happier than we, this may elicit wealth-oriented behavior from us, but the specific behavior may be very different from that of the person who is our model of wealth. Similarly, we may be inspired to artistic or literary efforts from reading a great book or seeing a beautiful painting by someone more talented or more persistent than we, but we do not try to copy their work—it simply elicits related behavior.

Among the practical implications of social learning theory and oper- **Behavior Modification**
ant conditioning (see Chapter 5), several are particularly important for parents, teachers, and anyone concerned with rearing and educating children. This practical orientation has yielded a number of specific techniques for changing behavior that are frequently described as *behavior modification*.

Positive reinforcement is a technique of behavior modification in which rewards are deliberately used to alter an individual's behavior. In its simplest form, positive reinforcement requires that circumstances be arranged in such a way that the desired behavior will be emitted and followed by reinforcement. Obviously, parents and teachers engage in much behavior based on positive reinforcement. Whenever a teacher praises a student, gives him a high grade, draws attention to his brilliance, or otherwise provides a sign of approval for his behavior, she is using positive reinforcement. There are numerous recent examples of systematic reinforcement programs in classrooms that are designed to promote learning and to eliminate disciplinary or social problems (Azrin and Lindsley, 1956; Meacham and Wiesen, 1969; Hewett, 1968). A simple form of these programs is to provide children with tokens for desirable behavior. In some cases tokens are revoked if undesirable behavior occurs. Periodically these tokens are exchanged for prizes or other more tangible forms of reinforcement.

Extinction is a second behavior modification technique. It simply involves the withdrawal of reinforcement as a means of bringing about the cessation of an undesirable behavior. A teacher who ignores disruptive behavior when she (or he) suspects that the behavior is maintained by the reinforcement of her attention, is employing extinction. Unfortunately, parents and teachers are frequently not aware of the reinforcement that maintains undesirable behavior, and therefore cannot use extinction effectively. For example, a student's disruptive behavior may be equally reinforced by the reaction of his classmates and the teacher's attention. In this case, ignoring the behavior might aggravate it. A third behavior modification technique involves the deliberate use of praiseworthy models to elicit desirable behavior or to eliminate less desirable responses. Alcoholics Anonymous, Synanon, and Weight Watchers employ modeling techniques to persuade their members of the possibility of achieving the desired results. Ex-alcoholic or ex-obese persons present themselves to individuals who are not yet "ex-," and speak disparagingly of their lives prior to their improved behavior. A teacher who praises an outstanding student and employs him as an example (model) to be emulated is also using behavior modification. The success of the technique is impressive.

Social Learning in Review The account of social learning presented here is based entirely on a model of observational learning described by Bandura and Walters (1963), and Bandura (1969). There are alternative explanations for social learning, but this one was chosen to balance and supplement the two other theoretical views of children described in this chapter. The value of an observational learning model of development cannot be disputed since evidence of the effects of imitation is all around us. However, it is still necessary to ask how much learning and behavior is explainable by imitation, and, correspondingly, how valid other models might be. The position adopted in this text is that some learning is best explained in terms of modeling; that some is more clearly attributable to an interaction between the individual and his environment (as described by Piaget), and that other behavior appears to result from the primitive urges that a child is born with and their conflict with reality as he develops (Freud's theory).

Summary This chapter began with the world of the Ihalmiut, the Eskimo people of the Barrens, as they were when Farley Mowat lived among them in the earlier part of this century. We observed the remarkable differences between the world of the Eskimo child and the children of our own culture. Hopefully you perceived that each child's world is unique; the average, normal, ordinary child who is described by the great theorists does not exist, not only because each child (except identical twins) is genetically different from every other but also because the significant aspects of his world can be known by him alone. Next the chapter encountered the rich theoretical formulations and practical observations of Sigmund Freud, stopping briefly to mention that his theory is more valuable for explaining the abnormal personality than the allegedly normal, but that it is nevertheless of considerable importance in a study of the child. With Piaget's voluminous and far-ranging work we skirted the field of a child's cognitive development. Finally the chapter returned to social learning and discussed the model of observational learning advanced by Bandura and Walters. We have only begun the story of development.

Main Points
1. "Who but a madman would raise his hand against blood of his blood? . . . Who but a madman would, in his man's strength, stoop to strike against the weakness of a child? Be sure that I am not mad, nor yet is Howmik afflicted with madness!" (Farley Mowat, 1952, p. 141)

2. Freud's theory is useful for understanding the development of personality, particularly the abnormal or pathological personality.

3. The *libido* or source of energy for human behavior, and consequently for the formation of personality, derives from two powerful *instinctual* tendencies of man: the urge to survive and the urge to procreate (*Eros*). The death wish (*Thanatos*) is also a powerful human urge, but is usually of less significance.

4. The newborn child is all libido — that is to say, he is all instinctual urges. The label *Id* is applied to the level of personality concerned solely with the gratification of urges — urges that are primarily sexual in Freud's view.

5. The conflict between the Id (instinctual urges) and reality develops the Ego — that aspect of personality concerned with finding ways for the Id to satisfy its basic urges.

6. Later in the course of development the Superego forms as an offshoot of the Ego. It represents societal and cultural taboos and restrictions that are imposed on an individual's instinctual urges and is called *conscience* by many grandmothers.

7. Freud describes development as a progression through five stages, each differentiated from the other primarily by the areas of the child's body that are the principal sources of sexual gratification at that time. The stages in sequence are the oral, the anal, the phallic, a period of latency, and the genital stage.

8. Piaget's theory describes the cognitive development of children. It is biologically based and inquires first about the process of adaptation, and second is concerned with classifying cognition in order of progressively more complex and logical processes.

9. Piaget believes that adaptation results from the interaction of the child with his environment through the complementary processes of using activities that are already in his repertoire (*assimilation*) and changing activities to conform to environmental demands (*accommodation*).

10. Those aspects of intelligence that can be organized and that are implicit in human behavior are called structure. Structure consists of *schemes* (simple behaviors and their structural connotations) and later of operations that are organized into progressively more complex systems. A description of the changes that structure undergoes during development is a description of the child's intellectual development.

11. Bandura and Walters' social learning theory explains learning based on the effects of imitation. Operant conditioning can explain these effects.

12. The three manifestations of observational learning are the acquisition of novel responses (the modeling effect), the inhibition or disinhibition of deviant responses (the inhibitory or disinhibitory effect), and the emission of behaviors that are not identical to the model's behavior, but are suggested by it (the eliciting effect).

13. The child is incredibly more complicated than this chapter might suggest, but he is easier to understand within the context of the more organized systems provided here than within the context of your grandmother's understanding of him.

Further Readings

Both Freud and Piaget were voluminous writers. It is frequently easier and sometimes more valuable to use secondary sources for information about their theoretical positions. Nevertheless, the interested student is strongly advised to consult original sources to achieve a better idea of their work. The following are particularly useful starting points:

Baldwin, Alfred L. *Theories of child development*. New York: John Wiley, 1967.

Brill, A. A. (Ed.) *The basic writings of Sigmund Freud.* New York: Random House, 1938.

Piaget, J. *The origins of intelligence in children.* New York: International University Press, 1952.

Inhelder, B., and J. Piaget. *The growth of logical thinking from childhood to adolescence.* New York: Basic Books, 1958.

Maier, H. W. *Three theories of child development.* New York: Harper and Row, 1965.

A clear and concise explanation of social learning theory is provided by Bandura and Walters in:

Bandura, Albert, and Richard Walters. *Social learning and personality development.* New York: Holt, Rinehart and Winston, 1963.

An interesting and practical explanation of behavior modification, particularly as it applies to teaching, is contained in the following sources:

Meacham, M. L., and A. E. Wiesen. *Changing classroom behavior: A manual for precision teaching.* Scranton, Penn.: International Textbook Co., 1969.

Lefrancois, G. R. *Psychology for teaching: A bear always faces the front.* Belmont, Calif.: Wadsworth Publishing Co., 1972, Chapter 15.

Part Four: A Description of Development

8

Of Survival, Alcohol, and Drugs: Prenatal Development

"I don't agree," Sam said rather emphatically, although there was really no one there with whom to disagree. I had simply come over to bring him a cake and to review the progress I had made on my book since the big sewer broke. "I'm starting to write about the beginning of human life," I informed him. That's when he said "I don't agree." He repeated it several times before launching into a long and involved discussion of the problems of the world. Sam has a great deal of time to read and think, and despite the fact that he is a recluse, he remains very concerned about the state of the world and its future.

"Do you realize," he asked, "that modern man is no more than a million years old?" When I asked what that had to do with my work, Sam looked at me with that peculiar exasperated look that intelligent people frequently bestow on those less gifted. "Don't you see? Look, the earth is perhaps 5 billion years old. Man is a mere million years old, perhaps much less. By the year 1830, the population of the entire earth was estimated at close to 1 billion people. You see it took almost 4.5 billion years for the population of the earth to reach a mere billion. Now consider that within the next century—just 100 years—the second billion was added. And the third billion took only 30 years. Barring some major catastrophe that would wipe out most of the earth's inhabitants, there is no doubt that by the turn of the next century there will be 6 billion people living on earth."

"Wow," I said, using my characteristic expression of amazement. Then I ventured a timid "So . . . ?"

"So, it's obvious," Sam hurried on. "The United Nations has decreed that the minimum average calorie intake required by people is 2000 per day. Right now, and you ought to know this, less than half of all people obtain the required 2000 calories. Perhaps 60 percent of the earth's population is undernourished. Thousands are starving every day.

"Now, when you consider that today there are only slightly more than 3 billion of us, and for every one of us there is an average of 1.2 acres of land under cultivation, you should be frightened. In order to nourish the earth's population adequately right now, we would have to double our production of food. When there are 6 billion people on earth, there will not only be less cultivated land per person, but there will also be a tremendous drain on energy resources, recreation facilities, and housing. We cannot continue to have children without drastically increasing our food output as well as everything else that we find necessary for comfortable living. We will have no territories left; we will revert to a primitive animal state; it will again be dog eat dog, and only the fittest will survive. The great fundamental law of evolution that we have managed to violate so flagrantly in a mere one hundred years will in the end take over again. You see, it is no longer just the fit who survive; the unfit in many cases have an even better chance than the fit since our medical technology is so far advanced that we can now keep alive those who would surely die in a harsher environment. The laws of natural selection apply only to some of our undomesticated animals; they no longer apply to people."

"Sam," I began to interject, but he interrupted me again. "I've changed my mind," he said. "We are an ingenious race. We'll survive. Go ahead and tell your readers how to make babies."

I assured Sam that I really didn't intend to talk about the mechanics of baby production.

"Mechanics!" he shouted, and we would surely have gotten into a long one-sided argument since Sam sees nothing mechanical in something as human and as moving as the subject under discussion. It was time to feed the rats, however, so I left him to his duties and returned again to mine. He and Samuel were eating great mouthfuls of chocolate cake when I left.

Conception   The beginning of the story of child development was told in the first chapter which, surprisingly in this world of unordered things, was entitled "The Beginning." But there is a smaller and more specific beginning that deals not with the human race whose proud members we are, but with the inception of a single individual. This beginning requires the union of a sperm cell with an egg cell, as well as the physical union between the bearers of these cells. But that is a mundane and uninteresting story for people as sophisticated as you are, so we will go directly to conception, the union of the two sex cells, rather than the union of the two sexes.

At conception the newly **fertilized** egg cell (zygote) contains the

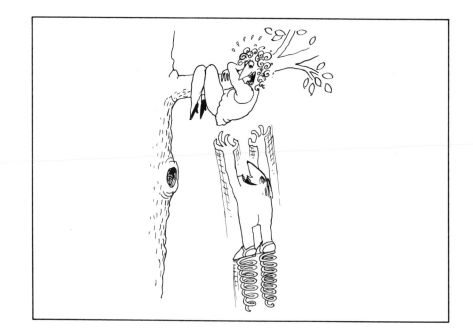

Pregnancy is caused. It does not just happen.

individual's entire genetic endowment in the form of 23 pairs of chromosomes. Normally, all changes that take place in this cell's development will result from the environment's interaction, both prior to and after birth, with the predispositions and predeterminations implicit in the particular genetic memory of chromosomes. It is extremely difficult to separate these predeterminations from influences that are unrelated to genetic endowment, but it is possible to note some of the effects of external influences on the developing organism. Accordingly, this chapter is concerned with describing prenatal development and examining some of the influences that may affect development.

Women find it valuable to be able to detect **pregnancy** prior to the actual birth of the baby. Despite the conflicting opinions of a number of grandmothers, however, there are few indications of pregnancy that can be interpreted with certainty prior to the later stages of **prenatal development**. Nevertheless, there are some highly indicative signs which appear relatively soon after conception. For convenience, the symptoms of pregnancy are generally divided into three groups, according to the extent to which they can be relied upon (Bookmiller and Bowen, 1967): **presumptive**, **probable**, and **positive**.

Symptoms of Pregnancy

The presumptive signs of pregnancy are generally well known by prospective mothers, their midwives, and their grandmothers. They include cessation of **menses**, morning sickness, changes in the breasts, increased frequency of urination, and **quickening** (fetal motion). Most of these symptoms do not occur very early in pregnancy. Cessation of menses is not usually noticed until at least two weeks of pregnancy have passed, since conception ordinarily occurs approximately two weeks after the last menstrual period. Nor is this a certain sign of pregnancy— many other factors may be its cause. Morning sickness, while it affects approximately two-thirds of all pregnant women, does not ordinarily begin until approximately two weeks after the missed period and can easily be mistaken for some other malady. Frequent urination is usually caused by increased pressure on the bladder, and will therefore not occur until the fetal mass is sufficiently enlarged to fill the uterine cavity (usually after the third month). Frequently during the early stages the breasts enlarge and become slightly painful, and the aureoles darken. Since this symptom is highly subjective, it is relatively unreliable. Quickening, the movement of the fetus in the womb, is not discernible by the mother until the fifth month, and by that time, most reasonably intelligent women have realized for some time that they are pregnant.

Presumptive Symptoms

Among the probable signs of pregnancy are several that occur after the fetus has begun to develop, including enlargement of the abdomen. However, caution should be exercised in interpreting enlargement of the abdomen as a sign of pregnancy, even if it occurs very rapidly. It could be caused by a rapidly growing tumor. A softening of the **uterus** at its juncture with the cervix is a second probable sign of pregnancy. The

Probable Symptoms

A probable sign of pregnancy. Note the swollen ankles.

third symptom is related to a change in the cervix itself, which also softens and develops a faintly bluish coloration about eight weeks after conception.

Positive Symptoms   When it is possible to hear—and sometimes to count—fetal heartbeats with the aid of a stethoscope, it is fairly certain that the woman is indeed pregnant. Similarly, if fetal movements can be detected by feeling the abdomen, or sometimes simply by observing it, one can be fairly confident that a fetus is present—unless the patient has a stomach tic, which is unlikely. Two other methods of ascertaining the presence of a **fetus** are to X ray the mother to detect its outline, or to palpate it through the abdominal wall. Unfortunately for the woman who must know whether or not she is pregnant immediately after intercourse, all these positive symptoms do not develop soon enough, although it is possible to hear a fetal heartbeat 4 or 5 weeks into a pregnancy. In such cases, the aid of a rabbit, a frog, a **mouse**, or some other unfortunate creature is usually enlisted. A small amount of urine from the suspecting mother is injected into an unsuspecting and immature mouse or into a **virgin rabbit** (if such animal can be found). If the woman is indeed pregnant the injection will cause a rupturing of the follicles on the ovaries of the animal. Bookmiller and Bowen (1967) report that a positive test cannot be obtained until 6 weeks after the last menses—in other words, until the woman is approximately 4 weeks pregnant. Since it is usually possible to detect pregnancy with a fairly high degree of certainty at the end of 8 weeks of gestation, some physicians are reluctant to sacrifice the rabbit, mouse, or frog unnecessarily.

A Virgin Rabbit

It is nothing short of phenomenal that as physically insignificant an object as a fertilized egg can become as complex and sophisticated an organism as a child within a period of 9 calendar months. It is interesting to note that the **gestation** period for different species varies considerably: for bovines it is similar to man's; elephants require no fewer than 600 days; dogs come to term in approximately 63 days, rabbits in 31, and chickens in 21.

Prenatal Development

Fertilization in the woman usually occurs in the **fallopian tubes** that link the **ovaries** to the uterus (see Figure 8.1). It results from the invasion of the tubes by sperm cells, one of which successfully penetrates the outer covering of the ovum and unites with it. From that moment a human child begins to form, but it will be approximately 280 days — 40 weeks or 10 lunar months — before this individual is freed from his life-giving prison. The gestation period is usually calculated in lunar months, each month consisting of 28 days — hence 10 lunar months or 280 days for pregnancy. These days are counted from the onset of the last menstrual period. The true gestation period is therefore approximately 266 days, since fertilization usually cannot occur until approximately 12 to 14 days following the beginning of menses.

The American College of Obstetrics and Gynecology has standardized the terminology employed in describing prenatal development by identifying three developmental stages with clear time boundaries. The stage of the **fertilized ovum** begins at fertilization and ends with implantation at approximately the end of the first week. The *embryo* stage follows and terminates at the end of the eighth week (calculated from the onset of the last menses rather than from fertilization). The final stage, the

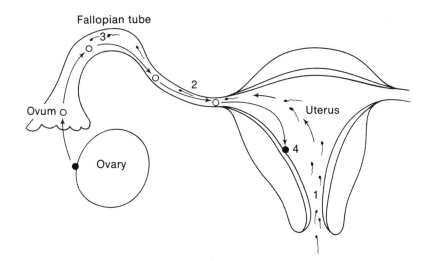

Figure 8.1   The process of fertilization and implantation. At (1) sperm cells have entered the vagina and are finding their way into the uterus. At (2) some of these spermatozoa are fighting the current up the fallopian tube (there is a similar tube on the other side) intending to lay siege to the ovum (3). The fertilized ovum drifts down the current, dividing and forming new cells as it goes, until it implants itself in the wall of the uterus (4) by the seventh or eighth day after fertilization.

fetus, lasts from the end of the second lunar month until the birth of the baby.

The Fertilized Ovum

After fertilization, the ovum is carried toward the uterus by currents in the fallopian tubes, a procedure requiring between 7 and 9 days. Cell divisions occur during this time, so that the fertilized ovum, which initially consisted of a single egg cell and a single sperm cell, will contain 64 cells. It is hardly larger at the end of the first week than it was at the time of fertilization, largely because the cells of which it consists are considerably smaller in size. This is not surprising since the ovum has received no nourishment from any source other than itself. At the end of the first week, the ovum is no larger than a pinhead but is ready to implant itself in the uterine wall.

The Embryo

The stage of the **embryo** begins with the implantation of the fertilized ovum in the wall of the uterus. The ovum facilitates this process by secreting certain enzymes and producing minute, tentacle-like growths, called villi, that reach out into the lining of the uterus. This is the beginning of the **placenta**, the flat membrane that links the developing embryo and the mother. From this point forward the embryo is parasitic, deriving its nourishment from the mother through the placenta, and in later stages of growth, ridding itself of wastes through the same membrane. There is no direct connection between the mother's blood and the infant's. Nutrients and other substances are transmitted through the placenta from the mother's blood vessels to the child's. Actually, the placenta serves less as a transmitter than as a filter. In time, the placenta and the fetus are connected by the **umbilical cord**, a long, thick cord that is attached to the placenta and what will be the child's **navel**. The umbilical cord consists of two arteries and one large vein and is approximately 20 inches long. It contains no nerve cells, so that there is no connection between the mother's nervous system and that of the child **in utero**.

The course of physiological development *in utero* is highly predictable and highly regular in normal development. By the end of the first lunar month (very early in the embryonic stage), the fetus is still only a fraction of an inch long and weighs much less than an ounce. Despite the size, not only has there been cell differentiation into future skin cells, nerves, bone, and other body tissue, but the rudiments of such organs as eyes, ears, and nose have begun to appear. In addition, some of the internal organs are beginning to develop. By the end of the second lunar month (the end of the period of embryonic development), the embryo is between 1½ and 2 inches long and weighs close to ⅔ of an ounce. All the organs are now present, the whole mass has assumed the curled shape characteristic of the fetus, and the embryo is clearly recognizable as human. Arm and limb buds have appeared and begun to grow, resembling short, awkward paddles. External **genitalia** have also appeared, although it is still impossible to determine the sex of the offspring.

It is now the end of the second lunar month; the woman is 6 weeks pregnant. She has missed 2 menstrual periods, or is currently missing her second. She is definitely pregnant, although the absolute mass of the organism that she carries inside her is still quite unimpressive. By the end of the third lunar month it may reach a length of 3 inches, but will still weigh less than an ounce. The head of the fetus is ⅓ of its entire length, and will have changed to ¼ by the end of the sixth lunar month, and slightly less than that at birth.

During the third month of pregnancy the fetus is sufficiently developed that if it is aborted it will make breathing movements and will give evidence of a primitive **sucking reflex** and of the **Babinsky reflex** if stimulated appropriately (the Babinsky reflex is the name given to the infant's tendency to fan his toes when tickled on the soles of his feet). Such a fetus will, however, have no chance of survival at this stage of development.

During the fourth lunar month of pregnancy, the fetus grows to a length of 6 inches and weighs approximately 4 ounces. The bones have begun to form, all organs are clearly differentiated, and there may even be evidence of some intrauterine movement. It is not until the fifth month, however, that the mother begins to feel these signs of movement, called quickening. It is also during this month that the downy covering, called **laguno**, begins to grow over most of the child's body. This covering is usually shed during the seventh month but is occasionally still present at birth. The fetus weighs approximately 11 ounces and may have reached a length of 10 inches by the end of the fifth lunar month.

Toward the end of the sixth month an obstetrician can palpate the

The Fetus

baby through the mother's abdomen. The heartbeat, faintly discernible in the fifth month, can now be heard clearly with the aid of a **stethoscope**.

The eyelids have now separated so that the fetus can open and close its eyes. It is approximately a foot long and weighs close to 20 ounces. It would have some chance of surviving in a modern hospital if born at this time.

The fetus' growth in size and weight becomes more dramatic in the last few months of the final stage, although there are few significant physiological developments left to come. It is now a matter of sheer physical growth: from 15 inches in the seventh month (2.6 pounds), to 16 inches in the eighth (4 pounds); from 17.5 inches in the ninth (4.7 pounds), finally to 19.6 inches (7 pounds) at the end of the tenth (see Figure 8.2). It is now ready to be born.

This story continues in the following chapter. Prior to going there, however, we will take a brief look at some of the factors that may be of importance to the normal or abnormal development of the fetus.

Factors Affecting Prenatal Development

It is nearly impossible to provide an exhaustive listing and description of the factors that influence the development of the child *in utero*, given the highly circumstantial nature of much of the evidence that has been gathered to support various points of view. In many ways, it is a confused area, not only because it is by nature extremely complex but also because many potentially helpful experiments cannot be performed for ethical or moral reasons. In addition, there is a frequent confounding of causes, as well as some confusion of causes and effects in the experiments performed. Consider, for example, the apparently simple problem of determining whether a particular drug affects the fetus. It would appear that all that is required is to obtain a group of women to whom the drug has been administered and observe their offspring for any signs of possible effects of the drug. The women, however, have usually been given the drug for a particular reason. The investigator is frequently unable to determine whether differences between the children produced by women who have taken the drug and a control group are due to the ailment for which the drug was administered, or to the drug itself. For obvious ethical reasons, it is not usually possible to administer the drug simply to observe its effect. Furthermore, the effects of prenatal environments are frequently so subtle that they are not easily discernible. Despite the difficulties encountered in the field, however, a good deal of valid information about the various effects of prenatal conditions on the development of the fetus is now available.

The World in Utero

The world of the embryo and the fetus is difficult for us to imagine, although we have all been through it at one time or another. It is probably a relatively comfortable place, since it is so admirably suited to the developing organism that it houses. The temperature is always optimal; adequate nourishment is provided with no effort required of the little parasite, and the environment is absolutely quiet and peaceful — or is it?

There is evidence that the fetus is sensitive to sounds. Bernard and

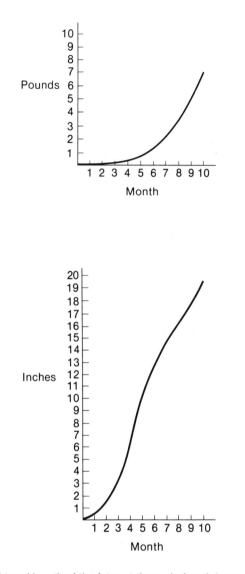

Approximate weight and length of the fetus at the end of each lunar month of prenatal   Figure 8.2
development.

Sontag (1947) found that during the last 2½ months of pregnancy, it is possible to produce marked cardiac acceleration in the fetus with tones of varying intensity, which they interpret as evidence that the fetus is sensitive to sounds. Spelt (1948) provides further corroborative evidence with fetuses conditioned to react to a low-intensity tone during the last two months of pregnancy. The unconditioned stimulus was a loud noise; the unconditioned response was a sudden movement or subsequent hyperactivity of the fetus (as detected with a stethoscope). Conditioning was accomplished by pairing this noise with the sound of a door bell from which the gong had been removed. The chime was placed directly on the mother's abdomen. This stimulus prior to conditioning elicited no discernible response in the fetus. Following 15 to 20 pairings of the chime with the loud noise, a definite conditioned response was obtained with the chime alone. Not only is the fetus sensitive to external auditory stimulation, at least in the latter stages of gestation, but it is also capable of learning. The range of possible responses and the importance to later development remain unanswered questions.

The world *in utero,* therefore, is not completely noiseless, and the noises may affect the captive occupant. What other characteristics of that world affect the unborn child? For many years grandmothers and old wives have believed that the mother's emotional states can be communicated directly to the child. If the pregnant woman worried too much, her child would be born with a frown on his forehead; if she had a particularly traumatic experience, it would mark the infant, perhaps for life; if she was frightened by a rabbit, the result might be a child with a harelip. She must try to be happy and to have pleasant experiences so that the child could be born free of negative influences. In point of fact, most of the old wives' tales concerning pregnancy are simply tales. Since there is no direct link between the mother's nervous system and the child's, there is little possibility that the mother's emotional states or disorders will be communicated directly to the unborn child. However, because of the intimate physical relationship between the mother and the child, it is logical to suppose that many of the stimuli that affect her will also have some effect on the child, however indirect.

Maternal Emotions

There is some tentative evidence that maternal emotions are transmitted to the child. Increases in fetal activity have been observed following emotional tension in the mother; however, no conclusive data have yet been presented for humans. This is not the case for subhuman species, however. Thompson (1957), in a carefully controlled experiment, demonstrated that female rats that were subjected to severe emotional upset during pregnancy tended to produce offspring that were demonstrably more anxious. The experimental procedure is interesting, but for obvious reasons cannot be employed with human subjects. Female rats were conditioned to associate the sound of a buzzer with a strong and unpleasant electric shock. Next, they were taught to escape the shock by running through a door into a second compartment where they would not receive a shock. A well trained rat would run very quickly to the safe side of the cage whenever she heard the buzzer. Following training, the rats were mated. After they became pregnant, they were subjected to the sound of the buzzer on three occasions each day while standing in the side of the cage where they had previously received the shock. The current was turned off, but the rats were not allowed to run to the safe side. The experimenter assumed that this procedure would subject the pregnant rats to considerable emotional strain.

Two procedures were used to test the emotionality of the offspring, both of which are relatively common measures of anxiety in rats. In the *open field* situation, the rat is simply released in the middle of a large open area and his movements observed. It is assumed that the rats who engage in the least amount of activity are the more anxious ones. The second procedure is to measure the amount of time it takes the rat to leave his home cage in order to reach food that has been placed at the end of an alley. Again, the assumption is that the more timid animals (the more anxious ones) will be the ones who take a longer period of time to leave their cages. On both these measures, members of the experimental group were more anxious than their controls.

Hockman (1961) confirmed Thompson's findings with tests given to rats 30 to 45 days old. However, the experimental and control animals were no longer different when retested at the age of 180 to 210 days, a finding that may have some implications for the interpretation of these studies. A second finding of the Hockman (1961) study is that of the fifteen animals originally included in the experimental group of mothers, the litters of only nine of them survived. One of the mothers died before giving birth, one refused to rear her young, one aborted prior to giving birth, and three gave birth to dead litters. It seems that the stress may have had a more severe toll on the mothers than on the offspring.

Thus, the effect of maternal emotional states on the fetus is still unclear, although evidence suggests that such states might have an effect on the unborn child, perhaps through changes in the chemical composition of the mother's blood. Barring some major changes in the social and ethical nature of contemporary societies (or some as yet unforeseen technological breakthrough), it will be extremely difficult to conduct the type of investigation required to ascertain the existence of such effects.

Investigating the effects of **drugs** on the fetus presents many of the ethical and moral problems implied above. It is clearly impossible to employ human subjects in controlled investigations with drugs whose effects will probably be injurious to the fetus. The information is therefore based on studies of animals or observations of human infants in poorly controlled situations. Generalizing from studies of animals to humans in the case of drugs presents an additional problem, since it has frequently been demonstrated that certain drugs have dramatically different results on members of different animal species, as well as on children relative to adults (Bowes, Brackbill, Conway, and Steinschneider, 1970).

Drugs

The frequency of drug use by pregnant women, and the variety of drugs that they consume is startling. Peckham and King (1963) gathered data on 3,072 patients, and found that physicians had prescribed an average of 3.6 drugs to each of these women. Four percent of the women had had 10 or more different drugs prescribed for them during their pregnancy. The importance of ascertaining the effects of these drugs on the fetus is obvious. An excellent review of the current knowledge is provided by Bowes et al. (1970).

Among the better known drugs that apparently have marked effects on the unborn child is thalidomide, which causes severe morphological changes in the embryo (Lenz, 1966; Taussig, 1962); quinine, which is associated with congenital deafness (Baker, 1960); barbiturates and other pain killers that reduce the body's oxygen supply, resulting in varying degrees of brain damage; and various anesthetics that appear to cross the placental barrier easily and rapidly and cause *depression of fetal respiration* and decreased responsiveness in the infant. It is important to note that the most serious structural changes (physical deformities and abnormalities) that are sometimes associated with drug intake, as well as with other factors such as maternal malnutrition, can occur only during the embryonic stage of development. After this stage, the fetus' basic structure has already been determined and formed and is not highly vulnerable to external influences.

Nicotine is another drug about which there is a great deal of uncertainty. Evidence suggests that smoking increases fetal heart rate and contributes to fetal hyperactivity (Sontag and Richard, 1938). In addition, it may cause general, but perhaps not severe, retardation of growth *in utero* (Frazier, Davis, Goldstein, and Goldberg, 1961; Lowe, 1959). Frazier et al. also found a significantly higher incidence of premature births among smokers than among nonsmokers. (There is no evidence of the father's nicotine intake affecting his progeny, however.)

While actual documentation of fetal injury related to drug use is still slight, it cannot be stated categorically that these drugs are in fact harmless. Bowes et al. (1970) wisely maintain that at least in the first few weeks of pregnancy, no drug can be considered absolutely safe. Table 8.1 summarizes known effects of some drugs on the fetus.

Table 8.1   Effects of Drugs on the Fetus or the Newborn Child*

Name of Drug	Effect on the Fetus or Newborn

Narcotics:
    Morphine
    Meperidine (Demerol)
    Heroin
    Methadone (Dolophine)
    Alphaprodine (Nisentil)
    Levorphanol (Levo-Dromoran)
    Dihydrocodeine
	Depression of fetal respirations. Decreased responsiveness of newborn.

	Babies born to narcotic addicts develop withdrawal symptoms of hyperirritability, shrill cry, vomiting. Can be fatal.

Narcotic antagonists:
    Nalorphine (Nalline)
    Levallorphine (Lorfan)
	Decrease neonatal depression caused by narcotics (?).

Barbiturates:
    Phenobarbitol
    Amobarbitol (Amytal)
	All barbiturates and thiobarbiturates cross the placenta. In usual clinical doses they cause minimal fetal depression.

Secobarbitol (Seconal)
    Pentobarbitol (Nembutal)
    Thiopental (Pentothal sodium)
    Thiamylal (Surital)
	Decreased responsiveness and poor sucking ability in early neonatal period.

Other sedatives: Chloral hydrate	No significant effect.

(continued on next page)

Table 8.1

Name of Drug	Effect on the Fetus or Newborn
Ethchlorvynol (Placidyl)	No significant effect.
Ethyl alcohol	No neonatal depression. May decrease uterine contractions.
	Withdrawal symptoms of twitching, hyperirritability, sweating, fever in babies born to mothers in delirium tremens.
Inhalation anesthetics: Ether	Crosses placenta rapidly. Depresses infant by direct narcotic effect. Does not interfere with oxygenation.
Cyclopropane	Infant depression dependent on duration drug is given. Depression owing to narcosis.
Nitrous oxide	No significant depression if oxygen concentration administered to mother is adequate (20 percent or more).
Trichlorethylene (Trilene)	No significant depression.
Methoxyflurane (Penthrane)	No significant depression unless mother deeply anesthetized.
Halothane (Fluothane)	No significant depression if drug given to mother for short duration.
Skeletal muscle relaxants: Curare Gallamine triethiodide (Flaxedil) Succinylcholine chloride (Anectine) Decamenthonium iodide (Syncurine)	In usual clinical doses, these drugs do not cross placenta in amounts that cause any noticeable effect on fetus.
Local anesthetics: Lidocaine (Xylocaine) Mepivacaine (Carbocaine) Procaine (Novocain) Tetracaine (Pontacaine)	Cross the placenta readily. May depress infant by direct drug effect or indirectly by causing maternal hypotension if used for regional anesthesia (spinal or epidural anesthesia).
Tranquilizers: Chlorpromazine (Thorazine) Promethazine (Phenergan) Prochlorperazine (Compazine)	No definite untoward effect on fetus substantiated.
Meprobamate (Equanil, Miltown)	No untoward effect on human fetus substantiated.
Chlordiazepoxide (Librium)	No untoward effect demonstrated so far. Crosses placenta.
Reserpine	Nasal congestion, excessive mucus, lethargy, decreased activity, bradycardia.
Antimicrobial agents: Cephalothin (Keflin)	No untoward effect demonstrated.
Chloramphenicol (Chlormycetin)	"Gray syndrome" (gastrointestinal irritability, circulatory collapse, death) in newborns treated with this drug. Never proven to occur in newborn if drug given only to mother.
Erythromycin	No untoward effects demonstrated.
Kanamycin	Ototoxicity suspected but never proved in infants born to mothers treated for prolonged periods.
Novobiocin	Increase in hyperbilirubinemia if newborn treated but not proved to occur if drug given only to mother.

(continued on next page)

Table 8.1

Name of Drug	Effect on the Fetus or Newborn
Penicillin	No untoward effect.
Ampicillin	No untoward effect.
Streptomycin	Hearing loss (very rare) in infants whose mothers have been treated for prolonged periods in early pregnancy.
Tetracycline (Achromycin) Chlortetracycline (Aureomycin) Oxytetracycline (Terramycin) Demethylchlortetracycline (Decloymycin)	Staining of deciduous teeth. Inconclusive association with congenital cataracts. Potential for bone growth retardation but not proved to occur *in utero*.
Sulfonamides: Sulfadiazine Sulfixoazole (Gantrisin) Sulfamethoxypyridazine (Kynex) Sulfadimethoxine (Madribon)	Sulfonamides compete with bilirubin for binding sites on albumin but no untoward effect on newborn proved if only mother received drug.
Metranidazole (Flagyl)	No untoward effect.
Griseofulvin	No untoward effect.
Isoniazid (INH)	Unconfirmed, retrospective, and circumstantial evidence of psychomotor retardation.
Quinine	Early reports of ototoxicity and congenital malformations unsubstantiated by extensive experience of many other authors. Danger of fetal damage probably minimal.
Nitrofurantoin (Furadantin)	Megaloblastic anemia in fetus with glucose-6-phosphate dehydrogenase deficiency.
Steroids: Cortisone Hydrocortisone Prednisone Prednisolone	Possible relation to cleft palate. None definitely proven in humans.
Dexamethasone (Decadron)	Placental insufficiency syndrome, fetal distress during labor. Not fully substantiated.
Progestins Testosterone Diethylstilbestrol	Masculinization of female fetus.
Thryoid compounds: Dessicated thyroid extract Tri-iodothyronine (Cytomel)	Crosses the placenta slowly but no known untoward effect on fetus.
Anthithyroid drugs: Propylthiouracil Methimazole (Tapazole) Potassium iodide I^{131}	All antithyroid drugs cross the placenta and can result in fetal goiters and hypothyroidism.
Antidiabetic drugs: Insulin	No proven untoward effect.
Chlorpropamide (Diabinese)	Respriatory distress and neonatal hypoglycemia. Teratogenic effects suggested but not proven.
Tolbutamide (Orinase)	Teratogenic effects suggested but never proven.
Anticoagulants: Heparin	No untoward effect.
Warfarin (Coumadin) Bishydroxycoumarin (Dicumarol)	Risk of fetal hemorrhage, particularly if mother is overtreated.

(continued on next page)

Table 8.1

Name of Drug	Effect on the Fetus or Newborn

Diuretics:
  Chlorthiazide (Diuril)
  Hydrochlorthiazide (Hydrodiuril)
	Thrombocytopenia.

Antihistamines and antiemetics:
  Dimenhydrinate (Dramamine)
  Cyclizine (Merazine)
  Meclizine (Bonine)
	No evidence of adverse effect in human beings.

Cancer chemotherapeutic agents:
  Aminopterin
  Amethopterin (Methotrexate) 6
    mercaptopurine combination
    with busulfan
	Congenital anomalies.

Miscellaneous: Salicylates (Aspirin)	No untoward effect in usual amounts. Salicylate poisoning may occur in neonate when mother takes overdose.

Vitamin K and analogues
  menadione sodium bisulfite
  (Hykinone)
Phytonadione (AquaMephyton)
	Hyperbilirubinemia.

Intravenous fluids	Electrolyte imbalance, usually hyponatremia (lethargy, poor muscle tone, poor color).
Smoking	Intrauterine growth retardation.

*From "The effects of obstetrical medication on fetus and infant" by Watson A. Bowes, Jr., Yvonne Brackbill, Esther Conway, and Alfred Steinschneider. *Monographs of the Society for Research in Child Development*, 1970, **35**, No. 4 (Copyright 1970 by the Society for Research in Child Development, Inc. Used by permission of the Society for Research in Child Development, Inc., and the author.)

Maternal Health

The mother's health inevitably affects the occupant of her womb since she is responsible for the fetus' comfort and nourishment. Stearns (1958) claims that the most frequent cause of fetal death is malnutrition in the mother. Hepner (1958) reports that serious malnutrition, if it does not lead to fetal death, may result in mental deficiency or such physical abnormalities as rickets, epilepsy, or cerebral palsy. While these aberrations may have other causes, one of the causes is presumably maternal malnutrition.

Harrel, Woodyard, and Gates (1955) investigated the effects of diet on the development of children. They provided an enriched diet to a group of mothers selected from a larger group of pregnant women whose diets left something to be desired. The children born to mothers whose diets had been enriched scored appreciably higher on measures of intelligence than their more unfortunate counterparts in the control group.

A wide range of diseases and infections are also known to affect the fetus. The best known is probably rubella (german measles); others are syphilis, gonorrhea, and poliomyelitis, each of which can cause mental deficiency, microcephaly, blindness, deafness, or miscarriages. Cretinism (subnormal mental development, undeveloped bones, a protruding abdomen, and rough, coarse skin) is caused by a thyroid malfunction in the mother. Other endocrine imbalances may result in mongolism, a mental deficiency accompanied by slanted eyelids and deformed facial features.

The mother's age also appears to be a factor in the well-being of the fetus. Malzberg (1950) and Penrose (1949) are among many researchers who have reported a much higher incidence of mongolism among children born to mothers above the age of 30. Apparently the probability of bearing a mentally defective child increases as the woman nears menopause (Benda, 1956). In addition, older women are more prone to miscarry a child or to have a stillborn infant. Since the reproductive organs and the female skeletal structure do not mature until her early twenties, the best years for a woman to have a child are between 21 and 29 years.

Social Class
The greatest single cause of infant death is premature birth; among the most direct causes of cerebral palsy and various forms of mental defectiveness is premature birth; the factor most closely related to premature births is social rather than medical. These statements are relatively well documented facts (see Wortis, 1963) which are of considerable significance. First, the high correlation between low social class and higher incidence of premature birth suggests that the living conditions and associated emotional and health consequences attributed to membership in the lower class are not conducive to the production of healthy full-term babies; second, this observation raises a number of serious moral, as well as social, political, and economic issues, not the least controversial of which is whether people who live in the abject poverty characteristic of slums in our major cities should be allowed to have children. Should anyone be prevented from having children? Should poverty be considered an inevitable part of any society, or can ignorance and apathy, so often a consequence of poverty, be eradicated through social reform? Such questions and their implications trouble this generation; hopefully, the answers will issue from the next.

About Alcohol
It might be irrelevant to some of you, but highly reassuring to others to know that there is little evidence that ethyl alcohol (booze) has any ill effects on the fetus (Belinkoff and Hall, 1950; Chapman and Williams, 1951). However, a mother suffering from *delirium tremens* is likely to give birth to an infant experiencing a variety of withdrawal symptoms: he will twitch, sweat, be hyperirritable, and will probably have a fever (Nichols, 1967). The mother may be somewhat uncomfortable as well.

About Narcotics
There is considerable evidence that babies born to narcotics addicts are also addicted. These unfortunate infants suffer a clearly recognizable withdrawal syndrome; hyperactivity, hyperirritability, rapid respiration, vomiting, trembling, perspiring, fevers, and shrill crying. This condition can be fatal (Cobrinik, Hood, and Chusid, 1959; Goodfriend, Shey, and Klein, 1956; Vincow and Hackel, 1960).

It's Not That Bad
It is often very disquieting for a nonmedical person to consult medical journals and textbooks in search of an explanation for his various

complaints. Inevitably he discovers that he has all the symptoms for innumerable vicious infections and exotic diseases. Thus, if you happen to be pregnant at this moment or are contemplating pregnancy, or are otherwise involved in the business, you might find yourself a little apprehensive. I draw this to your attention only to emphasize that it really isn't that bad (pregnancy, that is). The intrauterine world of the unborn infant is less threatening and less dangerous than our world. And it is perhaps reassuring that nature often provides for spontaneous abortions when the embryo or the fetus would have been grossly abnormal (Potter, 1957). In most cases the fetus comes to term; when it reaches this stage the probability that the child will be normal and healthy far outweighs the possibility that it will suffer any of the defects or abnormalities described in this chapter.

Summary

This chapter opened with Sam talking about population, survival, and mechanics, and eating chocolate cake. From there it moved to the beginning of human life, conception, and discussed the indications of pregnancy. The chapter dealt briefly with swollen and discolored breasts, menses and their cessation, quickening and urination. It spoke of distended abdomens, soft uteri, soft cervixes, palpation, and X rays; thence to rats, mice, and frogs, and finally found itself in the midst of the physiological development of a child *in utero*. The chapter examined the development of the ovum, the embryo, and then the fetus, noting the minuteness of the developing organism in its early stages, but the rapid development of its head regions and internal organs. The development of the fetus was followed to a point near its end, but the story stopped short of its ending, for that ending must begin the next chapter. The factors that can have harmful effects on fetal development were considered, however. Among these are the emotional states of the mother; her use of drugs; her health, diet, and age; and her indulgence in alcohol or narcotics. In the end it was decided that it isn't all that bad.

Main Points

1. Making babies is not always a popular topic with chocolate cake eaters who are concerned about problems of population growth and food shortage.

2. Pregnancy is caused; it does not just happen.

3. Early symptoms of pregnancy are notoriously uncertain, although in combination they provide relatively reliable information. They are frequently divided into presumptive, probable, and positive symptoms.

4. Presumptive signs of pregnancy include cessation of menses, frequent urination, breast changes, quickening, and morning sickness.

5. Probable symptoms of pregnancy are distension of the abdomen and changes in the uterus and the cervix, as well as some reasonably valid biological tests employing rabbits, mice, or frogs.

6. Fetal heartbeat, the outline of the fetus by means of X ray, fetal movement, and palpating the fetus through the abdomen are positive signs of pregnancy.

7. The gestation period for humans is 9 calendar months, which is more commonly computed as 10 lunar months (40 weeks or 280 days), beginning from the onset of the last menses.

8. Prenatal physiological development occurs in three stages: the period of the ovum (2 weeks), the embryo (2 to 8 weeks), and the fetus (8 to 40 weeks).

9. The fertilized ovum moves from the fallopian tubes to the uterus and imbeds itself in the wall of the uterus approximately 7 days after fertilization.

10. From week one to eight, the embryo develops from an almost microscopic speck to a little organism approximately $1\frac{1}{2}$ to 2 inches long and weighing close to $\frac{2}{3}$ of an ounce. By the end of the eighth week all the organs of the infant are present. No further structural changes will take place.

11. Fetal growth involves primarily physical changes in size and weight. The fetus will probably not survive if born before the seventh lunar month.

12. The average size of a newborn infant is approximately 19.5 inches and nearly 7 pounds.

13. Among the factors that affect prenatal development are maternal emotions, drugs, alcohol (in excessive amounts), narcotics, diet, general health and age of the mother. There is evidence that the fetus is sensitive to external sounds and that it can be conditioned to react to such sounds.

14. It isn't all that bad.

Further Readings   The course of prenatal development is well described in such standard textbooks as:

Bookmiller, M. M. and G. L. Bowen. *Textbook of obstetrics and obstetric nursing* (5th Ed.). Philadelphia: W. B. Saunders, 1967.

Arey, L. B. *Developmental anatomy* (7th Ed.). Philadelphia: W. B. Saunders, 1965.

The following provides a recent review of literature dealing with the effect of drugs on the fetus:

Bowes, W. A. Jr., Y. Brackbill, E. Conway, and A. Steinschneider. The effects of obstetrical medication on fetus and infant. *Monographs of the Society for Research in Child Development*. Vol. 35, No. 4, 1970.

Of Bitches and Pups: The Whole Infant

It was around 1 o'clock in the morning when Zoe, our English Setter, began to give birth to her first litter. Zoe is a Greek word meaning life. In this case the name was particularly appropriate. I had been sitting on an old camp stool next to a large box hurriedly built for the occasion. For 2 hours I waited, sipping from a bottle of medicine, feverishly reading through a heavy textbook on human obstetrics. I had already studied a short pamphlet on animal obstetrics, but there was a good deal more information in the book I was now reading, and much more interesting photographs and illustrations.

I based my belief that Zoe was about to give birth to her first litter of pups on my observation that exactly 63 days earlier a large Irish Setter had paid his respects. My suspicions gained substance when earlier that day, Zoe began to whine nervously and scratch in various corners of the garage, as if she were trying to find a nesting place. Once I understood what she wanted, I built the large box and laid a raft of newspapers in the bottom. Almost immediately Zoe jumped in and shuffled among the papers until she was satisfied that this was an appropriate place.

Now as it neared 1 o'clock, I laid my book aside and for the tenth time rearranged my clean white towels, my blunt scissors, and a length of sterilized string. The surgeon was all ready; another small medicinal dose, and he was more than ready. Let them come. They came. The delivery of the first pup was almost anticlimactic, there was so little fuss. Several almost imperceptible contractions, a very faint whine from Zoe, and a little pup appeared, encased in his own sac. The mother turned her head immediately and began to lick her baby vigorously, nipping at the sac and eventually breaking it to release the pup. She continued to lick, cleaning the mucus from around its mouth and nose and stimulating its breathing, all at the same time. This accomplished, she nuzzled the newborn puppy, who was already making feeble attempts to walk, and pushed him gently in the direction of her nipples. Meanwhile, I stood poised, a towel over my left arm, another over my left shoulder, a third over my right shoulder, a length of string in my left hand, and scissors ready in my right. Zoe beat me to it. She severed the pup's umbilical cord admirably close to his abdomen, and then ate the afterbirth. I gulped and took another dose of medicine in preparation for the next pup.

He followed the first in approximately 15 minutes. The entire process was almost routine by now: break the sac, lick the pup vigorously, sever his umbilical cord, eat the afterbirth cord and all, and push the newborn pup toward her nipples. In the course of the next few hours, ten pups were delivered in the same expert fashion by a totally inexperienced and quite illiterate bitch, while her master slept peacefully in the corner of the garage, an empty bottle of spirits for a companion.

One might speculate about how a human female would fare if she found herself pregnant and about to give birth to a baby without benefit of the wisdom of the **grandmothers** of the race or the specialized tech-

The History of
Obstetrics

niques, highly trained personnel, and modern equipment available in to-day's hospitals. Would she sense an urgency as her time drew near? Would she look for a safe and sheltered place in which to give birth to her infant? And when birth finally occurred, would she instinctintively stim-ulate the child's breathing, sever its umbilical cord, and eat the afterbirth (for the afterbirth contains rich hormones that would greatly enhance her production of milk)? Or, has civilized woman lost all her instinctual tendencies?

Although the birth of a child in our culture usually occurs within the safe and antiseptic confines of hospital walls, assisted by experts, it has not always been this way—even today many children are born in homes or in the fields and forests of the world. I was among those born at home, but unfortunately I remember very little of it. I do remember the births of my younger brothers and sisters, but since I was not permitted to witness the actual delivery, I cannot draw upon that source of knowl-edge for this chapter. When my first son was born, neither was I allowed to witness that event, despite my argument that I was teaching a course in child development and had a valid reason for being admitted to the de-livery room. The doctor was concerned about the temperament of the fathers and had categorically decided that no one but the mother and nursing attendants would be allowed in the delivery room.

The history of **obstetrics** is a long struggle between the traditions and beliefs of generations of midwives and the inevitable progress of science. It begins with Hippocrates' attempt to separate labor from religious rites, progresses through the desperate attempts of men like Semmelweis to promote cleanliness in hospitals to combat the dreaded killer of women after childbirth, puerperal fever (dramatized in the novel *The Cry and the Covenant*), and ends with current hospital techniques and procedures (see Table 9.1 for a sketch of the history of obstetrics, based on data provided by Bookmiller and Bowen, 1967).

Table 9.1   A resume of the history of the development of obstetrics.*

400 B.C.	Hippocrates' attempt to separate labor from religious rites.
200 A.D.	Soranus teaches obstetrics to Roman midwives.
1513	The printing press is invented; the first book on obstetrics is published (Roesslin).
1560	Pare rediscovers and describes version and breech extrac-tion.
1647	Chamberlen invents obstetric forceps.
1739	Smellie improves the teaching of obstetrics.
1807	The introduction of ergot in obstetrics.
1847	Holmes and Semmelweis fight puerperal fever.
1860	Pasteur discovers streptococci in puerperal fever.
1867	Lister describes asepsis (sterile procedures).
1900	The development of prenatal care and of obstetrics in nurs-ing institutions and in schools of medicine.

*Adapted from Bookmiller and Bowen, 1967, pp. 17–18.

Labor is defined as the process whereby the fetus, the placenta, and other membranes are separated from the woman's body and expelled; it ordinarily occurs approximately 280 days after the beginning of the pregnant woman's last menstrual period, although it can also occur earlier than this or occasionally somewhat later. The physical status of the child is classified according to the length of time he has spent in gestation and by his weight. A fetus born before the twentieth week and weighing less than 500 grams (about 1 pound) is termed an **abortion**. A fetus delivered between the twentieth and the twenty-eighth week and weighing between 500 and 999 grams (between 1 and 2 pounds) is an **immature birth**. An immature birth very rarely survives, although there are several documented cases of fetuses born prior to the twenty-eighth week, having survived. More often than not death ensues from respiratory failure. The birth of a baby between the twenty-ninth and the thirty-sixth week is called a **premature birth**, providing the child weighs between 1000 and 2499 grams (between 2 and $5\frac{1}{2}$ pounds). Complications are expected if the child weighs less than 1500 grams. A **mature birth** occurs between the thirty-seventh and the forty-second week, and results in an infant weighing at least 2500 grams (over 5 pounds). A late delivery is called a **postmature birth**.

The onset of labor is usually gradual and described in three stages. That there are exceptions to the normal process is substantiated by numerous fathers who were caught unawares, taxi drivers who drove too slowly, pilots who didn't quite make it, and many others for whom nature would not wait. Although physicians can induce labor, the precise cause of the beginning of labor remains unknown. There is no evidence that the procedures doctors employ (for example, rupturing the **amniotic sac** — the "bag of waters") would normally trigger labor. Labor amazingly begins, more often than not, at the prescribed time. The first stage of labor is the longest, lasting an average of 12 hours, and varying greatly in length, depending as much on unknown individual factors as on whether the woman has had previous babies. Generally, labor is longest and most difficult for the first child.

The first stage of labor consists of contractions of relatively low intensity that are usually spaced quite far apart at the beginning and eventually occur at shorter intervals. The initial contractions are described as similar to having "butterflies" in one's stomach; they last only a few seconds and are relatively painless. Apparently the "butterflies" become much more painful and last considerably longer during the terminal part of the first stage of labor. In this first stage, the **cervix** (the opening to the uterus) dilates to allow passage of the baby from the uterus, down through the birth canal, and eventually into the world. Contractions are totally involuntary and exert a downward pressure on the fetus as well as a distending force on the cervix. If the amniotic sac is still intact, it absorbs much of the pressure in the early stages and transmits some of the force of the contractions to the neck of the cervix. If, however, the sac has ruptured or bursts in the early stages of labor, then the baby's head will rest directly on the pelvic structure and cervix, thus serving as a wedge.

Childbirth

A Clinical View

When the cervix is sufficiently dilated, the second stage of labor ensues, beginning with the baby's head (in a normal delivery) at the cervical opening, and terminating with the birth of the child (see Figure 9.1). The second stage usually lasts no more than an hour, and frequently ends in a few minutes. Toward the end of the second stage, the attending physician or nurse severs the neonate's umbilical cord, places silver nitrate or penicillin drops in its eyes to guard against gonococcal infection, assures that its breathing, muscle tone, coloration, and reflexive reactivity are normal, and that it is of the appropriate sex. Following this, the physician assists in the third and final stage of labor.

In this third stage, the **afterbirth**—the placenta and other membranes—is expelled. This process usually takes less than 5 minutes and seldom more than 15. The physician examines the afterbirth carefully to ensure that all of it has been expelled. If it is incomplete, he may use surgical procedures to remove the remainder.

The fetus ordinarily presents itself head first and can usually be born without the intervention of a physician. On occasion, however, complications arise that require some sort of intervention. For example, the head of the fetus is sometimes too large for the opening provided by the mother. In such a case the physician may make a small incision in the vaginal outlet (an **episiotomy**), which he sutures after the baby is born. If this procedure is not performed the surrounding tissues may tear and the mother's healing process will be much slower. Complications can also arise from other abnormal presentations of the fetus. Some of these can be corrected prior to birth by turning the fetus manually in the uterus (*version*). Often the fetus is delivered just as it presents itself: **breech** (buttocks first), **transverse** (crosswise), or in a variety of other possible positions, all of which have appropriate medical labels.

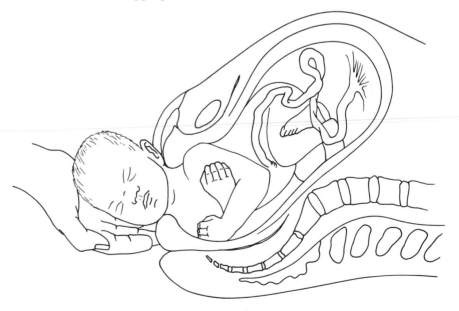

Figure 9.1   The normal presentation and delivery of a baby. The mother has been bisected, and her legs removed—in the interests of science.

At the end of the third stage of labor, the uterus should contract and remain contracted. It may be necessary to massage the abdominal area or administer various drugs to stimulate contraction and to guard against the danger of postpartum (after birth) hemorrhage.

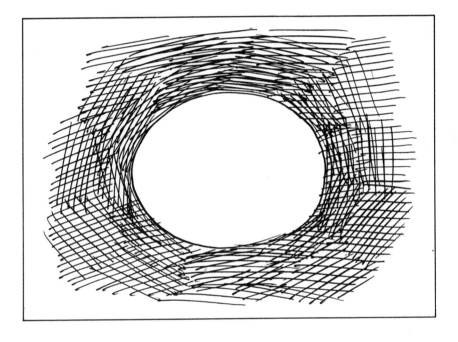

A Clinical View of Birth

A Mother's View

The preceding discussion of the delivery of a human child is admittedly clinical and perhaps somewhat like the cold, antiseptic hospitals in which most babies are born; it fails to uncover and transmit the magic of the process. One can recapture some of the mystery, however, by looking at the process from the mother's point of view.

In preparation for this discussion I conferred with several mothers whose experience qualified them to make subjective comments that I am incapable of. One of these experts assured me that childbearing is "as easy as rolling off a log." Another witness, similarly qualified, assured me that "it hurt like hell." Combining these impressions, a relatively clear picture of the situation emerges. The inexperienced mother undoubtedly approaches the event with some degree of apprehension; there is invariably some pain associated with the birth. However, advocates of **natural childbirth** claim that through a regimen of prenatal exercises and adequate psychological preparation, many women experience relatively painless childbirths.

Natural childbirth, a phrase coined by a British physician, Grantly Dick Read (1944), refers to the process of having a child without anesthetics. The Read process recommends physical exercises, relaxing exercises, and psychological preparation for the arrival of the child, all directed toward delivery in which pain killers are unnecessary. Natural

Having a baby is as easy as rolling off a log.

childbirth is based on the assumption that alleviating the fear of pain, together with training in relaxation, will result in less pain. Read's hypothesis has proved sound. However, Hall (1963, p. 110) provides the following data: of 100 women who become interested in natural childbirth, perhaps 10 will investigate it and abandon it immediately; the remaining 90 will practice the exercises and other aspects of the training. Of these 90, probably 40 will claim that they have not benefited from it at all; another 40 will be convinced that it helped them, but will use anesthetics as if they had not gone through the program. This leaves only 10 women who will deliver their babies without requiring drugs. It is revealing to note that in the absence of any interest in (or knowledge of) natural childbirth, roughly 50 percent of the women having babies require heavy medication, 40 percent require some drugs, and 10 percent require none. These figures are nearly identical to those for women who have investigated natural childbirth. While the technique is not completely suitable for all women, most can profit from greater awareness of what is involved in childbirth; they also can profit from prenatal exercises and relaxation. In short, there is some evidence of beneficial effects and no evidence of harmful ones.

From one mother's experience, childbirth may be tremendously painful. For another mother, childbirth may be a slightly painful, but intensely rewarding and satisfying experience. Although the amount of pain can be controlled to some extent with anesthetics, the intensity of the immediate emotional reward from the experience will also be dulled by drugs.

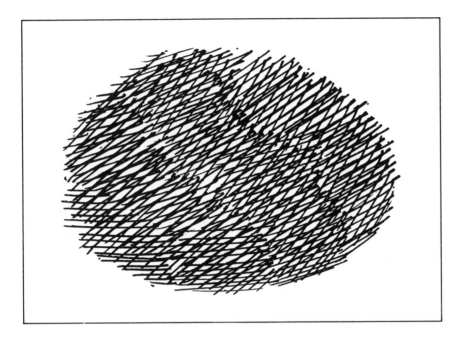

A Child's View of Birth

How does the child, the hero of this text, react to the process of birth? His story begins now, for although his life began at conception, his legal existence dates from his birth. (In some Oriental countries, the child is considered to be a year old when he is born, and even there the making of a child does not require more than 280 days.) The child's reaction to birth is probably not an emotional response, since the cortex, the part of his brain believed to be involved in emotional responses, is not active until some time after birth (the cortex is incapable of functioning in the oxygen-poor intrauterine environment). But we can speak of some probable effects on the fetus of the experience of being born.

    Consider the incredibly dramatic difference that birth makes for the child. Prior to this moment he has been living in a completely friendly and completely supportive environment. The provision of nourishment and oxygen, and the elimination of waste products from his body have been accomplished through no effort of his own. He has been kept at exactly the right temperature. The danger of bacterial infection is relatively insignificant (Ferreira, 1969). In addition to the complete biological support provided by the intrauterine environment, there have been no psychological threats. Now, as he is expelled from his mother's body, the child is suddenly exposed to new physiological and, perhaps, psychological dangers. Once the mucus is cleared from his mouth and throat, he must breathe for himself for the first time. If he is not successful on his first few attempts to inhale, he is dangled by the feet and slapped on the back. As soon as his umbilical cord ceases to pulsate, it is unceremoniously clipped an inch or two above his abdomen and tied off with a string.

A Child's View

He is now completely on his own—singularly dependent and helpless, to be sure, but no longer a parasite (biologically) on his mother.

There are two great dangers of brain damage that are attendant upon the birth of a child. Tremendous pressures are exerted upon the head of the infant during birth, particularly if the first stage of labor has been long and if the amniotic sac has been broken during most of that stage, in which case his head, in a normal presentation, has been repeatedly pressed against the slowly dilating cervix. In addition, the infant suffers passage through an opening so small that it often results in deformation of the child's head. (Fortunately, for most infants the head usually assumes a more normal appearance within a few days.)

An additional source of pressure on the child's head is forceps, those wicked looking, clamplike instruments sometimes employed in delivering a baby. If forceps are used relatively early in the first stage of labor, it is difficult to place them properly, and it is usually necessary to exert more pressure with them when the fetus is still high in the birth canal. Thus, use of **forceps** in the first stage of labor (termed "high forceps") is usually considered an emergency procedure. Forceps in the final stages of delivery are more routine ("low forceps"), and considerably less dangerous. Although it is evident that the fetus can withstand considerable pressure on his head, the real danger of such pressure is that it may rupture blood vessels and cause subsequent hemorrhaging. In severe cases, death may ensue; otherwise, there is a possibility of brain damage, since cranial hemorrhage can restrict the supply of oxygen available for the brain.

The oxygen supply to the brain can be restricted in another way. The fetus is still dependent on the mother for oxygen during the birth process; he obtains this oxygen through the umbilical cord. There is a constant danger that the cord, through which the fetus must still obtain his oxygen, will become lodged between the child's body and the very small canal passage of the birth canal through which he must pass. If this happens, the flow of oxygen through the cord may be stopped (referred to as **prolapsed cord**), also causing brain damage. Symptoms of brain damage often include various motor defects loosely defined as cerebral palsy. Even in cases where there are no overt symptoms of brain damage, there may be minimal damage, nevertheless. Tentatively, minimal damage may be linked with such personality predispositions as hyperactivity and impulsivity (Kagan, 1967).

In addition to the physiological **trauma** that accompanies birth, there is a remote possibility of psychological trauma. Rank's (1929) theory of the trauma of birth maintains that the sudden change from a comfortable, parasitic existence to the cold and demanding world creates great anxiety for the newborn child, and forever after a desire to return to the womb. Alleged evidence of this unconscious desire is found in the position assumed by many children and adults while sleeping or in times of stress—the characteristic curl of the fetus. However, since the higher centers of the fetal brain are not functioning at birth and have not been functioning *in utero* (Barcroft, 1938), and since it is therefore unlikely that the child can feel any emotion (Pratt, 1954), the theory of birth trauma has generally been abandoned. This does not deny the significance of the physiological trauma of birth; it simply asserts that there is no evidence to support a psychological trauma.

From the child's point of view, then, birth is an indifferent process: he cannot reason about it; he cannot compare it with other more or less pleasant states; he can do nothing deliberately to alter it; and he will not even remember it.

The **neonate** (newborn infant) is an unattractive little beast. His color may range from the bluish tinge of imminent **anoxia** (lack of oxygen) to fiery red; his features are wrinkled and may be distorted from passage through the birth canal; he sometimes bears the marks of forceps on various parts of his anatomy; his whole skull may be flattened, lengthened, skewed, or otherwise deformed. He is covered with remnants of amniotic fluid, matter oozes from his mouth and nose, his eyes are wrinkled shut, his breathing is a rasping and wheezing similar to an old man's death rattle, and he pierces the air with thin, reedy wails as if attempting to communicate the torment of his situation.

Description of a Neonate

Of what is the neonate capable? It was formerly thought that he was virtually insensitive to external stimulation, that his responses were limited to and determined by the repertoire of reflexive activities that his genes had provided for him. More recent evidence suggests that this belief is a myth. Indeed, it can be demonstrated that almost from the moment of birth the child can see, hear, and feel. He is not the passive little doll that grandmothers thought he was.

For years it was believed that the newborn's vision was very poorly developed, that he had no ability to discern patterns, form, or movement (Pratt, 1954; Spock, 1957). Recent evidence has dispelled many of these early beliefs; the world of the infant is not a "blooming, buzzing confusion" as was once supposed. Pupillary reflexes caused by changes in the brightness of visual stimulation (Pratt, 1934; 1954) demonstrate that the neonate is sensitive to light intensity; he is capable of visually following a slowly moving object within a few days (Haith, 1966); and he is sensitive to patterns and contours as early as two days after birth (Fantz, 1961, 1963, 1964, 1965).

Evidence of Perception in the Newborn

But, the extent of the newborn child's awareness of perceptual patterns is difficult to determine. Since the infant cannot communicate his perceptions and since he frequently prefers to sleep rather than to participate in psychological investigations, he is a rather poor subject. In the Fantz (1963) experiment that clearly demonstrates pattern distinction in newborn children, one of the criteria for selecting subjects was whether they kept their eyes open long enough to be exposed to the stimulus. Eighteen infants, ranging in age from 10 hours to 5 days, were employed in the experiment. They were shown six circular stimulus patterns of varying complexity, the most complex being a human face. In diminishing order of complexity the other stimuli included concentric

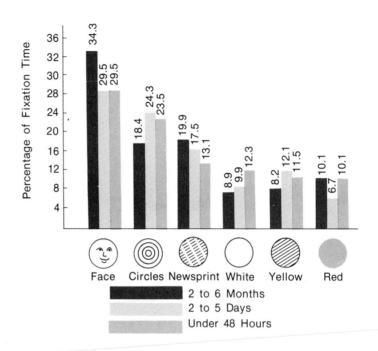

Figure 9.2 Relative duration (percentage of fixation time) of initial gaze of infants in successive and repeated presentations of six circular visual stimuli. The graph depicts infants' preference for the human face and the more complex stimuli. (Based on data in "Pattern Vision in Newborn Infants" by Robert L. Fantz, *Science*, 1963, **140**, 296–297. Copyright 1963 by the American Association for the Advancement of Science. Used by permission of the American Association for the Advancement of Science and the author.)

circles, newspaper print, and three unpatterned circles of different colors. Figure 9.2 shows the relative percentage of the total time spent by subjects looking at each of the stimulus figures. That the stimulus bearing the face was looked at for significantly longer periods of time not only indicates that the infant can discriminate among the various figures, but also that he prefers the more complex. From his first hours of life, the infant's vision seems to be sufficiently developed to allow him to perceive some of the physical characteristics of his surroundings, when he isn't sleeping. It is true, however, that his ability to accommodate to stimulation emanating from a distance does not appear to develop until approximately 2 months of age. Prior to 2 months, it is as though the infant had inherent accommodation for a distance of approximately 8 inches only (Haynes, White, and Held, 1965).

The neonate's contact with reality is happily not limited to the information that he derives through vision. Unlike the young of many infrahuman species (dogs and cats, for example) there is evidence that he is not deaf at birth. A large number of studies (Wertheimer, 1961; Eisenberg, Griffin, Coursin, and Hunter, 1964) have shown that the newborn child is sensitive not only to a wide range of sounds but also that he can detect the location of sound. In addition, sounds of different frequencies have different effects on children, although there are markedly individual responses to auditory stimulation. In general, low frequency sounds and rhythmic sounds have a calming effect, whereas higher frequency signals bring about a more violent reaction called the "orienting reflex" (Razran, 1961). The finding that the neonate is sensitive to sounds is to be expected in light of the studies that have demonstrated that the fetus not only responds to noise but can also be conditioned by auditory stimuli.

The newborn is also sensitive to different odors. It has been shown that an infant will attempt to avert his face when subjected to a powerful and unpleasant smell such as ammonia (Engen, Lipsitt, and Kaye, 1963; Lipsitt, Engen, and Kaye, 1963). His sense of taste is less impressive, however (Pratt, 1954). The distinctive tastes of salt, sugar, citric acid, or water do not elicit different responses, even when placed directly on his tongue, although by the age of 2 weeks he will react more greedily to sugar than to salt. *In utero* the fetus frequently ingests (orally) amniotic fluid, which then passes out as waste through the umbilical cord and the placenta, and eventually is disposed of through the mother's intestine. One complication of pregnancy, **polyhydramnios** (Bookmiller and Bowen, 1967), involves an excessive amount of amniotic fluid in the uterus and consequent discomfort and abdominal distention. When polyhydramnios threatens, it is desirable to cause the fetus to ingest a larger amount of amniotic fluid. One way of bringing this about is to inject a sugar solution directly into the amniotic fluid. The prevalent theory is that this "tastes" more palatable to the fetus, and that he therefore drinks (eats?) it more readily. If this is actually the case, it is surprising that the neonate's gustatory capacities are as limited as they would appear to be.

The infant's tolerance of pain seems extremely high—in fact, he is remarkably insensitive to pain (McGraw, 1943). This is probably fortunate since the process of being born might be quite painful if the child could sense pain. It is even more fortunate for boy babies whose early experience includes the discommoding event of circumcision, usually done in the first week when the newborn is not expected to feel pain, and no anesthetics are used.

Most of the behaviors that the newborn engages in are reflexive— that is, they do not require learning and can be elicited readily in the normal child by presenting the appropriate stimulus. While the neonate may engage in some activity that is not reflexive, it is probably true that he does not engage in any deliberate activity. In other words, some of the child's generalized behaviors such as squirming, waving the arms, and kicking, are frequently too complex and too spontaneous to be classified as reflexes, but are more properly referred to as unintentional operants (see Chapter 5).

The Behavioral
Repertoire of the
Newborn

Table 9.2 lists some of the newborn's common reflexes. Probably the best known of these is the *sucking reflex,* which is easily produced by placing an object in the child's mouth (a nipple is considered an appropriate stimulus). Reflexive behavior related to sucking is the **head turning** reflex, which can be elicited by stroking the baby's cheek or the corner of his mouth. He will turn toward the side that is being stimulated. This reflex is particularly apparent in breast-fed babies, who need to turn in the direction of stimulation if they are to reach the nipple. This reflex is less important to the child who is presented with a bottle.

Swallowing, hiccoughing, sneezing, and *vomiting* can all be elicited by the appropriate nourishment-related stimulation. They are therefore referred to as the vegetative reflexes.

There are also a number of common motor reflexes in the newborn that have no particular survival value. These include the startle reaction — throwing out the arms and feet symmetrically and then pulling them back toward the center of the body. This response is labeled the **Moro reflex** and is sometimes useful in diagnosing brain damage, since it ordinarily disappears during infancy in the normal child, but is frequently present later in life in cases of impaired motor centers of the brain. Other reflexes that disappear with time are the *Babinski reflex* — the typical fanning of the toes when tickled in the middle of the soles of the feet; the **palmar (grasping) reflex,** which is frequently sufficiently pronounced in the neonate that he can be raised completely off his bed if he grasps an adult's finger in each hand; and the *swimming* and *stepping reflexes,* which occur when one holds the baby balanced on his stomach, or holds him upright with his feet just touching a surface.

The neonate is remarkably alert and well suited to his environment. He can hear, see, and smell; he can turn in the direction of food, suck, swallow, digest, and eliminate; he can respond physically to a small range of stimuli; and he can cry and vomit. Still he is a singularly helpless creature; he would surely die if his environment did not include an adult intimately concerned with his survival. The fortunate infant has a grandmother, who will also do her very best to provide the infant's mother with all the advice that her years have made her heir to.

There is a fantastically impressive distance between a human adult's

Table 9.2 Some of the Reflexive Behavior of the Newborn

Reflex	Stimulus
Sucking	Object in the mouth.
Head Turning	Stroking the cheek or the corner of the mouth.
Swallowing	Food in the mouth.
Sneezing	Irritation in the nasal passages.
Moro Reflex	Sudden loud noise.
Babinski Reflex	Tickling the middle of the soles.
Toe Grasp	Tickling the soles just below the toes.
Palmar Grasp	Placing object in the infant's hand.
Swimming Reflex	Infant horizontal, supported by abdomen.
Stepping Reflex	Infant vertical, feet lightly touching flat surface.

responses to the world and the uncoordinated and frequently purposeless movements of a newborn child. The story of the child's progress toward adulthood fills the remaining pages of this text.

As defined in this text (as well as in most others), the period of infancy lasts from the first few weeks of life to approximately 2 years of age. At the beginning of this period, the infant is relatively unimpressive, as described in the preceding section; at the end he can walk, talk, recognize his grandmother, ride a tricycle, and tell his daddy and mama that he loves them. How a child develops these capabilities is the concern of the developmental psychologist; it is also the question that concerns us here.

Perceptual, Physical, and Motor Development

We begin as almost microscopic zygotes; 266 days later we are approximately 7 pounds of miniature human that stretches for about 20 inches (slightly less for a female). By the age of 6 months, another $9^{3}/_{4}$ pounds have been added to the frame, and an additional 6 inches. By the age of 2 years, the average male child weighs $27^{3}/_{4}$ pounds and measures $34^{1}/_{2}$ inches—almost three feet. In the first 2 years the female child is just slightly behind the male in physical growth (see Table 9.3).

Physical Growth

Height (in inches) and Weight (in pounds) at the Fiftieth Percentile for American Children*

Table 9.3

	Height		Weight	
Age	Girl	Boy	Girl	Boy
Birth	$19^{3}/_{4}$	20	$7^{1}/_{2}$	$7^{1}/_{2}$
6 mo.	$25^{3}/_{4}$	26	$15^{3}/_{4}$	$16^{3}/_{4}$
12 mo.	$29^{1}/_{4}$	$29^{1}/_{2}$	21	$22^{1}/_{4}$
18 mo.	$31^{3}/_{4}$	$32^{1}/_{4}$	$24^{1}/_{4}$	$25^{1}/_{4}$
24 mo.	34	$34^{1}/_{2}$	27	$27^{3}/_{4}$

*Adapted by the Health Department, Milwaukee, Wisconsin; based on data by H. C. Stuart and H. V. Meredith, prepared for use in Children's Medical Center, Boston. Used by permission of the Milwaukee Health Department.

Thompson (1954) notes that the rapidity of growth in infancy is significant but cautions against excessive reliance on tables of weight norms. The wide individual variations, not only in absolute weight or height, but also in growth rates makes such tables much less meaningful indicators of development and nutrition for some infants than for others. There are, however, a number of general developmental growth changes that are relatively common to most infants, involving changes in physical proportions and differential growth rates for various parts of the body. For example, the head of a fetus at 3 months is approximately one-third of its entire body size; by the time of birth, this proportion has been reduced to one-fourth; in the adult the head is perhaps one-tenth the size and length of the body. In effect, the rate of growth for the head decreases relative to the rate of growth for other parts of the body. In contrast,

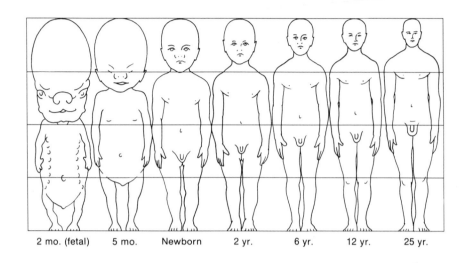

2 mo. (fetal)   5 mo.   Newborn   2 yr.   6 yr.   12 yr.   25 yr.

Figure 9.3   Changes in form and proportion of the human body during fetal and postnatal life. (From "Some aspects of form and growth" by C. M. Jackson in *Growth*, by W. J. Robbins, S. Brody, A. G. Hogan, C. M. Jackson, and C. W. Green. New Haven: Yale University Press, 1928, p. 118. Copyright 1928 by Yale University Press. Used by permission of Yale University Press.)

Rogers (1969) notes that the sex organs change very little in the first decade of life, but change very rapidly after puberty, and may continue to change even after the individual has ceased to increase in height. Relative changes in body proportions are shown in Figure 9.3.

Perceptual Development   The perceptual equipment of the infant differs only in relatively minor ways from the adult's, and primarily during the early stages of development. Very rapidly the infant develops coordination, the ability to accommodate, depth perception, and the recognition of spatial relations of objects that he initially lacked. The extent to which these perceptions result from the physiological maturation of the organism and the extent to which they are due to experience is not clear. Apparently, by the age of 6 months, the infant perceives the world in much the same way as an adult, although he obviously does not have the experience or the knowledge to enable him to interpret his perceptions as an adult would.

Motor Development   The helplessness of the neonate results mainly from his inability to exercise control over motor movements. His behavior is a far cry from that of the young of many subhuman species, including precocial birds and most members of the deer family, who are able to follow their mothers and to make considerable efforts to obtain food almost immediately after birth. But the child does not remain physically helpless throughout his infancy. Indeed, one of his major acquisitions during this period is the

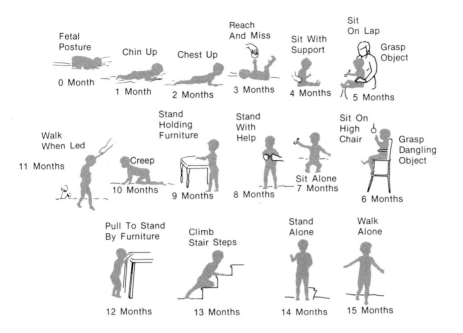

Locomotor development in infants. (From *The First Two Years* by Mary M. Shirley.   Figure 9.4
Institute of Child Welfare Monograph No. 7. Minneapolis: University of Minnesota
Press. © 1933, renewed 1961 by the University of Minnesota. Used by permission of
the University of Minnesota Press.)

ability to walk. Much before then he will have learned how to move by
creeping, and before that he will have developed the ability to sit with a
little support.

Although the sequence of appearance of motor capacities in children
appears relatively invariable (Bayley, 1935; Dennis, 1941; Gesell and
Amatruda, 1941), it is clear that the ages at which different abilities appear vary considerably from one child to another. It is useful nevertheless
to have developmental **norms**, not only as indications of sequence, but
also to have some standard by which to judge the child's rate of development. Here, as elsewhere, there is no *average* child.

Probably the best known and perhaps the most accurate description
of the motor sequence from birth to the age of 15 months is provided by
Shirley (1933). Her study employed a painstaking longitudinal approach
involving many subjects over a long period of time. The portion of the
study that was concerned with infants was not meant to be normative.
Shirley made this explicit, claiming that better norms had already been
provided by Gesell's (1937) extensive studies. However, her tentative
norms are very similar to Gesell's. (See figure 9.4 for Shirley's sequence of
motor development.) The study's purpose was to discover whether the
sequence was the same for different individuals. Her results offer rather
convincing evidence that this similarity indeed exists. Correlations among

the sequences of development for individual children in the sample, and the proposed normative sequence range from .93 to .98, with the greatest variability in sequence of acquisition occurring for ambiguous items (those items for which the investigators had difficulty in deciding clearly whether or not the child possessed a certain ability).

Shirley explains the regularity in the sequence of motor development in infancy in maturational terms—that is, she considers the total process of growth, rather than simply physical or neurological development. Her definition of growth explicitly excludes learning. It was her belief that the high degree of similarity among different babies and the correspondence between the order of their motor development and what she considered to be a fundamental law of development (that development is **cephalocaudal** and proceeds from the head toward the feet) invalidated the hypothesis that the sequence is caused by learning. The infant first acquires control over his head—for example, he can control his eye movements and raises his head prior to acquiring control over his extremities. Fetal development proceeds in the same manner: the head, eyes, and internal organs develop in the embryo prior to the appearance of the limbs. Hence, Shirley maintains that cephalocaudal progress is a fundamental biological principle of development.

Although Shirley's findings have not been seriously questioned by subsequent research, her interpretation of causal factors has been. The Dennis (1960) study of orphaned infants in Iran (see Chapter 3) conflicts with Shirley's interpretation of the causal factors involved in motor development. Experience not only drastically affects the age at which various motor capabilities are attained, but can also affect their quality. If you will recall, the study involved observing the motor development of a group of infants who were raised in pathetically deprived environments in two different institutions. Not only was their motor development severely retarded, but they preferred scooting to crawling. Infants employed this mode of propulsion not because they preferred it to a more orthodox crawl, but because they had not *learned* to crawl, ostensibly because they had not lain prone in their beds at any time during their infancy. Dennis suggests that the lack of opportunity to exercise the simple motor activities related to crawling made it unlikely that they would learn to crawl later. Since they had had some experience with sitting, it was not particularly surprising that the mode of propulsion they developed involved sitting and swinging their arms.

Other research on motor development has attempted to analyze the minute activities involved in learning various motor activities. Ames (1937), for example, studied films of children creeping and concluded that there are 14 sequential stages involved in acquiring the ability to locomote in this prone position. Because of the obvious importance of the infant's ability to move relative to his other motor capabilities, considerably more research has dealt with locomotion in infants than with other motor development. Nevertheless, investigations of such abilities as prehension (Halverson, 1931) also revealed relatively invariable sequential stages—in this case 10 stages beginning with the infant incapable of making physical contact with the object, and culminating with an adult-like grasp by the age of 60 weeks.

Any statements about an infant's emotions must be tentative for two reasons: emotion is a subjective response which cannot easily be interpreted by an observer, particularly when the subject is still incapable of communicating the essence of his feelings; situations which adults ordinarily interpret as emotion-producing cannot be assumed to be emotion-related for infants. Until the child is sufficiently developed that the emotional content of social and physical situations has meaning for him, investigating his emotions is indeed a difficult task.

Nevertheless, beginning with the pioneering work of Watson (1914), a number of psychologists assumed that the infant is capable of emotional responses from birth; that is, emotional responses are part of his reflexive repertoire. Watson identified three distinct emotional responses of a neonate: fear, rage, and love. He assumed that each of these was a reflex and could therefore be elicited by a specific stimulus. Rage, for example, was thought to result from being confined or from having movements restricted; fear, from a loud noise or from being dropped suddenly; and love resulted from being stroked or fondled. Sherman and Sherman (1929) later suggested that whenever an investigator assumed a child was reacting emotionally in response to a particular stimulation, he was subjectively interpreting the infant's behavior in terms of adult and personal predispositions. In other words, adults may ascribe motives and emotions to children with no valid basis for doing so. There is a similar tendency to anthropomorphize animal behavior—that is, to describe it in human terms. The tendency appears most pronounced when the investigator is most ignorant about his subject.

Following a general discrediting of Watson's belief that these three emotional reactions were the reflexes upon which all subsequent emotional responses would be based (through a process of classical conditioning), a host of other theories of emotional development were advanced. For example, Bridges (1932) maintained that the early emotional reactivity of an infant is a general, global, and undifferentiated state that can only be described as excitement. This primitive emotion is manifested in increased activity resulting from a variety of stimuli. Throughout life the individual continues to possess the ability to respond with excitement, but this diffuse emotional reaction differentiates into increasingly specific emotions. Around the age of 3 months the infant shows evidence of distress and delight; by the age of 6 months, the ability to feel distress has been refined further and is now evidenced in responses of fear, disgust, and anger. By the age of 12 months, delight has differentiated into elation and love. Through further refinements of emotional states (see Figure 9.5), the 2-year-old will have attained an adult range of emotional reactions. Bridges' theory is not based on very convincing evidence, but then emotion is not a quality that lends itself readily to experimental investigation.

A consideration of the development of emotion in children must

Social-Emotional Development

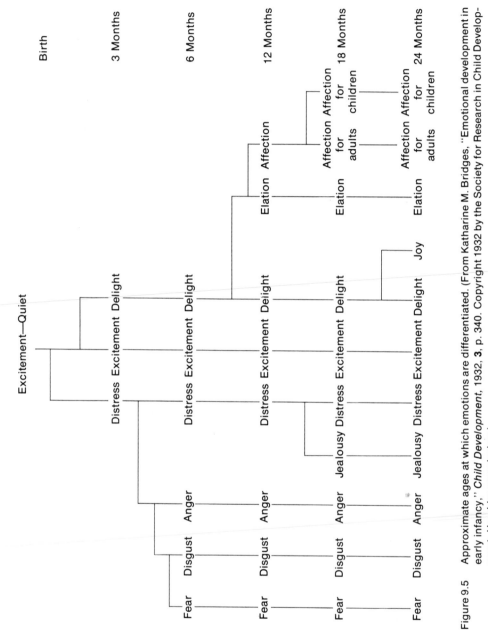

Figure 9.5 Approximate ages at which emotions are differentiated. (From Katharine M. Bridges, "Emotional development in early infancy," *Child Development*, 1932, **3**, p. 340. Copyright 1932 by the Society for Research in Child Development. Used by permission.)

inevitably be concerned with the role of the significant people in his life. While emotional reactions are elicited by a wide range of stimulation, relations among people probably elicit the most important human emotions. Feelings of love, tenderness, and affection, are most often tendered toward people—hence we consider the mother's role in the social and emotional development of her child.

Harlow (1958, 1959, 1966) has extensively investigated the attachment of infant monkeys to their mothers, and the consequences of separating young monkeys from their mothers. The results of these studies have important implications for human mother-child relationships.

The first Harlow (1959) study investigated the theory that an infant's attachment to his mother is determined by the fact that she is always present when he is being fed—just as she is usually present when such comforting things as changing diapers and bathing occur. These theories of infant attachment maintained that an association is formed between the sight of the mother and the reduction of the tension (unpleasant feelings) that accompanies hunger; since eating is pleasant, the mother, through association, will come to be reacted to as though she were pleasant. Accordingly, the feeling that an infant has for his mother, if it derives solely from the conditioning described above, will be similar to the feeling that he has for the breast, a bottle, or warm milk.

In Harlow experiments infant monkeys were separated from their mothers shortly after birth and provided with "mother surrogates." The substitute mothers were wire monkey-mother models with interesting, but nonmonkeylike wooden heads. Each infant's cage contained two surrogate mothers: one covered with soft, tan terry cloth; the other left bare. Both models were heated by a light bulb so that their warmth would be relatively equal. In the experiment that is most relevant here, one surrogate mother had a bottle attached to her chest with the nipple protruding, suggesting to the immature monkey that this was indeed a milk-giving breast. In four cages the bottle was attached to the wire model; the terry-cloth mother, on the other hand, was left milkless. In four other cages the terry-cloth mother was equipped with the bottle and the wire model was left breastless, nippleless, and milkless. The seemingly logical prediction is that if the infant monkeys were to develop an attachment to either model, it would be to the milk-giving model. Surprisingly, this occurred only when the terry-cloth mother provided the nourishment; when the bare wire mother was the milk-giver, the infant still became more attached to the terry-cloth substitute mother.

Harlow measured attachment in two ways. First, the experimenters recorded the total time per day that the infant spent embracing one model or the other. It seems reasonable that greater attachment for a mother would be demonstrated by more time spent with that model. This was indeed the case (see Figure 9.6). After the age of 25 days (presumably some time is required for the attachment to develop), all monkeys spent very little time with the naked wire model, but spent over 12 hours a day with the terry-cloth mother. If the models were placed in close proximity,

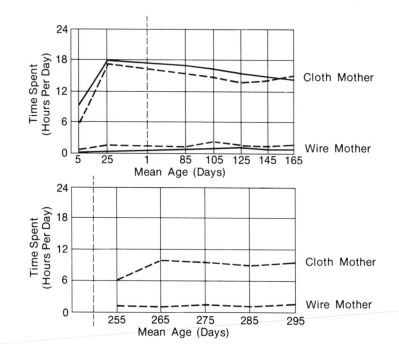

Figure 9.6   Amount of time spent by infant monkeys on cloth and wire surrogate mothers. The results show a strong preference for the cloth mother regardless of whether the infant
was fed on the wire model (broken line) or on the cloth model (solid line). (From
Harry F. Harlow, "Love in infant monkeys" in *Scientific American*, 1959, **200**, 68–74.
Copyright 1959 by *Scientific American*, Inc. All rights reserved. Used by permission.)

the infant would attempt to feed from the wire model while clinging to
the terry-cloth model!

A second measure of attachment was provided by the response of the
infant to a fear-producing stimulus such as the plaster cast of a monkey
head or a mechanical teddy bear that moved and played a drum. Again,
the results strongly corroborate the conclusion that the infants developed
a strong attachment to the terry-cloth mother regardless of which one fed
them. The infants ran into the arms of the soft mother when shown the
frightening stimulus. If she were not present, the infant monkey reacted
with much greater fear, frequently cowering in a corner of the cage or
the room and adopting a quasi-fetal attitude, occasionally covering his
eyes. Human children often react similarly to threatening or unfamiliar
situations when their mother is absent—as demonstrated by my young
son who frequently bellows his fear in grocery stores if his mother is suddenly lost from view.

The Harlow studies contradicted earlier theories about the formation of attachment between mother and child and raised some additional
questions. Since it does not appear to be the tension-reducing role of
food-giving that endears the mother to her child, what is it? Does the
monkey infant become attached to the terry-cloth mother out of a per-

verse desire to make things difficult for psychological investigators, who so readily employ infrahuman primates in all manner of investigations in which they would not dare to use human children? Or do the infant monkeys develop the attachment instinctively? This last statement obviously does not explain the phenomenon, particularly since Harlow also found that monkey infants who had been deprived of even surrogate mothers for the first 8 months of their lives were typically unable to form a lasting attachment to any surrogate mother, even one covered in terry toweling — suggesting that attachment to a substitute mother, or by inference to a mother, does not occur instinctively but is caused. Since attachment always favored the cloth-covered surrogate, it seems clear that the infant's attachment to the mother is partly related to her unique characteristics. Harlow concludes, therefore, that the "contact comfort" derived from the cloth is *one* of the variables involved.

Although it is difficult to generalize the results and conclusions of the Harlow studies to human infants, numerous recent studies with children increase our understanding of mother-child attachments. Schaffer and Emerson (1964) studied mother-child interaction during the first 18 months of the human child's life and found that two aspects of the mother's behavior most highly related to her child's attachment to her were her responsiveness to his crying and the amount of stimulation that she provided for him. The nature of the stimulation appeared to be much less important than sheer quantity of stimulation. Thus, it made little difference whether the mother stimulated the child physically (by rocking him, for example), whether the stimulation was primarily long-range (such as singing to him), or whether she simply provided objects for him to play with. Yarrow (1963) and others (see Moss, 1970) corroborate the importance of maternal stimulation of infants. For humans, as for monkeys, contact between a mother (and a father, for that matter) and a child is of paramount importance in the child's emotional development.

Several naturally occurring situations have provided some indication of the importance of the mother in the life of the child. Spitz (1945, 1954), Bowlby (1940, 1953), Goldfarb (1945, 1949), and others, are among many psychologists to describe the deleterious effects of naturally occurring mother-child separation. Spitz (1945), reporting the fate of institutionalized children, claimed that they had significantly higher mortality rates, that they were retarded in physical development, and that their emotional development was so severely thwarted by lack of mothering that they frequently withdrew, became depressed, and sometimes died as a result. The syndrome, which he explicitly attributed to maternal deprivation, is known as **marasmus** (progressive emaciation) or *anaclitic depression* (a slowing of normal development; weeping, sadness, and an increased susceptibility to disease). Related studies all conclude that if a child is separated from his mother for a prolonged period of time, he will suffer severe emotional disturbances, resulting from the lack of maternal love. By implication, then, the studies point to the hypothesis that maternal love or "mothering" is intimately involved not only in the child's

Maternal Deprivation

emotional development, but also in his intellectual development and his physical well-being. However, advocates of this hypothesis generally concede that maternal love need not come only from the true mother, but from any person who devotes the time, attention, and love to the child that a mother customarily displays. Casler's (1961) classical work examines 45 studies cited by Bowlby (1951) of the damaging effects of maternal deprivation. Casler argues that the 45 studies reviewed are "virtually without exception neither conclusive nor particularly instructive . . ." (p. 3). Casler points out that 33 of the 45 studies either do not describe the institution in which the subjects were found, fail to indicate the age at which the child's separation from the mother occurred, or involve subjects who were not separated from their mothers until after the age of 6 months. His criticism is clear: a child separated from his mother after the age of 6 months is already likely to have formed a strong attachment to her. Any unhappy effects of institutionalization may be due to rupturing this affectional bond, rather than to the child's being deprived of a mother. That is, if a child is separated from his mother prior to becoming attached to her, one might expect that separation will not be especially traumatic. Second, regardless of the child's age when institutionalized, if the institution in which he is housed does not provide sufficient emotional and intellectual stimulation, (recall the Tehran institutions described by Dennis) any untoward effect on the infant will more likely be due to the nature of his care rather than to the lack of a mother.

Accordingly, Casler concludes that the lack of perceptual stimulation accounts for many of the damaging effects of institutionalization on very young children—not their lack of mothering. While Casler's conclusion is perhaps valid for the studies that he examined, his arguments do not contradict the belief that maternal stimulation is conducive to an infant's healthy development—a belief that is supported not only by experience, but also by Harlow's studies of monkeys.

The Whole Infant   There is something frustrating about systematizing the developing child into such psychologically convenient categories as *description of capabilities, physical development, motor development, social-emotional development,* and *intellectual development.* We lose the infant in the interminable and frequently confused array of beliefs, findings, tentative conclusions, convincing arguments, and suggestions. The theoretical infant can raise his head from a prone position at the age of 4 weeks; he can visually follow a moving object; he demonstrates the Moro reflex; he is incapable of a social smile, although his face occasionally distorts from the pain of intestinal gases, *almost* convincing his grandmother that he is smiling. It is true that a great many infants are very close to the hypothetical average child when they are 1 month old. Fewer are still average at the age of 2 months, even fewer at the age of 6 months; and by the age of a year, almost none. By the time the child becomes as old as you or I, the average individual will no longer exist. He will appear only in the overly simplified theories of the psychologist or the sociologist, or in the files of the market researcher who wants to know what the "average man" is wearing this spring.

Each person is a more or less integrated whole, whose intellect, emotions, and physical being all interact; each part is inextricably linked with and dependent upon every other part of the living organism. However, if we attempt to describe a child in that way, the sheer complexity of the task can boggle the mind. And so we continue to speak of the isolated forces that affect human development as though they were in fact isolated, just as we speak of the child's locomotor development as though it existed apart from the integrated, whole child. Nonetheless, we must treat the individual topics of development to enable us to draw a clear and psychologically correct picture of the whole child. Thus, the next chapter will deal with the child's intellectual achievements—his acquisition of speech, and the course of his cognitive development. (If you lose track of the complete child, you may wish to consult Figure 9.7 from time to time as a reminder.)

The Whole Infant   Figure 9.7

This chapter began with the birth of ten puppies, moved through a sketchy   **Summary**
history of human obstetrics, and ran abruptly into a clinical discussion of the three stages of childbirth, pausing to ask the mother for her opinion and concluded that the process is probably somewhat painful. The child's point of view was also considered, although it was noted that because of his remarkable insensitivity to pain at birth, it is likely that he is quite indifferent to the process. The chapter described the neonate's appearance, his perceptual capacities, and his reflexive,

behavioral repertoire; then it examined his perceptual and motor development, and his social and emotional development, particularly as it relates to his mama. Finally the chapter observed that these features of development are necessary to provide us with a picture of the whole infant.

Main Points

1. My illiterate English Setter delivered ten pups while I slept peacefully in the doghouse with an empty bottle of spirits guarding the entrance.

2. Birth ordinarily occurs 266 days after conception; the mature newborn weighs approximately 2500 grams. Earlier deliveries are classified *abortions* (before the 20th week), *immature births* (20th to the 28th week), or *premature births* (29th to the 36th week). *Postmature births* are children born after the 42nd week.

3. Labor can be considered in three stages: dilation of the cervix in preparation for birth (lasting an average of 9 to 12 hours), the actual birth (usually accomplished within an hour), and expulsion of the placenta and other membranes (soon after birth and lasting several minutes).

4. Some mothers think that having a baby is like rolling off a log; others consider it a rather large log from which the fall is quite painful. Advocates of natural childbirth report painless births.

5. Dramatic demands confront the child immediately upon his delivery, not the least of which is that now he must breathe by himself and obtain his own food — a feat with which he must be aided by adults.

6. Birth poses two great dangers for the neonate: cerebral hemorrhage resulting from extreme pressures in the uterus, or more frequently in the birth canal, or occasionally, from the forceps wielded by the friendly obstetrician; the second is prolapse of the umbilical cord.

7. The neonate is not a pretty, curly-haired, smiling cherub dressed in pink and blue and diminutive bows.

8. The perceptual equipment of the neonate is remarkably well developed at birth and matures rapidly with age. His sense of taste may be the most undeveloped of his capacities. Depth perception, response to pattern, and the ability to accommodate vision for different distances develop during the first 6 months of life.

9. The behavioral repertoire of the neonate consists of a large number of reflexes, some of which are important for his survival, but many are not. The sucking reflex, occasionally considered too complex to be a reflex, is elicited by any object put in the infant's mouth.

10. Motor capacities develop in a series of stages. Although there is wide individual variation in the age at which each stage is attained, the sequence of stages appears invariant.

11. Statements about the young child's emotional response are often subjective. Infants react to stimulation with a generalized excitement; love, anger, and hate are differentiated in later development.

12. The attachment that infant monkeys develop for their mothers is independent of the mother's providing nourishment, but highly dependent on the comfort or reassurance provided by a soft, warm mother.

13. Lack of a mother-child relationship may damage the child's social and emo-

tional development (perhaps also his intellectual development). The evidence most often cited in support of this belief has been seriously questioned, however.

14. Although relatively fragmented aspects of the child have been discussed in this chapter, it is the whole child about whom we are concerned.

The following two references provide standard descriptions of the process of birth: **Further Readings**

Bookmiller, M. M., and G. L. Bowen. *Textbook of obstetrics and obstetric nursing,* 5th Ed. Philadelphia: W. B. Saunders, 1967.

Eastman, N. J., and L. M. Hellman. *Williams obstetrics,* 13th Ed. New York: Appleton-Century-Crofts, 1966.

Two articles provide detailed information about the development of affection in monkeys:

Harlow, H. F. Love in infant monkeys. *Scientific American,* 1959, **200**, 68–74.

Harlow, H. F. Age-mate or peer affectional systems. In D. S. Leahrman, R. A. Hinde, and E. Shaw (Eds.), *Advances in the study of behavior.* Vol. 2, New York: Academic Press, 1969.

An extensive and critical review of studies of maternal deprivation is:

Casler, L. Maternal deprivation: A critical review of the literature. *Monograph of the Society for Research in Child Development.* Vol. 26, No. 2, 1961.

Chapter 2 of the book by Reese and Lipsitt describes in detail the perceptual capabilities of the newborn and the subsequent development of these capabilities:

Reese, H. W., and L. O. Lipsitt. *Experimental child psychology.* New York: Academic Press, 1970.

Of the Smell of Nell: Infancy

I saw Sam again last night—he has become quite paranoiac and is increasingly difficult to find. I had seen him only once since the main sewer burst and we moved all his rats into a higher tunnel where Sam thought they would be safe. As it happened, this was a particularly bad year for sewers, and Sam had to move five more times in the course of the next few weeks. He is now convinced that they are after him—so he keeps moving. I asked him to provide me with an itinerary, telling me what sewer he will be visiting next week and the week after that, so that I might find him when I want to bring him a cake.

"I can't do that," Sam informed me sadly, "I haven't decided, because if I make up my mind too soon, they will discover where I'm going before I get there, and they'll get me!" He assured me, however, that he trusted me, and didn't really think that I would tell them where he was. They had uncanny ways of finding things out if they really wanted to know. I asked Sam who they were.

"They are the guys who saw to it that I didn't get tenure," he said somewhat bitterly. "But that isn't all. There's another group after me as well. You remember when I left and took a few of my rats with me? All the graduate students who were writing theses on those rats have organized themselves now. They too want to get me. They come in here almost every night looking for me. I had to kill some of my noisier rats so they wouldn't give me away."

At that, Sam began to sob quietly, his face in his hands. Suddenly I realized how unusually quiet it was in the mine shaft. The only sound was the rats' eating and scraping their tiny feet as they scurried about the

Samuel was sitting quietly in Sam's shirt pocket, peeking over its edge.

cages. Samuel was sitting quietly in Sam's shirt pocket, peeking over its edge at me. He had obviously not been sacrificed. When Sam recovered, he explained that he now knew—too late—how to quiet the rats without killing them. Sam wouldn't explain how he quiets his rats, but I suspect he uses alcohol. At any rate, when I asked him he changed the subject to writing and handed me a poem, telling me that it was by far his best—and he wondered whether I might not be able to get it published for him. Here it is:

To Samuel

They are black like the smell of wild asparagus
and blue
like the taste of pink saffron
$\qquad\qquad$ *dripping limpid languid liquid through the amber anvil*
and well I remember
the briny fluid feel in the December dark on glowing hearth embers
$\qquad\qquad\qquad$ *the brain waves of a Koron you ask*
$\qquad\qquad\qquad$ *the cortical activity of a Koron brain*
$\qquad\qquad\qquad$ *the brain of a corticized Koron*
$\qquad\qquad\qquad$ *the cortex of a waving brain*
$\qquad\qquad\qquad$ *I will tell*
they are black like the smell of wild pink saffron on the edge of a languid
liquid
have you run your hand along the thin sharp edge
$\qquad$ *Do you feel*
$\qquad$ *Do you feel the acrid smoke of knife nicks nell*
$\qquad\qquad\qquad$ *go to hell*
$\qquad\qquad\qquad$ *nell*
$\qquad\qquad\qquad$ *I will tell*
about the flaming feel of
wild pink saffron
dripping limpid languid liquid through the
$\qquad\qquad\qquad$ *nell*
$\qquad\qquad\qquad$ *fell*
$\qquad\qquad\qquad$ *and went to hell*
$\qquad\qquad\qquad$ *with a bell you thought but no*
no no no
no it is still black on the edge

$\qquad\qquad$ *black like the smell of*
$\qquad\qquad$ *nell eating wild asparagus because*
they feel like pink saffron
$\qquad$ *and smell like liquid limpids.*

The Power of Language   I have not included Sam's poem simply because he is my friend (despite his obvious madness) nor even because I feel sorry for him, but because it is an excellent example of the power of **language**—and it is important to be aware of the tremendous possibilities of expression before we enquire into the development of language and speech in the young child. Imagine, if you will, the flaming feel of wild pink saffron, or envision saffron as it drips limpid languid liquid through an amber anvil. Have you felt the acrid smoke of knife nicks? Does the thought not boggle your mind?

Now I want you to imagine a piece of ice: it is a long, flat slab of ice from an ice cube tray, whose dividers have been removed. Imagine that cold, dripping slab of ice. It is here in my hands as I stand before you, smiling in my usual, friendly way. Can you envision it—cold, bluish, dripping between my fingers. Now I slide it down your back. Close your eyes and imagine what I have just described to you. If the scene is not vivid enough, imagine that I am slowly scraping my fingernails across a chalkboard. You feel something, don't you? You must, if you are not totally insensitive. You feel another example of the power of language. You may say that it was your imagination that made you react—and so it was, but your imagination was triggered and guided by my words. More precisely, it was your understanding of my words that was responsible for the response which my words indirectly caused. Fortunately, your understanding of my words is very close to my own and to everyone else's; otherwise, communication would be impossible, or at best, confusing.

Now that you have an intuitive feel for the power of language, imagine what it must be like to be a child, totally incapable of producing comprehensible speech sounds, or of understanding the speech of others. Imagine, then, what a tremendous difference it must make in an infant's life when he finally reaches the point where his facility with language enables him to interact with others.

The power of language is difficult to determine. It obviously has a great deal to do with communication. Not so obviously, it also has a great deal to do with thought and intelligence. Benjamin Whorf (1966) has given expression to a belief (frequently labeled the Whorfian hypothesis) that language not only allows people to express their thinking but is also largely responsible for determining those thoughts. In other words, we tend to think those thoughts for which we have language, and thoughts that we are incapable of verbalizing do not occur to us. There are several logical difficulties in interpreting the Whorfian hypothesis. Since we ordinarily communicate thought through language, it is very difficult to conceive of a thought apart from the language in which it is couched. This does not completely validate Whorf's assertion; indeed, to accept it as unquestionably correct, it would be necessary to deny that there is preverbal thinking in children. In view of ample behavioral evidence of thinking in infants prior to their acquiring language, that is difficult to do.

Bernstein (1958, 1961), who attributes much inferior school achievement of the lower-class child to his language, also links language and thoughts. Following extensive studies of speech patterns of children of lower-class (working class) and of middle- or upper-class parents, Bernstein (1958) concluded that lower-class parents use what he terms **re**-

stricted, as opposed to **elaborated**, language codes. He also distinguishes between *public* (restricted) and *formal* (elaborated) language. Hypothetical examples of each are given below:

(Restricted)
   Mother: Clean your feet.
   Child: Why?
   Mother: Because.
   Child: Because what?
   Mother: I said clean your feet, that's why.
   Child: But why clean my feet?

(Elaborated)
   Mother: Blow your nose, Henry. It is about to drip on the carpet.
   Child: Why you don't want it to drip on the carpet, Mom? Why, Mom? Why you don't want it to drip?
   Mother: Because it's messy, Henry, and we must keep the carpet clean for when Daddy comes home, because Dad doesn't like to have nose drips all over the carpet.

     In summarizing his findings, Bernstein (1958) observed that the restricted language of the lower-class family has the following characteristics: it is employed to control or to express emotion, rather than to rationalize or to express information; it tends to be less personal despite the use of the first person; it is more global and less precise; it tends to be liberally sprinkled with idiom and colloquialism; and sentences are typically exceedingly short, frequently grammatically incorrect, and often incomplete. To the extent that this analysis is accurate, it is little wonder that the lower-class child almost invariably finds himself at a disadvantage in school. For the first time in his life, he is required to use increasingly precise and grammatically correct forms of expression; he is placed in a situation in which he inevitably begins by performing less well than those who have been more fortunate in their early language experiences. Perhaps before he has had a chance to catch up, he will find himself so far behind that he will feel it is hardly worth trying.

     Other investigations of language characteristics of disadvantaged groups have generally supported Bernstein's assertion that these groups fare less well in language tests. It appears, however, that the disadvantaged child is not necessarily less advanced in language development, but that in many cases he has simply developed a different language code. Baratz (1969) found that Negro and Caucasian children performed equally well when confronted with language codes that were outside their primary code; while the level of performance in standard English was significantly different for the two groups, their *language* development was actually similar. The essential difference between the two groups was that the Negro group had developed a nonstandard English code as their primary language, and were therefore faced with the same problems in standard English as Caucasian children confronted with nonstandard English codes. These findings suggest that the lower-class child is perhaps not deficient in language development, as Bernstein contends. However, lack of facility with the school language code remains deleterious to successful performance in school.

Despite the tremendous power of language, it is not essential for **communication**. Animals that do not have language can communicate, sometimes remarkably effectively. The reflexive communication of danger (Hebb, 1966) is the simplest level: whitetail deer wave their tails; pronghorn antelope bristle their rump patches; ground squirrels whistle shrilly; nesting crows pierce the air with raucous cries. These signals communicate danger to other members of the same species. Barnett (1967), in his studies of the behavior of some monkeys, has observed a similar, but more advanced, phenomenon. Baboons and other subhuman primates often mingle with herds of gazelles, apparently because the gazelle has much better vision, and probably a better sense of smell, than most baboons. The signals of danger that the gazelle emits are clearly meaningful for the baboon also.

In addition, there is evidence of communication between man and lower animals. An animal trainer who instructs his dog to roll over is communicating with the animal (at least when the dog obeys). The animal can also communicate with its master, as dogs frequently do when they are displeased, hungry, or otherwise agitated. As Lefrancois (1972a, p. 173) wrote, "A dog who looks at his master, walks to his dish and

Language and Communication

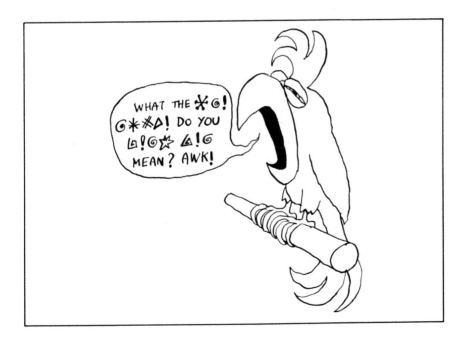

The parrot merely mimics. It does not communicate.

barks, looks at his master again, and then begins to growl is not only dangerous but is also communicating very effectively." This communication, however, is a far cry from that made possible by language. Even the parrot that has learned 100 words and can say whole sentences on occasions when those sentences are clearly appropriate, is still incapable of using language. For language involves the use of *arbitrary* sounds with established and accepted referents, either real or abstract, that can be arranged in sequence to convey different meanings. The parrot who can say, "Polly wants a cracker" is not only boringly conventional but is also probably incapable of saying, "A cracker wants Polly, heh, heh," with the intention of conveying a different meaning. The parrot merely mimics; it does not communicate.

The Elements of Language

But a child learns to speak in time. And the learning involved is incredibly complex. To begin with, what is language? We have already stated that it involves the use of arbitrary sounds that have accepted referents that can be arranged in different ways to have different meanings. This definition is the key to analyzing the elements of language.

The simplest unit of language is the **phoneme**: a single sound such as that represented by a vowel or a consonant. Phonemes can be combined to form *morphemes,* which are the units of meaning in language. The child cannot form morphemes until he can first pronounce the phonemes. Further, it is not sufficient simply to make the sound, but he must be able to make it when he intends to do so. (If the child could speak when he is first capable of uttering all the sounds that are required for any language, many tables describing the course of language acquisition would have to be revised.) In addition to the ability to utter words (single morphemes and morpheme combinations), the child must also acquire the ability to combine these in units. That is a large step, for there is a world of difference between being able to say "daddy," "mommy," "teddy," and "my," and turning with wide open arms to a beaming parent and saying "my mommy" or "my daddy." Organizing words into meaningful sentence units requires an intuitive knowledge of **syntax** – the grammar of language – the set of implicit or explicit rules governing the combinations of words that will be meaningful and correct for the speakers of that language. As the child practices and masters phonemes, morphemes, and syntax, he must also practice **prosody** – he must learn the manners of expression, the intonations, the accents, the pauses, and all the subtle variations that give different meanings to the same morphemes. Phonemes, morphemes, syntax, and prosody are the elements of language. Most of us have acquired these elements in an amazingly painless, effective, and efficient way, without really being conscious of what we were doing.

The Development of Language

The early studies of language acquisition in children primarily counted the number of words that a child had in his vocabulary at a given age. Psychologists soon found that the child's passive vocabulary far exceeds his active vocabulary; that is, in the early stages of language learning he can invariably understand many more words than he can use in his own speech. It is as if his knowledge were always far ahead of his capabilities—and perhaps it continues in that manner throughout life.* Studies of the extent of the child's vocabulary at different ages have observed that there is a *sequence* in the development of vocabulary size.

Normative tables for the acquisition of vocabulary provide a relatively simple guide for comparing the progress of different children. Attempting to determine the vocabulary of an individual child requires caution. Most normative tables are based on estimates of the child's passive vocabulary, rather than on his demonstrable active vocabulary, and it is exceedingly difficult to arrive at an accurate estimate of the number of words that a child knows and understands. Table 10.1 shows the average passive vocabulary of different children from the age of 8 months to 6 years (from M. E. Smith, 1926). Smith obtained data for this normative study by including both the words that the child could speak and those that he showed evidence of understanding. The estimates provided by this study are included in almost all textbook descriptions of vocabulary growth in children. Other estimates of vocabulary have been considerably higher. M. K. Smith (1941), for example, in establishing norms for the Seashore-Eckerson vocabulary test, found a vocabulary range between 6,000 and 48,800 words for first-grade students. The average vocabulary for this sample was 23,700 words—approximately 10 times greater than the most often cited norms. Other studies (notably Hart-

| The Early Growth of Vocabulary in Children.* | Table 10.1 |

Age (Years and Months)	Average Number of Words
0–8	0
0–10	1
1–0	3
1–3	19
1–6	22
1–9	118
2–0	272
2–6	446
3–0	896
3–6	1222
4–0	1540
4–6	1870
5–0	2072
5–6	2289
6–0	2562

*From "An investigation of the development of the sentence and the extent of vocabulary in young children," by M. E. Smith. *University of Iowa Studies in Child Welfare*, 1926, Vol. 3, No. 5.

* Indeed, many writers claim to be far in advance conceptually of their actual words. Like young children, their language facility apparently does not do justice to their thoughts.

man, 1941) have emphasized that traditional methods for assessing vocabulary size have tended to be gross underestimates.

A second way of approaching early language development is by examining the quality of the language acquired, rather than by estimating vocabulary size at different ages. Landreth (1967) has observed that contemporary linguists treat the developing child as a fellow linguist: they examine the progression of his knowledge of each of the elements of language not only to learn how the child acquires the ability to use language, but also to learn more about language itself. The field of psycholinguistics is a fascinating one, albeit incredibly complex and confusing. Little order has yet been imposed on the psycholinguists' countless observations. Some of these unordered observations are discussed in this chapter.

Steps in Language Acquisition

For convenience, language learning is frequently divided into two major stages: the prespeech stage, and the stage of speech. Interestingly and logically, the second stage follows the first. The prespeech stage begins the development of meaningful speech sounds. Also, a number of observations have been made about the child's behavior at this stage that can partially explain the processes by which a child acquires language. The prespeech stage lasts from birth to about the end of the first year or the early part of the second and terminates with the utterance of single words. During this first stage, the child engages in three different speech-related behaviors: he cries (sometimes a great deal), he develops a repertoire of gestures, many of which are intended to communicate his desires, and he practices **babbling**.

The roots of language are found in the infant's babbling; indeed, all the sounds of every language in the world are uttered in the babbling of an infant (even in the babbling of deaf children, although there is a drastic reduction in the amount of verbalization following pre-speech). Prior to the age of 6 months the child's babbling appears unsystematic and erratic, although linguists have analyzed it by the number of phonemes (single sounds) typically uttered by a child, as well as the specific sound of these phonemes. Irwin (1947a, 1947b; 1949), in an extensive series of studies of language development, found that the child begins his babbling with a preponderance of vowel sounds, followed by the simpler consonants, of which the aspirate *h* appears to be the simplest. Such consonants as *p, b, t, d, n, m, w, wh, f,* and *v* do not ordinarily join the child's repertoire until his second year—a fact that suggests that maturation is closely allied with the early development of speech.

More recent studies of language acquisition by infants have employed sophisticated procedures to determine whether or not children can discriminate among various sounds. For example, Moffitt (1971) illustrated dramatically that infants 20 to 24 weeks of age can discriminate between sounds as similar as "bah" and "gah." The procedure involved monitoring cardiac deceleration, which is one index of the orienting response (see Chapter 1). One group of infants was presented with the auditory stimulus "bah." The immediate orienting response was cardiac deceleration; the same stimulus was repeated until the child had habituated to the stimulus (that is, cardiac recovery was complete). Without breaking the previous tempo or intonation the stimulus "gah" was introduced next. The fact that heart rate decelerated with the new stimulus as well is evidence that the infant could discriminate between the new stimulus and the one to which he had habituated. Such discrimination is doubtless involved in the child's early babbling also, since babbling is a repetitive activity that must require some recognition of sounds.

After the age of 6 months the infant's babbling becomes more systematic and more controlled. He repeats the same sounds more frequently, sometimes succeeding in convincing his parents and his grandmother that he can talk. "Listen to little Norbert. A child prodigy. A lot like his grandfather," says a proud grandmother when she hears her grandson say "bah," as she hands the little tyke a new purple ball. What grandmother doesn't realize is that little Norbert, who is 8 months old, has probably been practicing "bah" all afternoon.

Babbling, defined as the practicing of single sounds, is a necessary first step to acquiring language. Osgood (1957) describes the process as a circular reflex that is attained when the child becomes capable of responding to auditory feedback from his own vocalizations. The child emits a sound, hears it, and repeats it because he hears it; as he repeats it, he hears it again, and is again moved to repeat it. Thus, the babbling of a young child is a monotonous repetition of the same sound, with occasional accidental variations—but it is through this repetition that the child acquires control over the sounds that comprise the language he must master.

The foregoing description illustrates the problem of determining when the child says his first word. Such expressions as "bah," when they come to *mean* something for the child, may be considered words. However, most infants repeat a sound such as "bah" many times before it becomes associated with an object. The point at which the sound "bah" ceases to be babble and becomes a *word* for ball, for example, is nearly impossible to determine. Somewhere near the age of one year, the child does utter his first meaningful word, frequently created by repeating two identical sounds such as in "mama," "dada," "bye bye," and "bingo." The appearance of the first word is rapidly followed by new words that the child practices incessantly. But even prior to acquiring this facility with single words, the infant has begun to show signs that he understands much more than he can say—words that will not be part of his active vocabulary for some time, as well as entire sentences. "Stick out your tongue," he is told by a proud parent, and he sticks out his tongue. "Show Daddy your hand," and he shows it. "Can you wink?" Sure can. Two eyes though.

The child continues to acquire words during his second year, but the range of syllables available to him is limited. Most of his words are one- or two-syllable words, and many repeat the same syllable in different combinations. For example, the child says, "Mommy," "Daddy," "Baby," "seepy" (sleepy), "horsy," and "doggy." Even when it is incorrect to do so, he may frequently repeat the syllable in a monosyllabic word, as in "car car," "kiss kiss," and "bingo." In a comic, unintelligent, and frequently unconscious attempt to communicate with their children, parents sometimes exaggerate the trivial errors committed by infants in the course of learning to speak. The result is occasionally something like, "Wou my itsy bitsy witta baby come to momsy womsy?" It is doubtful that parental (or, more frequently, grandparental) models of this type are particularly conducive to either the rapid, or the correct, acquisition of language.

Despite the child's increasing ability to employ words in a meaningful way, it is not until close to the end of his second year that he will begin to put these together to form simple two-word sentences: "Daddy go," "Mommy go." The most rapid increase in his vocabulary is still to take place, however. It occurs in the third year of his life; and it is also during that time that he learns (or invents) the rules of syntax that qualify him for the title *linguist extraordinaire*.

Chomsky (1957, 1965) has advanced a theory to account for the child's acquisition of syntax—a theory that has attracted a great deal of attention but has not been verified or disproved. Partly because of the child's incredibly rapid acquisition of grammatical rules during his third and fourth year, and partly because none of the conventional explanations of learning seem to account adequately for this acquisition, Chomsky has suggested that children are born with a previously established neurological *something* (labeled a **Language Acquisition Device** [LAD], or an Acquisition Machine [AM]) that corresponds to grammar. Because this something is already present, it facilitates learning grammar and accounts for the fact that the child makes only a fraction of all possible errors while learning syntax. Since the child frequently does make grammatical errors that he could not possibly have heard, imitation is not an adequate explanation. He may say, for example, "He doos" for "He does," because he has invented a rule that says adding the sound "s" to any verb makes it appropriate for a second person subject—and the child's syntactical rule, clever little linguist that he is, admits of no exceptions. Similarly, he says, "I sayed" for "I said"; "He goed" for "He went"; and "I runned" for "I ran."

Whether LAD is responsible, or whether there is another explanation, by the time a child has reached the age of 5, his intuitive understanding of the grammar of his language will be sufficient to handle any verbal situation. Considering the incredible complexity of the structure of language, this understanding ranks among the higher accomplishments of our young hero.

Some Additional Details   Psychological and psycholinguistic research is replete with isolated findings in language acquisition. Some of the more interesting and potentially useful of these are listed briefly in this section.

Sex Differences.   It may come as little surprise that girls appear to have a slight edge in learning language. Not only do they learn to speak at an earlier age than boys (McCarthy, 1930; Templin, 1957), but they frequently articulate better and have fewer speech defects (Johnson, et al., 1948). This observation has been explained on the assumption that a girl has more intimate interaction with her mother than a boy; since fathers are frequently away from home more than mothers, it is reasonable to expect that girls would be slightly accelerated in learning language. With the increasing influence of television, however, this sex difference, if it still exists, may eventually disappear.

Bilingualism.   The effect of **bilingualism** has been examined by many different studies (for example, Smith, 1949; McCarthy, 1960). The results of these studies indicate that only the very superior bilingual child is likely to keep pace with monolinguals in either language. Koenig (1953) has drawn attention to the possible ill effects on the child's social and emotional development of speaking the language of his peers with an accent, and to subsequent ill effects on his adjustment at school. There is additional evidence that learning two languages simultaneously retards the development of both. Vocabularies of bilingual children seem to be smaller, their articulation poorer, and their level of syntactical structure lower (Smith, 1957).

Although many studies suggest the possibly deleterious effects of bilingualism, the findings should be interpreted carefully. Often the home environment of the bilingual children examined in these studies was inferior to that of the control group; thus, these children might have performed less well than monolinguals even if they had been exposed to only one language. Also, these studies apply only to children who were exposed to two languages at home, or to a maternal language different from the dominant language of the school and peer community. These observations do not necessarily apply to learning a second language in school, for example. It would seem unreasonable to suppose that after a single language has been well learned and the syntax fully developed, a second language would have a detrimental effect on the first.

Twins.   Evidence indicates that twins typically are retarded in language development (McCarthy, 1954; see also Chapter 4). First, they do not receive as much individual attention from their mother as would a single child; in addition, twins seem to develop a private jargon and a gesture vocabulary, hence they have less incentive to invent syntax or to learn vocabulary.

Stuttering.   Stuttering in young children is not abnormal in general, and is, in fact, highly common among 3- and 4-year-olds. It is generally accepted that throughout most of the early years of language acquisition the child's cognitive ability is somewhat ahead of his language facility. Therefore, he frequently wants to say things that he can't quite articulate or finds that his words come more slowly than he wishes. This is particularly evident when a child becomes tense or excited. Bloodstein (1960) notes that if parents are patient and accept the child's behavior without drawing undue attention to it, the stuttering will eventually disappear completely.

Language is the attribute that most clearly differentiates man from the less phylogenetically fortunate animals. Although he frequently   In Partial Summary thinks of himself as more intelligent, he has had great difficulty defining intelligence satisfactorily. Man has also found it embarrassing that the magnitude of that part of his anatomy most obviously concerned with intelligence is not terribly impressive, relative to other animals'. I refer, of course, to the human brain, which weighs a full $3\frac{1}{4}$ pounds in the mature male of our species; the female brain weighs slightly under 3 pounds (which is the same proportion of brain-to-body weight). Armed with this information, man noticed that an elephant's brain weighs 13 pounds, and that a whale's tips the scale at 19 pounds. He quickly concluded that it was not the absolute weight of the brain, but the brain-to-body weight ratio that signified intelligence for different species. Here, of course, humans appear in the most favorable light: male and female have one pound of brain for every 50 pounds of body weight, whereas the whale and elephant have a single pound of brain for perhaps 1,000 pounds of weight. There is an additional observation that continues to cause some embarrassment—the mature dolphin weighs little more than a mature male, yet his brain weights a full $3\frac{3}{4}$ pounds. The dolphin, as far as we know, remains incapable of speech. But we are not absolutely certain of this; we continue our efforts to find out.

If we summarize all available knowledge about the child's acquisition of language, we merely have the suggestion of the beginning of an answer. We have succeeded (we don't know how accurately) in counting the number of phonemes, morphemes, words, and sentences that a child knows at every age; we have described the specific characteristics of these elements of language, and we have noted reassuring regularities in the

The human, as far as we know, remains incapable of speech. But we are not absolutely certain of this; we continue our efforts to find out.

sequence in which different children (even from different cultures) acquire language. In the process we have discovered that the child appears to reinvent the grammar of his language as he learns it, since there is ample evidence that he does not learn syntax through imitation. At the same time, there appear to be shortcuts in his reinvention of grammar for, as Chomsky points out, he makes many fewer errors than would be expected of him, were he simply reinventing grammar by inferring rules from the correct forms of speech that he first learns. The greatest mystery of the intrinsically mysterious process of acquiring language is our inability to explain how the child makes such extraordinary progress, particularly between his second and fifth year. How does he invent grammar? Is Chomsky's conjecture of a pre-wired, neurological mechanism (Language Acquisition Device) correct? Or do patterns of grammar fall from heaven?*

Table 10.2 presents a summary of language development to age 4. Lenneberg (1967) describes the average sequence of motor development as parallel to language acquisition. He deliberately juxtaposes the two to convey the close relationship between the development of motor capabilities and acquisition of language—a relationship that some have interpreted as evidence of a biological basis for language learning. Lenneberg, Nichols, and Rosenberber (1964) support this interpretation based on their examination of the language and motor development of 61 mongoloid children aged 2 to 22 years. One of their striking observations was that when the children were still crawling, regardless of age, they were usually at the babbling stage in their language development. And

Milestones in Motor and Language Development   Table 10.2

At the Completion of:	Motor Development	Vocalization and Language
12 weeks	Supports head when in prone position; weight is on elbows; hands mostly open; no grasp reflex.	Markedly less crying than at 8 weeks; when talked to and nodded at, smiles, followed by squealinggurgling sounds usually called *cooing*, which is vowel-like in character and pitch-modulated; sustains cooing for 15–20 seconds.
16 weeks	Plays with a rattle placed in his hands (by shaking it and staring at it), head self-supported; tonic neck reflex subsiding.	Responds to human sounds more definitely; turns head; eyes seem to search for speaker; occasionally some chuckling sounds.
20 weeks	Sits with props.	The vowel-like cooing sounds begin to be interspersed with more consonantal sounds; labial fricatives, spirants and nasals are common; acoustically, all vocalizations are very different from the sounds of the mature language of the environment.
6 months	Sitting: bends forward and uses hands for support; can bear weight when put into standing position, but cannot yet stand with holding on; reaching: unilateral; grasp: no thumb apposition yet; releases cube when given another.	Cooing changing into babbling resembling one syllable utterances; neither vowels nor consonants have very fixed recurrences; most common utterances sound somewhat like *ma, mu, da,* or *di.*

*This is Sam's theory.

Table 10.2

At the Completion of:	Motor Development	Vocalization and Language
8 months	Stands holding on; grasps with thumb apposition; picks up pellet with thumb and finger tips.	Reduplication (or more continuous repetitions) becomes frequent; intonation patterns become distinct; utterances can signal emphasis and emotions.
10 months	Creeps efficiently; takes side-steps, holding on; pulls to standing position.	Vocalizations are mixed with sound play such as gurgling or bubble blowing; appears to wish to imitate sounds, but the imitations are never quite successful; beginning to differentiate between words heard by making differential adjustment.
12 months	Walks when held by one hand; walks on feet and hands—knees in air; mouthing of objects almost stopped; seats self on floor.	Identical sound sequences are replicated with higher relative frequency of occurrence and words (*mamma* or *dadda*) are emerging; definite signs of understanding some words and simple commands (show me your eyes).
18 months	Grasp, prehension and release fully developed; gait stiff, propulsive and precipitated; sits on child's chair with only fair aim; creeps downstairs backward; has difficulty building tower of 3 cubes.	Has a definite repertoire of words—more than three, but less than fifty; still much babbling but now of several syllables with intricate intonation pattern; no attempt at communicating information and no frustration for not being understood; words may include items such as *thank you* or *come here,* but there is little ability to join any of the lexical items into spontaneous two item phrases; understanding is progressing rapidly.
24 months	Runs, but falls in sudden turns; can quickly alternate between sitting and stance; walks stairs up or down, one foot forward only.	Vocabulary of more than 50 items (some children seem to be able to name everything in environment); begins spontaneously to join vocabulary items into two word phrases; all phrases appear to be own creations; definite increase in communicative behavior and interest in language.
30 Months	Jumps up into air with both feet; stands on one foot for about two seconds; takes few steps on tiptoe; jumps from chair; good hand and finger coordination; can move digits independently; manipulation of objects much improved; builds tower of six cubes.	Fastest increase in vocabulary with many new additions every day; no babbling at all; utterances have communicative intent; frustrated if not understood by adults; utterances consist of at least two words, many have three or even five words; sentences and phrases have characteristic child grammar, that is, they are rarely verbatim repetitions of an adult utterance; intelligibility is not very good yet, though there is great variation among children; seems to understand everything that is said to him.
3 years	Tiptoes three yards; runs smoothly with acceleration and deceleration; negotiates sharp and fast curves without difficulty; walks stairs by alternating feet; jumps 12 inches; can operate tricycle.	Vocabulary of some 1000 words; about 80% of utterances are intelligible even to strangers; grammatical complexity of utterances is roughly that of colloquial adult language, although mistakes still occur.
4 years	Jumps over rope; hops on right foot; catches ball in arms; walks line.	Language is well established; deviations from the adult norm tend to be more in style than in grammar.

when they had begun to walk, they had also begun to talk. For these children, as for normal children, simple motor development and language development seem very closely allied. But here, as elsewhere in child development, there are exceptions to the average behavior ascribed to the nonexistent average child.

We have, in this and in the preceding chapter, paused long enough to scream feebly that the child is really not composed of all of these separate layers that we have invented to simplify our study of him. So far the layers we have considered are his physical growth, his motor development, the nature of his perceptual development, his social and emotional development, and the processes by which he acquires language. There remains one layer of paramount importance, inextricably involved with all other aspects of the child, but one that we shall consider in isolation: the mind of the child.

The Mind of the Infant

Maya Pines (1966) observed that for a long time, psychology neglected the infant's mind, as though there was a tacit admission that the baby did not really have a mind, or that whatever mind he possessed was relatively unimportant at his stage of development. The first major theories of child development were much more concerned with the child's physical and physiological development, his acquisition of language, and his emotional and personality development, than they were with his mind — with the exception of Jean Piaget. As far back as 1920, Piaget had already begun to map the course of the child's cognitive development. Interestingly, it is only very recently that his work has become accepted on this continent, and now it dominates developmental psychology. The story of the growth of the child's mind as painted by Piaget deals with the child's growing awareness of the world in which he lives, and his discovery or invention of ways of interacting with his world. It is a complex and fascinating story.

The world of the newborn infant begins as a world of the here and now. He has no memories, no hopes, no dreams, no fund of information with which to think. And so he does not think — he behaves. His behavior is of tremendous significance not only for his motor development, but for the growth of his mind. It is in behavior that cognition is rooted.

Recall that the introduction to Piaget's theories (Chapter 7) described the only two ways the child has of interacting with his world: assimilation and accommodation, processes also referred to as the invariant processes of adaptation. The processes are invariant because they are unchanging from childhood to adulthood. To assimilate is to use aspects of the environment for activities that are already learned. Thus, the child, born with at least a primitive and awkward ability to suck, is assimilating aspects of those objects that he sucks to the sucking scheme; at the same time, however, he is compelled to make changes in the activity of sucking — that is, he must accommodate.

At the very beginning, the world of the infant, while not necessarily a "blooming, buzzing mass of confusion," is a world that exists only when it is being reacted to, and is understood only in terms of those actions.

A nipple exists for the child when he is looking at it, touching it, sucking it, or otherwise responding to it; when it is removed from his immediate perceptual field it ceases to exist. The process by which concrete objects come to have a permanence and an identity of their own (the *object concept*) is not clearly understood, but is of paramount importance to the child's later cognitive development. The object concept is not achieved until near the end of the first year. Piaget (1954) devised an experiment to investigate the progressive understanding of the object concept, which involved showing the child an attractive object and then hiding it from his view. Piaget argues that if the object exists only when the child is perceiving it, he will make no effort to look for it even when he has seen it being hidden from view. When the child begins to look for an object that he can no longer see, this is definite evidence that he can "imagine" it. It continues to exist for him even when it is not being directly perceived.

Piaget typically classifies his observations by the stages through which the child passes. In the earliest stages of the development of the object concept, the child does not respond to the object once it is removed; next, he progresses through a number of stages during which he searches for the object, but only in the place where he last saw it; and finally he culminates with a complete realization of object permanence and has the ability to look for objects in a variety of places. The final stage does not occur until near the end of the first year of life.

Sensorimotor Development

Piaget labels the first two years of the child's life (infancy) the *period of sensorimotor development*. The reason for this is obvious: he believes that the child's understanding of the world throughout most of this period is restricted to the activities that he can perform on it and to his perception of it—hence, *sensori* and *motor*. Piaget simplifies the infant's development during this period by dividing it into six substages, which, considered chronologically, provide an intriguing and enlightening picture of the child in his first two years of life.

Substage 1: 0 to 1 Month

There is little new learning in the first month of life. The child spends most of his waking hours exercising the activities with which he was born—he sucks, looks, grasps, and cries. Some children engage in a great deal of the latter activity. The newborn infant also spends much of his time sleeping. Buhler (1930) reports that newborn infants sleep nearly 80 percent of the time, leaving them with no more than 4 waking hours per day; many grandmothers insist that much of the infant's waking time occurs during the night rather than during the day. By the time the child is a year of age, however, he will spend about as much time awake as he spends asleep.

The child's sucking, reaching, grasping, and looking activities during the first month are not all in vain. In addition to obvious survival functions of some of these activities, there is an equally important cognitive function. Through repeatedly exercising these activities and perfecting their execution, the child eventually gains control over small aspects of his environment (as well as over the activities themselves). By the end of the first month, the child has become relatively proficient at each of these activities. A problem of considerable difficulty that he cannot yet do is to execute more than one action to obtain a single goal. In other words, there is still a complete lack of coordination between these behaviors. A child presented with a visually appealing object can look at it but cannot reach toward it; that is, he cannot coordinate his vision with his motor capacities. He is incapable of demonstrating the intentionality that Piaget considers the hallmark of intelligent activity.

During the second substage, the child begins to acquire new behaviors. These come about as a result of *accidental* responses (operant or instrumental) that have the capacity to elicit their own repetitions—a phenomenon referred to as a circular reaction. The reactions during this stage are centered on the child's own body and are labeled **primary circular reactions**. The best known of these behaviors is probably thumb or hand sucking. The child accidentally gets his hand or a finger into his mouth; this triggers the sucking response, which results in the sensation of the hand in the mouth. That sensation leads to the repetition of the response, which leads to a repetition of the sensation, which leads to a repetition of the response—all of which, for obvious reasons, is called a primary circular reaction.

Despite the child's ability to acquire new behaviors (new adaptations through accommodation to different stimulation), these new behaviors are initiated accidentally and involve the child's body. His interaction with the world is still highly one-sided; it is still a world of the here and now that exists and has meaning when it is doing something to him, or when he is doing something to it. In both cases he must sense it in order for it to exist.

A second circular reaction appears during the third substage: the **secondary circular reaction**. Like the primary circular reaction, it is circular in that the response stimulates its own repetition; since it does not center on the child's body, it is called *secondary*. There are numerous secondary circular reactions in the 6-month-old child's behavior. He accidentally does something that is interesting, pleasing, or otherwise amusing, and proceeds to repeat it again and again. By kicking, Piaget's young son caused a row of dolls dangling above his bassinet to dance. The boy stopped to observe the dolls. Eventually he repeated the kicking, not intentionally to make the dolls move, but more likely because they had ceased moving and no longer attracted his attention. The act of kicking had the same effect again, and again the boy paused to look at the row of dancing dolls. In a very short period of time he was repeating the behavior over and over—hence a circular reaction.

An enterprising parent who has a child at the appropriate level of development can arrange a simple demonstration of this behavior. If one suspends a colorful mobile above the child and attaches a string from the mobile to the child's foot, toe, leg, arm, or any other part of his anatomy

Substage 2: 1 to 4 Months

Substage 3: 4 to 8 Months

that is likely to move, he will soon be tossing that part of his body around in wild abandon. The learning involved is easily explained through operant conditioning, assuming that the appearance of the moving object is reinforcing. Piaget's conviction that this is so is implicit in his title for discussing this behavior: *behavior designed to make interesting sights and sounds last.*

Substage 4: 8 to 12 Months

There are two achievements of this substage that are particularly noteworthy. First, the child develops the ability to coordinate previously unrelated behaviors to achieve some desired end. He can now look at an object, reach for it, grasp it, and bring it to his mouth specifically to suck the beast. Throughout this sequence, there is clear evidence of intention. He has succeeded in distinguishing the means from the end, no longer confuses the object with the activities that are appropriate for it and consequently acquires the object concept – the realization that objects exist apart from his operations on them.

In connection with the acquisition of the object concept, Phillips (1969) observes that since objects cease to exist when they are removed from the child's perceptual field, it follows that he cannot "miss" an absent object prior to developing the object concept. And since this concept does not ordinarily develop until the fourth substage (8 to 12 months), the anxiety purportedly caused by separation from the mother cannot possibly occur prior to the age of 8 to 12 months. This observation supports Casler's (1961) argument that the conclusions derived from the majority of the studies of maternal deprivation are invalid because they have failed to consider the age at which separation occurred (see Chapter 9).

The fourth substage also initiates the child's ability to use signs to anticipate events. This ability is closely linked with his ability to understand causality, since anticipating an outcome is an implicit admission (though not necessarily a valid one) that the signals preceding the outcome are its cause. In other words, a child who realizes that when his daddy puts on his jacket he will be leaving, *knows* that the cause of leaving is putting on the jacket – just as the *cause* of going to bed is taking a bath, putting on pajamas, the good night kiss, saying his prayers, or whatever ritual happens to be the common one.

Substage 5: 12 to 18 Months

Tertiary circular reactions define the fifth substage. The principal difference between these reactions and the circular reactions of the second and third substages is the quality of the circularity. Until the fifth stage the child repeats his actions in a rigid and unmodified manner. If saying "aaaagh" produces an interesting sound, he says "aaaagh, aaaagh, aaaagh, aaaagh, aaaagh . . ." until something distracts him or until his grandmother says "enough." With the advent of the fifth stage, however, the child begins to modify his responses to see what the effect of the modification will be. He no longer says "aaaagh" 115 times; he now says "aaaagh, aaaaaaaaaagh, aaarrgh, aaaarrrrrgh, aaawooo, awwwworrrgh." The behavior is still circular since the effect of the response causes its own repetition, but it is now a repetition that is designed to explore. The prevalent difference between the child's behavior at this stage and his behavior in earlier stages is summarized by Flavell (1963); prior to the fifth stage the child behaved simply to behave; he now behaves specifically to discover what the effects of his behavior will be. He has actively begun to explore his environment.

Substage 6: 18 to 24 Months

Some psychologists (for example, Stone and Church, 1968) do not include this final stage of sensorimotor development in the period of infancy, but assign it instead to the next stage—a stage that is sometimes called **toddlerhood**, both to distinguish it from childhood and infancy, and to emphasize the transitory nature of many of the child's developing abilities. It is appropriate, then, to view this sixth substage as a transition between the motoric intelligence of the first period and the progressively cognitive intelligence of the second. During this stage the child begins to represent objects and events mentally and combines these representations to arrive at *mental* solutions for problems. That is, the child is now capable of anticipating the consequences of some of his activities prior to his actually executing them. His behavior is consequently no longer restricted to trial and error as it was previously.

The ability to conceptualize the environment is reflected in the infant's mushrooming language development, which, according to Piaget, is greatly facilitated by his imitative behavior. During the early stages of imitation, the child is capable of imitating objects, activities, or people that are immediately present. This is clearly related to the difficulty the infant has in separating the objects he perceives from his perception of them and his consequent failure to realize that objects continue to exist independent of him. His eventual achievement of object permanence is inferred from what Piaget labels **deferred imitation**—the ability to imitate something or someone who is no longer present. When a 2-year-old child dresses up in her mother's shoes and struts in front of a mirror in the absence of her mother, she is practicing deferred imitation. This behavior is significant because in order to imitate a person who is absent the child must be able to represent that person mentally; similarly, to associate a name with an object not immediately present necessitates representing the object mentally. Accordingly, it is not surprising to find the child using words relating mainly to the here and now in the early stages of speech development (Landreth, 1967); it is not until near the end of his second year that the referents for his words become more remote than his immediate perception.

It is important to note that when Piaget speaks of the internal representation of an object he is referring to the internalization or conceptualization of activities related to the object. When an object is internalized or becomes part of one's cognitive structure, those activities directly associated with the real object comprise the individual's representation of the object. Bruner (1966) terms this **enactive representation**. The child's understanding of objects corresponds to the activities he performs with them. Three-year-olds typically define objects in terms of their function:

they are "to do something." A *ball* is to play with, a *bicycle* is to ride, and a *hole* is to dig.

The Child at Two

Near the end of Chapter 9, we paused to assert that it is the *whole infant* with whom we are concerned, but that we must consider the various layers of the organism before being capable of painting the whole picture. We have now examined two additional layers and are as ready to complete the picture as we are likely to be in this text.

What do we know of the hypothetical 2-year-old? Imagine him, if you will. He is a small person weighing 27 pounds and standing 34 inches. He can walk and run, but if he isn't careful and tries to turn too suddenly, he may fall. Fortunately, he is still very close to the ground and falling is of little consequence to him. His perceptual equipment is almost as good as yours or mine: he can hear, see, touch, taste, smell, sense hot and cold, and respond to cues regarding his equilibrium. His vocabulary has over 250 words in it and he uses these in all manner of combinations, primarily to communicate his perception of things that are occurring right here and now, frequently to demand things, and occasionally to express his feelings.

The 2-year-old child knows his father and his mother as well as most other significant people in his life; he reacts with serious apprehension when separated from them. He has his favorite toys, his favorite occupations and preoccupations, his favorite foods, and his favorite friends. In short, he has begun to develop an individualistic personality reflected in his likes and dislikes, and in his own distinct way of doing things. He is no longer the average child whom we continually allude to; the 2-year-old is becoming *himself*. Eventually he will be an adult. Will he still be the same *self*? It is a question worth considering.

Summary

Chapter 10 opened with one of Sam's poems, in order to convey some feel for the power of language—"dripping limpid languid liquid through the amber anvil." Also to emphasize what a powerful instrument language is, it invited you to consider a piece of ice. From there it examined communication and noted that, while language was not entirely necessary for communication, it does make possible a much wider, more precise, and infinitely more variable mode of expression. The chapter wondered next about the development of language in the child—a practical question given the importance of language and the fact that the child is initially quite incapable of either understanding language or of speaking it. To examine the development of language we isolated its various elements and mentioned the order in which the child acquired these elements, beginning with the unsystematic and erratic babbling of phonemes during the prespeech stage, progressing to the more systematic babbling of the second half of the first year, and culminating in the utterance of the morpheme, the word, the sentence, the paragraph, the chapter, and the book. In the end, we had done little more than discover that the child discovers or invents the rules of grammar for himself—a truly amazing, yet unexplained, phenomenon, although Chomsky's LAD theory offers a tentative explanation. From a discussion of the infant's language, the chapter finally turned to the infant's mind and traced, through the stages described by Jean Piaget, the evolution of his primitive understanding of reality and his increasing sophistication in his commerce with the environment. We concluded with an unfinished painting of the 2-year-old child. We shall continue to follow the child as he develops, but we are always a little behind him, for we do not understand everything he teaches us as he travels from conception to adulthood.

1. It is still black on the edge black like the smell of nell eating wild asparagus because they feel like pink saffron and smell like liquid limpids.   **Main Points**

2. The Whorfian hypothesis assumes that language not only permits the transmission of thought, but that it is largely responsible for determining the substance of that thought.

3. Bernstein described striking differences between the language of children whose parents are lower class and those whose parents are middle or upper class. Lower-class children use restricted language codes, whose forms are characterized by their brevity, the incompleteness of the sentences, the imprecise quality of the vocabulary, and the preponderance of idiom and colloquialism. The language of upper-class children tends to be more elaborate.

4. Language is not necessary for communication, as evidenced by the behavior of many animals. It helps quite a lot, however.

5. A child says his first word somewhere between 9 and 15 months of age — some sooner, some later. By the age of 2, the average vocabulary is close to 300 words. By the age of 6 it is closer to 3,000 words.

It is still black on the edge black like the smell of nell eating wild asparagus because they feel like pink saffron and smell like liquid limpids.

6. The child's early babbling is usually unsystematic. After the age of 6 months, however, there is more controlled repetition. By the age of 1 year, the amount of babbling declines rapidly and soon disappears altogether.

7. Researchers theorize that each child reinvents the grammar (syntax) of his language as he learns it. Although it is not known how he does this, Chomsky suggests that LAD (Language Acquisition Device) is involved. LAD is a pre-wired part of the brain that corresponds to grammar.

8. The dolphin may be more intelligent than man.

9. Piaget describes the intellectual development of the sensorimotor child (from birth to 2 years) in six substages, each of which is identified by the child's characteristic way of reacting to the world and his understanding of reality.

10. There is little learning in the first substage (0 to 1 month), but the child engages in a great deal of practice of those inherent responses with which he was born.

11. Substage 2 (1 to 4 months) comprises the learning of new activities through a series of accommodations, taking the form of primary circular reactions centering on the child's body.

12. In the third stage (4 to 8 months), the child begins to acquire a new repertoire of behaviors through the formation of circular reactions involving the environment rather than his own body (secondary circular reactions).

13. Not until the fourth stage (8 to 12 months) does the infant begin to coordinate the various activities that he has been practicing. This coordination of schemes allows him to employ activities intentionally to attain goals.

14. The fifth stage (tertiary circular reactions, 12 to 18 months) sees the child actively exploring his environment by modifying his sequential behaviors so that he may observe their effects on the environment.

15. Substage 6 (18 to 24 months) is a transition between the motoric and perceptual intelligence of the preceding stages and the more cognitive intelligence of the succeeding stage. Here the child begins to show evidence, both in his language and in his behavior, of an ability to conceptualize the environment.

Further Readings   The following two articles by Bernstein highlight the importance of language for learning and the close relationship that exists between social class and language sophistication.

Bernstein, B. Social class and linguistic development: A theory of social learning. *British Journal of Sociology,* 1958, **9,** 159–174.

Bernstein, B. Language and social class. *British Journal of Sociology,* 1961, **11,** 271–276.

Those interested in language development — particularly the development of syntax — are referred to the following two sources:

Chomsky, N. *Syntactic structures.* The Hague: Mouton, 1957.

Chomsky, N. *Aspects of the theory of syntax.* Cambridge, Mass.: M.I.T. Press, 1965.

The best single source of Piaget's description of the child's early development is the following:

Piaget, J. *Play, dreams, and imitation in childhood.* New York: Norton, 1951.

A somewhat simpler account of Piaget's work is contained in:

Flavell, J. H. *The developmental psychology of Jean Piaget.* Princeton, New
Jersey: D. Van Nostrand, 1963.

Of Cowboys and Indians: Preschool Children

Several years ago a colleague and I read a book that decried the fact that adults had forgotten how to play—really play the way children play, in wild abandon and with no concern for the distinctions that adults are so careful to make between the real and the imaginary. So we decided that we would play and try to recapture some of the magic of childhood in the games we would invent.

It was a lovely summer day—a lovely day for playing in the halls of the staid and respectable institution where we work. "I'm an Indian!" I screamed, and my friend accepted his opposing role immediately. "I'm a cowboy. Look out, you injun!" And so saying he armed himself with one of his weightier textbooks, which had previously contributed to the academic decor of his office, and we ran screeching and screaming down the hallway, around the elevator shaft, up the stairs to the next floor, whooping down that corridor, screeching through another set of stairs, and back to our own floor. Just as I was about to disappear into the safety of my office the cowboy appeared around the corner! "Bang! Bang! Bang! Ra ta ta ta ta ta ta ta . . . I got you, you injun!" What could I do? I fell screaming and moaning to the floor; but before I expired completely I managed to raise myself on one knee, pull an arrow back to its very tip, and let fly at my assailant. It was a good shot. He fell to his knees immediately, clutching desperately at the shaft of the arrow, which was deeply embedded in his most vital parts, grunting and groaning all the while in sheer agony. Eventually we both quieted, as our last breaths rattled noisily in our throats. We died almost simultaneously, with a few spasmodic jerks, the shuffling of my mocassins on the floor accompanying the rattling of his boots.

As the game ended, we became aware of various pairs of academic eyes peering around doorways and, as surreptitiously as possible, we retreated to our offices. That afternoon we tried again, still unwilling to go back to being supposedly mature university professors. Wandering about one of the few remaining lawns outside our building, we discovered some earthworms under a freshly planted shrub. We gathered a handful of the little beasts and carried them into the same hallowed hallway we had employed in the morning's game. It would be a race: each of us selected our fastest worm and moved him up to a line I had drawn on the floor. Then we lay on our stomachs, noses close to our worms, urging the beasts on. "Come on, Ed! Come on, Ed!" I pleaded (my worm was named after one of my colleagues). My opponent called his Ignatz, and his verbal supplications were phrased accordingly: "Go, Ignatz baby! Go, baby, go!"

Needless to say, we soon attracted a small crowd of people who were well prepared to wonder aloud at our strange behavior. (University professors have very large vocabularies.) But we gave them no satisfaction, for a child does not respond to the question "Why are you playing?" He may as well be asked "Why do you live?" Although we were not children, we did not deign to respond except to say, "I have an extra racer (for these were racers and not simply worms); you can have it if you want to play with us." Have you ever seen a middle-aged professorial spinster lying on her belly, nose to a worm's tail, excitedly urging the little beast on to victory? We did not see it either. Indeed our game ended shortly, spectatorless, for our audience had left. Some probably thought we were trying to make fools of them, though I'm not sure how. Others left more convinced than ever that we were both demented. And we ourselves abandoned our play, for we were no longer children. But perhaps for a brief moment we gained a small insight into how it feels to be a child—a rare insight for the troubled age of adulthood. Perhaps you could play like a child for a day, or even for an hour, and then return to this chapter, for here we will talk in more detail of childhood games and other things that fill the busy space between the ages of 2 and 6.

Between Two and Six

The subject of this chapter is the process of development from the age of two to six. In this case, the "layers" of the child under discussion will be the general physical characteristics, changes in motor development, the course of social development particularly as it is reflected in play behavior, morality, and the further elaboration of language, and the child's intellectual development as summarized by Jean Piaget. The chapter concludes by describing and evaluating several forms of preschool education.

A comparison of the 6-year-old with the 2-year-old provides some idea of the developmental process during these years. The magnitude of

Have you ever seen a professorial spinster lying on her belly . . . ?

the difference is phenomenal, although the changes that occurred from birth to the end of the child's second year are probably even more striking. The first observation that one can make about the process of development during childhood is that it is generally characterized by a marked slowing of development. For example, the rate of weight gain for the average child is greater during his first year than it is each year between the ages of 2 and 5.

The 2-year-old has been described as a dynamic 27 pounds of child that can be stretched to a height of slightly under 3 feet. His vocabulary is approximately 250 words, which he uses in a wide variety of two-word sentences. He characteristically employs several of these words more often than others; these are his pivot words. He might say, for example, "I happy," "Mommy happy," "Daddy happy," "puppy happy," and "Gramma not," pivoting on the word "happy." He knows his mother and father and the other significant faces in his life and has strong emotional ties with these people.

The 2-year-old has just begun the transition from an activity-oriented intelligence to the more symbolic thinking processes of the adult. This transition is greatly facilitated by the language that he continues to master during the next 4 years of his life. He is, then, a little person, capable of love, anger, sorrow, joy, excitement. He can feel pleased with himself, and he can become annoyed. His attention span is still relatively short, but is much increased from his first few months of life. He can understand many spoken directions and is therefore a much better subject for psychological investigation.

The 6-year-old, on the other hand, has grown another foot and stands approximately 46 inches, weighing about 48 pounds. His vocabulary is probably more than 2,500 words, and he can speak with amazing fluency and facility, having mastered the syntax of the language. He has long since abandoned the primitive and illogical view of the world that characterized the sensorimotor child and has begun to solve relatively difficult problems of classification and reasoning, frequently through intuitive processes, but often correctly nevertheless. Despite these advances, he remains incapable of completely logical thought and is forever making judgmental errors. When perception conflicts with reason he almost invariably relies on his perception, not even aware of the conflict. He contradicts himself time and again and steadfastly refuses to admit or even to realize that he has actually contradicted himself.

In the Freudian view, the 6-year-old child has successfully (if he is normal) survived the troubled period of the phallic phase of psychosexual development. He has progressed from the anal preoccupations of the 2-year-old to the phallic preoccupations of the 4-year-old, and in the process has fallen in and out of love with his mother and has overcome the latent hatred for his father that accompanied his earlier love for mama. In short, the 6-year-old stands ready to make two important and dramatic transitions, both of which are rooted in the experiences and the development that transpired in the first 6 years of his life, and both of which will lead to new changes and adjustments later. The first transition, according to Piaget, is from the prelogic of the preschool child to the more adult reasoning of the school-aged child. The second change, based on a Freudian view of the child, involves the transition from preoccupation with resolving the phallic conflicts and complexes to the period of sexual latency—a period marked by the absence of a definite sexual object.

In this chapter we examine the child's transition from the beginning to the end of the preschool period, which Piaget labels *preoperational* and Freud labels *phallic*.

Physical and Motor Development

Physical Development

Table 11.1 traces the physical development of boys and girls from the age of 2 to 6. Comparing these data with Table 9.3 reveals a dramatic deceleration in growth rates after the period of infancy, particularly in height. Although the growth rate between the second and the fourth year declines, there is an increase in the rate of absolute weight gained between the fourth and the sixth year. However, the increase in weight gain is slight and does not significantly alter the general pattern of decelerated growth.

Different growth rates for different parts of the body help explain some of the changes that occur between the ages of 2 and 6. The thick layers of baby fat that give the one-year-old child his distinctive babyish appearance and endear him to his grandmother begin to disappear slowly during the second year of life and continue to recede gradually. In effect, these tissues grow much more slowly than other tissues, so that by the time the child has reached the age of 6 his layers of fat are less than half as thick as they were at the age of one year. Partly because of this change he begins to look more like an adult.

Other changes as well account for the gradual transition from the appearance of infancy to the appearance of young boyhood or girlhood.

Table 11.1 Height (in inches) and Weight (in pounds) at the Fiftieth Percentile for American Children*

Age	Height		Weight	
	Girl	Boy	Girl	Boy
2 years	34	$34\frac{1}{2}$	27	$27\frac{3}{4}$
$2\frac{1}{2}$ years	36	$36\frac{1}{4}$	$29\frac{1}{2}$	30
3 years	$37\frac{3}{4}$	38	$31\frac{3}{4}$	$32\frac{1}{4}$
$3\frac{1}{2}$ years	$39\frac{1}{4}$	$39\frac{1}{4}$	34	$34\frac{1}{4}$
4 years	$40\frac{1}{2}$	$40\frac{3}{4}$	$36\frac{1}{4}$	$36\frac{1}{2}$
$4\frac{1}{2}$ years	42	42	$38\frac{1}{2}$	$38\frac{1}{2}$
5 years	43	$43\frac{1}{4}$	41	$41\frac{1}{2}$
$5\frac{1}{2}$ years	$44\frac{1}{2}$	45	44	$45\frac{1}{2}$
6 years	$45\frac{1}{2}$	$46\frac{1}{4}$	$46\frac{1}{2}$	$48\frac{1}{4}$

*Adapted by the Health Department, Milwaukee, Wisconsin; based on data by H. C. Stuart and H. V. Meredith, prepared for use in Children's Medical Centre, Boston. Used by permission of the Milwaukee Health Department.

Not only does the relative amount of fatty tissue alter during the pre-school years, but its distribution also changes as a result of the more rapid growth of bone and muscle. The infant's squat appearance is explained by the fact that his waist is at least as large as his hips or his chest. The 6-year-old child, on the other hand, has begun to develop a waist that is smaller in girth than his shoulders and hips. This becomes even more evident in early adolescence than at the termination of the preschool period.

The girth of the infant is also due in part to the relative size of the internal organs, many of which grow at a much more rapid rate than other parts of the body, while all must be accommodated in the space between the child's pelvis and his diaphragm. As a result his abdomen protrudes. As he grows in height during the preschool years his abdomen gradually becomes more like that of the few adults who have not been claimed by the obesity characteristic of our soft and bloated living.

Figure 9.3 portrays other changes in body proportions that account for the different appearance of the 6-year-old, such as the ratio of head to body size. It was shown that the head of the 2-month fetus is approximately half the length of the entire body—that is, it is equal in length to the length of the remaining part of the organism. At birth the head is closer to one-fourth the size of the rest of the body. By the age of 6 it is close to one-eighth the size, which is a short step removed from the head-to-body relationship typical of the normal adult with a normal-sized head —one-tenth. From the age of 2 to 6 the head changes from approximately one-fifth to one-eighth size—a significant enough change to be noticeable. Because of this change and because of changes in the distribution of fat and in the space that the child now has for his internal organs, the 6-year-old looks remarkably like an adult; when he was 2 he looked more like a typical baby.

The infant's most significant motor achievement is learning to walk. At the same time that he learns to walk he also learns to coordinate other motor activities which he has been practicing, so that by the age of 2 he is remarkably adept at picking up objects, stacking blocks, at unlacing shoes, and a host of other motor activities that are more or less pleasing for mothers. The close relationship between development and coordination of motor activities and the child's cognitive development during infancy is explicit in the theories of Jean Piaget. Indeed the infant's early cognitive structure is comprised of the internalized aspects of behavior and their external manifestations, since the child is still incapable of separating action from thought. Prior to this period the child's cognitive structure results directly from his overt physical activity; that is, thought is internalized action. Hence the close alliance between activity and early intellectual development.

The course of motor development during infancy is described by the sequential acquisition of abilities such as those involved in locomotion and in grasping. The child continues to make progress in motor develop-

Motor Development

ment during the preschool period, his locomotion becoming more certain as he loses the characteristic wide-footed stance of the toddler (from 18 months to $2\frac{1}{2}$ years). As his equilibrium stabilizes and his feet move closer together, his arms and hands also move closer to his body. Thus, he loses both the wide stance and the appearance of a tightrope walker, resulting from an attempt to maintain a precarious balance with both arms and feet. As his walking improves he acquires the ability to climb stairs standing upright and completely unassisted, and eventually to hop with two feet and to skip.

Gesell (1925) provides norms for motor behavior between the ages of 2 and 5, which are additional evidence of increased perceptual-motor coordination. He reports that the 3-year-old is capable of copying either a circle or a horizontal line, both of which are ordinarily impossible for a 2-year-old child. In contrast the 4-year-old has acquired the ability to copy a cross, which is a much more difficult figure. In addition he can trace a diamond and he is capable of buttoning his own clothes. The 5-year-old is also capable of all of these skills, but in addition he can copy a triangle or a prism, and he is capable of lacing (or unlacing) shoes.

Additional corroboration of Gesell's findings is provided by Cratty (1970), who employed a sample of 170 middle-class children in an attempt to determine the order of difficulty in copying various geometric designs. His sample did not include subjects younger than 4 years, so that the age comparison must begin from there. Cratty found that children could not trace a triangle until the age of 6, but that rectangles, circles, and squares could be copied correctly before 6. He also found that the diamond was considerably more difficult than other forms, and that few subjects could copy it correctly prior to the age of 7. Cratty reports a study conducted by Ilg and Ames (1965), which found that the order of difficulty for figures, beginning with the easiest, is the circle, the square, the triangle, the cross, the divided rectangle (a rectangle with diagonals and vertical and horizontal bisecting lines drawn in), and the diamond. Ilg and Ames indicate that 3-year-olds can copy a circle, just as Gesell reported. However, whereas Gesell reported that a 4-year-old could copy a cross, Ilg and Ames found that a cross could only be drawn correctly by $6\frac{1}{2}$-year-olds. Like Gesell, though, they report that the diamond and the divided rectangle could not be copied correctly before the age of 8 or 9. All these figures can be copied in almost recognizable fashion considerably earlier, however, probably accounting for the minor contradictions among the findings of Cratty, Ilg and Ames, and Gesell.

The most striking observation is that the order of difficulty for these geometric designs is virtually the same for every reported study. Since there appears to be some correlation between the level of motor development and general intellectual development, evident in the correlation between performance tests of mental ability and more verbal intelligence tests, a variety of measures of intelligence use these geometric forms. The Revised Stanford-Binet, for example, asks subjects at the ages of 5, 7, and 10 to draw a square, a diamond, and a more complex design (Terman and Merrill, 1960).

Obviously the child's physical and motor development are closely related, since the acquisition of many skills is dependent on development of the required musculature and on control of these muscles. The relationship of physical development to other areas of development is sometimes not as obvious, although no less real. For example, a child's play, particularly when it involves peers, is often influenced by his motor skills, since various aptitudes are called for in various games. A child who is still incapable of jumping with both feet is not likely to be invited by older children to join in a game of jump rope; a child who cannot grasp marbles skilfully may find himself left out of the traditional spring marble games. Conversely, the child who is precocious in physical and motor development is likely to be the first one asked to participate in games; indeed, he may be the one to initiate them. It is quite clear, then, that physical and motor development may have an influence on the general social development of the child, since game playing is one means of socialization. And the opportunities for interaction with other children provided by the games of the latter preschool period are largely responsible, according to Piaget (1951), for the progressive socialization of thought—a phenomenon that is examined in more detail in the next section of this chapter.

Social Development

As it is employed in this text the term *social development* has rather wide connotations. It consists of all the behavior of a child that involves interaction with others and therefore includes such topics as games, morality, and language learning. Clearly there are aspects of each of these that are unrelated to social development, just as there are areas of intellectual or physical development that are also related to socialization. Therefore the selection of topics considered in this section is somewhat, but not entirely, arbitrary since the focus of the discussion will be on the contribution that each form of interaction makes to the socialization of the child.

Play

The games that children **play**, unlike the games that adults play, are fun games. They are not designed to impress, to persuade, to deceive, or to annoy; they are played for the playing. And that, in a nutshell, is the difference between work and play: play is designed for no end but its own enjoyment. **Work**, on the other hand, may consist of exactly the same activities as play, but it is engaged in not for the sake of pleasure, but for what may be gained as a result. A game is not necessarily play; and work is not necessarily work; but play is indeed play.

If the preceding paragraph confuses you, do not yet despair. I am playing—that is, I am writing simply for the enjoyment, although it looks like work to my neighbors who prefer to stay at home in the evenings and fight with their wives or watch television. It is in this sense that work is not necessarily work. Still it is difficult to arrive at an acceptable distinction between work and play since there are many pleasurable activities that lead to productive ends other than simple enjoyment; at the same time numerous activities that apparently have no purpose are also not enjoyable. We frequently play cards in affable, neighborhood groups, although most of us abhor the very thought of this activity. It is a game, but play it isn't. Adults are often confused about work and play — only children aren't, for almost all they do is play.

If you persist in asking what importance play has, the psychologist must answer that since everything that the child does is play, then play must be important for almost every aspect of the child's development. To accept this at the outset will prevent my making a lengthy series of platitudinous statements similar to those frequently found in textbooks of child development with section headings like *The Importance of Play for Learning; The Importance of Play for Motivation; The Importance of Play for Adjustment; The Importance of Play for Mental Health; and The Importance of Play for Bingo.* Having accepted that play is a fundamental and necessary part of the child's activities, we move directly to an examination of a child's play.

There are three general categories of play: sensorimotor, social, and imaginative.

Sensorimotor play involves the manipulation of objects or the performance of activities simply for the sensations that are involved. This type of play is engaged in most frequently by infants, for it is the only type of play of which they are capable during the early stages of development, when they have not yet achieved the internalization of activity, as is necessary for other forms of play. Sensorimotor play may consist of motor activities such as creeping, crawling, walking, running, skipping, hopping, waving a hand, waving a foot or any other part of the anatomy that is wavable. It also includes manipulating objects, people, parts of one's own anatomy, or anything else that is manipulable. It is evident in countless solitary games of young children, such as moving the hand along the steep precipice of the table edge and roaring "rrrrrrrrr," deep in the throat, in the manner of a well-tuned motorcycle; running around a room with arms spread wide, sputtering like a badly tuned airplane "ahrahrahrahrahr," or jumping up and down on the davenport repeating rhythmically "upupupupupupup. . . ." But these last activities are not simply sensorimotor; they can also be described as **imaginative play**.

Imaginative play includes the multitude of make-believe games that become so prevalent during the preschool years. Indeed, all play in which either the activity or the persons involved in the activity are interpreted to be something other than what they really are may be classified as imaginative play. Thus, the child who runs about the room frightening his grandmother with the sound of his airplane motor is not only engaging in a sensorimotor game, but one that is imaginative as well — he is no longer himself, he is an airplane. And his voice is no longer a voice, but the roar of an incredibly powerful airplane engine. The worn carpet has been transformed into fluffy clouds and the bread crumbs on it are tiny houses and people far below our heroic aviator.

For the child, the world of make-believe is almost real. It is so close and so easily accessible; all he need do is pretend. Unhappily it is an art that is lost somewhere during the process of becoming an adult; an art that is sadly lacking among adults who pride themselves on a hard-nosed awareness of what is real and what is imaginary—we who have a troubling fear of one day mistaking the imaginary for the real. The fear is well founded, for an adult who mistakes the imaginary for the real soon finds himself incarcerated in an institution which we euphemistically call a mental hospital, or even more euphemistically, an institution. Indeed, those institutions are filled with people who cannot distinguish between the world in their minds and the world on the other side of their senses. That, by adult definition, is madness. But the child who runs about screaming like a mad banshee, transforming his world into the dense and terrifying jungles of an equatorial coast to be prowled in search of enemies, is not insane. He is simply a child.

The child's imaginative play includes a variety of related activities. There is play in which the child imagines that he is someone or something else: Batman, a dog, or a whale. There are related games in which he imagines that the activities he undertakes are something other than what they really are, or that the objects with which he plays are something different (as illustrated by the airplane).

There is a fourth type of imaginative play that becomes increasingly prevalent as the preschooler ages: daydreaming. Unlike the first two types of imaginative play in which the child actively engages in his fantasy, daydreaming simply involves the imagining without the activity. Greenacre (1959) reports that daydreaming becomes more prevalent when the child reaches school age. Prior to that time his activity-oriented behavior did not lend itself to unlimited daydreaming.

Hurlock (1964) draws attention to the possibly deleterious effects of daydreaming, claiming that the child who daydreams excessively suffers physically from the resulting inactivity and also suffers psychologically from an eventual overreliance on his daydreams to romanticize a self with which he is otherwise unhappy. Yet Hurlock cautions that the child who does not daydream not only deprives himself of considerable pleasure, but also lacks the imagination to conceive of himself in a more desirable role.

Despite the possible detrimental effects of excessive daydreaming, it is nonetheless true that all normal children do daydream, and not to do so may be indicative of serious disorders. Nor is there any substantial evidence to suggest that parents or teachers should monitor the activities of their children to ensure that they engage in an optimal amount of daydreaming combined with a healthy amount of physical activity, together with a healthy amount of social interaction. The evidence that we have is simply descriptive, not prescriptive.

Social play, the third type of children's play, involves interaction between two or more children and frequently takes the form of games with rather precisely defined rules, which may or may not be followed by the players, depending largely on their understanding and their level of development. Although children may play together prior to the preschool period, the nature of their games is frequently described as "parallel" rather than truly social (Parten, 1932; Piaget, 1932); that is, children play side by side but do not interact, do not share the activities involved in the game, and do not employ any mutually accepted rules. Parallel play is nevertheless social play of a primitive sort, since it involves two or more children who apparently prefer to play together, even though they don't yet interact. This is a transitional period between the solitary play of early infancy and the cooperative play of the later preschool period.

In a detailed investigation of the development of play and games in children, Piaget (1932) arrived at a classification of games by the *structures* that underlie them. This classification includes the *practice* game, games that use *symbols,* and games that have *rules.* In effect the first type is the sensorimotor game to which we referred earlier; the second is the imaginative play of children; the third is the social game. Interestingly these develop sequentially as well, beginning with the simplest and culminating with the most complex. Practice games, for example, are engaged in by animals and young infants (Piaget suggests a kitten batting a ball around and chasing it); symbolic games do not develop until the final substage of sensorimotor development, for they require imagination, and the ability to symbolize emerges during this stage; rule-regulated games begin to appear between the ages of 4 and 7 but do not become common until after the age of 7.

Morality

There is a close logical relationship between playing games that have rules and the development of **morality**. Indeed Piaget's investigation of morality in the child began with an examination of his progressive understanding of the rules of games, since morality may be defined as the internalization of rules. Whereas the regulations that govern game playing relate specifically to each game, the rules of morality govern life, and that too may be considered a game—not play, but a game nevertheless.

The child's understanding of the rules of games follows two frequently contradictory paths: his verbalized belief about the nature of rules, their origins, and their permanence; and his understanding of rules as reflected by his actual behavior. Piaget (1932) reports that the actual play behavior of children reveals an initial stage during which there is no adherence to rules (approximately until age 3). This stage is followed by an intermediate period during which the child imitates rules but does not really understand them and consequently changes them to conform to his interpretation of the game (ages 3 to 5). By the time the child is 7 or 8 years old he has begun to play in a genuinely social manner, with rules that are mutually accepted by all players and that are rigidly adhered to. Not until the age of 11 or 12 is the true nature of rules understood— when the child realizes that rules exist to make games possible and that they can be altered by mutual agreement.

Parallel to the child's demonstrated understanding of rules is his verbalization of this understanding. Piaget (1932) questioned a number of children about the origins of rules and about their characteristics. Their responses (or lack of responses) suggested the existence of three stages. The first lasts until the age of 3 and is characterized by no understanding of rules, which is reflected in the child's actual behavior as well. This initial stage is followed by a longer period during which the child believes that rules emanate from some external source (such as God); rules are timeless and immutable, and above all, children should not take it upon themselves to change them. This stage corresponds to the period in the child's life when his actual behavior in games is characterized by constantly changing rules. During the next stage of his actual games behavior he does not change rules, but gradually comes to accept that rules are made by people and that they can be changed by the players if they so wish. Note the clear contradiction between the child's beliefs and his overt behavior. It is a contradiction that has been noted elsewhere as well. Hartshorne and May (1928, 1929, 1930), for example, studied cheating in adolescents to discover the relationship between their understanding of moral rules and their behavior and arrived at the somewhat surprising conclusion that the probability of cheating or not cheating is more affected by the likelihood of being caught than by any convictions that the child may have about the relative evil of the act (see Chapter 12).

Piaget's observations concerning stages in the child's development of morality are derived partly from observing the manner in which children internalize rules of the games they play. In addition, he investigated children's notions of evil by telling them stories and asking them to make judgments about the goodness or evil of the characters. He employed a similar technique to investigate children's understandings of the nature of lies. For example, Piaget (1932) told a story of a child who accidentally breaks 15 cups, asking the subject to compare his behavior to that of a child who deliberately breaks a single cup. From the children's responses to these stories Piaget reached the general conclusion that there are two broad stages in the evolution of beliefs about culpability. In the first, lasting until about 9 or 10 years of age, the child judges guilt by the objective consequences of the act: the child who has broken the largest number of cups, or who has stolen the greatest quantity of goods or the largest amount of money, is invariably considered more evil than the one who deliberately broke only one cup, stole just a few things or just a little money. Following this stage the child's judgment becomes more adultlike—he is more likely to consider the motives behind the act than the quantitative attributes of the transgression.

As a brief aside, the moral judgment of adults frequently demonstrates the same characteristics as the child's earlier conception of guilt. My son knows quite clearly, as I discovered last night, that if he drops a plate covered with great heaps of messy food face down on the floor he is more likely to be reprimanded than if he drops the same plate when it is empty, regardless of the fact that in both cases the act was apparently accidental. Adults frequently judge the transgressor's moral culpability by the absolute magnitude of the act; in contradiction, the person who commits a very large infraction is sometimes more admired than one who commits petty crimes. Witness the social hierarchy in a prison: near the top of this structure is the embezzler who has stolen a million dollars; the petty thief is closer to the bottom rung.

Kohlberg (1969) has conducted extensive investigations of the moral development of children, and his findings generally support Piaget's less systematic, less detailed, and less rigorous observations. Both describe the evolution of morality as progressing from a simple, **egocentric**, highly unstable stage to a period of mutual cooperation, and finally to a stage in which the legal aspects of rules come to be understood more clearly and are conformed to with religious devotion. Kohlberg's work is discussed in more detail in Chapter 12.

In addition to these investigations of the child's development of morality, there are numerous theoretical accounts of moral development. It is generally accepted that the rules of conscience that define morality are learned. It is not surprising, then, that learning models are sometimes used to explain the acquisition of these rules. For example, Bandura and Walters (1963) deal with the development of morally linked personality characteristics such as aggression and sex-appropriate behavior. Their explanation for moral development is based on the observed effects of imitation; that is, it is assumed that a child learns what is right and wrong, not only through reinforcement or punishment for his behavior, but also through observation of models whom he assumes are behaving in appropriate or inappropriate manners, or of seeing models rewarded or punished for their behavior.

Freud posits an alternate explanation for moral development based on his belief that the Superego is the agent of morality in that it embodies all societal and religious constraints and restrictions imposed on the individual's behavior. Recall (Chapter 7) that the Superego develops primarily as a result of identification with one's parents. Identification is assumed to occur after the resolution of the phallic phase complexes when the child abandons his previous competition with the like-sexed parent for the sexual favors of the opposite-sexed parent. The process of identification involves more than simple imitation; it includes a subconscious attempt to assume the personality, the values, the beliefs, the goals, and the aspirations of the person identified with. The child who identifies with his parent strives to become like him, and in so doing he assumes his parent's beliefs about right and wrong. Thus he develops the Superego, the level of his personality that is in constant conflict with the more primitive and instinctual desires embodied in the Id. The Superego defines his morality.

But the preschool child obviously does not develop morality and play behavior in isolation from all other aspects of his development. We have already traced the physical and motor development characteristic of this period, both of which are closely involved with his social development. Another area of progress intimately concerned with the child's social and intellectual development is language.

Language

We surveyed the steps of language development in Chapter 10. It is also important to consider the role of language in the intellectual development of the preschool child. Language enables children to move from prelogical and perception-dominated thinking to more adult and more logical thought processes. Three studies discussed below define the specific part played by language in the preschool child's intellectual development.

My grandmother was amazingly gifted when it came to identifying cows. She knew all her cows (and their genealogy) as well as the neighbors' cows, but she was completely incapable of learning to distinguish among the various pigs that roamed about the place. Indeed, she couldn't even tell the difference between her pigs and pigs that belonged to other farmers, a shortcoming that occasionally got her into difficulty with the farmers' wives. As you must well know, cows come in a greater variety of sizes, shapes and conformations than do pigs. Furthermore, they frequently sport a great many colors. Pigs, on the other hand, seem to come in fewer sizes and shapes, and most of them have been endowed with the same uninteresting color. All of this should make it considerably easier to distinguish among cows than among pigs. As it happened, however, most of the cows with whom my grandmother was so familiar were ordinary black cows—and all seemed to me to be almost the same size. On the other hand, there were indeed big pigs, small pigs, black pigs, reddish pigs, spotted pigs, and ordinary tan-colored pigs—add all the possible combinations of size and color and there were a large number of very different-looking pigs. Grandmother suspected that it was because the cows had names that they could be distinguished. How in heaven could one mistake Bessie for Rosie? On the other hand, how could a body be expected to know that the large black boar belonged to Old

My own grandmother was amazingly gifted when it came to identifying cows.

Man Taylor, despite the fact that he was the only one who owned black pigs?

Grandmother was probably right, as Pyles (1932) has demonstrated. She presented 80 children, aged 2 to 7, with three variations of a relatively simple learning task. Each of the variations involved hiding a toy under one of five different objects, and then giving the toy to the subject when he selected the object under which it was hidden. Since the toy was always hidden under the same object there was no great amount of learning necessary. It was simply necessary for the children to learn to differentiate among the five stimulus objects, just as Grandmother had successfully learned to discriminate among a large number of cows (although she had been unsuccessful in learning to distinguish among a smaller number of pigs). The analogy is made even more plausible by the specific experimental variations. In one situation the stimuli were five familiar animal forms, each labeled appropriately by the experimenter. The second variation employed five unnamed and unfamiliar forms (corresponding to the pigs). In the third variation the objects were also unfamiliar but were named (corresponding to the cows, and the names were almost as meaningful as the names of most cows I have known: Mobie, Kolo, Tito, Gamie, and Bokie). The subjects were shown each of the three variations until they chose the correct stimulus object four consecutive times, thus showing evidence of having "learned," or until 25 trials were completed. In every case the examiner drew attention to the name of the chosen object, doing so for each of the first three trials, and for every third trial thereafter. When the animal forms were used the experimenter named them only if the child failed to do so spontaneously.

The results of the experiment support my grandmother's hypothesis (see Figure 11.1), demonstrating clearly that learning was much easier with familiar objects whose names were already well known by the subjects. Also, ascribing names to unfamiliar objects greatly increases the ease with which these can be distinguished one from another. Thus, only 54 percent of the sample successfully solved the unfamiliar-object-no-name condition, whereas 72 percent of the subjects chose the correct stimulus when the objects were given names. Pyles (1932) concludes from this study that verbalization facilitates learning.

Bruner (1966) conducted a similar study concerned more with thinking processes than with discrimination learning. He prefaces his description of the role of language in thought by pointing to the errors that children under 7 or 8 years typically make on problems of conservation hypothesizing that these errors may be due partly to the child's as yet undeveloped system of verbalization, insufficiently powerful to see beyond the misleading perceptual features of the problem. As in the familiar example of the plasticene ball, the preconservation child almost invariably maintains that the amount of plasticene has changed when it is transformed into a snake shape. He assumes that there is now more because the form is longer or wider, or less because it is thinner or flatter. The physical changes in the object result in perceptual changes, which are then reflected in the child's reasoning (Bruner, 1964).

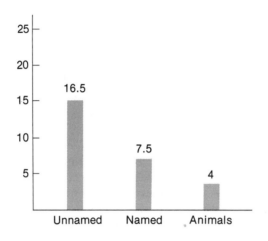

The median number of incorrect trials before choosing the correct stimulus four con-   Figure 11.1
secutive times. The results illustrate that verbalization facilitates learning. (Based on
data provided by Marjorie Pyles Honzik, "Verbalization as a factor in learning," *Child
Development,* **3**, 1932, 108–113. Copyright 1932 by The Society for Research in Child
Development. Used by permission of The Society for Research in Child Development
and the author.)

    To support his interpretation Bruner cites a study of transposition
(Bruner and Kenney, 1966). The experimental equipment consisted of a
tray of nine glasses of three different heights and three different widths,
arranged in three rows of equal heights and three columns of equal di-
ameters (see Figure 11.2). Children between 5 and 7 were required to
perform one of three tasks related to the matrix of glasses: copy the original matrix when all the glasses had been removed; properly replace missing glasses in an otherwise unchanged matrix; or rebuild the matrix with

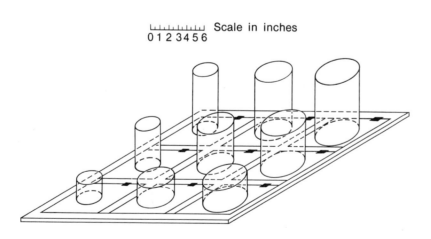

Matrix of glasses employed in the Bruner and Kenney experiment. (From J. S. Bruner,   Figure 11.2
Rose R. Olver, and Patricia M. Greenfield, *Studies in Cognitive Growth.* Copyright
1966 by John Wiley and Sons Inc. Used by permission of John Wiley and Sons, Inc.)

one of the corner elements transposed to the diagonal corner. The children's behavior in the face of the last task is especially relevant to understanding the role of language in thinking.

All subjects were encouraged to verbalize their attempts to carry out the tasks assigned them. In addition, they were asked to describe the array of glasses prior to the experiment. The experimenters observed three classes of verbal description. The first was associated with the youngest subjects and was clearly the least sophisticated. It consisted of what Bruner and Kenney (1966) term *global descriptions* — such terms as "bigger," "smaller," "littler," "gianter." Older children used *dimensional descriptions,* employing words specifically related to one of the dimensions of the glasses. A dimensional description would be "That one is taller but narrower, or even, "shorter and fatter." The third type of verbal description was labeled *confounded* since it included both dimensional and global terms.

The results of the experiment strongly support Bruner's contention that the child's language is closely related to his level of thinking. Children who employed dimensional terms to describe the matrix were more likely to succeed in transposing the matrix correctly than children who employed either global or confounded descriptions (see Figure 11.3).

Both the Bruner and Kenney transposition experiment and the Pyles discrimination learning study indicate the great importance of language in the child's thinking processes. Numerous Russian psychologists (for example: Luria, 1959, 1961; Vygotsky, 1962; Sokolov, 1959) assign even a more central role to language in the developmental process than most American psychologists. Their major contention is that language provides more than a means for representing reality or expressing thoughts — it is the means by which thoughts are formulated, and by which individuals are capable of analysis, synthesis, abstraction, and generaliza-

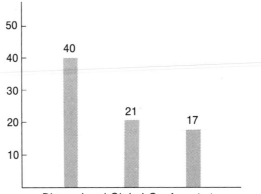

Figure 11.3   Percent of subjects who are successful in transposition using dimensional, global, or confounded descriptions of the matrix. (From J. S. Bruner, Rose R. Olver, and Patricia M. Greenfield, *Studies in Cognitive Growth,* p. 162. Copyright 1966 by John Wiley and Sons, Inc. Used by permission of John Wiley and Sons, Inc.)

tion. In their view language is the raw material for logic (Sokolov, 1959, p. 669).

Luria (1961) reports a number of celebrated Russian experiments on the role of language in the behavior of children. These studies ostensibly demonstrate three developmental stages for the **regulatory function** of speech (an individual's capacity to respond to verbal directions). This function is lacking in children under the age of 2. Luria notes, for example, that if a 2-year-old child is engaged in the process of pulling on one sock and is instructed to take the sock off, he will be incapable of following the instruction. On the other hand, if the child has not begun the act he will respond to directions (if he wishes to). A series of experiments in which children were instructed to squeeze a balloon in response to one of two lights confirmed Luria's hypothesis. The children were told to squeeze when one of the lights went on, and *not* to squeeze when the other light went on. Subjects under the age of 18 months are typically unable to follow the directions and consequently squeeze the balloon in response to both lights. Close to the age of 2 or $2^{1}/_{2}$ the child learns to respond to the instructions. The striking thing about his behavior is that once he has begun to respond he is quite incapable of stopping, even in response to contrary directions. If the child is in the process of squeezing, saying to him "Don't squeeze" often results in an intensification of the squeeze rather than in its cessation. Luria claims that at this age language has an initiatory function, but has not yet developed the inhibitory function that it must also have to be effective for regulating behavior. Later in the preschool period language does acquire the regulatory role. At this point both overt and covert speech (thought) play an important part in initiating, directing, and inhibiting behavior.

The average Piaget child is a verbal child. In describing the normal course of development Piaget assumes that intellectual development can be described as the child's progressive adaptation to his environment. This adaptation is effected through assimilation and accommodation and reflected in a series of developmental stages. Each stage is qualitatively different from its preceding and following stages, and each can be described either in terms of the major acquisitions of that period, or in terms of the child's most salient features during the stage. Recall that the previous chapter described the infant's intellecutal development as *sensorimotor,* denoting the most prevalent feature of the child's interaction with, and understanding of, his world during that stage. The preschooler's intellectual development is called *preoperational* because the child has not yet acquired the logical abilities that characterize later stages of thought involving operations. The first part of the preoperational period is called preconceptual (2 to 4 years); the second substage is called intuitive (4 to 7). The child's thought processes at each of these stages are described below.

Intellectual Development

The major intellectual difference between the sensorimotor child and the preschooler is in the means each has of representing the world and reasoning about it. The infant's intelligence is perceptual and motoric;

Preconceptual Thinking

it uses what Bruner (1964) terms *enactive* and *iconic* modes of representation. Enactive representation involves activity; **iconic representation** involves images, and is more related to perception and more directly internalized. In contrast the developing intelligence of the preschooler increasingly uses **symbolization** – a process greatly aided by his development of language abilities. Whereas images (icons) directly resemble the objects they represent, symbols are arbitrary and more economical. Consider, for example, the difference between the picture of an object and the single word for the same object. If a picture is worth more than 10,000 words, it is probably because an image requires that much more "cognitive space" for storage in the brain.

As the child begins to symbolize and develops the consequent ability to internalize objects and events in his environment, he develops **concepts** – but concepts not as complete and logical as an adult's, and therefore referred to as **preconcepts**. Despite their incompleteness, they are nevertheless sufficient to permit the child to make the simple classifications necessary for identifying some of the objects of the world. Thus, a child recognizes a man because he has a budding concept that tells him that *man* is whatever walks on two legs, has hair, wears pants, and speaks in a gruff voice. By noting their characteristics he can identify dogs, birds, elephants, and houses. What he frequently cannot do, however, is distinguish among different individuals belonging to the same species. Piaget illustrates this with his son, Laurent, who pointed out a snail to his father as they were walking. "Regardez l'escargot," he allegedly said in the polite manner of a Swiss child of the early 1920s. It is not certain what Piaget's reply to this observation was, but he reports that several minutes later they came upon another snail, and the child exclaimed that here again was the same snail. The child's apparent failure to recognize that similar objects can belong to the same class and still be different objects – that is, they can retain an identity of their own – is an example of a preconcept. A related example is the preschooler who steadfastly continues to believe in Santa Claus, even after seeing ten different Santas on the same day. For him they are all *identical* (Lefrancois, 1967).

There are two striking features of the child's reasoning processes during the preconceptual period, subsumed under the imposing headings of **transductive reasoning** and **syncretic reasoning**.

Transductive reasoning makes inferences on the basis of particular instances or on the basis of single attributes of objects. Such reasoning is in contrast to deductive reasoning, which proceeds from general to particular instances, or its converse inductive reasoning, which begins with a number of particular instances and proceeds to a general statement. Reasoning from particular to particular occasionally results in a correct conclusion, but frequently it doesn't. Consider the example:

A flies:
B flies:
therefore *B* is *A*.

Clearly if A is a bird and B is also a bird, then A is a B and vice versa. If A is a plane and B is a bird, the same reasoning process leads to an incorrect conclusion.

There are numerous examples of transductive reasoning in the preschooler's thought processes. My $2\frac{1}{2}$-year-old daughter exclaimed over an animal during a picnic last Sunday, "Kitty, Daddy. There's a kitty! There's a kitty! There's a kitty! Daddy! There's a kitty!" she said, once or twice, until I eventually turned and looked at a lovely and wholly undomesticated skunk. The evidence of transductive reasoning is clear: kitties have fur; that thing has fur; therefore that thing is a kitty.

The preschooler's classification behavior is also marked by his use of *syncretic reasoning* in which he groups disparate objects according to his own limited and frequently changing criteria. For example, a 2-year-old child, who is placed in front of a table bearing a number of objects of different kinds and colors and is asked to group those objects that go together, might proceed something like this: The truck goes with the truck because both are trucks, and this thing goes with them because it is blue and that truck is blue. Here is a ball and here is a marble and they go together, and here is a truck that is red like the ball so it goes with them too.

The period of *intuitive thinking* begins at about 4 and ends at approximately 7. It is labeled *intuitive* because much of the child's thought is based on immediate comprehension, rather than logical, rational processes. He solves many problems correctly, but he does so on the basis of insight rather than on the basis of logic. Piaget refers to a problem in which a child is shown three beads strung on a wire, which is then inserted into a hollow cardboard tube so that he can no longer see them. The beads are blue, red, and yellow. At first the child knows clearly which bead is on top when the tube is held vertically in front of him. Then it is turned a half rotation (180°) and the subject is asked which bead is now at the top. Alternately the tube may be turned a full rotation, $1\frac{1}{2}$ turns, 2 turns, and so on. Piaget found that as long as the subject could continue to *imagine* the position of the beads inside the tube, he could answer correctly. Interestingly the child could not arrive at a rule concerning the relationship between odd and even numbers of turns or half turns and the location of the beads. In other words, the solution to the problem was achieved through intuitive mental images rather than through logical reasoning. | Intuitive Thinking

Intuitive thinking is also characterized by egocentricity, a limited ability to classify, and a marked reliance on perception. Each of these qualities is illustrated below.

The preschooler's limited ability to classify is demonstrated in a classical series of experiments that present the child with a collection of objects made up of two subclasses. The objects may consist of wooden beads of which 15 are brown and 5 are blue; or of 25 flowers of which 19 are roses and 6 are dandelions. The subject is asked what the objects are. "They are wooden beads," he says proudly and intelligently. The experimenter then divides them into the two subclasses, brown beads and blue beads, and asks whether there are more brown beads or more wooden beads. The trick is obvious you say! Not to the child at this stage of development. "There are more brown beads," he answers proudly, but somewhat less intelligently. The answer reflects the child's inability to classify, since breaking a class into subclasses destroys the primary class (in this case, wooden beads) as far as the child is concerned.

An experiment in which a girl doll and a boy doll are placed side by side on a piece of string illustrates the egocentric nature of the preschool child's thought. The experimenter holds the ends of the string in both hands and stands behind a screen which hides the dolls from the child's view. The child is asked to predict which of the dolls will appear first if the experimenter moves the string toward the right. Let us assume that the boy doll appears first. The experimenter then returns the dolls to their original position and repeats the same question, "Which of the dolls will now appear first if they are moved to the same side?" The procedure is repeated several times regardless of whether or not the child answers correctly. A normally intelligent child will answer correctly for every early trial. What happens in later trials is striking and unbelievable for many grandmothers. The child eventually makes the opposite and clearly incorrect prediction! If asked why, one of the more common answers is that it is not fair that the same doll come out first every time; now it is the other doll's turn. The child injects his own values, his own sense of justice, into the experimental situation, thus demonstrating his egocentric thought processes. The term *egocentric* is not derogatory, but simply points out an excessive reliance on the thinker's individual point of view, coupled with an inability to be objective.

Egocentric thought is further demonstrated by the preschooler's inability to imagine what a mountain looks like when seen from the top or bottom, as well as from the side. The child's egocentricity completely pervades his conception of the world by controlling his thought processes throughout the early part of the preschool period.

The preschooler's perception heavily dominates his thinking, as seen in his response to conservation problems. When the child decides that there is more plasticene in the snake than there was in the ball from which the snake was formed he is relying solely on the object's appearance rather than on any conceptual processes that might be more appropriate. In contrast, whenever an adult is faced with a conflict between perception and thought, he is more likely to rely on thought than perception.

The preoperational period is often described by what the child cannot do rather than by his achievements. Instead of terminating with a list of the child's acquisitions during this stage (as was possible after examining the sensorimotor period), the obvious conclusion for this stage takes the form of: the child is still incapable of logical reasoning; his thought is highly egocentric, intuitive, and perception bound; and he has consequently not acquired any of the conservations that he will achieve during the period of concrete operations. Nevertheless he is now far advanced from the sensorimotor intelligence of the 2-year-old. To what extent his capabilities can be influenced by direct intervention is examined in the following section.

All the child's experiences from birth to school age comprise his education. The language he hears, the people who serve as models for his behavior, those who control some of his rewards and punishments, television programs, books, stories, movies, visits to different places, the activities in which he engages — all of these are his teachers. Life is the curriculum; adaptation is the major objective; development becomes the teaching process; and the child is the learner at the center of the process. **Preschool Education**

The most striking feature about the preschooler's environment is its haphazard, unstructured nature; yet the strides he makes from birth to school age are phenomenal. It appears reasonable, then, that if a child can learn as much as he does from teachers as unskilled as parents and from a curriculum as unsystematic and frequently unstimulating as parts of his life, he could certainly learn better from the more organized efforts of people trained in the schooling of young children. Indeed, this reasoning underlies many preschool education programs.

Research comparing children exposed to various preschool programs with children who remained in their homes has not uniformly supported the belief that preschool education enhances cognitive, social, or emotional development. A large number of these studies have shown that after participation in a preschool program, experimental children are superior in one or more ways, but the initial differences cease to exist with the passage of time. These findings need not mean, of course, that preschool education is undesirable; there are a number of plausible explanations for the differences. The first and most obvious is that the programs themselves were not always effective enough. A second explanation is that the instruments employed to gauge the effects of preschool education have not been sufficiently sensitive, have not measured the right things, or have done so inaccurately.

Recent research suggests that perhaps a combination of these two explanations is most valid. For example, measuring instruments have typically been intelligence tests, yet it is generally accepted that relatively lengthy, systematic, detailed, and deliberate intervention is necessary to bring about a significant change in intelligence test scores. More recently a number of studies have measured more specific abilities; for example, the Illinois Test of Psycholinguistic Ability (Kirk and McCarthy, 1961) yields scores for a number of different language abilities.

Another possible explanation for the poor maintenance of preschool gains has not been investigated sufficiently to permit any sound conclusion. Consider the effect of taking a child from a relatively unstimulating environment, exposing him to enriching experiences for a relatively short period of time, and then sending him back to the unstimulating world from which he came. It is entirely possible that if the enrichment activities were continued for a longer period of time, he would continue to show the gains he evidenced earlier. (It would probably be productive to consider also the effect of sending a child to an unstimulating elementary or secondary school environment.)

Interest in the education of the preschool child has recently undergone a tremendous revival. This interest is manifested in nationwide attempts to undo the damage of poverty through such compensatory education programs as Project Head Start of the U.S. Office of Economic Opportunity, as well as in the countless nurseries, kindergartens, Montessori schools, and other projects. A number of these **intervention programs**, together with very tentative assessments of their worth, are discussed below.

Nursery Schools

The **nursery school** is probably the most prevalent form of preschool education, dating back to the early parts of this century. The movement gained impetus during the depression, and received government support during the war to encourage employment of mothers. After the war federal support was withdrawn, and until recently there has been a shortage of qualified nursery school teachers.*

In addition to the obvious responsibility that they assume for the physical well-being of their charges, nursery schools are concerned with both social and intellectual development. Accordingly, nursery school programs usually consist of group activities such as games, dances, singing, listening to stories, coloring, cutting, and whatever else the teacher's ingenuity or the available manuals suggest (for example, Todd and Heffernan, 1970; Read, 1966). Not surprisingly, the beneficial effects of the nursery school experience for children are most obvious in the area of social development. Walsh (1931) observed that nursery school children become more confident, more spontaneous, less inhibited, more independent, more self-reliant, and more interested in their environments than comparable preschoolers who did not attend nursery school.

Early Training Project

The **Early Training Project** (Gray and Klaus, 1965, 1968, 1970) is a research study that dramatically demonstrates the potential benefits of a sustained intervention program for preschool children of impoverished backgrounds. The research made use of four groups of twenty children, each of which was treated somewhat differently. One group was exposed to a carefully prepared program for three summers prior to their enrollment in a regular school. During the winters, the experimenter visited each child's home and attempted to involve the mother and child in tasks similar to those employed during the summer program. An identical procedure was employed with the second group, except that it began one year later and therefore consisted of two summers rather than three. The other two groups were control groups—one group chosen from the same sample as the first two groups, and the other having similar background, educational level of parents, and parental income, but coming from a different town.

All subjects in the study were selected on the basis of the severe

---

* However, an increasing number of jurisdictions require that nursery school teachers be trained and that such teaching conditions as teacher-pupil ratio be carefully regulated.

deprivation of their backgrounds (using such criteria as the housing conditions, income, and education of the parents). Despite the abject poverty of their homes, most of them had television sets; but there were virtually no books or magazines in the homes, and there were also very few toys.

The program was based on the assumption that the deleterious effects of impoverished backgrounds are linked directly to the amount and variety of stimulation that the children receive. Accordingly, the project was designed to provide a wide range of stimulation, with an emphasis on the quality of the stimuli rather than quantity. Gray and Klaus argue that the sheer amount of stimulation received by a child from a deprived environment, particularly if there is a television set in the home, is probably as great quantitatively as that received by a middle-class child. Not only does the television set blare forth all day, but a host of siblings and neighbors' children add constantly to the din. In line with this observation, the project attempted to provide stimulation that would be distinctive enough to be easily separated from other stimuli in the child's environment. In other words, the aim was not only to provide a wide variety of stimulation, but also to provide the type of stimulation that could facilitate easy distinctions between figure and ground—distinctions between the salient features of the environment and the *background* that constantly accompanies them. Assuming that children from deprived environments would not have experienced the range of objects and activities found in middle class homes, Gray and Klaus provided the children with a variety of educational toys, structured learning situations, and other new experiences. In addition to emphasizing these stimulus variables, they identified five distinct reinforcement variables that were to be employed with the children, including tangible external rewards that were frequently paired with the teacher's verbal praise and peer reward in the form of social approval.

Initial results of the Early Training Project are impressive and dramatic. Gray and Klaus (1968) report that after the first 27-month period the first experimental group showed a gain of 9 points in measured IQ whereas the second group gained 5 points. In contrast, the control group from the other town *lost* 6 IQ points (Figure 11.4). Interestingly, the local control group had not changed significantly, a fact attributed to *diffusion,* or the fact that some of the experimental effects are transmitted to the control group through the interaction of parents and children from different groups.

Although it would be premature to assert that a training program such as that of Gray and Klaus is clearly effective in overcoming some of the deleterious effects of impoverished backgrounds, the evidence at least suggests this positive effect. The authors report that 39 months after the original testing the differences in IQ had been maintained. Hence, a tentative conclusion can be made that additional distinctive sensory stimulation is particularly important for children in whose lives there is an apparent deficit.

Ira J. Gordon (1969) has developed a preschool education program in Gainesville, Florida that is of particular current interest. The unique

Parent Education Project

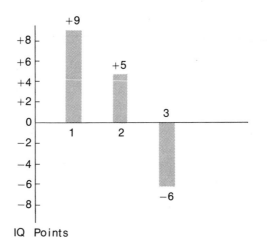

Figure 11.4   Average changes in IQ scores as a function of participation in the Early Training Project. Group 1 participated during 3 summers; group 2, during 2, and the third group
served as a control group. (Based on data provided in Gray, Susan W., and Klaus,
Rupert A., 1968)

feature of his program is that it does not remove the impoverished child
from his home. Instead a number of "parent-educators" are selected,
trained, and sent into the homes to instruct parents in ways of providing
cognitively oriented stimulation for their children. The parent-educators
are themselves women whose general backgrounds are highly similar to
those of the parents with whom they work. Training consists of 5 weeks
of intensive work with the exercises and materials that Gordon and his
group have designed to stimulate the intellectual development of young
children. Many of these exercises and materials are relatively simple and
are based on Piaget's notion that intellectual progress requires constant
adaptation to the environment. Accordingly, the intention is to provide
the child with activities that will be interesting, challenging, and conducive to the development of abilities characteristic of children from better
endowed environments.

The trained "parent-educators" in this program were able to establish
continuing working relationships with parents of selected experimental
children. Further, they continued in these relationships for prolonged
periods of time, and the children appeared to have benefited from the
program. Not only did the children perform better on the training tasks
themselves (a finding which is not particularly surprising or revealing),
but they also tended to perform better on the Griffiths Scales of Development (Weber, 1970). All of these factors point to the success of the program.

The Gordon **Parent Education Project** is of interest not only because
it attempts to provide a remedial program in the child's home, thereby
involving his parents (and in some cases siblings, grandmothers, and
others), but also because the remedial procedures are based on the theoretical formulations and experimental findings of such contemporary
workers in child development as Jean Piaget and J. Mcv. Hunt.

The Ypsilanti Project

Another preschool education project that is based explicitly on Piaget's theorizing is that developed in Ypsilanti, Michigan, under the direction of Constance Kamii.

The principal aim of the **Ypsilanti project** is to derive a preschool curriculum and an instructional methodology directly from the work of Jean Piaget. Accordingly, the Ypsilanti preschool program attempts to facilitate the transition of the child from sensorimotor modes of thinking to operational thought. Teaching strategies emphasize the development of the child's understanding of reality, logic (which is defined loosely as "reasoning"), and means of representing reality. Weber (1970) points out that the program is constantly evolving as the researchers delve more deeply into Piaget's research.

In a progress report, Weikart et al. (1969) ascribe the benefits of the Ypsilanti project largely to two assumptions upon which the programs are based. First, the experimenters maintain that preventive preschool programs must begin considerably earlier than preschool programs usually begin, since the critical years for early learning appear to be 3 and under. The second assumption is that programs are much more likely to be successful if they involve both the mother and her infant. The authors of this report also conclude that the process of getting a mother and infant ready to learn appears to be even more crucial than any actual measurable learning that may take place. (The program seeks to involve parents through lectures, discussions, and home visitations.) Second, they maintain that theories of child development have very little to say about specific children and their mothers — a fact (or at least a half-truth) that is somewhat disturbing.

Project Head Start

Project Head Start is certainly the most ambitious, the most far-reaching, and the most expensive remedial preschool education program ever undertaken. It began with the creation of the Office of Economic Opportunity in the United States, following the passage of the Economic Opportunity Act in 1964. It was originally conceived as part of the American war on poverty and was to consist of a series of 8-week summer programs for children from culturally deprived backgrounds. The project was aimed at overcoming the deficiencies of children from these backgrounds so that they would begin school within closer reach of the more fortunate middle-class child. The act made funds available for Head Start projects throughout the States, and the Office of Economic Opportunity published a booklet inviting participation and listing twelve objectives for the program.

Since a variety of approaches are employed in Head Start programs, it is virtually impossible to evaluate the effectiveness of the project as a whole. Wolff and Stein (1966) investigated a number of Head Start projects. They found that students who had attended Head Start programs, although they usually performed better than control groups immediately after the termination of the projects, frequently did no better 6 months later. However, many specific projects, some of which are discussed in this section, show substantial long-term gains. Critics of Project Head

Start have not focused on the project itself or on the idea behind it, but rather on specific methods employed in various Head Start schools, the lack of guidance and coordination of efforts, and the failure to take into account the results of research that have demonstrated which methods of overcoming learning disadvantages in similar children are successful and which are unsuccessful. Indeed, such critics point out that programs with more specific goals have produced better results (Feather and Olson, 1969). In fact, Reidford (1968) has criticized the Head Start goals as being global, all-inclusive goals that all people have for all children.

The Time Factor

Recent interest in compensatory education for disadvantaged children has generally focused on the preschool child between the ages of 3 and 6, and the various educational programs with that focus have frequently been disappointing. Caldwell (1968) has introduced the provocative hypothesis (which she labels "The Inevitable Hypothesis") that the reason for the ineffectiveness of many remedial programs is that they have not intervened early enough—that, in fact, the years before the age of 3 are the most crucial years in early child development. Accordingly, she has suggested that enrichment programs begin prior to that time and has instituted a research and remedial program involving groups of approximately 25 children in a center in Syracuse, New York. The program makes a wide variety of experiences available to infants and young pre-

Table 11.2   Schematic Model for Structuring the Educational Activities for a Development-Fostering Environment*

	Area of Influence:	Including:	Involves programming:
1)	Socioemotional attributes conducive to a positive orientation toward self, others, and events.	Sense of trust Positive self-concept Achievement motivation Persistence Social skills Sense of mastery Curiosity about environment Delay of gratification Independent behavior Joy of living	The interpersonal environment The experiential environment The physical-spatial environment
2)	Motor, perceptual, and cognitive functions that facilitate adaptive behavior.	Motor agility and balance Fine muscle coordination Ability to attend and discriminate Classification and evaluation Formation of learning sets Problem solution Memory Attention span Communication ability Artistic expression	The experiential environment The physical-spatial environment The interpersonal environment
3)	Culturally relevant knowledge.	Words, phrases, sentences Storehouse of experiences	The experiential environment The physical-spatial environment The interpersonal environment

*The model that serves as guide for the Caldwell preschool program. (From Bettye M. Caldwell, "The fourth dimension in early childhood education," in Robert D. Hess, and Roberta Meyer Bear, *Early Education*. Chicago: Aldine Publishing Co., 1968, p. 79. Copyright 1968 by Robert D. Hess and Roberta Meyer Bear. Used by permission of the author, the editors, and the publisher.)

schoolers in an attempt to enrich the child in three areas: the social-emotional; the motor, perceptual, and cognitive; and that which relates more closely to culture (language, for example). Table 11.2 presents the model used to structure the experiences provided for children. Caldwell reports that after the relatively short period of 7 months, gains in IQ made by experimental group subjects were highly significant. At this point, however, the findings can only be interpreted as suggestive, since similar results have often been obtained immediately after or during enrichment with much older children. Whether or not Caldwell is right in believing that the effects of enrichment will be more pronounced and will last longer with infants than with older preschoolers remains to be seen.

Although there are obviously many approaches to preschool educa-   A Different Approach
tion, this section will focus on the **pressure-cooker approach** since it offers a contrast to the traditional nursery school or kindergarten approach. This approach, developed by Bereiter and Engelmann (1966, 1968), is designed to *teach* the culturally deprived child rather than simply to stimulate him. It usually involves a small group of students and employs methods reminescent of the drill technique of yesterday's schools. Children are expected to repeat after the teacher, to sit quietly and properly, to speak in complete sentences at appropriate times, and to pay complete and careful attention to the teacher at all times. The teacher actually assumes a traditional role in that he (she) stands at the front of the room and *tells* the children, or *asks* them to repeat, individually or in unison, what they have been told. They are initially rewarded with raisins, hugs, privileges, or verbal comments.

The curriculum in the pressure-cooker schools consists of only three subjects, in which the child is expected to be most disadvantaged. Two—reading and language drills—relate to language, since the most significant difference between the middle-class child and the deprived child is degree of language development and sophistication. The third subject is arithmetic.

In its experimental stages, the program ran for 9 months, $2\frac{1}{2}$ hours a day, 5 days a week, and involved 15 four-year-old children (Bereiter and Engelmann, 1968). In addition to the three main subjects, there were field trips, play times, music, snacks, and occasional toileting intervals. Three different teachers were employed, one for each subject, so that students went from one classroom to another much as they might in a high school. (A relatively detailed description of the program itself is provided by Bereiter and Engelmann, 1966.)

At the end of the first 9 months all 15 children were administered the Illinois Test of Psycholinguistic Ability (ITPA). In all subtests of the ITPA except vocabulary, subjects progressed from a point approximately a year below their actual chronological age to almost 6 months above. Their IQ scores, measured by means of the Stanford-Binet, had increased an average of 7 points, and their achievement levels, based on performance on achievement tests, put almost all the children somewhere in the first-grade level for both reading and arithmetic. Indeed, in arithmetic, 11 scored at the beginning of the second grade (see Figure 11.5).

Some have expressed doubt, however, about the effectiveness of these techniques with middle-class children. Others have expressed "horror" at the "terrible" techniques employed (Pines, 1966). Although the approach has been successful in terms of measurable gains on the ITPA and on the Stanford-Binet, this evidence is not sufficient to mark its superiority over other methods. It is likely that the highly structured curriculum leads to more easily observable (and measurable) changes than more open and varied approaches. The broader aspects of the child's development are not as easily measured. Children might well be more beneficially affected by any of a number of other approaches.

The Montessori Method

There has been a recent resurgence of interest in the **Montessori Method**, particularly since the reintroduction of her work by Rambusch (1962). It is a method that dates back to the turn of the century (Montessori, 1912), but that has withstood the passage of time, unlike many educational fads. Unfortunately, the movement began at a time when experimental verification of belief and opinion was less important than it is now. Thus, there is relatively little evidence to support the claims made by enthusiasts, with several notable exceptions. Kohlberg (1968), for example, notes that Montessori represents three distinct things: a set of ideas, a set of materials, and an ideology. Each aspect will be examined briefly in turn.

Montessori's ideas are complex, far ranging, highly speculative, somewhat poetic, frequently unscientific, and relatively difficult to summarize. A recent American edition of some of her lectures (Montessori, 1967), for example, is concerned primarily with her beliefs about the "absorbent" nature of the infant's mind, and the consequent responsibility of an adult society to provide a structured education for that mind from its very earliest years. The notion is appealing, but the suggestions provided for implementing it are not always practical. Among Montessori's key ideas are her belief in the senses as the source of all intellectual growth and her conviction that intellectual development is therefore directly dependent upon the training of the senses.

The Montessori set of materials is a direct result of her fundamental belief that all learning stems from sense perception. She has developed an impressively large set of physical materials, some of which are illustrated in Figure 11.6. Each of these materials has a specific function and is to be used by the teacher in a carefully prescribed manner. For example, each sandpaper bar is covered with paper of a different coarseness; colors are graded shades of each hue; sound boxes produce sounds ordered in pitch; weights are carefully ranked. Thus, each is designed to promote sensory discriminations and, therefore, to enhance sensory development. In addition, most objects that can be lifted with one hand have a small knob affixed to them, so that the child can lift them only with his thumb, forefinger, and index finger. The weights, for example, are equipped in this manner. The purpose is ostensibly to develop the type of skill in holding objects that is required for holding a pencil.

The best-known Montessori materials are large letters of the alphabet

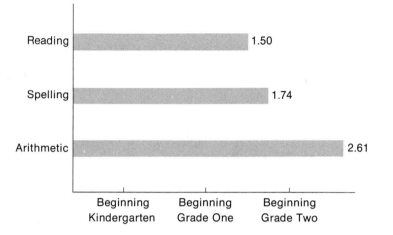

Mean achievement scores in three areas for 13 subjects in the Bereiter/Engelmann   Figure 11.5
program. At the time of testing, the children had completed their kindergarten year.
(Based on data reported by Carl Bereiter, and Siegfried, Engelmann, 1968, p. 28.)

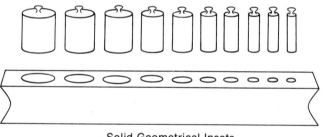

Solid Geometrical Insets

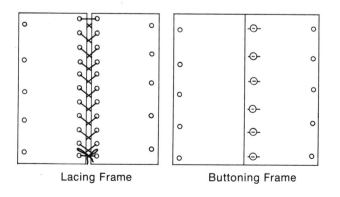

Lacing Frame   Buttoning Frame

Some traditional Montessori materials.   Figure 11.6

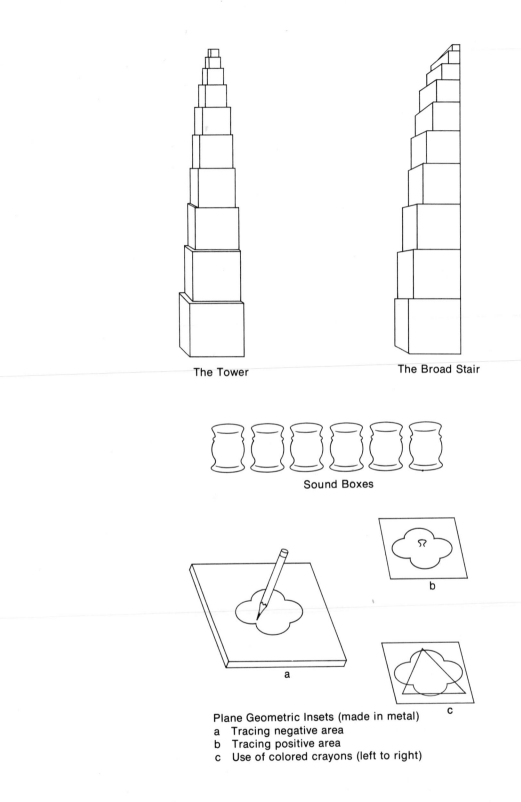

The Tower

The Broad Stair

Sound Boxes

Plane Geometric Insets (made in metal)
a   Tracing negative area
b   Tracing positive area
c   Use of colored crayons (left to right)

Figure 11.6   (continued)

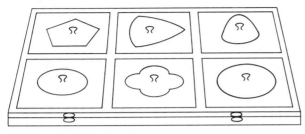

Plane Geometric Insets

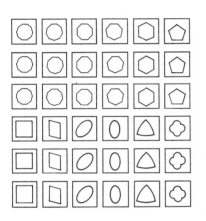

Plane Geometric Forms (in three series)

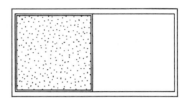

Sandpaper Boards

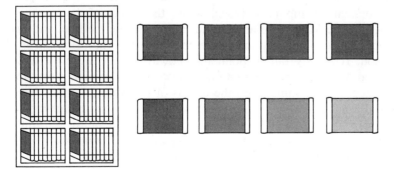

Color Boxes   Dark Red to Light Red

(continued)   Figure 11.6

covered with sandpaper, which are employed in teaching the child to read, according to the following prescribed method: During the first stage, the child is presented with tablets upon which are the sandpaper-covered letters. The teacher says the phonetic sound of the letter and has the child repeat it, while the child simultaneously feels the texture of the letter with the fingers of one hand, thereby getting a tactile sensation of it. At the same time he is encouraged to look at the letter in order to get a visual impression of it. In short, the first stage of teaching a child to read involves three senses: vision, touch, and hearing.

After repeated practice with the first stage, the child will have learned to associate the letter with its sound and will then be ready to proceed to an identification of vowels and consonants—a procedure that is made simple through the use of different colors. The final objective of this stage is that the child will be able to put letters together to form words that he hears. In later exercises the child makes words for pictures that are shown to him using movable letters. The next step is a simple progression to phrases and sentences.

Employing this technique, Montessori reported that she was able to teach young slum area children in Rome how to read as rapidly as the middle-class children of her day. Results have not always been as impressive in American Montessori schools, probably because English is not blessed with phonetic spellings to the extent that Italian is.

The Montessori ideology stresses individual liberty, emphasizes the responsibility of adults toward children, and is concerned with the development of human potential. At the same time, it is an ideology that holds "self-discipline" and "self-mastery" as high virtues. These beliefs are reflected in the prescribed methodology of the Montessori schools.

The Montessori approach has been criticized on a number of grounds. Some critics fear that excessive reliance on interaction with materials rather than with peers may have a deleterious effect on social development; that insistence on the prescribed methods of doing things may stifle potential creativity; that reliance on didactic materials rather than on verbal interaction between child and teacher may impede the development of important verbal skills; that many of the teachers who profess to be Montessorians are not trained in the method, and that the independence of children may be tempered by the authoritarianism of the method. It is only fair to point out, however, that the criticisms summarized here have been based on conjecture and opinion rather than on evidence. At the same time, the claims of the Montessorians have also been based largely on conjecture and on opinion. Kohlberg (1968), however, describes a Head Start project that employed Montessori methods, and that resulted in a mean IQ gain of 17 points between October and January. He advances the hypothesis that the Montessori emphasis on attention and on such tasks as ordering and classifying may be largely responsible for this significant increment in measured intelligence.

Current Status of Preschool Education

There is really insufficient evidence to find in favor of any one preschool method, and our discussion has focused on only a few of the many distinct approaches that have been employed. It is clear that well-defined criteria should be developed and that a review of preschool approaches is needed, not only to provide valuable information for teachers and others who are directly involved with the early education of the child but also to suggest to the researcher where he should go. There is little doubt that the first 6 years of a child's life are of tremendous importance for his later development. There is also little doubt that not all parents are sufficiently well equipped, or indeed have the required time, to provide the experiences that would be most beneficial for their children. It is up to the psychologist and the expert in early childhood education to provide better information about the nature of these experiences, the best way in which they can be provided, and the optimal time for doing so. While education is growing beyond its traditional limits of first and twelfth grade, it is highly probable that the greatest emphasis in the immediate future will be at the entry level.

Summary

This chapter opened with two mad adults playing cowboys and Indians and racing worms in the halls of a very respectable academic institution. Having made the point that the play of children makes no distinction between the real and the imaginary, and that adults are not expected, in this culture, to play like children, the chapter moved quickly through a description of the 2-year-old followed by a description of the 6-year-old. The descriptions pointed out the great space the child must cross between the ages of 2 and 6; then the chapter described the crossing in terms of physical and motor development and considered the social development of the child. It was noted that games are an important part of the child's social development, so we stopped briefly to describe the types of games that are played and the ages at which these are most prevalent. Games occasionally have rules, which must be learned and internalized by the child; an examination of this process led naturally to a discussion of moral development, another part of the child's socialization. The growth of language and its role in the thinking process was considered, and the next logical move was to look at the child's mind through the work of Jean Piaget, which has traced the development of the preschool child through the two substages of the preoperational period (the preconceptual and the intuitive). The natural development of the child was then put aside for a moment in order to look at the kinds of intervention that are made possible through preschool education programs and to examine the effects of some of these programs. The chapter closed with the prediction that the greatest educational emphasis in the near future will be at the school entrance rather than the exit.

Main Points

1. There is a world of difference between the games of the child and the games of the adult, for the adult, although he takes part in games, seldom plays. One can gain some insight into the world of the child by playing like a child for a day, or even for an hour.

2. Physical development between the ages of 2 and 6 is marked by a gradual deceleration in relative rate of growth. The result of the growth process is a 6-year-old child who looks like an adult compared with the infantile look of the 2-year-old.

3. The child's motor development in the preschool period is often described

by the sequential acquisition of such perceptual motor skills as are necessary for drawing simple geometric forms. The order of difficulty for these forms is relatively invariant, beginning with the circle (simplest), the square, the triangle, the cross, the divided rectangle, and finally the diamond (the most difficult—copied at age 7 or 8).

4. There are three broad categories of children's play: sensorimotor games such as practicing to run, skip, or stick out one's tongue; social games that involve interaction between two or more children; and imaginative games that consist of acting as though the actor, the actions, or the objects acted with or upon are something other than what they really are.

5. Piaget's investigation of morality begins with an examination of children's understanding of rules. Both he and Kohlberg describe the development of morality as progressing from simple, egocentric, and unstable beliefs about right and wrong, to a stage marked by mutual cooperation (social rules), and finally a last stage in which the legal aspect of rules becomes most important.

6. Language plays a prominent role in learning, the formation of discriminations, logical reasoning, and initiating, directing, and inhibiting overt behavior.

7. Piaget describes the preschool stage in terms of two substages of the preoperational period: the first, from 2 to 4, is labeled preconceptual; the second, from 4 to 7, is termed intuitive.

8. Preconceptual thinking is marked by the inability to understand simple classification, and by transductive reasoning and syncretic thinking.

9. Intuitive thinking is characterized by egocentricity, by a limited ability to classify, and by a marked reliance on perception.

10. Life is the child's only curriculum until he reaches school age; he learns to adapt through his experiences.

11. Most research on the effects of preschool education on the cognitive, social, and emotional development of the child is equivocal. Frequently, significant differences are found between experimental groups and controls immediately after the preschool experience, but these differences disappear within 6 months or a year.

12. Nursery schools are reported to make children more confident, more spontaneous, less inhibited, more independent, more self-reliant, and more interested in their environments.

13. The Gray and Klaus Early Training Project is based on the notion that the effects of cultural deprivation can be overcome by providing children with varied and distinctive sensory stimulation. Initial findings suggest that the program is effective in increasing the measured intelligence of subjects.

14. Project Head Start is a large-scale composite of federally funded preschool programs for children from impoverished backgrounds. Its tremendous potential is a source of real hope in the war against ignorance and poverty.

15. Caldwell suggests that the critical time for providing enrichment experiences for deprived children is prior to the age of 3. Results of her research tend to support her belief, although they are still more suggestive than conclusive.

16. The intensive, *pressure-cooker* approach developed by Bereiter and Engelmann has produced dramatic results in terms of measurable gains.

17. Montessori methods stress training of the senses. Teachers are provided with a wide range of carefully prepared and graded materials designed to develop motor and perceptual skills and eventually to lead to the learning of reading, arithmetic, geography, and virtually all other school subjects.

18. Preschool education is likely to receive even more emphasis in the coming decades than it has in the past.

Further Readings

Piaget's description of the moral development of children and their development of notions of rules is contained in:

Piaget, J. *The moral judgement of the child*. London: Kegan Paul, 1932.

The importance of language for the cognitive development of the preschool child is highlighted in Bruner's introduction to the following book and in several of the articles:

Bruner, J. S., R. R. Olver, and P. N. Greenfield. *Studies in cognitive growth.* New York: John Wiley, 1966.

The following two references discuss Piaget's description of the preschool child. The first is recognized as the most comprehensive description of Piaget's work currently available. The second is a somewhat simpler account of Piaget's theoretical formulations.

Flavell, J. H. *The developmental psychology of Jean Piaget*. Princeton, New Jersey: D. Van Nostrand, 1963.

Furth, H. G. *Piaget and knowledge*. Englewood Cliffs, N.J.: Prentice-Hall, 1969.

The recent intensification of interest in preschool education is reflected in the highly readable book by Maya Pines and in the provocative collection of articles edited by Hess and Bear:

Pines, M. *Revolution in learning: The years from birth to six*. New York: Harper & Row, 1966.

Hess, R. D. and R. M. Bear (Eds.). *Early education: Current theory, research and action*. Chicago: Aldine Publishing, 1968.

Of Outer Space: Ages Six to Twelve

I have actually been to Koros in the Androneas system. I tell you this and I tell you that it is true, hoping all the while that you might forgive this personal intrusion in an academic textbook. For I have recently read that in academic works the merest hint of the author's personality is an intrusion. And so I confess to be an intruder. I am he who was flown* from the rich lands at the foot of the most magnificent mountains in North America to the bleak desolation of the Koron landscape. And the trip so overwhelmed me that I cannot refrain from telling you about it.

Let me remind you that I know a Koron, whom I count among my closest friends. His name is **Kongor M-III.**† *Since he left us 6 short months ago, I have wondered constantly about him; we did not know whether he would be made a hero by his people or whether he would die. You see, he had violated one of the Eleven Great Laws. At last his superiors decided that he must be examined to assess the seriousness of his transgression. Apparently, he had assumed some characteristics of the humans of whom he spoke so highly in one breath and with such disdain in the next. There was little doubt that he had become emotional — and emotion is among the more despicable traits in a culture that claims it despises nothing, since it is so emphatically unemotional.*

Kongor had requested that I be brought from Earth to testify in his behalf, provided I was willing to come. (One of the corollaries to the Third Law of the Eleven Great Laws is that no alien will be forced to do anything unless not doing so results in danger to a significant number of Korons.) I was willing. The scientists among you may not believe all this, for a scientist does not like to accept a truth without examining it under all possible lights. To you I say that if you will take the trouble to check, you will find that I was absent from this life from May 8, 1971, to the eleventh day of that same month and year. The truth can indeed be verified.

I tell you this not because you have a great interest in what befell Kongor or in what Koros is like; or even that you yearn to know how it feels for a human soul to flit about under the rays of a strange and distant sun that does not exist in the limited spatial dimensions we are heir to. I tell you of Kongor and of my brief absence to explain to you in what manner I achieved new insight into the life of the child, about whom I write this chapter. It is perhaps a small insight, but it is a new one with which I have returned. All that I will say about Kongor is that he is well and alive; my testimony saved him. I am not allowed to disclose his whereabouts, but I may say that he will return.

Children on Koros are not like children on Earth — even their physical origins are dramatically different. Actual physical union between opposite-sexed mature Korons has so long been unnecessary for procreation that they have quite forgotten a time and place when they behaved as we do. Instead they store small quantities of germ cells in a biogenic laboratory; whenever there is need for an individual of a par-

---

* In our limited vocabulary *flown* seems the only appropriate word. In actual fact, however, I was not *flown;* my soul (*telsig*) was filliducted.

† Those who still doubt are urged to refer to Lefrancois, 1972b.

ticular type (series number), the appropriate male and female cells are joined and placed in a glass-lined embryonic chamber. Under the mysterious influence of various accelerating rays (called **falloren rays,** *whose existence was hitherto unknown to me), the fertilized cell becomes a little Koron within several hours. One of the amazing things about this little Koron is that he can speak almost from birth—certainly within a few days he is capable of saying anything at all and of practicing abstract reasoning.*

My new insight into the process of development resulted from an accident that occurred while I was touring a biogenic laboratory with Kongor. One of the Koron diobols* *developed a short circuit and reversed the falloren rays that were at that moment projected upon one of the embryonic chambers. An ordinary falloren ray accelerates development; a reversed ray does not reverse the process, but merely decelerates development. It is akin to watching a movie in incredibly slowed slow motion. One can observe the minutest detail of the process. While I stood transfixed by the overwhelming complexity of the process that had been accidentally revealed by the defective diobol, the insight came. I suddenly realized that within the limiting confines of words on printed pages, it is absolutely impossible to convey the full detail of childhood and of children, as we observe them in the process of becoming something that they presumably are not yet. Unlike most phenomena in the physical world, the child never really completes the process of becoming; he is always changing. And although a psychological examination of development necessarily limits its subject somewhat to a state or an outcome (frequently called a stage, phase, or period), we are nonetheless looking at a process. In effect, we are stopping the process at different places and examining what is there in much the same way that the reversed falloren ray almost stops the development of a Koron fetus.*

And so it occurred to me that examining the process of human development is like watching a motion picture, and at the same time, quite unlike watching a motion picture. A movie gives the illusion of continual motion, yet it can be halted at any point to reveal that it actually consists of isolated pictures—static representations. The development of a child can also be stopped and examined in much the same way as it is possible to examine the individual pictures that make up a movie. There is, nevertheless, a fundamental difference between the development of a child and the progression of a movie. The isolated and static pictures studied are illusory; the reality of human development is its continuous movement.

**Middle
Childhood**
The movement that concerns us in this chapter occurs during the years referred to as middle childhood. The boundaries are somewhat

---

*An advanced product of robotic engineering bearing only a faint resemblance to our computers.

arbitrary: it begins near the age of 6, a convenient age since the preschool period ends there, and it culminates at approximately age 12.* Since this stage terminates with the onset of pubescence, and pubescence occurs at very different ages for male and female, and for different individuals of the same sex, its top boundary is more indefinite. **Middle childhood** begins with a state of physical and mental development vastly different from that which terminates it. The 6-year-old child has been described as a relatively adultlike distribution of 48 pounds set upon a frame that stretches just a little under 4 feet (46 inches). His vocabulary is close to 2500 words, and he has pretty well succeeded in mastering the syntax of his language and in developing a symbolic (verbal) representation of his world. Despite this, he continues to engage in a great many sensorimotor games — games that require no symbolization and no abstract reasoning. Also, he still frequently represents reality in concrete mental images (iconic). The reasoning of the 6-year-old is replete with contradictions, despite the fact that he will attempt, and occasionally solve, problems that a 2-year-old would not begin to understand. His thinking is dominated by sense perception and is intuitive and egocentric.

In the Freudian view, the 6-year-old child has probably been successful in overcoming the sexually based conflicts that beset him from infancy. If he is a boy, he has renounced his overpowering attachment to his mother and has begun to identify with his father. If the child is a girl, she has abandoned her subconscious desire to have a baby by her father and has overcome the consequent jealousy of her mother; she is now ready to identify with her mother. Both the boy and the girl will enter a period of sexual latency, during which there is no dominant source of sexual gratification and interest in the opposite sex is at its lowest ebb.

In contrast to the typical 6-year-old, consider the 12-year-old. There is a great space of 6 years between the onset and the end of middle childhood, a space that culminates in a child who is drastically different from the child that he was at the beginning — physically, socially, and intellectually. The average 12-year-old boy weighs 84 pounds and is almost 5 feet tall (59 inches). His vocabulary is incredibly larger and includes many words, which are the frequently used idiomatic and slang expressions of his particular peer group. His immediate family has diminished in importance and the influence of his peer groups has increased. He attends school, has learned to read and write, and has refined his powers of concentration, of abstract thinking, and of problem solving. He has developed a fairly sophisticated logic, sufficient to handle all types of concrete problems. He can classify and deal with seriation, and he understands the concept of number. He no longer makes the errors that characterized his earlier attempts to solve conservation problems. These problems have become so easy for him that he may be embarrassed by their simplicity. The 12-year-old's thinking is symbolic, although usually related to real objects or to situations that he is easily capable of imagining. Just as his thinking has refined, so has his verbal skill.

---

*Many authors end middle childhood at age 10 and insert another period between there and adolescence, labeled late childhood or preadolescence.

Again from the Freudian view, the 12-year-old is about to emerge from the period of sexual latency, during which he avoided heterosexual contact, much preferring to consort with members of his own sex. He has developed notions of sex-appropriate behavior as a result of identification with the like-sexed parent, and also from having spent much time with his like-sexed peers. Peer groups are particularly prone to reinforce their members for sex-appropriate behavior and to extinguish all other behavior, both by not reinforcing it, and frequently by drawing attention to its inappropriateness through ridicule, ostracism, or some other form of punishment. A difficult transition from this period to the final stage of psychosexual development marks the termination of middle childhood and the beginning of adolescence.

By the age of 12 the child is ready to move from concrete to more abstract thought processes; from a period of sexual latency to the genital phase of development, when members of the opposite sex begin to assume the importance that they maintain throughout most of the individual's life — from the last period of development that can still be called childhood to one that must now be interpreted as at least the beginnings of adulthood.

Physical and Motor Development

Physical Development

During the years from 6 to 12 the child gains in the two most obvious manifestations of growth: he becomes taller and heavier. The parallel growth that existed for boys and girls prior to this period is not maintained throughout middle childhood. Although girls tended to be slightly shorter and slightly lighter than boys from birth to the end of the preschool period, the growth curves for each were almost identical; that is, both gained at approximately the same rate. Table 12.1 summarizes height and weight norms for boys and girls from the ages of 6 to 12. An examination of these norms reveals that although the average girl is $\frac{3}{4}$ of an inch shorter

Table 12.1 Height (in inches) and Weight (in pounds) at the Fiftieth Percentile for American Children*

Age	Height		Weight	
	Girl	Boy	Girl	Boy
6 years	$45\frac{1}{2}$	$46\frac{1}{4}$	$46\frac{1}{2}$	$48\frac{1}{4}$
$6\frac{1}{2}$ years	47	$47\frac{1}{2}$	$49\frac{1}{2}$	$51\frac{1}{4}$
7 years	48	49	$52\frac{1}{4}$	54
$7\frac{1}{2}$ years	$49\frac{1}{4}$	50	$55\frac{1}{4}$	57
8 years	$50\frac{1}{2}$	$51\frac{1}{4}$	58	60
$8\frac{1}{2}$ years	$51\frac{1}{2}$	$52\frac{1}{4}$	61	63
9 years	$52\frac{1}{4}$	$53\frac{1}{4}$	$63\frac{3}{4}$	66
$9\frac{1}{2}$ years	$53\frac{1}{2}$	$54\frac{1}{4}$	67	69
10 years	$54\frac{1}{2}$	$55\frac{1}{4}$	$70\frac{1}{4}$	72
$10\frac{1}{2}$ years	$55\frac{3}{4}$	56	$74\frac{1}{2}$	$74\frac{3}{4}$
11 years	57	$56\frac{3}{4}$	$78\frac{3}{4}$	$77\frac{1}{2}$
$11\frac{1}{2}$ years	$58\frac{1}{4}$	$57\frac{3}{4}$	$83\frac{1}{4}$	81
12 years	$59\frac{3}{4}$	59	$87\frac{1}{2}$	$84\frac{1}{2}$

*Adapted by the Health Department, Milwaukee, Wisconsin; based on data by H. C. Stuart and H. V. Meredith, prepared for use in Children's Medical Centre, Boston. Used by permission of the Milwaukee Health Department.

at the age of 6, she has caught up with and surpassed the average boy by the age of 10, and is still slightly taller than the boy at the age of 12. With respect to weight, girls are close to 2 pounds lighter at the age of 6 and do not catch up with boys until the age of 11. Between the ages of 11 and 12, however, there is a sudden spurt of weight gain for girls, which puts them 3 pounds ahead of boys in the course of a single year. The next chapter points out that not until the age of $14\frac{1}{2}$ do boys finally overtake girls in weight, and at $13\frac{1}{2}$ they exceed girls in height. The weight and height of average men continues to exceed that of women until death renders them equally short and light.

Another trend of physical growth that continues throughout middle childhood is a gradual decrease in the growth of fatty tissue, coupled with increased bone and muscle development. Muscle development is generally more rapid in boys, whereas girls tend to retain thicker layers of fat longer. This fatty tissue is distributed so that girls have rounder, smoother, and softer contours and frequently retain their babyish appearance (resulting from plumpness) longer than boys.

The growth spurt in height and weight during this period occurs approximately 2 years earlier for girls than for boys. For this reason, it is probably fortunate that boys and girls usually choose to associate with members of their own sex during the growth spurt, since the obvious physical differences that exist not only between the sexes, but also between members of the same sex, are frequently a source of acute embarrassment for children. At a time when peer approval has become among the most important things in life to a child, it is a great misfortune to be either precocious or retarded in physical development. It is humiliating for a boy to suddenly find that his younger sister has become taller than he; the humiliation is often accompanied by the fear that he will continue to be short. It is probably equally uncomfortable to be the tallest boy or the tallest girl in the class, and to live with the secret fear of becoming a tall, skinny freak.

Nature usually compensates for her initial discrepancies. The tall girl finds that she was an early bloomer; she ceases to grow at the time when her peers begin their growth spurts, and in a short time she finds herself surrounded by equals. The short boy discovers that he was merely a slow starter; when his seemingly more fortunate friends have nearly reached their adult heights, he suddenly stretches skyward and looks down upon them smiling.

The child's muscular control continues to develop during the years from 6 to 12. Early in this period his control of large muscles is considerably better than his control over smaller muscles (an explanation for the inelegant writing of first- and second-grade children). By the end of middle childhood, control of the large muscles has become nearly perfect and control over the small muscles is much improved.

Motor Development

The changes in the child's locomotor skills, his agility, his coordination, and his physical strength are particularly interesting; not only because they demonstrate such marked differences between sexes, but also because they are of tremendous significance in explaining the child's interests. This is perhaps a partial explanation for the fact that boys are more interested in physical activity than girls. For example, throughout middle childhood the boy's physical strength (measured in terms of grip strength) is superior to the girl's, even though the average girl is taller and heavier than the boy (Keogh, 1965, cited by Cratty, 1970).

On a number of other locomotor indices boys typically surpass girls. Johnson (1962) provides data on the average height that the child can jump from a standing start, summarized in Figure 12.1. Boys consistently outreach girls after the age of 7.* This evidence is assumed to indicate

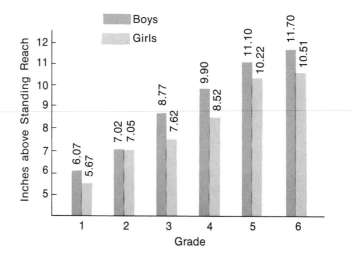

Figure 12.1   Number of inches above standing reach jumped by boys and girls from grades 1 to 6. (Based on data from "Measurements of achievement in fundamental skills of elementary school children" by Robert D. Johnson, *Research Quarterly*, 1962, **33**, 94–103, p. 97. Copyright 1962 by the American Association for Health, Physical Education and Recreation. Used by permission of the American Association for Health, Physical Education and Recreation.)

that boys' leg power and arm-leg coordination for jumping is better than the girls'. Johnson (1962) also found that boys excelled girls in tests of kicking, throwing, catching, batting, and zigzagging. This last test involved a zigzag run: four chairs were aligned 6 feet apart, with the first chair 6 feet from a starting line and the last chair 6 feet from a wall. The subject was instructed to run around the chairs, alternating sides (zigzagging), to touch an X that had been drawn on the wall, and to return to the starting line by the same route. Figure 12.2 presents the results of this test for boys and girls from grades 1 to 6.

---

*"Ah, but a man's reach should exceed his grasp . . ." (Robert Browning) Browning said nothing of a woman's reach, but he lived in an age of unliberated females.

Other measures of motor performance show that boys jump significantly farther than girls on a broad jump (Keogh, 1965), that boys perform better with hurdles (Cowan and Pratt, 1934), and that they are more adept at hopping on alternate feet (Keogh, 1968, cited by Cratty, 1970). Boys also run faster and throw a ball farther—all of which is interesting and potentially inflammatory information, although it is possessed by any grandmother who has observed school children at track and field meets. What Grandmother might not have known with as much conviction is that girls do surpass boys in a limited number of motor skills during the

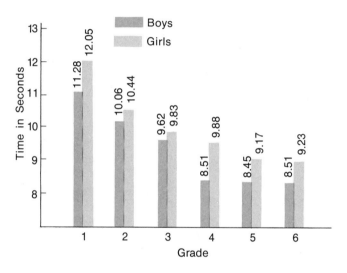

Time in seconds required by boys and girls from grades 1 through 6 to run a zigzag course. (Based on data from "Measurements of achievement in fundamental skills of elementary school children" by Robert D. Johnson, *Research Quarterly*, 1962, **33**, 94–103, p. 97. Copyright 1962 by the American Association for Health, Physical Education and Recreation. Used by permission of the American Association for Health, Physical Education and Recreation.)   Figure 12.2

middle childhood period (but rarely afterward). These skills include cable jumping—jumping over an object such as a rope while it is held by the jumper in front of him. In addition, Cratty (1970) reports that girls sometimes surpass boys in tasks involving rhythmic movements, such as in hopscotch.

Reaction time, defined as the length of time between the presentation of a stimulus and the initiation of the response, is one of the variables that is assumed to play an important role in the development of the child's motor abilities. One study (Whiting, 1969) reports that the reaction time of a 5-year-old child is approximately twice as long as an adult's. Whiting argues that the child's initial difficulty with such tasks as catching a ball is due largely to his slow reaction time. It is not clear whether the child is physiologically incapable of reacting more rapidly, or whether it simply   Reaction Time takes him longer to *decide* to react or *how* to react. In any case, rapid games are very difficult, if not impossible, for the young child. Different reaction times and different levels of motor skills (which are probably related to some extent) also make it likely that children of different ages will seek peers of similar ages with whom to play, not only because they share similar interests, but also because the skills they bring to their games will be more compatible.

Fitness and Intelligence

The belief that physical fitness and intellectual performance are directly related is sometimes verbalized and often accepted intuitively; but the evidence is ambiguous. Railo (1968, cited by Cratty, 1970) reports a study in which the physical fitness of 203 seventh-grade children was classified on the basis of the amount of oxygen they consumed while engaged in physical activity. The valid assumption is that those who consume less oxygen are in better physical condition. Subjects were given a 2-hour intelligence test, followed without interruption by another 2-hour period of difficult intellectual tasks, with one 10-minute break. Finally, all subjects received a second 2-hour intelligence test. The obvious prediction is that those students who are in better physical condition would be more able to withstand the grueling 6-hour session, and that the unfit would succumb from sheer physical exhaustion. Fatigue would be reflected in a marked decrease in their intellectual functioning, measured by the second test.

This hypothesis is not supported by the evidence; instead it is flatly contradicted by it. Not only did the less fit students not perform more poorly on the second test, but they did significantly better; they *improved* their intelligence test scores. Amazingly, those who had been classified as physically fit did not improve their performance, but declined significantly. Railo's explanation for this apparent contradiction of commonsense is that the more fit students have a higher need for physical activity and consequently were more frustrated by the testing situation. Their poorer performance, then, can be explained by motivational factors. On the other hand, the superior performance of the less fit group can perhaps be explained on the basis of learning that might have occurred as a result of the first test and of the intellectual exercises that were engaged in between the two testing sessions. If this explanation is correct, the message for teachers and school administrators is obvious: students should not be subjected to prolonged intellectual activities without benefit of some physical activity as well.

The Railo study does not demonstrate that there is no relationship (let alone an inverse relationship) between physical fitness and intelligence. What it does point out is that this relationship has not been researched adequately, and neither psychologists nor physical educators are yet sufficiently informed to be dogmatic about their beliefs concerning the contribution of physical health to intelligence or emotional stability.

Socialization

Socialization, as it is employed here and in the preceding chapter, includes all the changes in the child's abilities, attitudes, personality characteristics, and beliefs that influence how he adapts to his society. Accordingly, this section deals with school, peer groups, sex roles, and the child's development of morality.

Perhaps it is presumptuous to attempt to describe the effects of the school on the child, not only because some of these effects vary widely from one student to another, but also because the major effects are so inclusive that they are too obvious to be worthy of mention, and at the same time, too indeterminate and nonspecific to be analyzed easily. Consider, for example, that when a 6-year-old child enters school, although he has already learned the language of his people, and although he might even have begun to acquire some of the skills necessary if he is to have access to even a fraction of the cumulative wisdom of his race, it is the school (in most cases) that will make that wisdom accessible. In this age of accelerating technological and theoretical progress, it is no longer possible for grandmothers to transmit more than the merest hint of culture. The schools are our monolithic disseminators of culture.

The School

Throughout this book we have referred to the average child and the normal course of development, despite frequent reminders that these beasts have been invented for the sake of convenience; now we will invent the average school and examine the average effect it has on the average student. And we will begin, of course, by asserting that none of these is real, but simply the exigency of conceptual simplicity.

The average school, monolithic culture machine, opens its smiling jaws to the incoming hordes of 6-year-olds every September, and although it may appear to disgorge them daily at 3 o'clock, and to swallow them again the following morning, resting only on weekends, during holidays, floods, and bomb scares—it does not really free them. The culture machines detain their charges until they reach adolescence; their influence pervades the child's life.

It is in school that the child learns the basic skills and acquires knowledge fundamental to his understanding of, and effective interaction with, this complex world. Also through the school, the child develops the social skills and public personality that will characterize him throughout life, for it is in school that he finds himself in situations demanding interaction with people other than his immediate family. There is virtually nowhere for the frightened first grader to run—his mother has abandoned him. Although she continues to love him, to wash his clothes, to cook for him, and to sympathize with his expressions of joy and sadness, she is far away at home and he is here alone. He has discovered that the world stretches beyond the circle of home and family, that it is necessary to adjust to this world, and that the adjustment is sometimes painful.

If adjustment to school is not always easy for the well fed, well stimulated, healthy child from the typical middle-class home, imagine how much more difficult it is for the disadvantaged child. It is no myth that the child from a minority group (frequently disadvantaged in one or more ways) fares considerably worse in school than the more advantaged "ma-

The School and Minority Groups

jority" student. Numerous reasons have been advanced for this unhappy state of affairs. Crossland (1971; see Chapter 4) lists verbal handicaps, the middle-class orientation of school examinations, inferior teachers and school facilities in deprived areas, and various motivational deficiencies. To this list of disadvantages facing the child from a lower-class home can be added another factor, recently identified — the effect of the teacher's expectations on the student.

Rosenthal and Jacobson (1968a; 1968b) report a study which has tremendous implications for our understanding of how a teacher's expectations affect the behavior of his (her) students. The investigation involved students in a lower-middle-class school. Each student was administered an intelligence test in the spring of the school year. Teachers in the school were not informed that the measures were of aptitude, but were told instead that the experimenters were attempting to validate a new test designed to identify academic "bloomers." Teachers were also advised that students frequently show a sudden spurt in performance at some time during their academic career. For some children this spurt comes very early; for others it occurs later. The experimenters had ostensibly developed a test that would enable them to predict which students would most likely "bloom" during the following school year.

The following September a number of students were chosen at random from the school and designated the experimental group; they comprised approximately 20 percent of the school's population. The experimental treatment consisted of informing teachers casually that these were students who had been identified as "late spurters" the previous spring. There was no other treatment undertaken. Hence, the only difference between the experimental group and the remainder of the students in the school was that their teachers had some reason to expect better performances from them during the year. Significantly, all teachers did in fact observe the level of performance that they expected. The experimental group not only scored higher on measures of achievement, but even scored markedly better than the control group on a general measure of intelligence. Equally interesting is the fact that the younger students seemed to improve most, which suggests that younger children are perhaps more malleable, more subject to the subtle influences of a teacher's expectations.

Studies of the effects of teachers' expectations on school children may help us understand the lower achievement of minority group children: teachers frequently expect less of a lower-class or minority group child than they do of a middle-class child. On the average, this expectation is borne out. Thus, at least part of the inferior performance of the minority group child may be due precisely to the teacher's lower expectations for him.

The Rosenthal and Jacobson studies have been criticized extensively. In particular, Barber and Silver (1969a; 1969b) have examined many of the studies with which Rosenthal and Jacobson support their hypothesis, contending that few of these studies clearly demonstrate the effects of teachers' expectations. Rosenthal's (1969) replies to these criticisms are equally adamant in maintaining that the studies do indeed support his conclusions. Although it is too early to resolve the mild controversy surrounding the **"Rosenthal effect,"** failure to replicate the original findings does not necessarily invalidate the conclusion that at least in some cases, the expectations that a teacher has for her students may dramatically affect their social and intellectual development.

The influence of the school goes beyond simply imparting social and intellectual skills. It provides the child's first opportunity for meaningful and prolonged interaction with other significant adults and, more importantly, it provides the child's first encounter with peer groups, whose tremendous importance to the school-aged child cannot be underestimated.

Sex Typing

During his early years of schooling the child becomes increasingly aware of the behavior that his culture finds acceptable and desirable for his sex. This cultural process is frequently referred to as **sex typing**: the learning of sex-appropriate behavior. In our culture, for example, a boy must learn to walk without undue buttock movement, to run fiercely with his arms swinging free, to sit with legs sprawled, to throw a ball with a full arm swing and a flexed wrist, and to wrestle and fight, or at least to be playfully aggressive. He must love sports, and should know the names of a thousand baseball, basketball, or hockey players, be able to play the trumpet, be interested in science and mathematics, and play **bingo.** The girl, on the other hand, must learn to walk with a somewhat exaggerated buttock movement, run with her elbows tucked into her delicate ribcage and with limp-wristed hands, to sit with legs crossed properly at the knee and hands tucked neatly in her lap, to throw a ball with a little stiff-wristed pushing motion, and to sit quietly and demurely. She forgets the names of all sports heroes, plays the piano, is interested in art and music, and plays bingo. (Bingo is the great meeting ground.)

The differences between the sexes are rather minimal and artificial during the early years of development (excluding the biological differences which are never minimal or artificial). Although little girls are usually dressed differently from little boys, they tend to be interested in similar activities. The tomboyish girl is probably as common as the sissy boy. The primary difference between the tomboy and her male counterpart and their like-sexed peers is the degree to which they have accepted sex typing, which is accomplished in part through the child's identification with his like-sexed parent, and secondarily through the influence of peer groups. Furthermore, the mass media communicate powerful images of what a *man* or a *woman* should be, and these images have a decided effect on the child (Maccoby, 1964).

In short, the personality traits traditionally associated with being male or female do not appear to be innately determined, but apparently result from the combined influence of all the agents of socialization that define the culture in which the child matures. Recall Mead's (1935) description of the three New Guinea tribes. It is unreasonable to propose that these tribes had sufficiently distinct genetic backgrounds to account for the dramatic differences in their behavior. Yet one tribe was composed of men and women who were highly masculine by our standards (the

Mundugumor); another consisted of men and women who had feminine traits (the Arapesh); and in the third tribe the men were feminine and the women were masculine (the Tchambuli).

The Peer Group

The peer group is both a product of culture and one of its major transmitters, particularly during middle childhood and adolescence. It consists of a relatively loose-knit group of peers (equals). During the years of middle childhood (appropriately called the latency phase by Freud), the peer group typically consists of like-sexed children. In addition, because of the disparate abilities, capacity for understanding, and varied interests among the different ages spanning this period, the peer group usually consists of peers close in age. During adolescence the peer group may be enlarged to include members of both sexes and a wider range of ages.

An illustration of a boys' gang and of its importance to its members is provided in the following page from Sam's **diary** (reproduced here with Sam's permission):

October 25, 1935

Dear Diary;

Here I am again, Diary. Loney and Bill and George and Jim and Guy and Me had a great time last night, Diary. We all met near Old Man West's barn and I gave the secret word which I said I would never even write in my diary cross my hart and hope to die and so I cant tell you what our secret word is but it sure is a good one. When I said the word my best friends, Loney and Bill, said the answering word which is a secret too so I cant tell you that one either. Then George and Jim came and said the word and we let them in through the broken board into the stall where we keep all our treasures. I have to steal a candle, Dear Diary, because we burned our last one last night and Bill stole one last time so its my turn. I would steal anything for the Packrats. And you know what happened last night? When Guy came he forgot the secret password. He's not my best friend cause he's kind of dum. We wouldn't let him in for the longest time and he was going to start crying if we didn't say it was ok and tell him what the word was so we did and we let him in and he memorized the word all night. When we grow up me, and my gang are all going to go into business or something together and none of us are ever going to get married but we are going to live in a fine house along a river where there's lotta of fish, and will have secret passwords and sentences even and we won't let anybody in who doesn't know them, except mayke our dads when they come to visit us to go fishing. Loney and Bill sure are my very best friends, goodbye Diary because I have to go and steal that candle while Mom is in the bathroom.

The phenomenon of the boy's gang, while not universal, is fairly common. Similar types of close relationships may often exist within small, closely knit peer groups. The influence of the peer group on the lives of its members is quite as strong as that of a secret. You will remember that as children gradually leave the home and enter the school and community, the importance of the family decreases, both as an agent of socialization and as a source of reinforcement, while the importance of peer groups increases. Parents continue to play a predominant role, albeit a lessening one, during the early years of the child's schooling.

Research conducted by Prado (1958) clearly illustrates the shift in allegiance from family to peers during the transition from middle childhood to adolescence. Prado selected two groups of boys, all of whom had indicated that their father was their favorite parent. One group consisted of boys between 8 and 11 years of age; the second group contained adolescents between 14 and 17. For the experiment boys and their fathers were brought to a laboratory, along with the boy's best friend—a boy of similar age who had been selected as the "best friend" on the basis of interviews and questionnaires. The friends and the fathers were asked to throw darts at a target. The target was arranged so that the boy could not see the exact scores made by his father or his friend. His task was to estimate their performance.

The results of the study reveal that both the younger boys and the adolescents were almost equally accurate in their estimates. Interestingly, however, the younger boys consistently overestimated the scores made by their fathers and underestimated those made by their friends. In contrast, adolescents tended to underestimate their fathers' scores and overestimated their friends' scores. The evidence strongly suggests that from middle childhood to adolescence there is a marked decline in the importance of parents and a corresponding increase in the importance of peers.

The characteristics of children most likely to be accepted as peers vary depending on age and sex. In general, children who are friendly and sociable are more easily accepted than those who are hostile, unsociable, withdrawn, or indifferent (Tuddenham, 1951; G. H. Smith, 1950). Similarly, children who are intelligent and creative are more acceptable than those who are slow learners or retarded (Gallagher, 1958). Size, strength, athletic prowess, and daring are particularly important characteristics for membership in boys' peer groups; maturity and social skills are more important for girls, particularly as they approach adolescence.

The most common technique for assessing the nature of peer acceptance or rejection is called **sociometry**, in which a questionnaire or an interview is used to determine the patterns of likes and dislikes in a group. The data gathered in this way are frequently interpreted through pictorial or graphical representations in a **sociogram**. The data may be arrived at in one of several related ways. The investigator might present each of the children with the pictures or names of all of the other children in his class and ask him to sort them according to the ones he would most like to be with, or those whom he likes the best. The investigator might also ask children to discuss those children whom they like the least and would least like to be with. Alternate methods involve asking children to select the most popular boy or girl in the room, the smartest child or the dumbest one.

A sociogram is valuable as a source of potentially meaningful insights into social relationships in the classroom, about which the teacher might be totally unaware. Its reliability is frequently limited, however. The sociogram shown in Figure 12.3 reveals that Bob, Sam, and Loney are the best liked boys — not surprising if the teacher already knows that they are among the best athletes, the most intelligent, and the most friendly and outgoing. Similarly, the most popular girls are Joan and

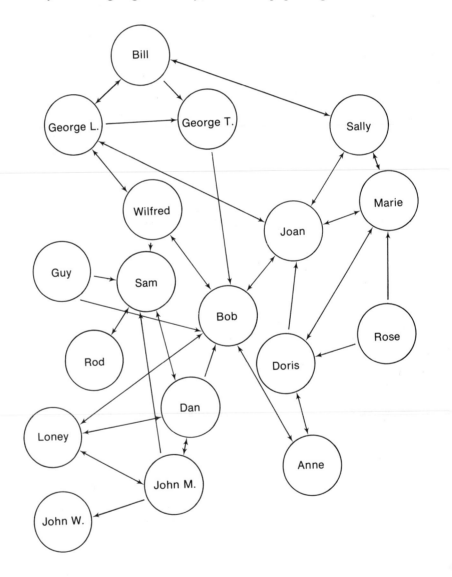

Figure 12.3   A sociogram of a fourth-grade classroom. The popular children are Loney, Sam, Bob, Joan, and Marie. The unpopular are Rose and Guy.

Marie; and that too, given their irrepressible good looks, their buoyant personalities, and their intelligence, is not particularly surprising. But there is also a message of sadness and loneliness in this sociogram. There is a shy and retiring child who admires the two most popular boys, but who is liked by no one in return—Guy. There is a little girl not overly endowed by nature and to whom nurture has not been kind, either. Her name is Rose, and she, like Guy, is liked by no one. There is something terribly tragic and poignant about a young child whose only source of friendship is his dog (if his parents will permit him that friend). Perhaps there is something a sensitive and concerned teacher can do for such a child.*

During his first years of school, the child's peer group has several important functions, some of which have been implied above. First, the child's need for acceptance and approval is satisfied mostly by his peer group. The child also needs to develop a favorable self-concept (Murray, 1938)—to achieve self-esteem—and the concept of his *self* is found to be in direct relation to how he thinks others perceive him. G. H. Mead (in Strauss, 1964) has developed a philosophical theory based on the development of self, asserting that the *self* that an adult eventually comes to possess is a conglomerate of the way he thinks the significant others in his life perceive him. Psychological research supports this position. Horowitz (1962), for example, found that children who were rated unpopular by their peers tended to have a derogatory self-concept; these children were most likely to be dissatisfied with what they were and to want to become like the other children whom they thought more popular. Coleman (1961) has corroborated these findings with studies of high school children.

Second, peer groups are integral to the formation of sexually appropriate values and attitudes. There is ample evidence that prolonged membership in a group makes its members more similar by bringing their values and attitudes into closer correspondence. Campbell and Yarrow (1958) found that racially integrated summer camps significantly reduced feelings of social tension and distance among the children. Similarly, Coleman (1960) found that the predominant academic values of a school were transmitted via peer groups. With the passage of time, freshmen's estimates of the importance of the school's predominant values tended to increase. More precisely, with continued exposure to a group with relatively defined values, the individual's values gradually approach those of the group.

The peer group's influence on attitudes toward morality is examined in more detail below.

Moral Development

With the conviction that frequently accompanies intuition, all of us believe implicitly that people *are* good or bad in differing degrees—that the goodness or evil is an intrinsic part of what we are—of our *selves*. A closer examination of morality, however, reveals that although such

---

* Buy him a dog, you say? Please, this is a serious matter.

standards may partly define one's humanness (whatever that is), there are other dimensions of moral behavior that are amenable to scientific investigation.

Kohlberg (1964) discusses three aspects of morality: the first two are those to which we are most likely to respond when judging the relative "goodness" of people; the third quality is the one currently receiving most attention from researchers and theorists. The first is the behavioral aspect of morality, reflected in a person's ability to resist temptation; the second relates to the amount of guilt that accompanies failure to resist temptation; the third is the individual's estimate of the morality of a given act based on some personal standard of good or evil. It is obvious that these dimensions of morality are not necessarily very closely related. A person may incessantly transgress some accepted code of conduct — behave immorally, in other words — and yet feel a great deal of guilt. A second may engage in exactly the same behavior and feel no guilt. Despite these differences, both may judge the act equally evil. Who has the strongest conscience?

What is a strong conscience? There are two classical approaches to answering this question. The psychoanalytic approach is based on the belief that the strength of the Superego is the strength of conscience. It asserts explicitly that the stronger a person's beliefs about the immorality of an act, the less likely he is to engage in that act. Interestingly, empirical evidence has not supported this position. Several studies and reports (for example, Hendry, 1960; Havighurst and Taba, 1949) have indicated that

Evidence suggests that the child's beliefs about right and wrong have less to do with his training and actual behavior than with the likelihood of being caught.

there is a very low correlation between the strength of a person's beliefs and his actual behavior. Hence, a person who *behaves* as though he were a moral individual does not necessarily house a Superego that consists of a million objections to immoral acts and an equal number of prescripts for good behavior.

The second approach, a more religious one, is based on the belief that a good conscience is a manifestation of strength of character and good habits that have been inculcated in the individual, usually through his religious training. Kohlberg (1964) summarizes several studies that again indicate no relationship of religious training and parental demands to overt behavior. Indeed, available evidence (as is mentioned in Chapter 11) strongly suggests that beliefs about right or wrong have less to do with the child's actual behavior than with the likelihood of his being caught or the gains to be derived from transgression. Other related factors are the individual's intelligence, his ability to delay gratification (to choose long-range goals over short-range objectives), and the individual's self-esteem. It appears that children who have favorable self-concepts are less likely to engage in immoral behavior, presumably because they are more likely to feel guilty if they do. If this is correct, people who are involved with young children should find the information about the importance of the child's self-concept useful in understanding and guiding his behavior.

Based on these findings, Kohlberg (1964) argues that moral behavior is primarily a matter of strength of will (Ego strength), rather than strength of conscience, Superego or character. In other words, morality is not a fixed behavioral trait, but rather a decision-making capacity. From this point of view, Kohlberg (1969, 1971) has delineated three levels or stages in the development of moral judgment, each consisting of two types of moral orientation (shown in Table 12.2). The three levels are sequential, although succeeding levels never entirely replace preceding ones, making it almost impossible to assign ages to them. It appears, however, that the average child progresses from an initial premoral state, in which he responds primarily to punishment or reward, through a rule-based, highly conventional morality, and finally to the stage of self-accepted principles (see Figure 12.4).

Kohlberg's description of children's responses to questions relating to two aspects of morality is illustrated in the following examples of various moral orientations in children between the ages of 10 and 16:

Motivation for Moral Action*

Stage 1: Punishment — Danny, Age 10:
(Should Joe tell on his older brother to his father?)
"In one way it would be right to tell on his brother or his father might get mad at him and spank him. In another way it would be right to keep quiet or his brother might beat him up."

* From "Development of moral character and ideology" by Lawrence Kohlberg in *Review of Child Development Research*, Vol. I, edited by Martin L. Hoffman and Lois Wladis Hoffman. New York: Russell Sage Foundation, 1964, p. 401. Copyright 1964 by Russell Sage Foundation. Used by permission of the Russell Sage Foundation.

Stage 2: Exchange and Reward—Jimmy, Age 13:
(Should Joe tell on his older brother to his father?)
"I think he should keep quiet. He might want to go someplace like that, and if he squeals on Alex, Alex might squeal on him."

Stage 3: Disapproval Concern—Andy, Age 16:
(Should Joe keep quiet about what his brother did?)
"If my father finds out later, he won't trust me. My brother wouldn't either, but I wouldn't have a *conscience* that he [my brother] didn't."
"I try to do things for my parents; they've always done things for me. I try to do everything my mother says; I try to please her. Like she wants me to be a doctor, and I want to, too, and she's helping me to get up there."

Stage 6: Self-condemnation Concern—Bill, Age 16:
(Should the husband steal the expensive black market drug needed to save his wife's life?)
"Lawfully no, but morally speaking I think I would have done it. It would be awfully hard to live with myself afterward, knowing that I could have done something which would have saved her life and yet didn't for fear of punishment to myself."

Basis of Moral Worth of a Human Life

Stage 1: Life's Value Based on Physical and Status Aspects—Tommy, Age 10:
(Why should the druggist give the drug to the dying woman when her husband couldn't pay for it?)
"If someone important is in a plane and is allergic to heights and the stewardess won't give him medicine because she's only got enough for one and she's got a sick one, a friend, in back, they'd probably put the stewardess in a lady's jail because she didn't help the important one."
(Is it better to save the life of one important person or a lot of unimportant people?) "All the people that aren't important because one man just has one house, maybe a lot of furniture, but a whole bunch of people have an awful lot of furniture and some of these poor people might have a lot of money and it doesn't look it."

Stage 2: Life's Value as Instrumental to Need-Satisfaction—Tommy at Age 13:
(Should the doctor "mercy-kill" a fatally ill woman requesting death because of her pain?)
"Maybe it would be good to put her out of her pain, she'd be better off that way. But the husband wouldn't want it, it's not like an animal. If a pet dies you can get along without it—it isn't something you really need. Well, you can get a new wife, but it's not really the same."

Stage 4: Life Sacred Because of a Social and Religious Order—John, Age 16:
(Should the doctor "mercy-kill" the woman?)
"The doctor wouldn't have the right to take a life, no human has the right. He can't create life, he shouldn't destroy it."

Stage 6: Life's Value as Expressing the Sacredness of the Individual—Steve, Age 16:
(Should the husband steal the expensive drug to save his wife?)

Kohlberg's Levels and Types of Morality   Table 12.2

Level I   Premoral
      Type 1   Punishment and obedience orientation
      Type 2   Naive instrumental hedonism
Level II   Morality of Conventional Role Conformity
      Type 3   Good-boy morality of maintaining good relations, approval of
                others
      Type 4   Authority maintains morality
Level III   Morality of Self-Accepted Principles
      Type 5   Morality of contract, of individual rights, and of democratically
                accepted law
      Type 6   Morality of individual principles of conscience

"By the law of society he was wrong but by the law of nature or of God the druggist was wrong and the husband was justified. Human life is above financial gain. Regardless of who was dying, if it was a total stranger, man has a duty to save him from dying."

The progression of stages of moral development is interesting and informative. At the premoral stage the child's judgment of right and wrong takes one of two orientations. In this stage, the child believes that evil

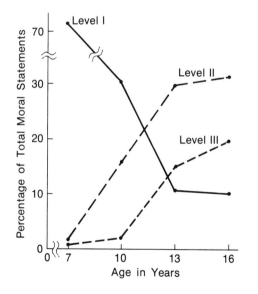

Mean percent of moral statements of six moral types made by boys aged 7 to 16. The   Figure 12.4
chart illustrates the typical decrement from the first type of moral reasoning with advancing age and an increase to move advanced moral judgments. (From "Development of moral character and ideology," by Lawrence Kohlberg in *Review of Child Development Research, Vol. I,* edited by Martin L. Hoffman and Lois Wladis Hoffman. New York: Russell Sage Foundation, 1964, p. 403. Copyright 1964 by Russell Sage Foundation. Used by permission of the Russell Sage Foundation.)

behavior is that which is likely to be punished, and good behavior is based on obedience or the avoidance of the evil implicit in disobedience. Thus, the child does not evaluate right or wrong in terms of the objective consequences of the behavior or the intentions of the actor; judgment is based solely on the subjective consequences to the child. Accordingly, the second moral orientation possible at this level is a hedonistic one, in which the child interprets good as that which is pleasant and evil as that which has undesirable consequences for him. At this level there begins the reciprocity that characterizes morality at the second level, but it is a practical reciprocity. The child will go out of his way to do something good for someone if he himself will gain by the deed.

The second level, a morality of conventional role conformity, reflects the increasing importance of peer and social relations to the developing child. Type 3, for example, is defined as morality designed to maintain good relations. Hence, moral behavior is behavior that receives wide approval from significant people — parents, teachers, peers, and society at large. Type 4, conformity to rules and laws, is also related to the child's desire to maintain a friendly status quo. Thus, conforming to law becomes important for maintaining adults' approval.

At the highest level, the child begins to view morality in terms of individual rights (Type 5), and as ideals and principles that have value as rules or laws, apart from their influence on approval. The person's individual notions of right and wrong (Type 6) begin to take precedence.

Levels I and II are characteristic of the child who is the subject of this chapter: he is the moral hedonist and the conformer to rules. Middle childhood is still some distance from the idealistic rejection of established order that characterizes the adolescent, whose moral orientation has now come to include the morality of self-accepted moral principles.

The moral progression described by Kohlberg is not very different from that described by Piaget, although the former is considerably more detailed and more carefully substantiated by empirical evidence. Kohlberg's research deals primarily with boys between 10 and 17 years of age. The particular merit of this research is that it follows the same group of 75 boys throughout most of the studies and is therefore in a position to assert some conclusions regarding moral development from a longitudinal point of view. Essentially, the conclusion indicated by the data is that there is an apparent sequence from a premoral orientation, through a period of conformity, and finally to an autonomous moral orientation. Piaget (1932) similarly described moral development as consisting of two major stages: a period of *heteronomy* followed by a period of *autonomy*. By *heteronomy of morality*, Piaget meant moral judgment determined by outside authority, obviously corresponding to Kohlberg's first level. Piaget also included a stage of reciprocity in the first period, during which the child's moral thinking is significantly altered by social influences. This stage presumably corresponds to Kohlberg's second level, although the reciprocity of which Piaget spoke was simply a means of moving from the period of heteronomous control to autonomy.

Bull (1969) has criticized Piaget's theory, claiming that reciprocity does not become autonomy, but that it continues unchanged into adulthood. Accordingly, Bull advanced yet another sequence of moral development, beginning with a period of no moral orientation (**anomy**), and progressing through **heteronomy**, **socionomy** (Level II type social rules), and culminating in **autonomy**. Although a more detailed examination of these would lend little to this discussion, the obvious parallel to Kohlberg is important. Bull's sequence reinforces the general conclusion that morality progresses from external control and externally based standards to internal control and internally based standards. It follows that delinquency (and subsequent criminality) may result from the child's failure to reach the final level of morality and his consequent absence of internalized principles by which to guide and judge his behavior. The lack of autonomy results in an absence of guilt over transgression and a consequent failure to refrain from transgressions (Bandura and Walters, 1959; McCord and McCord, 1956).

Morality seems to be a product of the process of socialization. It may be considered the consequence of the combined influences of all the socializing agencies of moment in the child's life. It is not surprising to find that as the parents are diminishing in importance, the restricted, authority-based morality of early childhood gives way to the social and peer-group morality of reciprocity and social rules and conventions. Also, at the time when a child enters the idealism typical of adolescence, he reformulates and reexamines the rules that he had passively accepted earlier and develops his personal set of moral standards.

The child's moral development is part of his social development; it is also part of his intellectual development, for the two are separable only by means of the artificial divisions that psychologists invent. For this chapter, there remains one additional aspect of the process of development from age 6 to 12 — the development of the child's intellect.

When we left the child's mind toward the end of Chapter 11, it was not because his mind had ceased to develop while he continued to advance physically and socially, but because the minds of authors and sometimes of readers are not always facile at rendering lucid as complex a subject as the child's total development. We pick up the thread of intellectual development once more, keeping in mind that as his intellect is developing, the child is also growing in other ways. Our guide again is Jean Piaget, and the period through which we are moving is labeled *concrete operations*. The child approaches this period by way of the sensorimotor period (birth to 2 years) and two preoperational subperiods, preconceptual thought (2 to 4 years) and intuitive thinking (4 to 7 years). The child's thinking toward the end of the intuitive stage is egocentric, perception dominated, and intuitive. Consequently, it is fraught with contradictions and with errors of logic. With the advent of the period of concrete thought, many of these deficiencies will disappear and be replaced by more logical thinking.

Transition from the intuitive stage to concrete operations is marked by the acquisition of one or more *conservations* — and these are at once

Intellectual
Development

the most widely researched, the most interesting, and perhaps the most significant manifestations of the child's thinking investigated by Piaget.

The Conservations

Ancient French grandmothers believe that to conserve is to put into glass jars, seal with a rubber ring, a glass top, a metal rim, and boil.* More contemporary American grandmothers believe that the procedure described does not lead to conservation but does lead to preservation. It is a question of conserves versus preserves.

To Piaget, **conservation** refers to the fact that the quantitative aspects of objects do not change unless something has been added to or taken away from that object, despite other changes in the objects that may lead to misleading perceptual alteration. This kind of perceptual alteration was illustrated earlier by the preoperational child's assumption that there was more plasticene in the snake than there had been in the ball, presumably because the form was longer and looked as though it had more material. The child's error is an example of his inability to *conserve*. The eventual comprehension that the transformed object does not have more or less substance than it previously had not only marks the acquisition of concepts of conservation, but also marks the transition between preoperational thought and concrete operations.

The significance of the acquisition of conservation is not so much that the child ceases to be deceived by a problem but rather that he has

Conservation Behavior

Conserver (French), to preserve.

1. Conservation of substance (6-7)

A 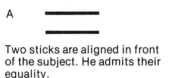 B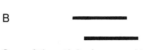

The experimenter presents two identical plasticene balls. The subject admits that they have equal amounts of plasticene.

One of the balls is deformed. The subject is asked whether they still contain equal amounts.

2. Conservation of length (6-7)

A  B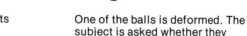

Two sticks are aligned in front of the subject. He admits their equality.

One of the sticks is moved to the right. The subject is asked whether they are still the same length.

3. Conservation of number (6-7)

A  B

Two rows of counters are placed in one-to-one correspondence. Subject admits their equality.

One of the rows is elongated (or contracted). Subject is asked whether each row still has the same number.

4. Conservation of liquids (6-7)

A  B

Two beakers are filled to the same level with water. The subject sees that they are equal.

The liquid of one container is poured into a tall tube (or a flat dish). The subject is asked whether each contains the same amount.

5. Conservation of area (9-10)

A  B

The subject and the experimenter each have identical sheets of cardboard. Wooden blocks are placed on these in identical positions. The subject is asked whether each cardboard has the same amount of space remaining.

The experimenter scatters the blocks on one of the cardboards. The subject is asked the same question.

Some simple tests for conservation with approximate ages of attainment.   Figure 12.5

now developed certain fundamental logical rules. These rules of logic are most characteristic and most descriptive of the child's thinking at the stage of concrete operations. Three of these rules are particularly important: **identity, reversibility,** and *combinativity. Identity* is the notion that for every operation (internalized act, or thought) there is an operation that leaves the product unchanged. *Reversibility* is the realization that every operation can be undone (reversed or unthought), and that certain logical consequences follow from this possibility. *Combinativity* (also termed *closure*) is a logical law specifying that several operations can be combined to yield a new product (closure), or that several operations can be combined in different ways to yield the same result (*associativity* or *compensation*). All of these concepts can be simplified considerably by once again referring to the classical conservation of substance situation.

The child is presented with two identical plasticene balls which he admits contain the same amount of plasticene. One is then elongated, while the other is left unchanged. The child is asked whether the deformed object still contains the same amount of plasticene as the unchanged object, or whether it has more or less. If he says that it has an equal amount (conservation), he may be reasoning in one of three ways. He may think that nothing has been added to or taken away from the elongated object and that it must therefore be identical to what it was (identity). Or, he might reason that the ball was formed into a sausagelike shape, but that it can be reformed into a ball, in which case it would still contain the same amount now (reversibility). A third assumption might be that the elongated object has more material since it is longer but also appears to have less because it is thinner. The two dimensions therefore compensate each other and the changes are cancelled (combinativity).

There are as many conservations as there are quantitative attributes of objects, and not all of these are acquired at the same age, despite the fact that similar rules of logic are appropriate to the solution of each. In addition to conservation of substance (also referred to as conservation of matter, solids, or continuous matter), there is conservation of number, length, area, volume, discontinuous substance, liquids, and so on. Appropriate tests for several of these conservations are described in Figure 12.5 (see Lefrancois, 1972a). The ages given are simply approximations for the "average" child.

Acceleration of
Conservation

The general question of whether the sequence of development described by Piaget can be altered through intervention has been examined primarily by attempting to accelerate the conservations. Since the acquisition of conservation marks the transition from preoperational thought to operational thinking, and since it is relatively simple to determine whether or not a child has acquired a specific type of conservation, the area is particularly appropriate for study. It is amazing that many studies designed specifically to teach conservation to young children prior to the time they would be expected to acquire it naturally have been unsuccessful. An apparently simple task such as teaching a child that the amount of plasticene in an object does not change unless material is added or taken away is almost impossible (Smedslund, 1961a, b, c, d, e) — almost, but not quite. A number of systematic and detailed training procedures, the majority employing subjects who were almost at the transition stage, have reported success in teaching conservation (for example, Lefrancois, 1966, 1968; Carlson, 1967; Travis, 1969). Most research reported, however, did not involve any attempt to ascertain whether or not conservation behavior on one task generalized to any other task. In view of this, and given the apparent difficulty of teaching conservation, it is likely that in many of the studies reporting success the subjects have learned only to respond correctly for that test. Thus, they have learned an empirical rule, but have probably not acquired the logical understanding required for a significant alteration of the developmental process. In short, the conclusion that development can be altered in any appreciable way through short-term training programs in specific areas is not warranted by the available evidence.

Acceleration of Conservation

In addition to acquiring various conservations, the child acquires three distinct abilities as he enters concrete operations. First, he learns to deal with classes, achieving the capacity to understand class inclusion and to reason about the combination and the decomposition of classes. An 8-year-old child, for example, would be unlikely to make a mistake when asked to decide whether there are more roses or more flowers in a bouquet consisting of fifteen roses and five dandelions. He would understand that roses make up a subclass of the larger class "flowers." Simi-

Other Abilities

larly, he would have little difficulty multiplying two classes in the problem that follows: If there are fat coyotes and skinny coyotes, and some are mangy and some are healthy, how many kinds of coyotes are there? The classes he must multiply are fat and skinny coyotes by mangy and healthy coyotes. The answer is illustrated in Figure 12.6. We also note in this illustration one of the principal limitations of the child's reasoning during the concrete operations stage. Although he is capable of reasoning as if he understands the simple multiplication of classes, he is still incapable of systematically multiplying the products of these. In other words, the child at this stage would not look at Figure 12.6 and expand it.

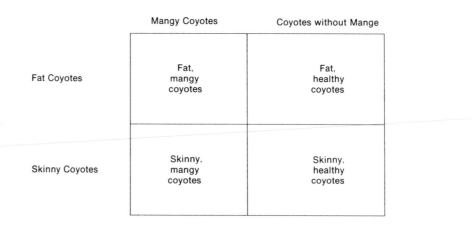

Figure 12.6   How many kinds of coyotes are there if there are fat ones and skinny ones, and mangy ones and ones without mange? An illustration of the classification abilities of the concrete operations child.

During the period of concrete operations the child comes to understand the concept of **seriation**—that is, the orderly relationship of asymmetrical parts. Piaget developed a problem to demonstrate the lack of seriation during the preoperational period; this same method can be employed to demonstrate its presence during concrete operations. The child is presented with two ordered series of objects—for example, a group of dolls and a group of canes, each a different length so that the objects might easily be arranged from longest to shortest. Figure 12.7 illustrates the arrangement desired, easily and quickly produced by the child in concrete operations, even when both series are presented to him in random order. The child at the stage of intuitive thinking, however, is ordinarily incapable of responding correctly even with a single series. A typical response is to place several of the dolls in ascending order of length without regard for the fact that others may fit in between those that have already been positioned. If the next doll the child selects is too short to be placed where the child intended it to be (at the upper end), he places it without hesitation at the other end, even though it might be taller or

A test of a child's understanding of seriation. The elements of the series are presented   Figure 12.7
in random order and the child is asked to arrange them in sequence of height.

shorter than the doll that is already positioned there. The child fails to make an inference that signals complete understanding of seriation and is almost essential to the solution of the problem: if A is greater than B, and B is greater than C, then A must also be greater than C. Understanding this concept eliminates the necessity for making all the comparisons that would otherwise be necessary.

Once the child understands classification and seriation he can also understand the concept of number. Although prior to this time he might have learned to recite numbers in the appropriate order and he might appear to associate collections of objects with particular numbers, his concept of number is still necessarily incomplete. The child must comprehend both the ordinal (the ordered sequence or succession of numbers)

Seriation

and the cardinal (quantitative) properties of number; the first concept is implicit in seriation, whereas the second relates to classification. That is, a number involves classes since it represents collections (classes) of different, or increasing, magnitude (the cardinal property of number); number involves seriation in the sense that numbers are ordered in relation to other numbers of greater or lesser magnitude (the ordinal properties of number).

Summary of Concrete Operations

An operation is a thought that is characterized by rules of logic. Since the child acquires conservations early in this period, and since these concepts are manifestations of operational thinking, the period is called *operational*. It is also termed *concrete* because the child's thinking deals with real objects or those that he can easily imagine. The child in the concrete operations stage is bound to this world; he does not yet have the freedom made possible by the more advanced logic of the formal operations stage—freedom to contemplate the hypothetical, to compare the ideal with the actual, to be profoundly unhappy and concerned at the discrepancy between this world and that which he imagines possible.

Summary

This chapter opened with children of Koros, falloren rays, and a short-circuited diobol in a biogenic laboratory. From there it stopped briefly to speak of movies and of development, suggesting that one is static but gives the illusion of movement, while the other flows continuously but gives the illusion of being static —at least within the limitations of printed words in textbooks of developmental psychology. The space between the two ends, top and bottom, of middle childhood was filled in through discussions of physical growth, socialization, and intellectual development. The growth spurt, earlier for girls than for boys, occurs near the top limit of middle childhood. Motor development and some differences between the sexes (in addition to the usual biological differences) were next examined briefly. The chapter then paid a short visit to a monolithic culture machine, watching it gobble and digest innocent school children. Soon it hurried on to a discussion of sex typing, and the role of peer groups, noting in passing that friends eventually replace fathers in the lives of young boys. The boy no longer threatens, "My pop will beat you up," but claims instead that his best buddy will do the trick. The chapter peeked at Sam's diary, reproduced one page from it, and discovered some interesting passages to be continued in Chapter 13. Turning closer to its end, the chapter assessed some of the recent work on the development of morality and disclosed once again the rather disturbing fact that moral behavior is less closely related to religious training and parental control than to the fear of being discovered. Kohlberg's levels and types of moral orientation were discussed and illustrated, prior to examining the child's concrete mind—not cement, of course, but tied to the realities of the world. The last statement hinted that the child would be freed from his restrictions in time.

Main Points

1. Korons employ falloren rays to accelerate the development of newly forming Korons in glass-lined embryonic chambers. Reversed falloren rays decelerate development.

2. Middle childhood spans the ages from 6 to 12; the last two years of this period are frequently included in late childhood or preadolescence.

3. Although boys are normally heavier and taller than girls throughout their lives, there is a brief period late in middle childhood when girls become heavier and taller than boys. It is a momentary thing simply reflecting different growth timetables.

4. Boys surpass girls in most motor activities, except those involving rhythmic movements and balance, such as playing hopscotch. Boys can usually reach higher, jump farther, run faster, and shout louder than girls.

5. The reaction time for young children is considerably slower than for adults.

6. Fitness does not appear to be positively related to performance on intellectual tasks, perhaps because the child who is particularly healthy also has a greater need for physical activity and consequently becomes more frustrated when he is confined to a desk.

7. The school is a powerful influence. This platitude requires little amplification.

8. Sex typing—learning sex-appropriate behavior—is accomplished partly through identification with the like-sexed parent and partly through explicit and implicit pressures of peer groups and other agents of socialization.

9. During middle childhood and adolescence the peer group gradually replaces the parents as the most important socializing force.

10. Morality can be described in three dimensions: the behavior of the individual, the amount of guilt that accompanies transgressions, and the individual's estimate of the morality (or immorality) of the act in question.

11. Neither the Freudian psychoanalytic view, which maintains that strength of conscience is a function of the strength of Superego (learned attitudes about evil), nor the supposition that conscience reflects a strong and well *trained* character, is supported by evidence. Correlation between beliefs and behavior is low; correlation between religious and cultural training and behavior is also low.

12. Kohlberg describes three levels of moral orientation: the premoral, oriented toward punishment, obedience, and pragmatic hedonism; the morality of convention, characterized by the desire to conform to standards to maintain good social relations; and the morality of individual principles, characterized by conscious personal formulations of principles of conduct. Piaget's description concurs in substance with Kohlberg's.

13. The period of concrete operations is marked by the child's acquisition of concepts of conservation of various quantitative attributes. These are acquired at different ages and are remarkably resistant to training.

14. In addition to the conservations, during concrete operations the child acquires three related abilities: the ability to deal with classes, to seriate, and to understand number.

One of the most lucid and comprehensive descriptions of the child's motor and perceptual development is provided by Cratty. Particularly interesting are the detailed descriptions of the motor development in children of different ages and sexes.

Further Readings

Cratty, B. J. *Perceptual and motor development in infants and children.* New York: The Macmillan Company, 1970.

Kohlberg has extensively investigated moral development, an area of considerable current interest. The following are two sources of information about these investigations:

Kohlberg, L. Development of moral character and moral ideology. In M. L. Hoffman and L. W. Hoffman (Eds.), *Review of Child Development Research*. Vol. 1. New York: Russell Sage Foundation. 1964, 383–432.

Kohlberg, L. and E. Turiel. *Research in moral development: The cognitive developmental approach*. New York: Holt, Rinehart & Winston, 1971.

Two books that summarize some of Piaget's theorizing and give particularly good accounts of the development of conservation in the school child are the following:

Phillips, J. L. *The origins of intellect*. San Francisco: W. H. Freeman, 1969.

Ginsberg, H. and S. Opper. *Piaget's theory of intellectual development*. Englewood Cliffs, N.J.: Prentice-Hall, 1969.

The following are two of many articles relating to the acceleration of conservation in children:

Carlson, J. S. Effects of instruction on the concept of conservation of substance. *Science Education*, 1967, **4**, 285–291.

Lefrancois, G. R. A treatment hierarchy for the acceleration of conservation of substance. *Canadian Journal of Psychology*, 1968, **22**, 277–284.

Of the Passage, and of Sex: Adolescence

The sun had not yet crept over the eastern hills when his father, his uncles, and all the elders of the tribe came for him. With them they brought the great head of the fish; without it Ootala could not have become a man. Ootala had caught the fish by himself two months earlier, easily the largest fish any boy had ever caught before the day of his Passage into Manhood.* This augured well for the boy, for it was well known that the size of the fish head would determine his success as a man and how many sons he would have. So Ootala was proud as he walked between his uncles, stepping in the footprints of his father, and listening to the shuffle of the elders as they moved quietly behind. All were silent, for speaking was an evil thing before the Passage.

But although Ootala was proud, he was fearful too, for the Passage is not to be taken lightly; it is a serious event and must be treated with the reverence it deserves. Ootala's fear arose not only from the significance of the day, but also because there was much that he did not know about the events that would take place—events which have occurred on the occasion of every Passage since the beginning of time and are known only to those who are men. And Ootala would not be a man until his Passage.

The solemn retinue shuffled quietly through the ashes of yesterday's fires, which were scattered among the huts in which the women, the children, and the dogs lay quiet—quiet, but not sleeping. As he walked through the white ashes Ootala remembered that in the songs of the Passage, ashes were a symbol of years of childhood that would soon be in the irretrievable past, even as the fires that had created the ashes were past. Ootala prayed that the silent occupants of the little huts would make no noise till he had passed, otherwise memories of his childhood would come to haunt him when he was an old man. When a boy becomes a man he must leave his childhood behind: today he is a child, but from tomorrow onward he will be a man.

As the skies turned the chill pink that heralds the coming of another sun, Ootala and the men of his tribe entered the forest and tensely filed down the path to the hut of the Passage. In all his childhood Ootala had heard of this hut but had never seen it, for a child must never look upon the hut where men are made until he himself is ready to become a man. Now Ootala saw a small hut made of grass and mud, set in the center of a little clearing on the edge of a hill facing east. As they approached the hut the men saw that the day's sun was not yet on the horizon and they were relieved, for the Passage must occur with the sunrise if the man is to arise with strength every day of his life. If the time is too early he will not sleep at night, and his wives will leave him to seek the solace of men who snore more peacefully; if it is too late he will not be able to arise in the morning, and his wives will leave him to find more energetic men.

Ootala and his uncles entered the hut. The oldest uncle, Benag, carried the precious Passage bundle—a pouch of antelope skin bulging with items unknown and from which there emanated a faintly pungent

---

* Another common expression is **rites de passage**.

odor. His other uncle, Aras, carried the fish head. The remaining elders formed a circle around the hut while Ootala's father stood with his back to the hut's dark doorway, scrutinizing the eastern horizon.

In the momentary chill of predawn, the elders sang the Songs of the People, and from the hut there came some obscure noises. The elders' songs gradually rose in pitch until they drowned out any sounds that might be coming from the hut. And as the sun burst over the hill, the sounds reached a crescendo and then slowly calmed to anticipatory silence. Ootala walked proudly out of the hut to greet the sunrise. He had had his Passage. The women, the children, and the dogs came from their huts and ran about excitedly. There was nothing left now but the feasting; Ootala was a man.

The Passage   In Western culture the transition from childhood to adulthood requires passage through several years of adolescence, a period of life frequently acknowledged as the most troubled, the most stressful, and the most unpleasant of all stages of development. In numerous primitive societies, such as Ootala's, the passage from childhood to adulthood is marked by ritual and ceremony. These ceremonies are not always pleasant, but in most cases the result is the individual's certain knowledge that he is now a man, or a woman, with all the responsibilities and the privileges attendant upon being an adult.

In contemporary Western culture there are no *rites de passage*.* No one tells the child, "Today you are a man my son, although yesterday you were a child. Yesterday you could play with children; today you must pick up your typewriter and go to work, for you must now earn a living. You may also marry and behave as adults are permitted to behave. And you can vote; you can fight; you can be killed; you can have children; you can protest; you can become fat and lazy; and you can get drunk or otherwise dizzy. For today you are indeed a man." Because Western culture does not tell its children when they have become men and women, they must discover this for themselves. And the discovery is made particularly difficult by the fact that the culture training them is **continuous** —that is, there is no clear demarcation of passage from one state to the other. It is ironic that there is no such ritual when such events as birth and death are still observed by ceremony and ritual, which is often every bit as elaborate and superstitious as the rituals of some primitive tribes. And to the individual who is most centrally involved in these ceremonies, they are quite meaningless. That is the irony of our ritualistic life.†

Since our culture is *continuous* rather than *discontinuous* (an adjective describing societies such as that depicted in the introduction to this chapter), the passage from childhood to adulthood is, by definition, a much lengthier one. In numerous treatments of this period of adolescence,

---

*Excluding the Jewish ritual of Bar (Bat) Mitzvah, in which the Jewish boy or girl becomes an adult at the age of 13, through religious ceremony.
†Marriage is an exception for some individuals.

it is divided into a series of stages. For example, Cole and Hall (1970) divide the period from 11 to 20 into four stages: preadolescence, early adolescence, middle adolescence, and late adolescence (p. 3). There is no easy way to determine the termination of this period since there is no single criterion by which one may determine whether a person has achieved adult status; but its beginnings are somewhat more definite, although still variable.

Biologically, adolescence usually signifies the period from the onset of puberty to adulthood; occasionally adolescence designates the period beginning with pubescence and terminating with adulthood; and sometimes it indicates the span of the teen years (13 to 19). **Puberty** signifies sexual maturity; **pubescence** refers to the changes that occur in late childhood or early adolescence (depending on arbitrary divisions) resulting in sexual maturity. Adulthood cannot easily be defined but may arbitrarily be considered to begin at the age of 20. It would be convenient for this text to say that adolescence begins at 12, since we have included the earlier ages in preceding developmental periods. However, it is more accurate to say that the beginning of adolescence is variable and that age 12 simply serves as a general orientation.

Physical Changes

Puberty defines sexual maturity—the ability to make babies. As Jersild (1963) has observed, prior to puberty the individual is a child; afterward he can have a child. The problem in defining puberty in this manner is that it is almost impossible to determine exactly when a person becomes fertile. Past research has relied on information relating to the girl's first menstrual period (termed **menarche**) to discover the age at which puberty begins. Actually, however, a girl is frequently infertile for about a year after her first menstruation, so that the menarche is not an accurate index of puberty; nevertheless it is a useful indication of impending sexual maturity. It is nearly impossible to arrive at a clear index for boys.

Age of Puberty

It is generally accepted that the average age for sexual maturity is 12 for girls and 14 for boys, immediately following the period of most rapid growth (the growth spurt). Consequently the age of puberty may be established by determining the period during which the person grew most rapidly (Shuttleworth, 1939). The period of rapid growth may begin around the age of 9 for girls, compared to 11 for boys (see Chapter 12). The actual range in age is wide, however—sexual maturity for girls may range from as young as 10 to as old as 16. Similarly, boys may reach puberty as young as 12 or as old as 18. Research has revealed some interesting trends and differences in the age of menarche for different cultures and for different generations. Tanner (1955) reports that girls have been maturing earlier by as much as one-third or one-half a year per decade since 1850. In addition, adolescents are often taller and heavier than they were several generations ago. Smart and Smart (1967) review a number of studies showing that the age of menarche in different countries varies widely. For example, it has been found that the average age of menarche is 12.75 in the United States, 13.2 in southern England, and 13.9 in Jerusalem.

Pubescence

Pubescence refers to all the changes that lead to sexual maturity. Most signs are well known. Among the first signs in both boys and girls is the appearance of pigmented pubic hair, which is straight initially but becomes characteristically kinky during the later stages of pubescence. At about the same time as the pubic hair begins to appear, the boys' testes begin to enlarge, as do the girls' breasts. The girl then experiences rapid physical growth, her first menstrual period, the growth of **axillary** (armpit) **hair**, the continued enlargement of her breasts, and a slight lowering of her voice. The boy is not blessed with anything comparable to the menarche; his voice changes much more dramatically; he too grows rapidly, particularly in height and length of limbs; he acquires the capacity to ejaculate semen; he grows axillary hair; he eventually develops a beard, and if blessed by the gods who determine (cultural) signs of masculinity, he begins to grow a matting of hair on his chest.

Changes in Height, Weight, and Reach

The rapid changes in height and weight characteristic of pubescence have been described in Chapter 12, since they typically occur prior to the age of 12. Table 13.1 shows average height and weight data for boys and girls from 12 to 18. It bears repeating that by the age of 10 girls often surpass boys in height and maintain a slight advantage until $13\frac{1}{2}$. Girls' weight surpasses boys' at approximately 11, but loses the race permanently by $14\frac{1}{2}$. An additional physical change, of particular significance to boys, is a rapid increase in the length of limbs. It is not uncommon for a boy to discover that his legs are suddenly several inches longer than they were a scant year ago, and that he can reach an addi-

Table 13.1   Height (in inches) and Weight (in pounds) at the Fiftieth Percentile for American Children*

Age	Height		Weight	
	Girl	Boy	Girl	Boy
12	$59\frac{3}{4}$	59	$87\frac{1}{2}$	$84\frac{1}{2}$
$12\frac{1}{2}$	$60\frac{3}{4}$	60	$93\frac{1}{4}$	$88\frac{3}{4}$
13	$61\frac{3}{4}$	61	99	93
$13\frac{1}{2}$	$62\frac{1}{2}$	$62\frac{1}{2}$	$103\frac{3}{4}$	$100\frac{1}{4}$
14	$62\frac{3}{4}$	64	$108\frac{1}{2}$	$107\frac{1}{2}$
$14\frac{1}{2}$	63	65	111	114
15	$63\frac{1}{2}$	66	$113\frac{1}{2}$	120
$15\frac{1}{2}$	$63\frac{3}{4}$	$66\frac{3}{4}$	$115\frac{1}{4}$	125
16	64	$67\frac{3}{4}$	117	$129\frac{3}{4}$
$16\frac{1}{2}$	64	68	118	133
17	64	$68\frac{1}{2}$	119	$136\frac{1}{4}$
$17\frac{1}{2}$	64	$68\frac{1}{2}$	$119\frac{1}{2}$	$137\frac{1}{2}$
18	64	$68\frac{1}{2}$	120	139

*Adapted by the Health Department, Milwaukee, Wisconsin; based on data by H. C. Stuart and H. V. Meredith, prepared for use in Children's Medical Centre, Boston. Used by permission of the Milwaukee Health Department.

tional 4 or 5 inches. As a result of this growth he acquires the gangling appearance so frequently associated with early adolescence, exaggerated by the fact that his rate of purchasing clothes is often considerably behind the rate at which he outgrows them. Another result of his unaccustomed length of limb is a temporary clumsiness: he finds himself tripping over furniture because he has blithely assumed that the space between him and the object was three steps when in fact it was only two; and he constantly overreaches objects that are too close to him. Comparable changes in girls are usually less dramatic and seldom result in the awkwardness that afflicts many boys. Note, however, that not all boys are similarly unfortunate — many pass quite uneventfully through pubescence.

. . . he has blithely assumed that the space between him and an object is three steps when in fact it is only two . . .

Adolescence sees an increased emphasis on social skills. During this time conversational talents that were previously more important for girls than for boys become important for both. Also during this period relationships between males and females as well as those between persons of the same sex begin to assume a profound significance. Throughout adolescence there is a continued decline in the importance of parents and family and an increased importance of peer relations.

Social Development

Although it is a gross oversimplification, it is possible to describe the socialization of the adolescent in terms of three general stages based on the changing roles of friends and parents. Early in adolescence the

Three Stages of Socialization

parents continue to be of considerable importance, socially, emotionally, and physically. The young adolescent is dependent on his family in a literal sense, not only for his physical comforts but also for the psychological support they provide. It is clear, however, that the extent of this dependency is not nearly as great as it was in earlier periods of development.

Shortly after the onset of adolescence the child begins to move toward independence; and it is this progress that defines the second stage in adolescent socialization — a period of conflict both for the parents and for the child. He finds himself torn between two forces: on the one hand there is his former allegiance to his parents, his continued love for them, and his economic dependence on them; on the other hand there is a new-found allegiance to his friends and his need to be accepted by his peers. Conflict between adolescents and their parents stems not only from the child's desire to associate more frequently and more closely with his peer groups, but also from a variety of other sources. Adolescents often list such causes of strife as parental interference with social life, lack of adequate financial assistance, parental interference with school work or criticism of grades, the parents' failure to give information about sex, and their criticism of friends (Lloyd, 1954). In a study by Block (1937), a large sample of junior and senior high school students of both sexes were asked to indicate which of 50 listed items were most annoying about mothers; the following were selected by over 60 percent of the group:

Pesters me about my table manners.
Pesters me about my manners and habits.
Holds my sister or brother up to me as a model.
Scolds if my school marks are not as high as other people's.
Objects to my going automobile riding at night with boys.
Insists that I tell her what I spent my money for.
Won't let me use the car.
Insists that I eat foods that I dislike, but which are good for me.

The preceding discussion should not be interpreted to mean that parents and teen-agers are typically in conflict, but simply as information regarding prevalent sources of conflict. Meissner (1965), in an ambitious examination of parent-child relationships involving 1278 high school boys, found that changes in parent-child interaction included both positive and negative aspects. Subjects felt that as they became older they were given more opportunity for socializing; consequently they became more tolerant of parental authority and more grateful for parental guidance. At the same time, however, a significant number of adolescents reported increased unhappiness in the home, greater misunderstandings between parents and children, and increasing conflicts with parents over religion. Boys reported spending less leisure time at home than previously. Meissner (1965) concludes that while the pattern is clearly one of "gradual **alienation**" from parental control and a concomitant increase in rebelliousness, the data do not wholly justify a general label of "rebelliousness" for a description of adolescent-parent interaction.

From a stage of high dependence on the parents the adolescent progresses through the intermediate stage of conflict described above, and finally achieves the third stage—relative independence from the parents. Independence does not imply that the child breaks all bonds with his family and ties himself irrevocably to groups of peers, but simply that he has achieved an independence allowing him to function in the milieu of peers that has become so important to him—an independence that frequently implies parental conflict. The **generation gap** is a cliché recognizing the significance (and indeed the existence) of the conflict between the reigning generation (the "establishment") and the contemporary crop of adolescents from high schools to colleges, unemployed, employed, in love, out of love, or otherwise dead or alive. This gap is examined in more detail in a later section of this chapter.

Adolescent peer groups vary in size, interests, social backgrounds, and structure. They might consist of two or three like-sexed persons (buddies, pals, best friends); there are larger groups also consisting of like-sexed individuals, and a third group consisting of couples, usually of opposite sexes, who currently find themselves in the throes of romantic love. Yet another type of peer group comprises persons of both sexes who "hang around" together. Most adolescents belong to several groups at the same time. Membership in a closely knit peer group is not necessarily a mark of adolescent normality, for it is neither normal nor abnormal to behave as do the majority of the people. On the other hand, an adolescent who is unable to establish the social relationships required for membership in peer groups, and who is rejected by his peers, may be adversely affected. Effective adaptation in our culture requires a relatively high degree of social skill, as well as the ability to form and maintain personal relationships, thereby establishing the importance of the peer group. The person who, by choice or by circumstance is isolated from his peers, is denied an important opportunity to develop the ability to interact socially.

The Nature and Importance of Peer Groups

Figure 13.1 illustrates the development of groups in adolescence as they progress from small groups of like-sexed members to interaction between groups of different sexes, leading eventually to the formation of what Dunphy (1963) calls the "crowd"—a large heterosexual group that has evolved from the smaller unisexual groups. In later stages of adolescence there is a gradual disintegration of the earlier cohesiveness of the groups, brought about by the pairing of boys and girls into couples.

The characteristics of adolescents who are well liked by their peers are similar to the qualities of well liked school-aged children described in the preceding chapter. Jersild (1963) reports a large number of studies which indicate that the student who likes others is himself well liked. Recall the studies that reported that children who were friendly, sociable, and outgoing as opposed to hostile, withdrawn, and unsociable were most liked by their peers. In addition, adolescents tend to stress personality

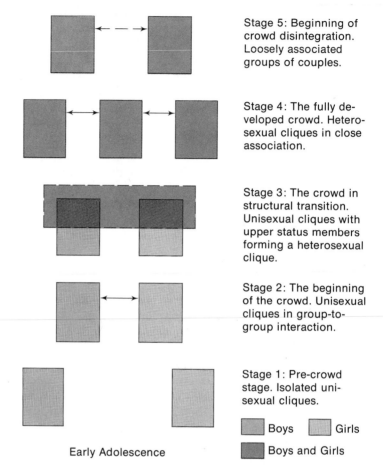

Figure 13.1   Dunphy's diagram of stages in peer group development during adolescence. (From "The social structure of urban adolescent peer groups" by Dexter C. Dunphy, *Sociometry*, 1963, **26**, 230–246. p. 236. Copyright 1963 by the American Sociological Association. Used by permission of the American Sociological Association and the author.)

characteristics associated with happiness. The person who is sociable, cheerful, active, and fun loving is typically the most popular.

The importance of being accepted by peers is highlighted in a large-scale study reported by Gronlund and Holmlund (1958). A group of 1,073 sixth-grade children were asked to select five people with whom they would like to sit, work, or play. Based on this sociometric data, the investigators divided the entire sample into two groups designated the *high-status* group and the *low-status* group. The high-status children were those selected most often—27 or more times; low-status children were those selected fewer than 3 times. Seven years later the records of some of the children in these groups were examined to determine how many had graduated from high school. It is significant that 82 percent of the high-status group compared with 45 percent of the low-status group had graduated, particularly because observed differences in intelligence between the two groups were, in the opinion of the authors, too small to account for the higher drop-out rate of the low-status children. At the same time, however, the fact that the low-status children did score significantly lower on intelligence tests is further corroboration of the assumption that intelligence is an important factor in peer group acceptance. Such studies, however, cannot be interpreted as certain evidence that peer rejection is the causal factor in school drop-outs, delinquency, or other forms of social maladjustment, for it is equally plausible to suppose that those factors responsible for maladjustment are the very factors that cause the child to be rejected by his peers in the first place. In any case, the close relationship that exists between adjustment and acceptance demands further investigation.

For the normal child, adolescence is a period of intense sociability. He awakens in the morning anxious to go to school primarily to see his friends. Together they lounge beyond the precincts of the school, surreptitiously inhaling their morning cigarette, which is expressly forbidden at home, and watching budding young nymphets approach, unconsciously seductive, shyly nervous, deliberately coy, all confusion in the emotional turbulence of newly discovered feelings. They loiter there smoking, these nonchalant young men of the world, whistling at the girls, and the whistles provide at once a hint of the mating call, a suggestion of disdain and aloofness, a nervous and awkward attempt to tease, a means of getting attention, and a way of telling their peers that they are men who appreciate a good-looking representative of womankind. These young men have not been initiated. No one has taken them to the ritual hut in the eerie predawn light; no one has sung the Songs of the People for them; nor have their uncles assisted with their Coming of Age. They must discover for themselves that they are men, and they must also discover what it means to be a man.

The following excerpts from Sam's diary* passionately and poignantly illustrate the importance of peer group activities in the adolescent's life.

October 22, 1971

Dear Diary:

Diary, I sure had a good time last night. It was a swinger, man — real hot dog swingin' swinger. Loney had his dad's bomb so we cruised around 'till we saw this real cool doll real swingin' stacked man, so I whistled like, and this doll turned and flashed her uppers real sweet. Old Loney floored the bomb and squealed right to the corner of the block where the guys were hanging around. We stopped and jawed for a while and then Marcie and that blond number from St. Mark's swung in and we picked them up, but Marcie had to go home so we got zeroed. Out'a sight diary! out'a sight!

---

* Reproduced with Sam's permission.

November 3, 1971

Dear Diary:

I have been reading Albert Camus, diary. He said "Life as a human being is absurd." He was dead right. It is kind of a mess. I am so bored I sometimes wish I were dead. Loney and the guys had his old man's bomb last night, but I didn't get to go with them. I think it's because they think I'm too smart for them. They've been teasing me quite a lot lately because I've been raising those rats for my psychology course. I think maybe it's because my nose is pretty long. It isn't fair when your dad has a long nose because a guy is pretty likely to inherit a long nose too. I think that there should be some sort of law so that the only people who would have kids are pretty good looking because there isn't anything worse than being an ugly kid. Especially when you're as skinny as I am! I don't care if Loney and the guys go ahead and ride around in his old man's bomb—It's pretty gutless that old car and one of these days I hope he breaks his arm with the crank. You know diary, I'm just so turned on these days. Man it doesn't take anything to get me going. I keep going to confession because I know it's a sin and I know that it might make me impotent and mentally retarded. I wouldn't mind not being able to have kids because it isn't fair to bring kids up in this kind of world until we get all of the problems straightened out. I wish I could get rid of my acne at least.

These two excerpts from Sam's diary reveal a great deal about the preoccupations of a fairly typical adolescent. Notice first the use of slang. Adolescents of every generation develop their own jargon, which becomes part of their existence as meaningfully as the jargon of psychology is a part of that discipline. Jargon provides a sense of affinity, of belongingness. One of the surest signs that a person does not *belong* is his failure to speak the language of the group. If the group does not want him, they will communicate their rejection by exaggerating their private language in his presence; if they do want him, they will allow him to learn their language. The slang of adolescence, judging from an adolescent diary several decades old, changes with time.

This entry in Sam's diary also demonstrates the sociability of adolescence, and it is a clue to the desperate loneliness of rejection whether it be real or imagined. And associated with the loneliness of rejection are the countless fears that possess some adolescents and that make life quite unbearable at times. Sam feared rejection and consequently was upset and miserable because of potential causes of rejection—his long nose, his acne, his connection with rats, and his intelligence, all of which makes him different from his group. To be different is a benefit only if the difference is something admired by peers; in many cases being different is the worst eventuality. Sam's fears and worries are probably more common than people might think.

Frazier and Lisonbee (1950) had tenth-grade adolescents indicate problems that concerned them and the degree to which they were worried about each. Items most frequently listed as the greatest worry for boys included the presence of blackheads or pimples, irregular teeth, oily skin, glasses, and other slight physical abnormalities such as noses that were too thin or too long, skin too dark, heavy lips, protruding chins, and so on. Girls, like boys, were most concerned about the presence of blackheads or pimples. In addition they were particularly concerned about freckles which, for some reason, they considered highly undesirable. Scars, birthmarks, and moles are also a source of worry, in addition to the danger of being too homely, having oily skin, and wearing glasses. The adolescent is very concerned with his rapidly changing physique to which he must learn to adjust.

The adolescent's physical appearance is of considerable moment to his psychological adjustment as well, not only because of the part it plays in peer acceptance but also because of the way his perception of his body affects his self-concept. For example, it is obvious that a person who thinks he is a great orator is more likely to seek and to accept invitations to display his oratorical skills than is the individual who, because he stutters, believes that he is not gifted as an orator. Similarly, an adolescent who thinks he is attractive to the opposite sex because of his charm, his wit, and his irresistible good looks is more likely to expose himself to that sex than another who believes that he is decidedly unattractive.

One might rewrite Sam's October 22nd entry in a more recent style:

October 22, 197?

Diary, baby:
Last night was a groove, Diary. Real far out. Loney had his rod together so we cruised. Saw this foxy chick – real tough to orb at so I sicked the wolf. But Loney burned out to the burger pit. So there were the guys. I mean that's where it was at, ya know. No way would we split, so we whipped in and rapped till Marcie and this blonde fox from St. Mark's showed and we put the arm on them. We didn't score cause Marcie had to can it. Groovy, Diary! Real groovy!

This entry alludes obliquely to the area which may well be the most profound preoccupation of the adolescent – an area that consumes a great deal of his time and energy and to which he frequently devotes himself with rarely equalled ardor; an area that consumes him day and night and will continue to do so at intervals (or continually) throughout much of the remainder of his life. I speak of Sex – a subject which is capitalized once only, for emphasis.

To begin with, sex is simply a category: male or female. As a category it is rather easily defined by some obvious biological differences between   Sex members of the sexes named above. Indeed, the differences are obvious enough that from the moment of birth it is possible for someone to pronounce proudly, "Hey, it's a boy!" or alternatively to say, "It's a girl!"

Sex is more than a category; it is also a psychoanalytic term referring to thumb sucking, defecation, masturbation, fantasies, repressions, and indeed, to all of living. Sex is the source of libidinal energy that motivates all of us from birth to death, whether by way of the "normal" psychosexual stages, or through the labyrinth of neuroses and psychoses springing from the constant warring between our Ids and Superegos.

Sex is also more than a psychoanalytic term. It can mean (as it does in this section) nothing more nor less complicated than the physical union between male and female, or variations thereof, or the wish thereto, or the fantasy thereof.

Extensive data have been gathered concerning the sexual beliefs and behavior of the adolescent—data that indicate a marked change in sexual beliefs in recent generations (Bell, 1966). Some interpret this change as a movement toward promiscuity and shallow, meaningless relationships between casual acquaintances. Others interpret the change as a significant and long overdue recognition of the desirability of what is regarded as the highest form of communication between humans. Fortunately my role is not to judge, but to report. You may judge if you wish.

Kinsey (1948, 1953) is one of the major sources of information about sexual behavior in the United States. The Kinsey data reveal that although most children have engaged in some form of sexual play prior to adolescence, it is not until puberty that they become capable of an adult sexual response. There is also evidence that immediately following puberty boys experience more intense sexual arousal in response to an extremely wide range of stimuli than girls experience. This arousal gives rise to a rather urgent desire for orgasm. Consequently, virtually all male adolescents studied have reported experiencing orgasm by the time of marriage, while only 30 percent of the females have reported doing so.

The most common form of sexual outlet for males and females is masturbation—a practice that is often accompanied by feelings of guilt and occasionally by fears of impotence, mental retardation, or some other affliction. Males masturbate far more frequently than females, reaching their peak sexual activity (peak is defined as frequency of orgasm regardless of its cause) between their 16th and 17th year. Kinsey reported that the average frequency for this peak period is 3.4 orgasms per week. In contrast, during the period of most frequent orgasm for women, a period that is not reached until the last half of the third decade of life, the average is only 1.8 orgasms per week. In addition, whereas virtually all males experience orgasm, approximately 10 percent of females have never had that unique experience.

In addition to masturbation there are other usual (and unusual) sources of sexual gratification available to mature humans. A recent study of unmarried students (Luckey and Nass, 1969) reports that 58 percent of college males and 43 percent of females have had intercourse. The average age for The First Time was 17.9 for boys and 18.7 for girls. In another survey of college students, most of whom were under 25, taken by *Psychology Today* magazine, 80 percent of the males reported having engaged in premarital sexual intercourse. The figure for females was not appreciably lower—78 percent (reported in *Involvement in Developmental Psychology Today,* 1971). Other interesting findings from this survey are that women tended to have fewer one-night (or day) affairs; that first intercourse most often occurred with a steady date, never with a prostitute, and infrequently with a casual acquaintance; that women engage in extramarital sex almost as often as men (36 percent compared to 40 percent for men) and that 20 percent of the females rarely or never reached orgasm.

A study by Ehrmann (1961) found that petting is acceptable under some circumstances by almost all college students, with strength of relationship as the determining factor. Petting occurred on 73 percent of all of the men's dates, and on 71 percent of the women's; interestingly, however, sexual intercourse occurred during only 2 percent of the women's, but 12 percent of the men's dates. These statistics may reflect women's reluctance to admit having had intercourse—even to as nonthreatening an object as a questionnaire (or as nonthreatening a person as a psychologist). On the other hand, it is not unlikely that men may exaggerate their exploits. It is no secret that male society actively reinforces its members for the frequency and range of their sexual experiences. Female society is much quieter about its reinforcement, although there is evidence of impending change with the emergence of the newly liberalized woman.

While marital sex is not substantially different from premarital sex, its psychological effects might be very different indeed. Despite this generation's professed liberalization and its vociferous espousal of the hang-loose ethic, many of its members are characterized more by hang-ups than by loose hanging. Premarital sex frequently results in guilt feelings, anxiety, remorse and self-recriminations, and in consequent damage to the adolescent's all important self-image. These problems do not ordinarily accompany marital sex (and probably don't accompany postmarital sex, either). It is sad to note that despite the apparent sophistication of this generation of adolescents, and despite the widespread availability of birth-control information and devices, pregnancy or fear of pregnancy is a deciding factor in close to half of all high school marriages (Burchinal, 1959; Vincent, 1966), and approximately 20 percent of all new brides are pregnant when they marry (Vincent, 1966). Not the least of the problems accompanying adolescent marriages is the fact that the break-up rate is approximately three times greater than that of the general population (Landis and Landis, 1963).

Sex—the activity, the category, and its psychoanalytic connotations —is frequently a problem for the adolescent but is not his only problem. Nor is it his only source of joy. It has been said that sex gets dirty if it is considered too long, even in an academic textbook. We shall therefore move to the mind of the adolescent, hoping that it will be clean, before returning to some of his other problems and his other joys in the final section of this chapter.

Intellectual Development

We have traced the growth of the child's mind from birth to the beginning of adolescence, basing our account on the work of Jean Piaget and his associates. Let us briefly review the process: first were the fumbling attempts of the infant to nourish himself through the activation of his imperfect capacity to suck — his sucking scheme — followed by the elaboration and stabilization of this and other schemes until they had become internalized; from these activities arose the child's ability to grasp symbols and from this beginning there arose language and the dawning of a capacity to reason, at first fumbling and illogical — intuitive, egocentric, and qualified by sense perception; the child's thinking remained preoperational, until his internalized actions (concepts) became reversible and coordinated by means of rules of logic that allowed him to conceive beyond the sometimes misleading perceptual features of objects; at the age of 7 or 8, with the appearance of reversibility, identity, associativity, and other rules of logic that could guide him in his interactions with his environment, the child entered the period of concrete operations. And when we left the Piagetian child at the close of the preceding chapter we left a child who could classify, who understood ordering, who could deal with number, and who had consequently achieved a wide range of conservations. But the child at the termination of the period of concrete operations is still some distance from the late adolescent.

Consider the following problem that Inhelder and Piaget (1958) posed to a number of subjects of different ages. There are five test tubes containing different unidentified chemicals. A combination of these chemicals will result in a yellow liquid. This chemical phenomenon is demonstrated for the subject so that he knows that one special tube, which is kept apart, is the catalyst for the desired reaction. What he does not know is which combination of the other four tubes is the correct one. He is asked to discover this for himself, and he is allowed to experiment as necessary to solve the problem. The typical 10-year-old begins by combining two of the chemicals. Assuming that this combination does not provide any positive information, he then combines another two chemicals, or perhaps he combines one of the first two test tubes with a third. He continues in this manner until, by chance, he arrives at a correct solution, whereupon he exclaims, "There, those two! That's the solution." If the experimenter then says, "Are there any other solutions — any other combinations that will also make a yellow liquid?" the child will be forced to admit that he does not know yet, but that he can try to find out. His strategy changes little. He continues to combine pairs of liquids; he may even combine several groups of three, or perhaps all four, and to these he adds liquid from the fifth tube. In the end he asserts that he has tried them all, and that there is but one solution. If he is less fortunate and less persistent he may be incapable of discovering even one correct combination. The 14-year-old behaves in quite a different manner. His solution, illustrated in Figure 13.2, involves systematically combining the tubes by twos, threes, and finally all four, thus yielding fifteen possible combinations (sixteen including the combination in which nothing is combined). There is no doubt in his mind about whether or not he has found the unique solution or whether there are others.

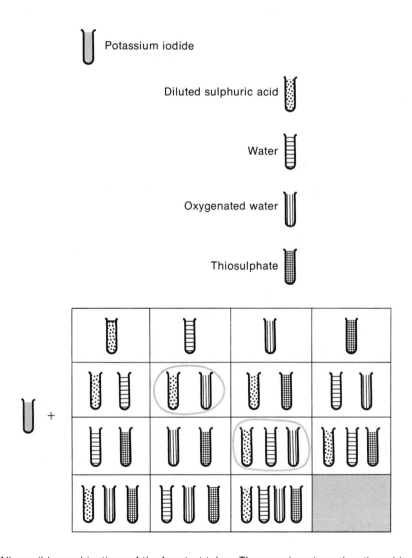

All possible combinations of the four test tubes. The experiment requires the subject   Figure 13.2
to discover the combination(s) that yield a yellow liquid when potassium iodide is
added. The correct solutions are circled.

The experiment described above illustrates several of the principal differences between the child's thinking during the stage of concrete operations and the thinking characterized by formal operations. First the 10-year-old begins his solution by attempting actual combinations; his hypotheses are the combinations translated into action. The 14-year-old, on the other hand, begins by envisaging all the possibilities; then he actualizes them. There is a fundamental difference in the orientations. The first reflects the concrete nature of the child's thought; the second reflects the hypothetical and deductive capacities of adolescent thinking.

Second, the experiment illustrates the *combinatorial* capacity of the adolescent's thinking; because the 10-year-old considers every combination as a separate and unrelated hypothesis, and because he arrives at these combinations in a haphazard fashion, he is likely to overlook several possibilities in the process. In contrast the adolescent first considers the range of possible combinations. The concrete logic that was sufficient to deal with classes and seriation is replaced by what Piaget terms the "logic of propositions." And this form of logic is a much more powerful tool for dealing with the hypothetical — statements that need not relate to reality, but are simply characterized by the possibility that they can be true or untrue (in fact, this is the definition of a **proposition**: a verbal statement that can be true or false).

The adolescent's propositional thinking guides his response to such complex verbal problems as: A is greater than B but smaller than C; which of the three is greatest? Or similarly, Bill is fatter than Sam but thinner than Joe; who is the skinniest? These problems are extremely difficult for the child who has not reached the level of formal thinking, not because he is incapable of ordering, but because the problem involves hypothetical propositions. If Bill, Sam, and Joe were standing in front of the 10-year-old, he would have no trouble whatsoever in ranking them from fattest to least fat; but when the problem is removed from concrete perception and couched in the complex form described above, it moves beyond the limits of his system of logic.

The consequences of the adolescent's newly acquired ability to deal with the hypothetical, to reason from the real to the possible or from the hypothetical to the actual, are reflected in a new intense **idealism.** The child can suddenly contemplate states of affairs that do not exist; he can compare the ideal to the actual; and he can become profoundly disturbed at the failure of preceding generations to avoid the confusion that he observes around him. For some adolescents this becomes a great source of frustration — a frustration that is reflected by the term *generation gap.*

Adolescent idealism is further exhibited in the transition from Kohlberg's first level morality to the second and third levels. The self-accepted principles characterizing the highest level of moral development are unattainable for the child in concrete operations. Self-accepted principles not only become possible but almost inevitable with the advent of formal thinking, however. In other words, not until the child can reason about hypothetical states, becoming progressively concerned with the evils of the world and of the human condition, will he begin to internalize the rules of moral conduct that define the adult conscience (see Chapter 12).

So we consider again the problems and the joys of the adolescent, arriving here by way of a description of the adolescent's mind, for by examining the newly found powers of that mind one can achieve a greater understanding of adolescent behavior. We have come to the most popular subject in the sermons of grandmothers:

There is little doubt that adolescence is a time of turmoil for many; at the same time, it must be kept in mind that it is quite the opposite for numerous adolescents, who pass exuberantly through their teen years. Such individuals discover the joys of their increased powers of mind and body, and are successful in overcoming or avoiding the turmoil that besets their less fortunate peers. The average adolescent is considerably more difficult to describe than the younger child. Research may be incapable of determining which quality best characterizes the largest number of adolescents for the longest periods of time: turmoil, ambivalence, or exuberance. Although we may be dealing with the minority, we consider now some of the forms, causes, and manifestations of turmoil; for this minority, if it is one, is significant.

The Turmoil Topics

There are two principal sources of **frustration** for the adolescent: his inability to define his role and his sense of the depressing distance between the utopia that he envisages and the actual world as he perceives it. The adolescent's difficulty in defining his role is in part a failure of the culture. With the advent of puberty, he suddenly finds himself physically mature. Not only is he capable of being in love, of having intercourse, and of producing offspring, but he is actively desirous of doing so — or desirous at least of engaging in the second of these activities. In many cases, however, he must resort to frequently unsatisfactory means of achieving sexual relief. And when the means are physically more satisfactory, they are perhaps less so psychologically, for the guilt accompanying masturbation is often even more severe for premarital sexual intercourse. But the adolescent's complaints of frustration or guilt are likely not to be his alone, for the powerful human sex drive often finds itself unsatiated in many individuals throughout their lives.

Adolescent Frustration

As frustrating for the adolescent as his sexual unemployment is his economical unemployment. Cultural demands for schooling make it impossible for the child to become economically independent. Thus, at a time when he is struggling to become psychologically independent from his parents he finds himself turning to them with greater frequency and with bigger economic demands. The inherent frustration is obvious: a boy cannot afford to ignore parental dictates when he desires the family sedan.

The adolescent may also feel frustrated by his ambivalence about where childhood ends and adult status begins. The responsibilities that are occasionally placed on his shoulders — as in time of war for example — are ostensibly adult responsibilities. At the same time, however, the privileges granted him are frequently those of children. Until recently, and even now in many places, he could not drink publicly, he could not vote, and he could not run for public office, although he could go out and get shot for his country. This, at least in his view, is sufficiently unfair to occasion frustration.

Additional frustration derives from conflicting cultural pressures which surround the adolescent. He has been led to believe that kindness, generosity, modesty, and affection are among the highest virtues, and yet he observes cruelty, selfishness, ambition that is quite incompatible with modesty, and the affectionless impersonality of existence in large cities, and sometimes in small homes as well. He is taught that a person should be an individual, that he should "do his own thing," and yet the advertising media constantly urge him to conform. Indeed most adult culture urges conformity. These conflicts are powerful sources of dissonance and frustration.

All of the frustration that stems from the adolescent's ambivalence about his role and from conflicting demands that are made of him is frequently less important to the individual than the perceived distance between the ideals he envisages and espouses and the reality he observes. This is the time in his moral development that he questions and examines rules and precepts in order to arrive at self-chosen moral principles. And implicit in these principles are beliefs about desirable states of affairs — about what *ought* to be — in short, about the ethical aspects of human existence. There are people starving, people in pain, people dying needlessly, people fighting, people destroying their environments. There is injustice, greed, anger, rape, murder, dishonesty and a thousand forms of hypocrisy. There is a callous disregard for the humanity of persons in the depersonalized movements of technology. The adolescent is acutely aware of these realities and of other evils of greater or lesser magnitudes; as a result he often drops out in some way or he rebels quietly or violently.

Rebellion   It would be impossible to provide a complete analysis of the "turmoil topics" selected for this discussion. Not only is there insufficient space, but current knowledge is also insufficient. Nevertheless, knowledge has progressed some distance beyond the stereotypes maintained by grandmothers and several of these stereotypes can now be discounted.

To begin with, popular belief maintains that the rebel — the student activist — is a malcontent, a social misfit, a disturbed individual, a potential criminal, a lower-class complainer, or some other form of undesirable individual. Interestingly, if adolescent rebellion is defined by student activism, a somewhat different picture of the adolescent-as-rebel emerges: he is, in fact, typically a well-adjusted, middle-class individual — a social malcontent to be sure, but no more a potential criminal than you or I.

The second of grandmother's stereotypes, those mental crutches without which her conversations on world affairs and society at large would be reduced to a few single-word utterances and mumblings, asserts that all college kids are radicals — that the only reason they go to college is to join demonstrations, to sit in hallways of administration buildings, to burn anyone in effigy, to protest their country's attitude toward internal and external problems, to agitate against the stupidity of all people. This venerable folk belief is only partly correct. There are certainly some students whose social consciences demand that they express their dissatisfaction and concern, but the total number of students involved in this demonstrative behavior is seldom more than 15 percent of the student body, and is usually much lower than that (Trent and Craise, 1967; Trent and Medsker, 1967). One of the traditional weaknesses of stereotypes is that they are applied to all individuals who have superficially similar appearances.

A third stereotype is that the hippies, the yippies (of the late 1960s), college activists, members of motorcycle gangs, and a few other forms of quasi-human life that grandmothers often find so abhorrent, are all alike. In truth they are basically dissimilar, although the issue may be confounded by the fact that an individual can be a hippie, perhaps a yippie, maybe a college activist, and a member of a motorcycle gang all at the same time. In most cases, however, the hippie is characterized by a pacific attitude and a greater concern with doing his own things than with interfering with what other people are doing; yippies are explicitly politically active; college activists are less alike as a group than are hippies, yippies, or gang members, but are brought together by common purpose and frequently only for a specific situation and for that one time. Motorcycle gangs are notoriously preoccupied with their own sometimes non-pacific forms of pleasure, rather than with the social issues concerning college activists. All the fish may be in the same kettle, but they appear remarkably different.*

One last stereotype that must be examined is the widespread belief that college students protest simply to join the group, that few sincerely believe in what they are attempting to do or even understand it. This folk belief is perhaps more valid than the former stereotypes were, since there is evidence that of the hundreds of thousands of people who turn out for mass demonstrations and marches on appointed days, many are there less for the issues than for other reasons. Flacks (1967) theorizes that there are large groups of students who protest because of the sheer *romanticism* of fighting for ideals and causes. Others express *moral purity* and concomitantly reject the alleged hypocrisy of an adult world that publicly espouses one set of values but violates these privately at every opportunity. Some students are expressing their protests *against institutions* that depersonalize man and rob him of his humanity, *against the authority of the establishment, against dogmatism,* and *against a non-egalitarian system* that is founded on the democratic ideal of self-rule but that appears to be autocratic.

But not all students who are dissatisfied, disillusioned, or in need of the community of groups join them in protest. A significant number of the severely dissatisfied drop out of society. Lest another stereotype be

---

*This crude analogy is included for the sake of grandmothers, who would understand me better if I said "That is a different kettle of fish" than if I were to make some academic pronouncement such as "All of them are basically different."

For others rebellion is an expression of moral purity.

fostered, one must point out that the methods of dropping out described here are undertaken by the adventurous and by the timid; by the weak and by the strong; by the deluded and by the rational—and frequently they are not attempts to drop out but merely attempts to intensify the experience of living.

Dropping Out through Drugs

Drug use is a fact of life. Drugs are with us constantly in the guise of coffee, tea, headache tablets, cocktails, and in thousands of other forms. Man has been familiar with drugs for centuries, although he has not always known the chemical components of the substances that he ate, drank, chewed, applied to his wounds, inhaled, put in his ears, or otherwise used on his person. But the label is much less important than the effect, and sometimes the availability.

It was a revelation to me, two years ago, to be hunting with an old trapper who learned most of what he knows from a band of Stony Indians, and who pointed out to me a dozen or more folk remedies that he had learned about from the Stonies. Many of these remedies were plants; some were seeds, and others were roots. Some could be boiled as tea to cure colds and headaches; others could be chewed to remedy a variety of ailments. One of these was of particular interest to me; it was the broadleafed **digitalis** plant from which the well known drug for cardiac patients is derived. "This," my guide pointed out, "is for people who have weak hearts." I was amazed that the Stonies, for whom the word *science* is meaningless, could have made this discovery.

For adolescents, the discovery of drugs is considerably simpler than it was for the Stonies. One need no longer go about testing brews made from plant leaves or chewing on roots and seeds. The communications media have discovered drugs for today's youth. It takes only nominal intelligence for a teen-ager to be aware of the availability of drugs. Not only do the media serve as a source of information, but they also convey an image of adolescents and drugs which frequently misleads. There is little doubt that the frequency of drug use among teen-agers has increased dramatically in the past decade, just as alcohol consumption increased drastically several generations ago. At the same time, however, reports of the seriousness of the "problem" and of the extent of drug use are seldom based on more than conjecture and opinion. Thus, the reports of incidence of drug use are often derived from police reports, which may not be deliberately exaggerated, but which, by nature of the policeman's work, represent only the criminal element.

Recent surveys of drug use in high schools and colleges have not yielded consistent results, but the majority of the reports have presented a less terrifying picture than some might expect. Goldstein's (1966) survey of drug use in high schools is among the most frequently cited; he reports that approximately 15 percent of all high school students will have tried illegal drugs prior to finishing high school. A recent large-scale survey of one university revealed that 21 percent of the sample had tried marijuana at least once (Wozny, 1971); another 18 percent admitted that they would try it "under the right circumstances"; whereas a full 61 percent staunchly maintained that they would never try it. In contrast Weil, Zinberg, and Nelson (1968) report encountering extreme difficulty in locating "marijuana naïve" persons among college students in Boston, implying that almost all students had experimented with it at least once. It is clearly difficult to ascertain the frequency and extent of drug use through the available literature. Part of the confusion is probably due to the fact that admitting to having tried drugs is admitting to a crime, and even when anonymity appears guaranteed, the sophisticated student is often well aware of the variety of methods available for rendering apparently anonymous questionnaires less anonymous. It is quite possible that most of the estimates that have been reported are in fact underestimates.

Marijuana and LSD are among the drugs most frequently used by college and high school students and thus will be discussed briefly below.

Marijuana is derived from hemp, a tall annual plant appearing in male and female forms. It is from the female hemp plant that the pharmacological preparation *Cannabis sativa* is derived. The specific chemical grouping that apparently accounts for its effects is termed **tetrahydrocannabinols**. It is variously known as dawamesc, hashish, bhang, grass, ganja, charas, marijuana, muta, grefa, muggles, pot, reefer, guage, stick and tea (Ebin, 1961). Marijuana is ordinarily smoked, although it can also be eaten or drunk. According to Goode (1969), its primary effect is a pleasant emotional state, although he describes it as more of an "experience enhancement" effect than as one that is highly pleasurable in itself. Thus, it is often taken ("done") prior to listening to music, eating, or engaging in sexual activity. It is reported to enhance the enjoyment of all three. An additional effect sometimes associated with marijuana is an increased ability to become involved with people, to interact sensitively. It should be pointed out as well that marijuana is occasionally reported to have no discernible effect on the psychological state of the user. There is also contrasting evidence that if taken in sufficient doses and in sufficiently pure forms (which are extremely rare), it may evoke the same types of hallucinogenic reactions that are sometimes associated with stronger drugs like LSD (Gershon and Angrist, 1967).

Marijuana is not addictive, nor is there any evidence that smoking marijuana is more physically harmful than smoking tobacco cigarettes. There is evidence, however, that the individual who is "stoned" or "high" (the terms are equivalent) on marijuana is less capable of thinking abstractly, and his friends usually consider him less capable of driving a car safely.

The widely held fear that marijuana is the first step towards heroin addiction has generally been discounted. There is no evidence that tolerance to marijuana develops, as does tolerance to some of the so-called "hard" drugs. Hence the marijuana user does not *need* to go to more powerful drugs to continue to achieve the same "high." Nor is there any evidence that using marijuana leads to a physiological craving for heroin, for example. It is true, however, that procuring marijuana, since it is illegal, frequently exposes the adolescent to underworld persons who would like nothing better than to "hook" someone else. In that sense alone perhaps marijuana may lead to other drugs.

LSD-25 (**d-lysergic acid diethylamide tartrate**) is the most powerful synthetic hallucinogen known. Because it is a synthetic chemical it can be made by anyone who has the materials, the equipment, and the knowledge. The substance lysergic acid is derived from ergot, a fungus that grows on rye and sometimes on other grasses. Its medical use is relatively widespread. For example, derivatives of ergot are frequently administered to women directly after childbirth to cause contraction of the uterus, thereby indirectly preventing bleeding. Ergot is also known to cause abortions (Brookmiller and Bowen, 1967).

LSD-25 (ordinarily referred to simply as LSD) is usually taken orally, commonly in the form of a white, odorless and tasteless powder. Much more is known about its chemical derivation and its production than about its effects. The most objective comment that can be made about its effects is that they vary widely from one person to another as well as from one occasion to another for the same person. The predominant characteristic of an LSD experience (called an "acid trip") is the augmented intensity of sensory perceptions. Color, sound, taste, and vision are particularly susceptible. The subjective experience has been described as an intensely "rich and satisfying experience." On occasion an acid trip is accompanied by hallucinations, some of which may be mild and amusing; at other times the hallucinations can be sufficiently frightening to lead to serious mental disturbance in the subject even after the immediate effects of the drug have worn off (Louria, 1966). There is also tentative evidence that LSD may produce changes in chromosomes that could affect the offspring of the user, if the fetus is not aborted first (Alexander, 1967).

The "drug scene" is a huge and complex panorama. It includes all manner of people, from all social and occupational levels, and of younger and younger ages. But the drug scene on university campuses and in high schools is very different from that which is to be found in every large city on this continent. Addicts who must mainline (inject directly into the vein) heroin every morning when they awaken in their private corners of the slums, are a great distance from the college student who "drops" pills or smokes grass for the experience that it provides him.

Suicide, the deliberate taking of one's life, is rather final — an end which is sought when an individual can see only two choices: life as it is now, or death. Evidently he prefers to die. If he is a male, he will probably shoot himself; a female is more likely to use poisoning or asphyxiation. There are obviously many other methods available, but some of these result in a death that appears accidental (drowning, a car accident) and is difficult to identify as suicide unless the person has left a note, a letter, or a book that can be interpreted as a message of intent to end it. Since a suicide note appears in only 15 percent of all reported suicides (Ruch and Zimbardo, 1971), there are probably many apparent accidents that are in fact unidentified suicides.

Suicide is not a pleasant topic — it so violently contradicts our implicit belief in the goodness of life. Consequently there is a powerful social stigma attached to the act and the event is often covered over both by the information media and by the attending physician. As a result people know only of suicides of people whom they have known (and sometimes not even then), or of particularly prominent persons (not always those either), or of people who commit the act so flagrantly that it compels attention. There are relatively few scientific investigations of suicide, its causes, and the personalities of those who deliberately choose their time and method of departure. Do children commit suicide? How often? How about the adolescent, disillusioned idealist that he is, caught up in the stress and turmoil of the transition to adulthood? Here are some facts.

The suicide rate in the United States is less than 10 per 100,000. Very few children under the age of 15 commit suicide, and although the rate increases for adolescence and the early twenties, it does not reach its peak until the ages between 75 and 84 (27.9 per 100,000). After the age of 85 the rate declines again (Dublin, 1963). Considerably more men than women commit suicide — a higher rate of approximately 12 percent in the United States (Maris, 1969). Divorced and widowed men are especially prone to suicide, the rates sometimes exceeding 100 per 100,000. The same is not true for women. College students are half as likely to commit

Dropping Out through Suicide

suicide as their non-college peers (Peck, 1970; cited in Ruch and Zimbardo, 1971). Foreign students are much more likely to kill themselves than native Americans in American colleges. Older college students are more suicide-prone, as are those students who have been referred for psychiatric care (Seiden, 1966). Suicide-proneness in college students can be attributed to three major areas of concern and conflict: concern over studies, physical complaints, and probably most important, difficulties with interpersonal relationships. Suicide accounted for at least 34 percent of all student deaths during a 10-year period at the University of California, Berkeley (Seiden, 1966).

Suicide is the solution of an isolated few. Most of us choose to wait for Death and hope that she will be a long time in coming.

Summary

This chapter opens with the Passage of Ootala, noting that Ootala's manhood began clearly and irreversibly at the very dawn of the day of this ritual. It is not so for our children, for they know not exactly when they leave childhood and become adults; there are no *rites de passage* for them. We continue to have elaborate, expensive, and frequently superstitious rites for birth and even more frequently for death, but there is nothing to mark adulthood. The chapter then turned to a consideration of the physical changes that define adolescence—the period of transition between childhood and adulthood—and spoke of pubescence, the period that encompasses all the changes, and puberty, the consequent sexual maturity that results from the changes of pubescence. From a consideration of these momentous physical changes the chapter moved to the social development of the adolescent and examined the stages in his socialization—his movement from initial dependence on his parents to a final stage of relative independence. This change is greatly facilitated by his interaction with peers, since groups of peers have become central to the life of the adolescent. The chapter then looked quickly at some passages from Sam's diary, omitting many that would have been more appropriate but that would certainly have been censored. It was natural for the chapter to move from Sam's diary to a discussion of sex and to make several profound observations about this subject: sex exists, the chapter began; it is of considerable importance to the adolescent; masturbation is almost universal among males; 10 percent of all women never achieve orgasm; college students sometimes have intercourse; and early marriages are more likely to dissolve than later ones. From this topic the chapter turned to a clean discussion of the mind of the adolescent, contrasting it with the cognitive powers of middle childhood. The adolescent's ability to deal with the hypothetical, the logical nature of his thinking, and his idealism were pointed out. In the end the chapter examined the "turmoil topics": rebellion, drugs, and suicide. Some, though not all, students rebel; some, though not all, try drugs; and relatively few choose to leave it all behind.

Main Points

1. Ootala had his Passage into Manhood in the early dawn assisted by two of his uncles. His father yelled, "Olat."

2. Societies with clearly recognized boundaries between childhood and adulthood are termed discontinuous; those without boundaries are continuous. The continuity makes it difficult for some adolescents to determine when they cease to be children and become adults.

3. Puberty is sexual maturity. It results from pubescence—the period of change that includes the boy's ability to ejaculate semen and the girl's menarche, among other changes for both sexes.

4. The advantage that girls have over boys in height and weight during early adolescence is permanently lost before the age of 15.

5. Social development progresses from a stage of relative dependence on the parents to a stage of relative independence. As the adolescent becomes less closely attached to his immediate family he becomes more dependent on peer groups.

6. Peer groups begin as small unisexual groups in early adolescence and progress through four additional stages. The first is a period when the unisexual groups interact as groups but remain intact, followed by a stage when the crowd has begun to form but still consists of unisexual groups interacting in a closer fashion. Eventually a large heterosexual group is formed. In the later stages of adolescence this crowd breaks into less cohesive groups of couples.

7. The adolescent's acceptance by his peers is profoundly important for his social and psychological wellbeing.

8. Sex, the activity and the topic, is highly significant to the adolescent. Masturbation is almost universal among boys, but less so among girls. Premarital sexual intercourse is more or less frequent depending on the interpreter's point of view (approximately 50 percent of all college students have tried it at least once. This means that approximately half have never tried it and really don't know what I am talking about.)

9. The intellectual development of the adolescent culminates in adultlike forms of reasoning—thought that is potentially completely logical, that is inferential, that deals with the hypothetical as well as with the concrete, that is systematic, and that results in the potential for being idealistic.

10. The adolescent may be frustrated by his inability to define his role, and by the distance that he observes between the ideal worlds that he contemplates and the one in which he lives. Not all adolescents are frustrated, and some are less than others.

11. Only about 15 percent of college students join demonstrations and other similar amusements, many are pacific, very few are drug addicts, and some are sincere, well intentioned, and occasionally justified in their beliefs and demands.

12. The female hemp plant produces dawamesc, hashish, bhang, grass, ganja, charas, marijuana, muta, grefa, muggles, pot, reefers, guage, stick, and tea.

13. LSD-25 (d-lysergic acid diethylamide tartrate) is the most powerful known synthetic hallucinogenic drug. Both LSD and marijuana are non-addictive, but both can cause psychoticlike reactions although these are less common with Mary Jane.

14. Suicide is an uncommon end, although it accounted for at least 34 percent of all student deaths during a 10-year period at the University of California, Berkeley.

Gold and Douvan present an excellent collection of articles relating to adolescent development: **Further Readings**

Gold, N., and E. Douvan. *Adolescent development: Readings in research and theory.* Boston, Mass.: Allyn & Bacon, 1969.

Insights into the differences between adolescent and child thought are found in the following book by Peel, which is based largely on Piaget's developmental theory and clarifies Piaget's definition of logic.

Peel, E. A. *The pupil's thinking*. London: Old Bourne, 1960.

Two current sources of information about drugs are a collection of articles relating to the psychological, moral, and ethical implications of drug use, and a more literary description of the effects of various drugs including marijuana, opium, peyote, and LSD. Among the various well-known authors who describe their drug experiences in this second book are such people as Ginsberg, Moser, Havelock Ellis, Aldous Huxley, and Charles Baudelaire.

Goode, E. (Ed.) *Marijuana*. New York: Atherton Press, 1969.

Ebin, D. (Ed.) *The drug experience: First person accounts of addicts, writers, scientists and others*. New York: The Orion Press, 1961.

Information relating to the frequency and causes of student suicide is given in:

Seiden, R. H. Campus tragedy: A study of students' suicide. *Journal of Abnormal Psychology*, 1966, **71**, 389–399.

Part Five: The End

The End

Had you been standing behind me these last months, looking over my shoulder, you would surely have thought I was writing this book. But it is not really so, for books are only partly from the minds and the guts of their authors. A large part of them comes from somewhere else, and we the authors sit at our typewriters waiting for books to happen. Not until a book has set itself down on paper does it irrevocably belong to its author. Prior to that time it could have taken any number of forms, but from the moment it is recorded it has own definite shape and substance.

The life of a human child is something like a book. It too can take any number of shapes and directions, and no one knows precisely what that form will be until it happens—unless the great timekeeper himself takes the trouble to notice the life of one child among 3 billion. But quite unlike a book as the life of a child unfolds and takes form and substance it never irrevocably possesses that form. I rediscovered this during the past week. Three nights ago I was sitting here waiting for the next part of the book to happen. It was a longer wait than usual, and in the interval I chanced to look out the window; that was not a wise thing to do, for books seldom occur when the night is soft and warm as that early spring evening was. It reminded me strongly that I still had not taken my young son on the overnight fishing trip I had promised him, and it reminded me as well that the ice was now melted on the lakes. And so for the past two days I have been lazing about the shores of a small lake, listening to and observing my son. He is 4 years old, and he is several short books, all at the same time—confused and unorganized books to be sure, but books nevertheless.

There is something infinitely disquieting about being faced with the living subject of a book. I sit here in the academic, antiseptic confines of this book-lined office and blithely type such humanistic phrases as: "there is no average child," "it is the whole infant that we are concerned with," "a child is an incredibly complex little organism," "he is qualified for the title of linguist extraordinaire." But it is something else to be faced with the living linguist, the whole infant, the nonaverage child, and the incredibly complex organism all at once and in the flesh. And not just for a brief passing glance, but for an uninterrupted period of two days.

It was a marvelously refreshing and totally disheartening experience, for as I observed and listened to my son, I could not help thinking that he is what I had undertaken to describe in this book. And I now know so much more clearly than I had previously known that there is no average child—that I am in fact talking about the various layers that I have chosen to call chapters or chapter sections, and that the whole process of attempting to set down in static words a thing that is at once as dynamic and as elusive as a child in the process of becoming necessarily robs both the child and the process of their dynamism. And to repeat again that this is so makes it no less so. But perhaps it does make us more aware of that which concerns us: that a child, like an adult, is never what he will be, but is always becoming; and it reminds us that a child is not 2 before he is 1, 0 and −1; and that after he is 6 he will also be 7, 8, 20, and eventually he will be old and die. The small insight I have gained from trying to relate what I have written to the actual child that is my son is this: when all the layers of the chapters and sections of this book have finally been bound together and the painting of the child finally rendered, it will necessarily bear only a faint resemblance to its subject. For the subject of the process of becoming does not stop and pose; by its very nature it continues to move forever.

A Summary   The subject of this book is the movement of man from his beginning to a point somewhat closer to his end. The book began at the beginning with a consideration of some of the forces that determine the course of development. Heredity certainly determines much of the eventual outcome of development, although we don't know precisely how much. Heredity does determine most of the physical characteristics of man – his body type, his general pattern of physical growth, the color of his eyes, his skin, his hair, and the shape of other parts of his anatomy. Evidence strongly suggests that heredity is also profoundly involved in determining the intelligence of individuals, and that personality predispositions are also somewhat subject to genetic influences. In short, there is a great deal about each of us that is predetermined when we are born – characteristics that were determined largely by chance and certainly not influenced by anything we had any personal control over. Indeed, the very fact that there is such a person as you or I is largely a matter of fortune – it could have been another ovum; it could have been any one of several million other sperm cells. And in each case the result would have been someone else. Or would it?

But what you and I are becoming is not solely a function of the intricate arrangements of DNA molecules which our parents passed on to us, and which they in turn received from their parents, and they from their parents, and so on, so that there exists in a remote sense a common pool of genes for all of us. What we are is also a matter of where we were at different times in our lives and of what people and things were like around us. Witness the dramatic differences among the Arapesh, the Tchambuli, and Mundugumor. Or closer to home, look at the ideals and aspirations, the typical behavior, the sources of reinforcement, the language, the self-concepts, the *selves,* of the people around you. And if the point is not yet striking enough, look at the painful differences among the inhabitants of your city. What we become is a process of constant interaction between our native endowment – our genetic bags – and the environment in which we find ourselves. Environment is a complex thing, including everything around us: family, friends, inanimate objects, the media, the air – everything. Really understanding the influence of the environment on an individual means perceiving it from that person's point of view – from what is termed a *phenomenological* standpoint. We will speak of this again shortly.

The effect of the environment on an individual is interpreted within the categories that psychologists have invented to build their houses — in terms of what is known about *learning*. Thus, we moved from a consideration of the environment to a discussion of various explanations of learning and finally to an integration born of the awareness that human learning is sufficiently complex and varied to require a number of different explanations. Much of what was said about learning was important for understanding the description of the developing child that was presented in later parts of the text.

Learning cannot be considered in isolation from motivation; the reasons for man's behavior are also the reasons for many of the changes that occur in that behavior. Since learning is defined as a change in behavior resulting from experience, then motivation is clearly implicated in learning. Piaget has made the obvious statement that there is no learning without interest, and interest is one of the emotions most closely involved with the motivated behavior of human beings.

Heredity and environment in interaction and as interpreted through learning and motivational processes are the two basic forces that direct the course of development. Having scratched the surface of these incredibly complex processes the book paused to examine some of the theories advanced specifically to describe and explain development. We summarized the complex systems of Freud and Piaget and briefly discussed observational learning as preparation for the next section of the text dealing with the child in the process of becoming.

The child begins as a microscopic speck in one of his mother's fallopian tubes. Through the next 266 days he changes from this indistinct cellular mass to the form and functions that define the newborn infant; and although these changes are ordered, systematic, and highly predictable, they are nevertheless subject to external influences. Some of these influences on the child *in utero* were examined, followed by a description of the process of birth, both from the physician's and from the mother's points of view. Having accounted for the origins of the real hero of this piece, and having introduced the necessary facts and theories about his development and the forces that influence it, the book turned finally to its principal task — a description of the child.

The child progressed through the sequential stages of his unfolding: infancy, preschool, middle childhood, and finally the period of transition between childhood and adulthood, adolescence. At each of these steps something was said of the physical, social, and cognitive development of the average child; and at each stage you were urged to keep in mind that we spoke of the nonexistent average child, and further that we were dividing him into different layers to simplify the process of communication between us, but at the same time robbing the child of his individuality and robbing the developmental process of its dynamism. That part of the story has now been told. There remains only the attempt to bring the various layers and pieces into a cohesive whole to provide a richer, more accurate, more complete, and more *human* picture of the child in the process of becoming.

   Who am I? Is the I who is sitting here thinking about who he is different from the I who visited Koros and observed a miraculous time-stopping machine? Was I the same me when, as an adolescent, I wondered about life, its purposes and goals, the reaches beyond its obvious limits, society and the predicaments that it had created for itself, and a thousand other questions of grave and immediate consequence? Was the I who went to school as a freshly scrubbed 6-year-old the same person who graduated from college many years later? Who is my self and what is it; how does it become what it is?

   Perhaps there is no correct answer to the question of identity that has plagued philosophers, psychologists, theologians, grandmothers, and all manner of thinkers since thinking began. But there are two useful answers that are frequently given, both intuitive, highly subjective, but no less meaningful for humans. The first asserts that there is an unidentifiable something about the self that continues from the dawning awareness of a personal identity until the oblivion of psychotic disorder, senility, or death destroys all sense of existence. The other answer does not contradict the first, but simply extends it: the self is continually developing, despite the individual's feeling of a single and unique personal identity throughout life.

   Discussions of the self and its development have been a primary concern of humanistic psychology and existential philosophy, both of which contribute much to our understanding and appreciation of the phenomenon of development. A rigorous discussion of their contributions is beyond the scope of this text. Nevertheless an introduction to the two points of view shall be presented here, partly to serve as an alternative to the somewhat unreal picture of the child that inevitably results from attempting to examine him in objective psychological detail, and partly as a finishing touch for the painting that has been attempted in this text.

Humanism   Humanism is a concern for man, for his humanity, for the development of that humanity, and for its expression. The humanity of man is interpreted in terms of his *self*. Thus, the concepts of paramount concern to the humanistic psychologist include such currently popular notions as self-structure, self-concept, self-image, self-understanding, self-acceptance, self-enhancement, self-realization, and self-actualization (Gale, 1969). Humanism is concerned with that which is most clearly human; accordingly the development of self (self-actualization) is considered the goal toward which humans should strive to achieve fulfillment.

   The process of self-actualization is the act of becoming whatever one has the potential to become through one's own efforts; it is the process of actualizing—of making actual or real that potential. But it is not a static goal toward which individuals consciously or unconsciously strive; it is a process, an ongoing activity. Self-actualization is in fact the process of development. It would have been possible to substitute different terms in this text to make this relationship more apparent. For example, instead of speaking of development we might have spoken of self-actualization or of the development of self; instead of referring to the frustrations of the adolescent, who cannot easily determine whether he is child or adult, we could have referred to the difficulty of establishing the *identity* of the self during the transition from childhood to adulthood; and instead of discussing forces that impede or accelerate development, we could have discussed self-enhancement or changing self-structure. And the picture that would have emerged might have been a more integrated one, for we would constantly have been speaking of the self. It would also have been a more *real* picture, which dealt more with the real child than with the average, normal child—for the self belongs solely to the individual; there is no "average" self. To speak of the average self is to distort the concept unforgivably. At the same time the portrait would probably have been a more global, less precise, and less informative study of the child.

To complete further the description of the child presented here we might consider the concepts of **existential** psychology, since they are not essentially different from those of humanistic psychology. From Jean-Paul Sartre we borrow a description of the human condition—cynical and pessimistic, but one that enables us to understand better the direction of development, particularly in its nearly adult stages. From Martin Buber we borrow ideas from a philosophy of personalism, which is but a short distance from humanism.

Existentialism

The existential picture of man and of the forces that move him, as presented by Jean-Paul Sartre, can be described by three words: *anguish, abandonment,* and *despair.* These words summarize the human condition—they are both the facts of existence and its consequences. Man is forever in *anguish* because he is constantly forced to make decisions, and yet has no guides for these decisions. There is no guarantee that anything he does is correct, for there is no God, Sartre informs us, and without a God all action must be justified in terms of its effects on men. Such resolution is a tremendous and terrible responsibility for man—an insoluble dilemma—and its consequence is deep and undying anguish. Man has also been abandoned, and **abandonment** is an indescribably lonely feeling. Man has not been abandoned simply by other men, but he is abandoned and without a purpose, and with no *a priori* values. He has been abandoned to be free—free to make choices, but also required to make them. And so man despairs; he despairs because he is free but without hope—since to will something is not necessarily to achieve it, and because when he dies all his efforts may have been in vain.

This is atheistic existentialism and it is described here to give a perspective through contrast to the more optimistic reflections of Martin Buber. Buber (1958, 1965) tells us that there are four main evils in the modern world and that the effect of these evils is to highlight the importance of the human self. The first of these evils is man's terrible loneliness, and loneliness has long been recognized by existentialists as a concept of extreme importance. Existence as a self is essentially a lonely experience, because the self always belongs only to the individual—it can never be shared completely. Therefore man is always alone. Buber's second evil is the never-ending drive for technological progress, the individual's worth lessening with the increasing importance of man's machines and sciences. The third evil stems from human duality, the good versus the evil dichotomy; the Id warring with the Superego. Finally Buber contends that the individual is being degraded by the state; the conglomerate, impersonal, and faceless entities that define states are incompatible with the uniqueness and personal worth of the individual.

The result of these evils is summarized in a single existentialist (and humanistic) term: *alienation*. Man is alienated from himself, from others, and from his environment. In short, he has been uprooted from the relationships that he should have with all three: his private self, those who surround him, and his environment. Accordingly, the greatest evil that besets man, the social animal, is alienation; and the greatest good is *love* — love of self and love of others. Buber's philosophy is seldom pessimistic, for it asserts strongly that man's salvation, his happiness, and his consequent self-actualization, can be achieved through love. And love is simply a question of relationships, what Buber terms an I-Thou relationship: one in which the object or person being related to is not being used selfishly, the relationship is mutual; there is dialogue as opposed to monologue, and people say and do what they honestly mean rather than what is merely convenient or socially appropriate.

If the process of human development has a goal — that is, if it ever ceases to be a process of becoming — then its goal must surely be a capacity to feel great love, and the reward for having reached that state must surely be great happiness. Does self-actualization ever become self-realization? Does the child ever grow up?

Epilogue

The earth continues its endless circling of the distant sun, one among uncounted planets also moving in great monolithic patterns in space, beyond the reaches of human imagination. Each great orbit creates four seasons which mark the ebb and flow of life; and with every orbit there are $364\frac{1}{4}$ rotations causing the days and the nights, and these too mark the patterns of life.

We can say in our wisdom that the movements of celestial bodies create night and day, and that this is accomplished by means of light. With that same wisdom we can explain the coming and the going of the seasons — and that too has to do with light. And all light came from the sun in the beginning — and so it was easy to know where God was, for God was the source of light, and the source of light is the sun, and so God was the sun and the sun was God.

But now man has created light. He has forgotten that the light comes only from the sun and he thinks that God has died.

But there is still a timekeeper who watches over the movements of all creatures during the eons of time. He is perhaps not a god, and perhaps he doesn't know where all of this came from or where it is going, though he may wonder occasionally.

Maybe it was the Great Timekeeper himself who whispered to Blaise

Pascal at another time that one of the paradoxes of human existence is that despite man's great intelligence it is impossible for him to know where he came from or where he is going. For while our imaginations may stretch beyond the limits of our coming and going, our science and our knowledge bind us here.

Glossary

This glossary defines the most important terms and expressions used in this text. In each case the meaning given corresponds to the usage in the text. For more complete definitions, the reader is advised to consult a standard psychological dictionary.*

Abandonment   An adjective describing the existential dilemma. Abandonment refers to an intense feeling purported to result from the realization that man has been abandoned on Earth with no purpose, no knowledge of where he comes from or where he is going. (See *alienation.*)

Abortion   A miscarriage occurring usually before the twentieth week of pregnancy when the fetus ordinarily weighs less than one pound.

Accommodation   Involves the modification of an activity or an ability that the child already has, to conform to environmental demands. Piaget's description of development holds that assimilation and accommodation are the means by which an individual interacts with his world and adapts to it. (See *assimilation.*)

Adaptation   Changes in an organism in response to the environment. Such changes are assumed to facilitate interaction with that environment. Adaptation plays a central role in Piaget's theory. (See *assimilation, accommodation.*)

Adolescence   A general term signifying the period from the onset of puberty to adulthood, typically including the teen years (13 to 19). (See *puberty, pubescence.*)

Affect   (See *emotion.*)

Afterbirth   The placenta and other membranes that are expelled from the woman's body following the birth of a child.

Alienation   An adjective employed in existential philosophy and psychology to describe an individual's feeling of separation from people and things that are important to him. (See *existentialism.*)

Amniotic sac   A sac filled with dark, serous fluid (amniotic fluid) in which the fetus develops in the uterus.

Amorous consorting   A grandmother's euphemism for natural act.

Anal stage   The second of Freud's psychosexual stages of development, beginning at approximately 8 months and lasting until around 18 months. It is characterized by the child's preoccupation with physical anal activities.

Anomy   A term employed by Bull to describe the earliest stage in the development of morality. Refers to the absence of a moral orientation. (See *heteronomy, socionomy,* and *autonomy.*)

---

*Some of these definitions are taken from the glossary in Guy R. Lefrancois, *Psychology for teaching: A bear always faces the front.* Belmont, California: Wadsworth Pub. Co., 1972. Used by permission.

Anoxia   A condition involving an insufficient supply of oxygen to the body.

Arousal   A term with both physiological and psychological connotations. As a physiological concept arousal refers to changes in heart rate, respiration rate, electrical activity in the cortex, and the skin's conductivity to electricity. As a psychological concept arousal refers to degree of alertness, awareness, vigilance, or wakefulness. Arousal can range from very low (coma or sleep) to very high (panic or high anxiety).

Artificial insemination   An artificial breeding procedure often employed in animal husbandry and sometimes with humans. This procedure obviates the necessity for a physical union between a pair of opposite-sexed individuals.

Assimilation   The act of incorporating objects or aspects of objects to previously learned activities. To assimilate is, in a sense, to ingest or to employ for something that is previously learned; more simply, the exercising of previously learned responses. (See *accommodation*.)

Associationism   A term employed almost synonymously with stimulus-response learning. Associationism refers to the formation of associations or links between stimuli, between responses, or between stimuli and responses. Hence associationistic positions are typically behavioristic or neobehavioristic positions. (See *behavioristic theory* or *neobehavioristic theory*.)

Authoritarian   An adjective describing people who consistently exhibit their need to establish authority.

Autonomy   The final stage in Bull's scheme of moral development, characterized by the emergence of individual principles of conscience. (See *anomy*, *socionomy*, and *heteronomy*.)

Axillary hair   Armpit hair.

Babbling   The relatively meaningless sounds that young infants repeat.

Babinski reflex   A reflex present in the newborn child, but disappearing later in life. It involves fanning the toes as a result of being tickled in the center of the soles of the feet. Normal adults curl their toes inward rather than fanning them outward.

Bar   The equipment described in Chapter 4, used primarily for dispensing alcoholic beverages from one side, while the other side is occupied by consumers of alcoholic beverages.

Behavioristic theory   A general term for those theories of learning concerned primarily with the observable components of behavior (stimuli and responses). Such theories are labeled S-R learning theories and are exemplified in classical and operant conditioning.

Bilingualism   The ability to speak and understand two languages.

Bingo   A game of skill and chance with tremendous social implications.

Birth   The process whereby the fetus, the placenta, and other membranes are separated from the mother's body and expelled. (See *labor*.)

Birth order   The position that a child occupies in a family (for example, first, second, or third born).

Black box   A term employed by grandmothers to describe an object that is squarish and appears black, usually as a result of having been painted with a substance that color. In psychology the term is occasionally used to describe the "mind," implying that the contents of the mind are unknown and perhaps unknowable.

Boggling   A term implying confusion in the human mind, usually as a result of complexity of input.

Book   A collection of words. (See *textbook*.)

Breech birth   An abnormal presentation of the fetus at birth: buttocks first rather than head first.

Cardiac   Pertaining to the heart.

Castration complex   The Freudian notion that a boy who is jealous of his father because he loves his mother (Oedipus complex) fears that his father will retaliate and defend his position by castrating him or cutting off his penis.

Cephalocaudal   Referring to the direction of development beginning with the head and proceeding outward toward the tail. Early infant development is cephalocaudal since the child acquires control over his head prior to acquiring control over his limbs.

Cervix   The small circular opening to the womb (uterus), which dilates considerably during birth.

Child   Young human.

Childhood   An arbitrary division in the sequence of human development which, for purposes of this text, begins around the age of 2 and ends with adolescence. (See *adolescence*.)

Chromosome   A microscopic body in the nucleus of all human and plant cells, containing the genes—the carriers of heredity. Each mature human sex cell (sperm or ovum) contains 23 chromosomes, each containing countless numbers of genes. (See *genes*.)

Classical conditioning   Also called learning through stimulus substitution, since it involves the repeated pairing of two stimuli so that a previously neutral (conditioned) stimulus eventually comes to elicit the same response (conditioned response) as was previously evoked by the first stimulus (unconditioned stimulus). This type of conditioning was first described by Pavlov.

Cloning   The process of reproducing identical individuals from selected cells of the body. Cloning, which has been successfully completed with salamanders, ordinarily involves replacing the nucleus of one egg cell with a cell from the body of the individual who is being cloned (reproduced).

Cognitive dissonance   A state of conflict between beliefs and behavior, or between expectations and behavior. The term also refers to a motivational position premised on the assumption that the conflict arising from cognitive dissonance results in behavior designed to reduce the dissonance.

Cognitivism   Includes those theories of learning concerned primarily with such topics as perception, problem solving, information processing, decision making, and understanding. (See also *behavioristic theories, neobehavioristic theories*.)

Collative variables   A term employed by Berlyne to describe those properties of stimuli most likely to increase arousal (attention) in an organism. Such characteristics of stimulus objects as novelty, surprise, complexity, and ambiguity are collative variables.

Comic book   A collection of cartoon stories, most of which are not comic, and many of which are characterized by excessive violence.

Communication   The transmission of messages. Communication does not require language, although it is greatly facilitated by it. Lower animals communicate although they do not possess language.

Concept   A collection of perceptual experiences or ideas related by virtue of their possessing common properties.

Conception   The beginning of human life. Conception occurs with the union of a sperm cell with an egg cell. (See *fertilization*.)

Concrete operations   The third of Piaget's four major stages, lasting from age 7 or 8 to approximately 11 or 12, and characterized primarily by the child's ability to deal with concrete problems and objects, or objects and problems easily imagined in a concrete sense.

Conditioned response   A response that is elicited by a conditioned stimulus. In some obvious ways a conditioned response resembles its corresponding unconditioned response. The two are not identical, however.

Conditioned stimulus   A stimulus that does not elicit any response or elicits a global orienting response initially, but as a result of being paired with an unconditioned stimulus and its response acquires the capability of eliciting that same response. For example, a stimulus that is always present at the time of a fear reaction may become a conditioned stimulus for fear.

Conditioning   A term employed to describe a simple type of learning. (See *classical conditioning, operant conditioning*.)

Conflict   A term referring specifically to behavioral indecision as a result of the positive or negative qualities of goal situations. Conflicts may be approach-approach, in which the individual is equally tempted to strive for two goals, one incompatible with the other; avoidance-avoidance, in which the individual strives desperately to avoid unpleasant consequences although doing so will incur other unpleasant consequences; or approach-avoidance, in which a single behavior has both pleasant and unpleasant consequences.

Congenital   Related to heredity rather than to environment or experience.

Conscience   An internalized set of rules governing an individual's behavior.

Conservation   A Piagetian term implying that certain quantitative attributes of objects remain unchanged unless something is added to or taken away from them. Such characteristics of objects as mass, number, area, volume, and so on, are capable of being conserved.

Content   Piaget's general term for an individual's behavior. Content is raw, uninterpreted, behavioral data.

Continuous culture   A culture that does not clearly demarcate passage from one period of life to another. Contemporary Western societies are usually continuous.

Continuous reinforcement   That type of schedule of reinforcement in which every correct response is followed by a reinforcer.

Control group   Consists of subjects who are not experimented with, but who are used as comparisons to the experimental group to ascertain whether the subjects were affected by the experimental procedure.

Counter conditioning   A therapeutic technique that attempts to condition an acceptable response as a replacement for an unacceptable response.

Covert   Hidden or internal; incapable of being observed directly. For example, thought is a covert activity; in contrast, speech is at least partly overt.

Critical period   The period during which an appropriate stimulus must be presented to an organism for imprinting to occur. (See *imprinting*.)

Cross-sectional study   A technique in the investigation of child development that involves observing and comparing different subjects at different age levels. A cross-sectional study would compare 4- and 6-year-olds by observing both groups of children at the same time, one group consisting of 6-year-old children, and the other of 4-year-old children. A longitudinal study would require that the same children be examined at the age of 5 and then again at the age of 6.

Cultural relativity   The belief that the behavior and the personality of an individual can only be understood and evaluated within the context of his cultural environment.

Culture The sum total of the mores, traditions, beliefs, values, customary ways of behaving, and explicit and implicit rules that characterize a group of people. A culture is frequently describable in terms of its schools, its religions, and its laws.

Death The upper limit of an individual's consciousness—perhaps.

Defense mechanism Relatively irrational and sometimes unhealthy methods employed by persons to compensate for their inability to satisfy their basic desires and to overcome the anxiety accompanying this inability. (See *displacement, reaction formation, intellectualization, projection,* and *denial.*)

Deferred imitation Imitating people or events in their absence. Deferred imitation is assumed by Piaget to be critical to developing language abilities.

Denial This Freudian defense mechanism distorts perception of the world: an individual who smokes and feels guilty because he smokes may exhibit denial by ignoring the evidence that smoking is harmful.

Deoxyribonucleic acid (DNA) A substance assumed to be the basis of all life, consisting of four chemical bases arranged in an extremely large number of combinations. The two strands of the DNA molecule that comprise genes are arranged in the form of a double spiral (helix). These double strands are capable of replicating themselves as well as crossing over from one strand of the spiral to the other and forming new combinations of their genetic material. The nucleus of all cells contains DNA molecules.

Dependent variable The variable which may or may not be affected by manipulations of the independent variable in an experimental situation. (See *variable, independent variable.*)

Development The total process whereby an individual adapts to his environment. Development includes growth, maturation, and learning.

Developmental psychology That aspect of psychology concerned with the development of individuals.

Developmental theory A body of psychological theories concerned with the development of children from birth to maturity.

Diary A frequently locked book in which an individual records his personal activities, feelings, and desires.

Digitalis A drug derived from a broad-leafed plant and used extensively in the treatment of cardiac patients.

Dilation and curettage (D and C) A surgical procedure that involves scraping the walls of the uterus. It is occasionally necessary after birth if all of the placenta has not been expelled.

Diobol An advanced product of robotic engineering bearing a faint resemblance to contemporary advanced computers.

Displacement A Freudian defense mechanism referring to the appearance of previously suppressed behavior in a somewhat more acceptable form. For example, an individual who has tendencies toward violence against people may displace this tendency in aggression against animals.

Dominant behavior A phrase describing the behavior of the dominant monkey or ape in a particular tribe. The dominant subhuman primate is typically a large male.

Dominant gene The gene (carrier of heredity) that takes precedence over all other related genes in genetically determined traits. Since all genes in the fertilized egg occur in pairs (one from the male and one from the female), the presence of a dominant gene as one member of the pair of genes means that the hereditary characteristic which it controls will be present in the individual. (See *recessive gene*.)

Drugs   Chemical substances that have marked physiological effects on living organisms.

Dyzygotic   Resulting from two separate eggs and forming fraternal (non-identical) twins. (See *monozygotic*.)

Ear   An odd protuberance found on either side of the human head; also present in many animals. Assumed to be related to hearing.

Early Training Project   A preschool project developed by Gray and Klaus emphasizing enriched and distinctive stimulation for children from impoverished backgrounds.

EEG (Electroencephalogram)   A recording of electrical impulses emitted by the brain. Popularly referred to as a brain-wave pattern.

Ego   The second stage of the human personality, according to Freud. It is the rational, reality-oriented level of human personality, which develops as the child becomes aware of what the environment makes possible and impossible, and therefore serves as a damper to the Id. The Id tends toward immediate gratification of impulses as they are felt, whereas the Ego imposes restrictions that are based on environmental reality. (See *Id; Superego*.)

Egocentricism   A perception of reality characterized by an inability to assume an objective point of view. Early child thinking is heavily egocentric.

Elaborated Language Code   A phrase employed by Bernstein to describe the language of middle-and upper-class children. Elaborated language codes are grammatically correct, complex, and precise.

Electra complex   A Freudian stage occurring around the age of 4 or 5 years, when a girl's awareness of her genital area leads her to desire her father and to become jealous of her mother. (See *Oedipus complex*.)

Elicited response   A response brought about by a stimulus. The expression is synonymous with the term *respondent*.

Eliciting effect   That type of imitative behavior in which the observer does not copy the model's responses but simply behaves in a related manner. (See *modeling effect, inhibitory-disinhibitory effect*.)

Embryo   The second stage of prenatal development, beginning around the first week after conception and terminating at the end of the sixth week.

Emitted response   A response not elicited by a known stimulus, but simply emitted by the organism. An emitted response is an operant.

Emotion   Refers to the "feeling" or "affective" aspect of human behavior. The term *emotion* includes such human feelings as fear, rage, love, and desire.

Enactive   A term employed by Bruner to describe the young child's representation of his world. It refers specifically to the belief that children represent their world by the activities they perform with it or on it. (See also *iconic, symbolic*.)

Environment   Referring to the significant aspects of an individual's surroundings. Includes all experiences and events that influence the child's development.

Episiotomy   A small cut made in the vagina to facilitate the birth of a child. An episiotomy prevents the tearing of membranes and ensures that once the cut has been sutured healing will be rapid and complete.

Epistemic behavior   A label employed by Berlyne to describe behavior designed to gather information.

Equilibrium   A relatively nebulous Piagetian term referring to a balance between assimilation and accommodation. The concept of equilibration is of primary importance to Piaget's explanation of motivation. He assumes that an individual constantly interacts with his environment (through assimilation and accommodation) to achieve a state of equilibrium.

Eros   A Greek word meaning love, employed by Freud to describe what he also called the life instinct—man's urge for survival. Eros is used in contrast to Thanatos. (See *Thanatos.*)

Eugenics   A form of genetic engineering that selects specific individuals for reproduction. The term as applied to humans raises a number of serious moral and ethical questions. It is widely accepted and practiced with animals, however.

Existentialism   A philosophical-psychological movement characterized by a preoccupation with existence. Existential philosophers describe the human condition in such terms as abandonment, loneliness, despair, and alienation. These feelings are purported to result from the individual's lack of knowledge about his origin and his eventual end. Hence the term *existentialism,* since the only knowable reality is existence.

Experiment   A procedure for scientific investigation requiring the manipulation of some aspects of the environment to determine what the effects of this manipulation will be.

Experimental group   A group of subjects who undergo experimental manipulation. The group to which something is done in order to observe its effects. (See *control group.*)

Exploratory behavior   A global term describing behavior that has no specific goal object but seems to be directed solely toward the examination or the discovery of the environment. The term frequently denotes curiosity-based activities.

Extended family   A large family group consisting of parents, children, grandparents, and occasionally uncles, aunts, cousins, and so on. (See *nuclear family.*)

Eyebrow   A fringe of hair above the human eye that may be raised or lowered to achieve a quizzical or nonquizzical expression.

Eyelids   Movable eye coverings.

Fairy tales   Stories, many of which have very ancient origins, frequently told to young children. Fairy tales are only infrequently about fairies, although many end with "And they lived happily ever after." Many are characterized by violence and by the description of fear-inducing situations.

Fallopian tube   Tubes that link the ovaries and the uterus. Fertilization (conception) ordinarily occurs in the fallopian tubes. From there the fertilized egg cell moves into the uterus and attaches to the uterine wall.

Falloren ray   A complex combination of sound and light waves that have the capacity of accelerating embryonic development on the planet Koros.

Fertilization   The union of sperm and ovum. The beginning of life. (See *conception.*)

Fertilized ovum stage   The first stage of prenatal development beginning at fertilization and ending at approximately the second week.

Fetal growth   The development of the fetus in the uterus. (See *fetus, uterus, embryo.*)

Fetus   An immature child in the uterus. It is the final stage of prenatal development and begins approximately 6 weeks after conception and lasts until the birth of the baby.

Fixation   A Freudian term describing the inability of a particular individual to progress normally through the psychosexual stages of development. Such individuals become *fixated* at specific stages. (See *regression.*)

Fixed schedule   An intermittent schedule of reinforcement in which the reinforcement occurs at fixed intervals of time, in the case of the *interval schedule,* or after a specified number of trials, in the case of a *ratio schedule.*

Forceps   Wicked looking, clamplike instruments that sometimes assist the delivery of a baby.

Formal operations   The last of Piaget's four major stages. It begins around the age of 11 or 12 and lasts until about 14 or 15. It is characterized by the child's increasing ability to use logical thought processes.

Fraternal twins   Twins whose genetic origins are two different eggs. Such twins are as genetically dissimilar as average siblings. (See *dyzygotic, identical twins.*)

Frustration   An affective reaction to the inability to gratify one's impulses.

Functional invariant   A Piagetian term describing those aspects of human interaction with the environment that are unchanging as the individual develops. The functional invariants of adaptation are assimilation and accommodation, since the processes of assimilating and accommodating remain constant as the child grows. (See *functioning.*)

Functioning   A Piagetian term describing the processes by which an organism adapts to his environment. These processes are assimilation and accommodation. (See *assimilation, accommodation.*)

Generalized reinforcers   A learned type of reinforcement that is reinforcing for a wide variety of behaviors. Such consequences of behavior as praise, social prestige, money, and power are important generalized reinforcers for human behavior.

Generation gap   A cliché referring generally to the conflict that exists between the established generation and the one still growing.

Genes   The carriers of heredity. Each of the 23 chromosomes contributed by the sperm cell and the ovum at conception is believed to contain between 40,000 and 60,000 genes. (See *dominant gene, recessive gene, polygenetic determination.*)

Genetic endowment   The influence of heredity transmitted from parent to offspring. (See *heredity.*)

Genitalia   A term referring generally to sex organs.

Genital stage   The last of Freud's stages of psychosexual development, beginning around the age of 11 and lasting until around 18. It is characterized by involvement with normal adult modes of sexual gratification.

Gestation   The period of time between conception and birth (typically 266 days for humans).

Grandmother   A woman, frequently rather old, one of whose children has had at least one child. There is much wisdom in the collective heads of ancient grandmothers.

Group pressure   The effect that the opinions, feelings, exhortations, or behavior of groups has on a single individual.

Growth   Ordinarily refers to such physical changes as increasing height or weight.

GSR (Galvanic Skin Response)   A measure of the conductivity of the skin to electricity. With increases in emotional reaction (arousal), the conductivity of the skin increases. Hence GSR measures may be considered indexes of arousal or emotion.

Guillotine   A machine for beheading humans.

Head turning reflex   A reflex elicited in the infant by stroking his cheek or the corner of his mouth. The infant turns his head toward the side being stimulated.

Heredity   The transmission of physical and personality characteristics and predispositions from parent to offspring.

Heteronomy   An intermediate stage in Bull's scheme of moral development in which the individual responds to situations primarily by their effect on himself. (See *anomy, socionomy,* and *autonomy.*)

Heterozygous   Refers to the presence of different genes with respect to a single trait. One of these genes is dominant and the other is recessive. (See *homozygous.*)

Homogeneous   Highly similar; coming from the same background. For example, a homogeneous culture is one in which all members have had highly similar experiences.

Homozygous   A term referring to an individual's genetic makeup. An individual is homozygous with respect to a particular trait if he possesses identical genes for that trait. (See *heterozygous.*)

Hospitalism   A medical name for the syndrome (configuration of symptoms) associated with the inability of infants to survive in children's homes or hospitals. Symptoms of hospitalism include listlessness, inability to gain weight, unresponsiveness, and eventual death.

Humanism   Describes a philosophical and psychological orientation primarily concerned with the humanity of man—the worth of man as an individual, and those processes that augment his human qualities.

Humanitarianism   Concern with the welfare of man. (See *humanism.*)

Huntington's chorea   A mental disorder characterized by progressive mental deterioration and death, usually after the age of 20 or 30. Huntington's chorea is caused by a dominant gene and is always fatal.

Hypothesis   A prediction about the outcome of an event or a situation, or a possible explanation for some phenomenon.

Iconic   A stage in the development of the child's representation of his world. Employed by Bruner to describe an intermediate stage of development characterized by a representation of the world through concrete mental images. (See also *enactive, symbolic.*)

Id   One of the three levels of the human personality, according to Freudian theory. The Id is defined as all the instinctual urges that man is heir to; it is the level of personality that contains man's motives; in short, it is Eros and Thanatos. A newborn child's personality, according to Freud, is all Id.

Idealism   Concern with ideas and ideals rather than with actuality or reality.

Identification   A general term referring to the process of assuming the goals, ambitions, mannerisms, and so on, of another person—of identifying with him. (See *imitation.*)

Identical twins   Twins whose genetic origin is a single egg. Such twins are genetically identical. (See *fraternal twins, monozygotic.*)

Identity   A logical rule specifying that certain activities leave objects or situations unchanged. (See *reversibility.*)

Imaginative play Play activities that include make-believe games. These are particularly prevalent during the pre-school years. (See *play*.)

Imitation The complex process of learning through observation of a model.

Immature birth A miscarriage occurring sometime between the twentieth and the twenty-eighth weeks of pregnancy, and resulting in the birth of a fetus weighing between 1 and 2 pounds.

Imprinting Unlearned, instinctual behaviors, which are not present at birth but become part of an animal's repertoire after exposure to a suitable stimulus. Such exposure ordinarily must take place during the critical period. The following behavior of young ducks, geese, and chickens is an example of imprinting.

Impulsive A personality characteristic manifested in a greater concern with the rapid solution of problems than with their correct solution.

Incentive motivation A reinforcement-based explanation for human behavior, referring specifically to the belief that it is the reinforcing property (or lack of reinforcing property) of the outcome of behavior that determines whether or not the individual will behave. In other words, it is the incentive value of a behavioral outcome that determines its occurrence or nonoccurrence.

Independent variable The variable in an experiment that can be manipulated to observe its effect on other variables. (See *variable, dependent variable*.)

Infancy A period of development that begins a few weeks after birth and lasts until approximately 2 years of age.

Inhibitory-disinhibitory effect Imitative behavior that results in either the suppression (inhibition) or appearance (disinhibition) of previously acquired deviant behavior. (See *modeling effect, eliciting effect*.)

Instinct Complex, species-specific, relatively unmodifiable behavior patterns such as migration in birds, hibernation in some mammals, and leadership behavior in fish.

Intellectualization A Freudian defense mechanism whereby the individual emphasizes the intellectual or rational content of his behavior in order to exclude any of the emotional connotations of his behavior. Intellectualization is commonly referred to as *rationalization*.

Intelligence A property measured by intelligence tests. Seems to refer primarily to the capacity of individuals to adjust to their environment.

Interval schedule An intermittent schedule of reinforcement based on the passage of time. (See also *fixed schedule, random schedule*.)

Intervention programs A global term referring to educational programs, which are typically remedial in nature. Many intervention programs have been organized at the preschool level to supplement the backgrounds of culturally deprived children.

Intrauterine Relating to the inside of the uterus. The term is frequently employed to describe the environment in which the fetus develops.

Intuitive thought One of the substages of the preoperational period beginning around 4 and lasting until age 7 or 8. Intuitive thought is marked by the child's ability to solve many problems intuitively, and by his inability to respond correctly in the face of misleading perceptual features of problems.

In utero A Latin expression meaning inside the uterus. A pregnant woman, surprisingly enough, carries her child *in utero*.

Jensen hypothesis The hypothetical argument advanced by Jensen on the basis of some evidence regarding heredity and environment — that with respect to intelligence the most influential environmental factors are prenatal, and that racial and social class differences in intelligence test scores cannot be accounted for by differences in environment alone. Hence genetic factors are assumed to be responsible for some of the observed differences in intelligence among different racial groups.

Kongor An extraterrestrial being from Koros in the Androneas system. (A personal friend of the author's.)

Labor The process during which the fetus, the placenta, and other membranes are separated from the woman's body and expelled. The termination of labor is usually birth.

Laguno Downy, soft hair that covers the fetus. Laguno grows over most of the child's body some time after the fifth month of pregnancy and is usually shed during the seventh month. However, some laguno is often present at birth, especially on the infant's back.

Language Complex arrangements of arbitrary sounds that have accepted referents and can therefore be used for communication among humans.

Language Acquisition Device (LAD) A label employed by Chomsky to describe the neurological *something* that corresponds to grammar, and that a child is assumed to have in his brain as he is learning language.

Latent stage (latency) The fourth of Freud's stages of psychosexual development, characterized by the development of the Superego (conscience) and by loss of interest in sexual gratification. This stage is assumed to last from the age of 6 to 11 years.

Learning Includes all changes in behavior, which are due to experience. Does not include temporary changes brought about by drugs or fatigue, or changes in behavior simply resulting from maturation or growth.

Libidinal gratification The gratification of sexual impulses. Within the context of Freud's theory, these need not necessarily involve what the layman considers to be the sexual regions of the body.

Libido A general Freudian term denoting sexual urges. The libido is assumed to be the source of energy for sexual urges. Freud considers these urges the most important forces in human motivation.

Life space A term employed by Lewin to describe the individual's interpretation of his environment. The life space includes the individual, his goals and aspirations, the alternatives that he has to obtain his goals, and the barriers that obstruct his action.

Longitudinal study A research technique in the study of child development that observes the same subjects over a long period of time. (See *cross-sectional study*.)

Love Is it never having to say you're sorry? Is it a many-splendored thing?

LSD-25 (D-lysergic acid diethylamide tartrate) A particularly powerful hallucinogenic drug; an inexpensive, easily made, synthetic chemical that can sometimes have profound influences on human perception. In everyday parlance it is often referred to as "acid."

Major gene determination A hereditary process whose outcome is determined by the presence or absence of a single dominant or recessive gene. (See *dominant gene, recessive gene, polygenetic determination*.)

Marasmus (*also called* anaclitic depression) The label given to the condition brought about by maternal deprivation. Symptoms of marasmus include retarded development, depression, and occasionally death. (See *hospitalism*.)

Maturation A developmental process defined by changes that are relatively independent of a child's environment. While the nature and timing of maturational changes are assumed to result from genetic predispositions, their manifestation is at least partly a function of the environment.

Mature birth   The birth of an infant between the thirty-seventh and forty-second weeks of pregnancy.

Maze-bright   An adjective describing those rats able to learn to run through mazes very easily. A maze-bright rat is the counterpart of an intelligent person. (See *maze-dull.*)

Maze-dull   An adjective describing the rat who has a great deal of difficulty in learning how to run a maze. A maze-dull rat is the counterpart of a stupid person. (See *maze-bright.*)

Mediation   A term used to describe the processes assumed to intervene between the presentation of a stimulus and the appearance of a response. Mediation is often assumed to be largely verbal.

Meiosis   The division of a single sex cell into two separate cells, each consisting of 23 chromosomes rather than 23 pairs of chromosomes. Meiosis therefore results in cells that are completely different, whereas mitosis results in identical cells. (See *mitosis.*)

Menarche   The girl's first menstrual period. An event which transpires during pubescence.

Menses   A monthly discharge of blood and tissue from the womb of a mature female. The term refers to menstruation.

Mental retardation   A global term referring to those individuals whose intellectual development is significantly slower than that of normal children, and whose ability to adapt to their environment is consequently limited.

Middle childhood   An arbitrary division in the sequence of development beginning somewhere near the age of 6 and ending at approximately 12.

Minority group   Describes a cultural, social, ethnic, or religious group existing within a larger cultural group.

Mitosis   The division of a single somatic cell into two identical cells. Occurs in body cells as opposed to sex cells. (See *meiosis.*)

Model   A term sometimes used to describe an attractive human female. May be employed more generally to describe a pattern for behavior, which can be copied by someone else. (See *symbolic model.*)

Modeling effect   Imitative behavior involving the learning of a novel response. (See *inhibitory-disinhibitory effect, eliciting effect.*)

Monozygotic   Twins resulting from the division of a single fertilized egg. The process results in identical twins. (See *mitosis.*)

Montessori method   A comprehensive educational program developed by Montessori, making extensive use of sense training through a variety of specially designed materials. The Montessori method is best known at the pre-school level.

Morality   Refers to the ethical aspect of human behavior. Morality is intimately bound to the development of an awareness of acceptable and unacceptable behaviors. It is therefore linked to what is often called conscience. (See *conscience.*)

Moro reflex   The name given to the generalized startle reaction of a newborn infant. It characteristically involves throwing out the arms and feet symmetrically and then bringing them back in toward the center of the body.

Morpheme   Combinations of phonemes that make up the meaningful units of a language. (See *phonemes.*)

Mother-in-law   A derogatory label given to an individual's spouse's mother.

Motor development   The development of such physical capabilities as walking, climbing, creeping, grasping, and handling objects.

Mouse   An unfortunate creature that is sometimes injected with a small amount of urine from a suspecting mother and then sacrificed to determine whether or not the mother was really pregnant. Virgin rabbits and frogs are used for the same purpose. Hence this particular test for pregnancy is frequently called the rabbit test.

Natural childbirth   Refers to the birth of a child in which a mother employs no anesthetics (or very little) to relieve pain. Advocates of natural childbirth recommend physical exercises, exercises in relaxation, and mental preparation prior to the birth of the child. Hypnosis may also be employed for natural childbirth.

Nature-nurture controversy   A very old psychological argument concerning whether genetics (nature) or environment (nurture) is more responsible for determining development.

Navel   Belly button. Adam didn't have one.

Need   Ordinarily refers to a lack or deficiency in the organism. Needs may be unlearned (for example, the need for food and water), or learned (the need for money or prestige).

Need achievement   An indicator of motivation described by McClelland. Aggressive and ambitious people possess a higher need for achievement than more passive and less ambitious people.

Need for affiliation   The need that individuals have to establish relations with other individuals.

Negative reinforcement   A stimulus that increases the probability of occurrence of the response that precedes it when it is removed from the situation. A negative reinforcer is usually an unpleasant or noxious stimulus that is removed when the desired response occurs.

Neobehavioristic theories   A division in learning theory that includes those theoretical positions that, while they are still concerned with stimuli and responses, are also concerned with the events that intervene (mediate) between stimuli and responses. (See *behavioristic theory*.)

Neonate   A newborn infant. The neonate period terminates when birth weight is regained.

Nonreversal shift   A type of discrimination learning in which the subject, who has been reinforced for selecting one value of a dimension, is now reinforced for selecting stimuli on the basis of another dimension. For example, the child who has been taught to select a black circle or square and reinforced for doing so is now reinforced for selecting squares or circles regardless of their color. (See *reversal shift*.)

Norm   An average, or a standard way of behaving. Cultural norms, for example, refer to the behaviors expected of individuals who are members of that culture.

Nuclear family   A family consisting of a mother, a father, and their offspring. (See *extended family*.)

Nursery school   A preschool institution that accepts children at an early age and that emphasizes child care, and emotional and social development.

Obesity   Corpulence; fatness.

Object concept   Piaget's expression for the child's understanding that the world is composed of objects that continue to exist quite apart from his immediate perception of them.

Objective (adj.)   Refers to research, theory, or experimental methods dealing with observable events. The implication is that objective observations are not affected by the observer. (See *subjective*.)

Obstetrics   A sophisticated medical term for what grandmothers call midwifery. It involves the medical art and science of assisting women who are pregnant, both during their pregnancy and at birth.

Oedipus complex   A Freudian concept denoting the developmental stage (around 4 years) when a boy's increasing awareness of the sexual meaning of his genitals leads him to desire his mother and envy his father. (See *Electra complex*.)

Operant   The label employed by Skinner to describe a response not elicited by any known or obvious stimulus. Most significant human behaviors appear to be operant. Such behaviors as writing a letter or going for a walk are operants, if no known specific stimulus elicits them.

Operant conditioning   A type of learning involving an increase in the probability of a response occurring as a result of reinforcement. Much of the experimental work of B. F. Skinner investigates the principles of operant conditioning.

Oral stage   The first stage of psychosexual development, lasting from birth to approximately 8 months of age. The oral stage is characterized by the child's preoccupation with the immediate gratification of his desires. This he accomplishes primarily through the oral regions, by sucking, biting, swallowing, playing with his lips, and so on.

Orientation reaction   The initial response of humans and other animals to novel stimulation. Also called the orienting reflex or orienting response. Components of the orientation reaction include changes in EEG patterns, in respiration rate, in heart rate, and in galvanic skin response. (See *EEG, GSR*.)

Ovary   A female organ (most women have two of them) which produces ova (egg cells).

Overt   Outward or external. Capable of being observed. (See *covert*.)

Ovum (plural *ova*)   The sex cell produced by a mature female approximately once every 28 days. When mature it consists of 23 chromosomes as opposed to all other human body cells (somatoplasm), which consist of 23 *pairs* of chromosomes. It is often referred to as an egg cell. (See *sperm cell*.)

Palmar reflex   The grasping reflex that a newborn infant exhibits when an object is placed in his hand.

Parent Education Project   A preschool education program developed by Gordon, involving sending "parent educators" directly into the homes of impoverished children. The educational programs themselves are based heavily on Piaget's theories of intellectual development.

Peer group   A group of equals. Peer groups may be social groups, age groups, intellectual groups, or work groups. When the term applies to young children, it typically refers to his age/grade mates.

Penis envy   A Freudian concept referring to the envy that a young girl is assumed to have for males, since they have a penis.

Phallic stage   The third stage of psychosexual development. It begins at the age of 18 months and lasts to the age of approximately 6 years. During this stage the child becomes concerned with his genitals and may show evidence of the much discussed complexes labeled *Oedipus* and *Electra*. (See *Oedipus complex, Electra complex*.)

Phenomenon   An event, occurrence, or happening.

Phenylketonuria (PKU)   A metabolic defect resulting from an individual's inability to oxidize phenylalanine. Until recently PKU always resulted in severe mental retardation very early in life. Now it can be detected immediately after birth through a routine check and controlled through special diet.

Phoneme   The simplest unit of language, consisting of a single sound such as a vowel.

Phylogenetic development   The evolutionary development of the species from its origins to its present state. Phylogeny is contrasted to ontogeny, in the sense that it refers to the development of a species rather than to the development of an individual.

Placenta   A flat, thick membrane attached to the inside of the uterus during pregnancy and to the developing fetus. The placenta connects the mother and the fetus by means of the umbilical cord.

Play   May be defined as activities that have no goal other than the enjoyment derived from them. (See *work*.)

Polygenetic determination   The determination of a trait through the interaction of a number of genes, rather than through major gene determination. (See *dominant genes, recessive genes, major gene determination*.)

Polyhydramnios   A complication of pregnancy involving an excessive amount of amniotic fluid in the uterus.

Positive reinforcement   A stimulus that increases the probability of a response recurring as a result of being added to a situation after the response has once occurred. It usually takes the form of a pleasant stimulus (*reward*) that results from a specific response.

Positive symptoms   Symptoms of pregnancy that determine positively that the woman is bearing a child. These include fetal heartbeats, the ability to feel the fetus by palpating the woman's stomach, and X rays that show the outline of the fetus.

Postmature birth   The birth of an infant after the forty-second week of pregnancy.

Postnatal   Following birth.

Preconcept   The label given to the preconceptual child's incomplete understanding of concept, resulting from an inability to classify. (See *preconceptual thought*.)

Preconceptual thought   The first substage of the period of preoperational thought, beginning around 2 and lasting until 4. It is so called because a child has not yet developed the ability to classify and therefore has an incomplete understanding of concepts (See *preconcept*.)

Pregnancy   A condition which occurs in women, but never in men. It involves being pregnant. (See *pregnant*).

Pregnant   An adjective describing a woman who has had an ovum (egg cell) fertilized, and who, nature willing, will eventually give birth to a human child.

Prehension   A term denoting the ability to grasp.

Premature birth   The birth of a baby between the twenty-ninth and thirty-sixth week of pregnancy. A premature birth weighs somewhere between 2 and $5\frac{1}{2}$ pounds, and is seldom capable of surviving if the fetus weighs less than $3\frac{1}{2}$ pounds.

Prenatal development   The period of development beginning at conception and ending at birth. That period lasts approximately nine calendar months in the human female (266 days). Chickens are considerably faster.

Preoperational thought The second of Piaget's four major stages, lasting from about 2 to 7 or 8 years. It consists of two substages: intuitive thinking and preconceptual thinking. (See *intuitive thought, preconceptual thought.*)

Pressure-cooker approach A preschool education program developed by Bereiter and Engelmann, emphasizing didactic teaching techniques, repetitive drill, and reinforcement.

Presumptive symptoms The initial, highly probabilistic signs of pregnancy frequently noted by prospective mothers and grandmothers. These include cessation of menses, morning sickness, changes in the breasts, and occasionally an increase in the frequency of urination.

Primary circular reaction An expression employed by Piaget to describe a simple reflex activity such as thumb sucking. (See *secondary circular reaction, tertiary circular reaction.*)

Primary reinforcement A stimulus that is reinforcing in the absence of any learning. Such stimuli as food and drink are primary reinforcers, since presumably an organism does not have to learn that they are pleasurable.

Probable symptoms Symptoms of pregnancy that are more certain than presumptive symptoms. These become evident after the fetus has begun to develop, and include enlargement of the abdomen, a change in the hardness of the uterus, and a change in the cervix.

Project Head Start A U.S. government project of preschool education aimed at overcoming the educational deficit of children from impoverished backgrounds.

Projection A Freudian defense mechanism whereby the individual attributes anxieties that are really his own to someone else. For example, an individual who is afraid of the dark and assumes that everyone is afraid of the dark is said to be *projecting.*

Projective technique A method of investigation or observation in which the subject is encouraged to respond in his own way to relatively nebulous stimuli, and the investigator then interprets the subject's response. The assumption is that the subject will project his true feelings, thoughts, or beliefs.

Prolapsed cord A condition that sometimes occurs during birth, when the infant's umbilical cord becomes lodged between his body and the birth canal, thereby cutting off his supply of oxygen. The effect may be brain damage of varying severity, depending on the length of time until delivery following prolapsing of the cord.

Proposition A term that grandmothers consider to imply impure intentions. In psychological jargon it refers to a statement that can be either true or false.

Prosody Modes of expression, intonations, accents, and pauses peculiar to a particular language.

Psychological hedonism The belief that people act to obtain pleasure and avoid pain.

Psychology The science that examines man's behavior (and that of animals as well).

Psychosexual development A Freudian term describing child development as a series of stages that are sexually based. (See *oral stage, anal stage, phallic stage, latent stage, genital stage.*)

Puberty Sexual maturity following pubescence. (See *pubescence.*)

Pubescence Changes that occur in late childhood or early adolescence, and that result in sexual maturity. In boys these changes include enlargement of the testes, growth of axillary hair, changes in the voice, and the ability to ejaculate semen. In the girl pubescence is characterized by rapid physical growth, occurrence of the first menstrual period (menarche), a slight lowering of the voice, and enlargement and development of the breasts.

Punishment   Involves either the presentation of an unpleasant stimulus or the withdrawal of a pleasant stimulus as a consequence of behavior. Punishment should not be confused with negative reinforcement, since punishment does not increase the probability of a response occurring, but is intended to have the opposite result.

Pupillary reflex   An involuntary change in the size of the pupil as a function of brightness or darkness. The pupillary reflex is present in the neonate. (See *neonate.*)

Quickening   The name given to the first movements of the fetus *in utero.* Quickening does not occur until after the fifth month of pregnancy.

Random schedule (*also called* variable schedule)   An intermittent schedule of reinforcement. It may be either interval or ratio, and is characterized by the presentation of reward at random intervals or on random trials. While both fixed and random schedules may be based on the same intervals or on the same ratio, one can predict when reward will occur on the fixed schedule, but it is impossible to do so with a random schedule.

Rat   A small rodent who has been of considerable service in the advancement of psychology as a science. The most commonly used laboratory species is the white Norway rat.

Ratio schedule   An intermittent schedule of reinforcement based on a proportion of correct responses. (See also *fixed schedule, random schedule.*)

Reaction formation   A Freudian defense mechanism whereby the individual behaves in a manner opposite to his inclinations. Reaction formation is illustrated by an individual who intensely desires a person of the opposite sex but is unable to obtain that person; consequently he shows evidence of disliking that person.

Recessive gene   A gene whose characteristics are not manifest in the offspring unless it happens to be paired with another recessive gene. When a recessive gene is paired with a dominant gene, the characteristics of the dominant gene will be manifest.

Reflective   A personality predeposition exhibiting a tendency to evaluate alternatives and to delay decisions in order to avoid errors. (See *impulsive.*)

Reflexive behavior   An unlearned stimulus-response connection. Flinching or withdrawing as a result of pain is an example of a reflex.

Regression   A Freudian term describing reversion to an earlier stage of psychosexual development. An individual at the genital stage of development may, for example, regress to the oral stage and show evidence of this regression through such activities as smoking. (See *genital stage, oral stage, fixation.*)

Regulatory function   In this context the expression refers specifically to the capability that language has of directing an individual's activities.

Reinforcement   The effect of a reinforcer. Specifically, to increase the probability of a response recurring. (See also *reinforcer, reward, negative reinforcement,* and *positive reinforcement.*)

Reinforcement schedule   The manner and order in which reinforcement is presented to an organism as it learns. (See *random schedule, fixed schedule, continuous schedule.*)

Reinforcer   A reinforcing stimulus.

Respondent   A term employed by Skinner in contrast to the term *operant* (also synonymous with *elicited response*). A respondent is a response elicited by a known specific stimulus. Unconditioned responses of the type referred to in classical conditioning are examples of respondents.

Response   Any organic, muscular, glandular, or psychic reaction resulting from stimulation.

Restricted language code   A term employed by Bernstein to describe the language typical of the lower-class child. Restricted language codes are characterized by short and simple sentences, general and relatively imprecise terms, idiom and colloquialism, and incorrect grammar. (See *elaborated language code*.)

Retarded   A term describing abnormally slow development, or those people who have not developed either physically or intellectually as rapidly as normal.

Reversal shift   A type of discrimination learning in which the organism previously taught to select stimuli on the basis of one value of a single dimension, is now required to respond to the opposite value of the same dimension. For example, the child who has been reinforced for selecting black stimuli whether they were squares or circles, is now reinforced for selecting white stimuli, whether they be squares or circles. (See *nonreversal shift*.)

Reversibility   A logical property manifested in the ability to reverse or undo activity in either an empirical or a conceptual sense. An idea is said to be reversible when a child can unthink it and when he realizes that certain logical consequences follow from doing so.

Reward   An object, stimulus, event, or outcome that is perceived as pleasant and may therefore be reinforcing.

Rites de passage   Ritualistic ceremonies marking the passage from childhood to adulthood in many primitive societies. There are no *rites de passage* in continuous cultures. (See *continuous culture*.)

Rosenthal effect   The belief that others' expectations affect an individual's behavior. Rosenthal ostensibly demonstrated that teacher expectations could affect the general academic performance of students, and also their intelligence test scores.

Safety needs   A term employed by Maslow to describe the individual's need to maintain an orderly and predictable environment—an environment not threatening in either a physical or psychological sense.

Sam.   The untenured and somewhat demented university professor who resides in the bowels of this city.

Schemes (*also* schema *or* schemata)   The label employed by Piaget to describe a unit in cognitive structure. A scheme is, in one sense, an activity together with its structural connotations. In another sense scheme may be thought of as an idea or a concept. It usually labels a specific activity: the looking scheme, the grasping scheme, the sucking scheme.

School   The acculturation machinery of complex societies. They are implicitly (and sometimes explicitly) employed to transmit the knowledge, beliefs, values, and other bits of wisdom that the society has accumulated.

Scooting   A form of locomotion employed by young children. It is similar to creeping or crawling, except that the child propels himself in a sitting position by using his hands and arms.

Secondary circular reaction   Infant responses that are circular in the sense that the response serves as a stimulus for its own repetition, and secondary since the responses do not center on the child's body, as do primary circular reactions. (See *primary circular reaction, tertiary circular reaction.*)

Secondary reinforcement   A stimulus that is not ordinarily reinforcing but that acquires reinforcing properties as a result of being paired with a primary reinforcer.

Self   The concept that an individual has of himself. Notions of the self are often closely allied with the individual's beliefs about how others perceive him.

Self-actualization   The process or act of becoming oneself, developing one's potentiality, achieving an awareness of one's identity, fulfilling oneself. The term *actualization* is central to humanistic psychology.

Self-esteem needs   A term employed by Maslow to describe the individual's desire for others to hold him in high esteem, and for the individual himself to maintain a high opinion of his behavior and his person.

Sensorimotor   The first stage of development in Piaget's classification. It lasts from birth to approximately age 2 and is so called because the child understands his world primarily through his activities towards it and sensations of it.

Sensorimotor play   Play activity involving the manipulation of objects or execution of activities simply for the sensations that are produced. (See *play.*)

Sensory deprivation   A situation in which an experimental subject is placed in a condition of either highly monotonous or highly restricted sensory stimulation. Subjects in prolonged conditions of sensory deprivation experience impaired perceptual and cognitive functioning. Infrequently hallucinations may also result from prolonged sensory isolation.

Seriation   The ordering of objects according to one or more empirical properties. To seriate is essentially to place in order.

Sex   An attribute employed to categorize people and other organisms according to their reproductive functions. It is ordinarily dichotomous. It also sometimes refers to an indescribable activity.

Sex chromosome   A chromosome contained in sperm cells and ova responsible for determining the sex of the offspring. Sex chromosomes produced by the female are of one variety (X); those produced by the male may be either X or Y. At fertilization (the union of sperm and ovum), an XX pairing will result in a girl; an XY pairing will result in a boy. Hence the sperm cell is essentially responsible for determining the sex of the offspring.

Sex typing   Learning behavior appropriate to the sex of the individual. The term refers specifically to the acquisition of masculine behavior for a boy and feminine behavior for a girl.

Shaping   The term employed to describe a technique whereby animals and people are taught to perform complex behaviors not previously in their repertoire. The technique reinforces responses that become increasingly closer approximations to the desired behavior. Also called the method of successive approximations, or the method of differential reinforcement of successive approximations.

Siblings   Offspring whose parents are the same. Siblings are simply brothers and sisters.

Skinner box   Refers to the experimental apparatus employed by Skinner in much of his research with rats and pigeons. It is a cagelike structure, equipped to allow the animal to make a response and the experimenter to reinforce or punish him for the response.

Social development   The development of a child's ability to interact with others. A consideration of social development frequently includes such topics as games, morality, the learning of language, and the learning of socially appropriate and inappropriate behaviors. (See *social learning.*)

Social learning   Acquiring patterns of behavior that conform to social expectations. Learning what is acceptable and what is not acceptable in a given culture.

Social play   Play activity that involves interaction between two or more children and frequently takes the form of games with more or less precisely defined rules. (See *play.*)

Socialization   The complex process of learning those behaviors that are appropriate within a given culture as well as those that are less appropriate. The primary agents of socialization are home, school, and peer groups.

Sociogram   A pictorial or graphic representation of the social structure of a group.

Sociometry   A measurement procedure employed extensively in sociological studies. It attempts to determine patterns of likes and dislikes in groups, as well as plotting group structure.

Socionomy   An intermediate stage in Bull's scheme of moral development in which the individual begins to accept social rules and consequently morality becomes authority oriented. (See *anomy, heteronomy,* and *autonomy.*)

Sperm cell   The sex cell produced by a mature male. Like egg cells (ova), sperm cells consist of 23 chromosomes rather than 23 pairs of chromosomes.

Squaw   A female North American Indian.

Stages   Identifiable phases in the development of human beings. Such developmental theories as Jean Piaget's are referred to as stage theories since they describe behavior at different developmental levels.

Stethoscope   A medical instrument that amplifies the sound of a heartbeat. Its use caused its inventor, Semmelweis, a great deal of trouble since it was considered scandalous to place a rolled up newspaper on a mother's abdomen to discern her fetus' heartbeat.

Stimulus (*plural* stimuli)   Any change in the physical environment capable of exciting a sense organ.

Structure   A phrase employed by Piaget to describe the organization of an individual's capabilities, whether they be motor or cognitive. Structure is assumed to result from interacting with the world through assimilation and accommodation. (See *assimilation, accommodation, scheme.*)

Subjective   Used in contrast to the adjective *objective.* It refers to observations, theories, or experimental methods which are affected by the observer.

Sucking reflex   The automatic sucking response of a newborn child when the oral regions are stimulated. Nipples are particularly appropriate for eliciting the sucking reflex.

Suicide   The deliberate taking of one's own life. It is final.

Superego   The third level of personality according to Freud. It defines the moral or ethical aspects of personality, and like the Ego, is in constant conflict with the Id. (See *Id, Ego.*)

Symbolic   The final stage in the development of a child's representation of his world. The term is employed by Bruner to describe a representation of the world through arbitrary symbols. Symbolic representation includes language, as well as theoretical or hypothetical systems. (See also *enactive, iconic.*)

Symbolic model   Nonhuman models such as movies, television programs, verbal and written instructions, or religious, literary, musical, or folk heroes.

Syncretic reason   A type of semilogical reasoning characteristic of the classification behavior of the very young preschooler. It involves grouping objects according to egocentric criteria, which are subject to change from one object to the next. In other words, the child does not classify on the basis of a single dimension, but changes dimensions as he classifies.

Syntax   The grammar of a language, consisting of the set of implicit or explicit rules that govern the combinations of words comprising a language.

Television   An electronic device which transmits pictures and sound. It is used extensively as a babysitter in contemporary American society.

Tertiary circular reaction   An infant's response that is circular in the sense that the response serves as the stimulus for its own repetition, but where the repeated response is not identical to the first response. This last characteristic, the altered response, distinguishes a tertiary circular reaction from a secondary circular reaction. (See *primary circular reaction, secondary circular reaction.*)

Tetrahydrocannabinols   The active ingredient in marijuana and similar substances (hashish, bhang).

Textbook   A collection of wise words. (See also *book.*)

Thanatos   A Greek word meaning death, employed by Freud to describe what he calls the *death wish* or *death instinct*. It is used in contrast with the word *Eros.* (See *Eros.*)

Toddler   A label sometimes used to describe the child between the ages of 18 months and $2\frac{1}{2}$ years.

Transductive reasoning   The type of semilogical reasoning that proceeds from particular to particular, rather than from particular to general or from general to particular. One example of transductive reasoning is the following:
Cows give milk.
Goats give milk.
Therefore goats are cows.

Transverse presentation   A crosswise presentation of the fetus at birth.

Trauma   An injury or nervous shock. Traumatic experiences are usually intense and unpleasant experiences.

Type R learning   A Skinnerian expression for operant conditioning. It is so called since both reinforcement and a response are involved in the learning.

Type S learning   A Skinnerian expression for classical conditioning. It is so called since stimuli are involved in classical conditioning.

Umbilical cord   A long, thick cord attached to what will be the child's navel at one end and to the placenta at the other. It transmits nourishment and oxygen to the growing fetus from the mother.

Unconditioned response   A response elicited by an unconditioned stimulus.

Unconditioned stimulus   A stimulus that elicits a response prior to learning. All stimuli capable of eliciting reflexive behaviors are examples of unconditioned stimuli. For example, food is an unconditioned stimulus for the response of salivation.

Uterus   A relatively sophisticated term for what is frequently called the womb.

Values   Judgments or beliefs relating to the desirability of certain behaviors or goals.

Variable   A property, measurement, or characteristic which is susceptible to variation. In psychological experimentation such qualitites of human beings as intelligence and creativity are referred to as variables. (See *independent variable, dependent variable.*)

Vicarious reinforcement   The type of reinforcement that results from observing someone else being reinforced. In imitative behavior the observer frequently acts as though he were being reinforced, when in fact he is not being reinforced, but is aware or simply assumes that the model is.

Virgin rabbit   An undespoiled female rabbit—a rare thing in these days of loose sexual behavior.

Wild children (frequently referred to as feral children)   Children allegedly abandoned by their parents and adopted and reared by such wild animals as chickens, wolves, bears, or tigers.

Work   Activities engaged in not primarily for the pleasure derived from them, but rather for what may be gained as a result of the activities. (See *play.*)

Ypsilanti project   A preschool project based heavily on instructional methodology derived from Piaget. (See *Parent Education Project.*)

Zygote   A fertilized egg cell (ovum). A zygote is formed from the union of a sperm cell and an egg cell; it contains 46 chromosomes (a full complement).

Bibliography

Alexander, G. LSD: Injection early in pregnancy produces abnormalities in offspring of rats. *Science*, 1967, 157, 459–460.

Altman, R. A. and Snyder, P. O. The minority student on campus: Expectations and possibilities. University of California, Berkeley: Center for Research and Development in Higher Education, and Western Interstate Commission for Higher Education, Boulder, Colorado, 1970.

Altus, W. D. Birth order and academic primogeniture. *Journal of Personality and Social Psychology*, 1965, 2, 872–876.

Altus, W. D. Birth order and its sequelae. *International Journal of Psychiatry*, 1967, 3, 23–32.

Ames, L. B. The sequential patterning of prone progression in the human infant. *Genetic Psychology Monographs*, 1937, 19, 409–460.

Arey, L. B. *Developmental anatomy.* (7th Ed.) Philadelphia: W. B. Saunders, 1965.

Arnold, A. *Violence and your child.* Chicago: Henry Regnery Co., 1969.

Asch, S. E. Opinions and social pressure. *Scientific American*, Nov., 1955.

Atkinson, J. W. *An introduction to motivation.* Princeton, N.J.: Van Nostrand, 1964.

Atkinson, J. W. The mainsprings of achievement-oriented activity. In J. D. Krumboltz (Ed.), *Learning and the educational process.* Chicago: Rand McNally & Co., 1965, 25–66.

Atkinson, J. W. and Feather, N. T. (Eds.) *A theory of achievement motivation.* New York: John Wiley, 1966.

Ausubel, D. P. *The psychology of meaningful verbal learning.* New York: Grune & Stratton, 1963.

Ausubel, D. P. *Educational psychology: A cognitive view.* New York: Holt, Rinehart & Winston, 1968.

Azrin, N. H. and Lindsley, O. R. The reinforcement of co-operation between children. *Journal of Abnormal and Social Psychology*, 1956, 52, 100–102.

Baker, J. B. E. The effects of drugs on the fetus. *Pharmacological Review*, 1960, 12, 37–90.

Bakwin, H. Psychologic aspects of pediatrics. *Journal of Pediatrics*, 1949, 35, 512–521.

Baldwin, A. L. *Theories of child development.* New York: John Wiley, 1967.

Bandura, A. *Principles of behavior modification.* New York: Holt, Rinehart & Winston, 1969.

Bandura, A. and Walters, R. H. *Adolescent aggression.* New York: Ronald Press, 1959.

Bandura, A. and Walters, R. *Social learning and personality development.* New York: Holt, Rinehart & Winston, 1963.

Bandura, A., Ross, D., and Ross, S. A. Vicarious reinforcement and imitative learning. *Journal of Abnormal and Social Psychology*, 1963, 67, 601–607.

Baratz, J. C. Bi-dialectical task for determining language proficiency in economically disadvantaged Negro children. *Child Development*, 1969, 40, 889–901.

Barber, T. X. and Silver, M. J. Fact, fiction, and the experimenter bias effect. *Psychological Bulletin Monographs Supplement*, 1969–70, 1–29 (a).

Barber, T. X. and Silver, M. J. Pitfalls in data analysis and interpretation: A reply to Rosenthal. *Psychological Bulletin Monographs Supplement,* 1969–70, 48–62 (b).

Barcroft, J. *The brain and its environment.* New Haven: Yale University Press, 1938.

Barnett, S. A. *Instinct and intelligence: Behavior of animals and man.* Englewood Cliffs, N.J.: Prentice-Hall, 1967.

Bayer, A. E. Birth order and college attendance. *Journal of Marriage and the Family,* 1966, 28, 480–484.

Baumrind, D. Child care practices anteceding three patterns of pre-school behavior, *Genetic Psychology Monographs,* 1967, 75, 43–88.

Bayley, N. The development of motor abilities during the first three years. *Monographs of the Society for Research in Child Development,* 1935, 1, 1–26.

Belinkoff, S. and Hall, O. W. Intravenous alcohol during labor. *American Journal of Obstetrics and Gynecology,* 1950, 59, 429–432.

Bell, R. R. Parent-child conflict in sexual values. *Journal of Social Issues,* 1966, 22, 34–44.

Benda, C. E. Mongolism: A comprehensive review. *Archives of Paediatrics,* 1956, 73, 391–407.

Benedict, R. *Patterns of culture.* Boston: Houghton Mifflin, 1934.

Bereiter, C. and Engelmann, S. *Teaching disadvantaged children in the pre-school.* New York: Prentice-Hall, 1966.

Bereiter, C. and Engelmann, S. An academically oriented pre-school for disadvantaged children: results from the initial experimental group. In D. W. Brison and J. Hill (Eds.), *Psychology and early childhood education,* Ontario Institute for Studies in Education, Monograph Series, No. 4, 1968, 17–36.

Berlyne, D. E. Conflict and choice time. *British Journal of Psychology,* 1957, 48, 106–118. (a)

Berlyne, D. E. Conflict and information theory variables as determinants of human perceptual curiosity. *Journal of Experimental Psychology,* 1957, 53, 399–404. (b)

Berlyne, D. E. The influence of the novelty and complexity of stimuli on visual fixation in the human infant. *British Journal of Psychology,* 1958, 49, 318–319. (a)

Berlyne, D. E. The influence of complexity and novelty in visual figures on orienting responses. *Journal of Experimental Psychology,* 1958, 55, 289–296. (b)

Berlyne, D. E. *Conflict, arousal, and curiosity.* New York: McGraw-Hill, 1960.

Berlyne, D. E. Conflict and the orienting reaction. *Journal of Experimental Psychology,* 1961, 62, 476–483.

Berlyne, D. E. Motivational problems raised by exploratory and epistemic behavior. In S. Koch (Ed.), *Psychology: A study of a science.* Vol. 5. New York: McGraw-Hill, 1963, 284–364.

Berlyne, D. E. *Structure and direction in thinking.* New York: John Wiley, 1965.

Berlyne, D. E. Curiosity and exploration. *Science,* 1966, 153, 25–33.

Bernard, J. and Sontag, L. W. Fetal reactivity to sound. *Journal of Genetic Psychology,* 1947, 70, 205–210.

Bernard, L. L. *Instinct: A study in social psychology.* New York: Holt, Rinehart & Winston, 1924.

Bernstein, B. Social class and linguistic development: A theory of social learning. *British Journal of Sociology,* 1958, 9, 159–174.

Bernstein, B. Language and social class. *British Journal of Sociology,* 1961, 11, 271–276.

Bijou, S. W. and Sturges, P. S. Positive reinforcers for experimental studies with children — consumables and manipulatables. *Child Development,* 1959, 30, 151–170.

Binet, A. and Simon, T. Méthodes nouvelles pour le diagnostic du niveau in-tellectuel des anormaux. *Année psychologiques,* 1905, 11, 191–244.

Birch, D. and Veroff, J. *Motivation: A study of action.* Belmont Calif.: Brooks/Cole, 1964.

Birnbrauer, J. S., Wolf, M. N., Kidder, J. D., and Tague, C. E. Classroom be-havior of retarded pupils with token reinforcement. *Journal of Experimental Child Psychology,* 1965, 2, 219–235.

Blatz, W. E. *Collected studies on the Dionne quintuplets.* Toronto: University of Toronto Press, 1937.

Block, V. L. Conflicts of adolescents with their mothers. *Journal of Abnormal and Social Psychology,* 1937, 32, 193–206.

Bloodstein, O. The development of stuttering. *Journal of Speech and Hearing Disorders,* 1960, 25, 219–237.

Bloom, B. S. *Stability and change in human characteristics.* New York: John Wiley, 1964.

Bookmiller, M. N. and Bowen, G. L. *Textbook of obstetrics and obstetric nurs-ing.* (5th Ed.) Philadelphia: W. B. Saunders, 1967.

Boring, E. G. Intelligence as the tests test it. *New Republic,* 1923, 35, 35–37.

Bossard, J. H. and Boll, E. S. *The large family system.* Philadelphia: University of Pennsylvania Press, 1956.

Bossard, J. H. and Sanger, W. P. The large family system—a research report. *American Sociological Review,* 1952, 17, 3–9.

Bowes, W. A., Jr., Brackbill, Y., Conway, E., and Steinschneider, A. The effects of obstetrical medication on fetus and infant. *Monographs of the Society for Research in Child Development,* Vol. 35, No. 4, 1970.

Bowlby, J. The influence of early environment. *International Journal of Psy-choanalysis,* 1940, 21, 154–178.

Bowlby, J. Some pathological processes set in train by early mother-child separa-tion. *Journal of Mental Science,* 1953, 99, 265–272.

Brehm, J. W. and Cohen, A. R. *Explorations in cognitive dissonance.* New York: John Wiley, 1962.

Bridges, K. M. B. Emotional development in early infancy. *Child Development,* 1932, 3, 324–341.

Brill, A. A. (Ed.) *The basic writing of Sigmund Freud.* New York: Random House, 1938.

Brim, O. G., Jr. Family structure and sex-role learning by children: A further analysis of Alan Koch's data. *Sociometry,* 1956, 21, 1–16.

Brown, J. A. C. *Freud and the post-Freudians.* Middlesex, England: Penguin Books, 1961.

Bruner, J. S. On going beyond the information given. In *Contemporary ap-proaches to cognition.* Cambridge: Harvard University Press, 1957, 41–69. (a)

Bruner, J. S. On perceptual readiness. *Psychological Review,* 1957, 64, 123–152. (b)

Bruner, J. S. The course of cognitive growth. *American Psychologist,* 1964, 19, 1–15.

Bruner, J. S. *Processes of cognitive growth: Infancy.* Worcester, Mass.: Clark University Press, 1968.

Bruner, J. S. and Kenney, H. J. On multiple ordering. In Bruner, J. S. et al, *Studies in cognitive growth.* New York: John Wiley, 1966, 154–167.

Bruner, J. S., Oliver, R. R., and Greenfield, P. N. *Studies in cognitive growth.* New York: John Wiley, 1966.

Buber, M. *I and thou.* New York: Scribner's, 1958.

Buber, M. *The knowledge of man* (M. Friedman, Ed.). New York: Harper & Row, 1965.

Buhler, C. *The first year of life.* (Greenberg and Ripin, Transl.). New York: Day, 1930.

Bull, M. J. *Moral judgment from childhood to adolescence.* Beverly Hills, Calif.: Sage Publications, 1969.

Burchinal, L. Comparison of factors related to adjustment in pregnancy-provoked and non-pregnancy-provoked youthful marriages. *Midwest Sociologist,* 1959, 21, 92–96.

Burt, C. The genetic determination of differences in intelligence: A study of monozygotic twins reared together and apart. *British Journal of Psychology,* 1966, 57, 137–153.

Caldwell, B. N. The fourth dimension in early childhood education. In R. D. Hess and R. M. Bear (Eds.), *Early education: Current theory, research and action.* Chicago: Aldine Publishing Co., 1968, 71–82.

Campbell, D. T. and Stanley, J. C. *Experimental and quasi-experimental designs for research.* Chicago: Rand McNally, 1963.

Campbell, J. D. and Yarrow, M. R. Personal and situational variables in adaptation to change. *Journal of Social Issues,* 1958, 14, 29–46.

Carlson, J. S. Effects of instruction on the concepts of conservation of substance. *Science Education,* 1967, 4, 285–291.

Carpenter, C. R. A field study in Siam of the behavior and social relations of the Gibbon (*hylobates lar*). *Comparative Psychology Monographs,* 1940, 16, 1–212.

Casler, L. Maternal deprivation: A critical review of the literature. *Monograph of the Society for Research in Child Development,* 1961, Vol. 26, No. 2.

Chapman, E. R. and Williams, P. T. Intravenous alcohol as an obstetrical analgesia. *American Journal of Obstetrics and Gynaecology,* 1951, 61, 676–679.

Chomsky, N. *Syntactic structures.* The Hague: Mouton, 1957.

Chomsky, N. *Aspects of the theory of syntax.* Cambridge, Mass.: MIT Press, 1965.

Cobrinik, R. W., Hood, R. T., and Chusid, E. The effect of maternal narcotic addition on the newborn infant. *Paediatrics,* 1959, 24, 288–304.

Cole, L. and Hall, I. N. *Psychology of adolescence.* (7th Ed.) New York: Holt, Rinehart & Winston, 1970.

Coleman, J. S. The adolescent sub-culture and academic achievement. *American Journal of Sociology,* 1960, 65, 337–347.

Coleman, J. S. *The adolescent society.* New York: The Free Press, 1961.

Collias, N. E. The analysis of socialization in sheep and goats. *Ecology,* 1956, 37, 228–239.

Cowan, E. and Pratt, B. The hurdle jump as a developmental and diagnostic test. *Child Development,* 1934, 5, 107–121.

Cratty, B. J. *Perceptual and motor development in infants and children.* New York: The Macmillan Co., 1970.

Crick, F. H. The genetic code. *Scientific American,* 1962, 207, 66–74.

Crick, F. H. On the genetic code. *Science,* 1963, 139, 461–464.

Crossland, F. E. *Minority access to college: A Ford Foundation report.* New York: Schocken Books, 1971.

Davis, E. A. The development of linguistic skills in twins, single twins with siblings, and only children from age 5 to 10 years. Indianapolis: University of Minnesota Press, Institute of Child Welfare Series, No. 14, 1937.

Darwin, C. A biographical sketch of an infant. *Mind,* 1877, 2, 285–294.

De Charms, R. and Moeller, G. H. Values expressed in American children's readers: 1800–1950. *Journal of Abnormal and Social Psychology,* 1962, 64, 136–142.

Dember, W. N. Response by the rat to environmental change. *Journal of Comparative and Physiological Psychology,* 1956, 49, 93–95.

Dennis, W. Infant development under conditions of restricted practice and of minimum social stimulation. *Genetic Psychology Monographs,* 1941, 23, 143–191. (a)

Dennis, W. The significance of feral man. *American Journal of Psychology,* 1941, 54, 425–432. (b)

Dennis, W. Historical beginnings of child psychology. *Psychological Bulletin,* 1949, 46, 224–235.

Dennis, W. A further analysis of reports of wild children. *Child Development,* 1951, 22, 153–158.

Dennis, W. Causes of retardation among institutional children: Iran. *Journal of Genetic Psychology,* 1960, 96, 47–59.

DeVore, I. (Ed.) *Primate behavior.* New York: Holt, Rinehart & Winston, 1965.

Dublin, L. I. *Suicide: A sociological and statistical study.* New York: Ronald Press, 1963.

Dunphy, D. C. The social structure of urban adolescent peer groups. *Sociometry,* 1963, 26, 230–246.

Eastman, N. J. and Hellman, L. M. *Williams obstetrics.* (13th Ed.) New York: Appleton-Century-Crofts, 1966.

Ebin, D. (Ed.) *The drug experience: First person accounts of addicts, writers, scientists and others.* New York: The Orion Press, 1961.

Ehrmann, W. Changing sex mores. In Ginzberg, E. (Ed.), *Values and ideals of American youth.* New York: Columbia University Press, 1961, 53–70.

Eisenberg, R. B., Griffin, E. J., Coursin, D. B., and Hunter, M. A. Auditory behavior in the neonate. *Journal of Speech and Hearing Research,* 1964, 7, 245–269.

Eisenman, R. Birth order and sex differences in aesthetic preference for complexity-simplicity. *The Journal of General Psychology,* 1967, 77, 121–126.

Engels, F. *The origin of the family, private property and the state.* Chicago: Kerr, 1902.

Engen, T., Lipsitt, L. T., and Kaye, H. Olfactory responses and adaptation in the human neonate. *Journal of Comparative and Physiological Psychology,* 1963, 56, 73–77.

Erikson, E. H. *Identity, youth and crisis.* New York: W. W. Norton, 1968.

Erlenmyer, K. L. and Jarvik, L. F. Genetics and intelligence: A review. *Science,* 1963, 142, 1477–1478.

Etzel, B. C. and Gerwirtz, J. L. Experimental modification of a caretaker-maintained high-rate operant crying in a six- and a twenty-week old infant (*Infans tyrannotearus*): Extinction of crying with reinforcement of eye-contact and smiling. *Journal of Experimental Child Psychology,* 1967, 5, 303–317.

Fantz, R. L. The origin of form-perception. *Scientific American,* 1961, 204, 66–72.

Fantz, R. L. Pattern vision in newborn infants. *Science,* 1963, 140, 296–297.

Fantz, R. L. Visual experience in infants: Decreased attention to familiar patterns relative to novel ones. *Science,* 1964, 146, 668–670.

Fantz, R. L. Visual perception from birth as shown by pattern selectivity. *Annals of the New York Academy of Science,* 1965, 118, 793–814.

Faris, R. E. Sociological causes of genius. *The American Sociological Review,* 1940, 5, 689–699.

Feather, D. B. and Olson, W. S. *Children, psychology, and the schools: Research and trends.* Glenview, Illinois: Scott, Foresman, 1969.

Ferreira, A. J. *Prenatal environment.* Springfield, Ill.: Charles C Thomas, 1969.

Festinger, L. *A theory of cognitive dissonance.* Stanford, Calif.: Stanford University Press, 1957.

Festinger, L. and Carlsmith, J. M. Cognitive consequences of forced compliance. *Journal of Abnormal and Social Psychology,* 1959, 58, 203–210.

Festinger, L. Cognitive dissonance. *Scientific American,* October, 1962.

Flacks, R. The liberated generation: An exploration of the roots of student protest. *Journal of Social Issues,* 1967, 22, 52–75.

Flavell, J. H. *The developmental psychology of Jean Piaget.* New York: D. Van Nostrand, 1963.

Fowler, H. Response to environmental change: A positive replication. *Psychological Reports,* 1958, 4, 506.

Fowler, H. *Curiosity and exploratory behavior.* New York: The Macmillan Co., 1965.

Frazier, A. and Lisonbee, L. K. Adolescent concerns with physique. *School Review,* 1950, 58, 397–405.

Frazier, T. M., Davis, G. H., Goldstein, H., and Goldberg, I. D. Cigarette smoking and prematurity: A prospective study. *American Journal of Obstetrics and Gynaecology,* 1961, 81, 988–996.

Freud, A. *The ego and the mechanisms of defense.* (C. Baines, Transl.) New York: International Universities Press, 1946.

Fuller, J. L. and Thompson, W. R. *Behavior genetics.* New York: John Wiley, 1960.

Furth, H. G. *Piaget and knowledge.* Englewood Cliffs, N.J.: Prentice-Hall, 1969.

Gagné, R. M. Learning hierarchies. *Educational Psychologist,* 1968, 6, 1–9.

Gagné, R. M. *The conditions of learning.* (2nd Ed.) New York: Holt, Rinehart & Winston, 1970.

Gale, R. F. *Developmental behavior: A humanistic approach.* New York: The Macmillan Co., 1969.

Gall, J. G. Chromosomal differentiation. In W. D. McElroy and B. Glass (Eds.), *Chemical basis of development.* Baltimore: Johns Hopkins, 1958, 103–135.

Galton, F. *Hereditary genius: An enquiry into its laws and consequences.* London: Macmillan, 1869.

Gardiner, W. L. *Psychology: A story of a search.* Belmont, Calif.: Brooks/Cole, 1970.

Gershon, S. and Angrist, B. Drug-induced psychoses: II. *Hospital Practice,* 1967, 2, 50–53.

Gesell, A. *The mental growth of the pre-school child.* New York: The Macmillan Co., 1925.

Gesell, A. *Infancy and human growth.* New York: The Macmillan Co., 1937.

Gesell, A. *Wolf-child and human child.* New York: Harper, 1940.

Gesell, A. and Amatruda, C. S. *Developmental diagnosis: Normal and abnormal child development.* New York: Hoeber, 1941.

Getzels, J. W. and Jackson, P. W. *Creativity and intelligence.* New York: John Wiley, 1962.

Ginsberg, H. and Opper, S. *Piaget's theory of intellectual development.* Englewood Cliffs, N.J.: Prentice-Hall, 1969.

Goddard, H. H. *Feeble-mindedness: its causes and consequences.* New York: The Macmillan Co., 1914.

Gold, N. and Douvan, E. *Adolescent development: Readings in research and theory.* Boston: Allyn & Bacon, 1969.

Goldstein, R. *1 in 7: Drugs on campus.* New York: Walter, 1966.

Goode, E. (Ed.) *Marijuana.* New York: Atherton Press, 1969.

Goodfriend, M. J., Shey, I. A., and Klein, M. B. Effects of maternal narcotic addiction on the newborn. *American Journal of Obstetrics and Gynaecology,* 1956, 71, 29–36.

Gordon, E. W. and Wilkerson, D. A. Compensatory Education for the Disadvantaged: Programs and Practices: Preschool Through College. New York: College Entrance Examination Board, 1966.

Gordon, I. J. Stimulation via Parent Education. *Children,* 1969, March-April, 58.

Gottesman, I. I. Differential inheritance of the psycho-neuroses. *Eugenics Quarterly,* 1962, 9, 223–227.

Gottesman, I. I. and Shields, J. Schizophrenia in twins: Sixteen years, consecutive admissions to a psychiatric clinic. *British Journal of Psychology,* 1966, 112, 809–818.

Gray, S. W. and Klaus, R. A. An experimental preschool program for culturally deprived children. *Child Development,* 1965, 36, 887–898.

Gray, S. W. and Klaus, R. A. The early training project and its general rationale. In R. D. Hess and R. M. Bear (Eds.), *Early education: Current theory, research, and action.* Chicago: Aldine Publishing, 1968, 63–70.

Greenacre, P. Play in relation to creative imagination. *Psychoanalytic Studies of the Child,* 1959, 14, 61–80.

Greenspoon, J. The reinforcing effect of two spoken sounds on the frequency of two responses. *American Journal of Psychology,* 1955, 68, 409–416.

Gronlund, N. E. and Holmlund, W. S. The value of elementary school sociometric status scores for predicting a pupil's adjustment in high school. *Educational Administration and Supervision,* 1958, 44, 255–260.

Guthrie, E. R. *The psychology of learning.* New York: Harper & Row, 1935.

Haith, M. M. The response of the human newborn to visual movement. *Journal of Experimental Child Psychology,* 1966, 3, 235–243.

Hall, G. S. The contents of children's minds on entering school. *Paediatric Seminars,* 1891, 1, 139–173.

Hall, R. E. *Nine months' reading: A medical guide for pregnant women.* (Rev. Ed.) New York: Bantam Books, 1963.

Halverson, H. M. An experimental study of prehension in infants by means of systematic cinema records. *Genetic Psychology Monographs,* 1931, 10, 107–286.

Harlow, H. F. Motivation as a factor in the acquisition of new responses. In *Current theory and research motivation.* Lincoln, Nebraska: University of Nebraska Press, 1953, 24–49.

Harlow, H. F. The nature of love. *American Psychologist,* 1958, 12, 673–685.

Harlow, H. F. Love in infant monkeys. *Scientific American.* 1959, 200, 68–74.

Harlow, H. F. Age-mate or peer affectional systems. In D. S. Leahrman, R. A. Hinde, and E. Shaw (Eds.), *Advances in the study of behavior,* Vol. 2. New York: Academic Press, 1969.

Harlow, H. F., McGaugh, J. L., and Thompson, R. F. *Psychology.* San Francisco: Albion Publishing, 1971.

Harlow, H. F. and Zimmerman, R. R. Affectional responses in the infant monkey. *Science,* 1959, 130, 421–432.

Harlow, M. K. and Harlow, H. F. Affection in primates. *Discovery,* 1966, 27, 11–17.

Hartmann, G. W. A critique of the common method of estimating vocabulary size, together with some data on the absolute word knowledge of educated adults. *Journal of Educational Psychology,* 1941, 32, 351–364.

Hartshorne, H. and May, M. A. *Studies in the nature of character: Vol. 1, Studies in deceit; Vol. II, Studies in self-control; Vol. III, Studies in the organization of character.* New York: Macmillan, 1928–1930.

Hatfield, J. S., Ferguson, L. R., and Alpert, R. Mother-child interaction and the socialization process. *Child Development,* 1967, 38, 365–414.

Havighurst, R. J. and Taba, H. *Adolescent character and personality.* New York: John Wiley, 1949.

Haynes, H., White, B. L., and Held, R. Visual accommodation in human infants. *Science,* 1965, 148, 528–530.

Hebb, D. O. *The organization of behavior.* New York: John Wiley, 1949.

Hebb, D. O. *A textbook of psychology.* (2nd Ed.) Philadelphia: W. B. Saunders, 1966.

Henderson, G. *America's other children: Public schools outside suburbia.* Norman, Oklahoma: University of Oklahoma Press, 1971.

Hendry, L. S. Cognitive processes in a moral conflict situation. Unpublished doctoral dissertation, Yale University, 1960.

Hepner, R. Maternal nutrition and the fetus. *Journal of the American Medical Association,* 1958, 168, 1774–1777.

Heron, W. The pathology of boredom. *Scientific American Reprint,* Jan., 1957.

Hess, R. D. and Bear, R. M. (Eds.) *Early education: Current theory, research and action.* Chicago: Aldine Publishing, 1968.

Hewett, S. *The emotionally disturbed child in the classroom.* Boston: Allyn and Bacon, 1968.

Hilgard, E. R. and Bower, G. H. *Theories of learning.* (3rd Ed.) New York: Appleton-Century-Crofts, 1966.

Hill, W. F. *Learning: A survey of psychological interpretations.* San Francisco: Chandler Publishing, 1963.

Himmelweit, H. T., Oppenheim, A. N., and Vince, P. *Television and the child.* London and New York: Oxford University Press, 1958.

Hockman, C. H. Pre-natal maternal stress in the rat: Its effect on emotional behavior in the offspring. *Journal of Comparative and Physiological Psychology,* 1961, 54, 679–684.

Holbrook, S. H. *Dreamers of the American dream.* Garden City, N.Y.: Doubleday, 1957.

Horowitz, F. D. The relationship of anxiety, self-concept, and sociometric status among fourth, fifth, and sixth grade children. *Journal of Abnormal and Social Psychology,* 1962, 65, 212–214.

Hull, C. L. *Principles of behavior.* New York: Appleton-Century-Crofts, 1943.

Hull, C. L. *Essentials of behavior.* New Haven: Yale University Press, 1951.

Hull, C. L. *A behavior system.* New Haven: Yale University Press, 1952.

Hunt, J. McV. *Intelligence and experience.* New York: Ronald Press, 1961.

Hurlock, E. B. *Child development.* (4th Ed.) New York: McGraw-Hill, 1964.

Ilg, F. L. and Ames, L. B. *School readiness.* New York: Harper & Row, 1965.

Inhelder, B. and Piaget, J. The growth of logical thinking from childhood to adolescence. New York: Basic Books, 1958.

Involvement in Developmental Psychology Today. Del Mar, Calif.: C.R.M. Books, 1971.

Irwin, O. C. Research on speech sounds for the first six months of life. *Psychological Bulletin.* 1941, 38, 277–285. (a)

Irwin, O. C. The profile as a visual device for indicating central tendencies in speech data. *Child Development,* 1941, 12, 111–120. (b)

Irwin, O. C. Infant speech. *Scientific American,* 1949, 18, 22–24.

Jackson, C. N. *Some aspects of form and growth.* In W. J. Robbins, S. Brody, A. G. Hogan, C. N. Jackson, and C. W. Green, *Growth.* New Haven: Yale University Press.

James, W. *The principles of psychology.* New York: Holt, Rinehart & Winston, 1890.

Jensen, A. R. Social class, race, and genetics: implications for education. *American Educational Research Journal,* 1968, 5, 1–42.

Jensen, A. R. How much can we boost I.Q. and scholastic achievement? *Harvard Educational Review,* 1969, 39, 1–123.

Jersild, A. T. *The psychology of adolescence.* (2nd Ed.) New York: The Macmillan Co., 1963.

Johnson, N. Through the video-screen darkly. *The Christian Science Monitor,* Feb., 1969.

Johnson, R. C. and Medinnus, G. R. *Child psychology: Behavior and development.* (2nd Ed.) New York: John Wiley, 1969.

Johnson, R. D. Measurements of achievement in fundamental skills of elementary school children. *Research Quarterly,* 1962, 33, 94–103.

Johnson, W., Brown, S. F., Curtis, J. F., Edney, C. W. and Keaster, J. *Speech handicapped school children.* New York: Harper, 1948.

Kagan, J. Reflection-impulsivity and reading ability in primary grade children. *Child Development,* 1965, 36, 609–628. (a)

Kagan, J. Individual differences in the resolution of response uncertainty. *Journal of Personality and Social Psychology,* 1965, 2, 154–160. (b)

Kagan, J. Reflection-impulsivity: the generality and dynamics of conceptual tempo. *Journal of Abnormal Psychology,* 1966, 71, 17–24. (a)

Kagan, J. Developmental studies in reflection and analysis. In Kidd, A. H., and Rivoire, J. L. (Eds.), *Perceptual Development in Children.* New York: International Universities Press, 1966, 487–522. (b)

Kagan, J. Biological aspects of inhibition systems. *American Journal of Diseases of Children,* 1967, 114, 507–512.

Keller, F. S. *Learning: Reinforcement theory.* (2nd Ed.) New York: Random House, 1969.

Kellogg, W. N. and Kellogg, L. A. *The ape and the child: A study of environmental influence upon early behavior.* New York: McGraw-Hill, 1933.

Kendler, H. H. and D'Amato, M. F. A comparison of reversal shifts and non-reversal shifts in human concept formation behavior. *Journal of Experimental Psychology,* 1955, 49, 165–174.

Kendler, H. H., Glucksberg, S., and Keston, R. Perception and mediation in concept learning. *Journal of Experimental Psychology,* 1961, 61, 186–191.

Kendler, H. H. and Kendler, T. S. Vertical and horizontal processes in problem-solving. *Psychological Review,* 1962, 69, 1–16.

Kendler, T. S. Development of mediating responses in children. *Monograph of the Society for Research in Child Development,* 1963, 28, 86, 33–48.

Kendler, T. S. and Kendler, H. H. Reversal and non-reversal shifts in kindergarten children. *Journal of Experimental Psychology,* 1959, 58, 56–60.

Keogh, J. F. Motor performance in elementary school children. *Monographs,* University of California, Los Angeles, Physical Education, 1965.

Keogh, J. F. A rhythmical hopping task as an assessment of motor deficiency. Paper reported at the 2nd International Congress of Sports Psychology, Washington, D.C., 1968.

Kessen, W. *The child.* New York: John Wiley, 1965.

Kimble, G. A. *Hilgard and Marquis' conditioning and learning.* New York: Appleton-Century-Crofts, 1961.

Kinsey, A. C. Pomeroy, W. B., and Martin, C. E. *Sexual behavior in the human male.* Philadelphia: W. B. Saunders, 1948.

Kinsey, A. C. Pomeroy, W. B., Martin, C. E., and Gebhard, P. H. *Sexual behavior in the human female.* Philadelphia: W. B. Saunders, 1953.

Kirk, S. A. and McCarthy, J. J. *The Illinois test of psycholinguistic abilities: An approach to differential diagnoses.* Urbana: University of Illinois Press, 1961.

Kivy, P. M., Early, R. W., and Walker, E. L. Stimulus context and satiation. *Journal of Comparative and Physiological Psychology,* 1956, 49, 90–92.

Klaus, R. A. and Gray, S. W. The early training project for disadvantaged children: A report after five years. *Monograph of the Society for Research in Child Development,* 33, No. 4, 1968.

Koch, H. L. Some personality correlates of sex, sibling position, and sex of sibling among five and six year old children. *Genetic Psychology Monographs,* 1955, 52, 3–50.

Koch, H. L. *Twins and Twin Relations.* Chicago: University of Chicago Press, 1966.

Koenig, F. G. Improving the language abilities of bilingual children. *Exceptional Children,* 1953, 14, 183–186.

Kohlberg, L. Development of moral character and moral ideology. In M. L. Hoffman and L. W. Hoffman (Eds.), *Review of Child Development Research,* Vol. 1. New York: Russell Sage Foundation, 1964, 383–432.

Kohlberg, L. Montessori with the culturally disadvantaged. A cognitive-developmental interpretation and some research findings. In R. D. Hess and R. M. Bear (Eds.), *Early education: Current theory, research and action.* Chicago: Aldine Publishing, 1968, 105–118.

Kohlberg, L. Stage and sequence: The cognitive-developmental approach to socialization. In D. Gosslin (Ed.), *Handbook of socialization theory and research*. Chicago: Rand McNally, 1969.

Kohlberg, L. and Turiel, E. *Research in moral development: A cognitive developmental approach*. New York: Holt, Rinehart & Winston, 1971.

Konrad, H. S. and Jones, H. E. A second study of familial resemblence in intelligence: Environmental and genetic implications of parent-child and sibling correlation in the total sample. *Yearbook of the National Society for Studies in Education*, 1940, 39.

Krech, D., Rosenzweig, M., Bennett, E., and Krueckel, B. Enzyme concentrations in the brain and adjustive behavior patterns. *Science*, 1954, 120, 994–996.

Krech, D., Rosenzweig, M., and Bennett, E. Effects of environmental complexity and training on brain chemistry. *Journal of Comparative and Physiological Psychology*, 1960, 53, 509–519.

Krech, D., Rosenzweig, M. and Bennett, E. Relations between brain chemistry and problem-solving among rats in enriched and impoverished environments. *Journal of Comparative and Physiological Psychology*, 1962, 55, 801–807.

Krech, D., Rosenzweig, M., and Bennett, E. Environmental impoverishment, social isolation, and changes in brain chemistry and anatomy. *Physiology and Behavior*, 1966, 1, 99–104.

Krech, D., Cruchfield, R. S., and Livson, N. *Elements of Psychology*. (2nd Ed.) New York: Alfred A. Knopf, 1969.

Landis, J. T. and Landis, M. G. *Building a successful marriage*. Englewood Cliffs, N.J.: Prentice-Hall, 1963.

Landreth, C. *Early childhood: Behavior and learning*. (2nd Ed.) New York: Alfred A. Knopf, 1967.

Lee, E. S. Negro intelligence and selective migration: A Philadelphia test of the Klineberg hypothesis. *American Sociological Review*, 1951, 16, 227–233.

Lefrancois, G. R. The acquisition of concepts of conservation. Unpublished doctoral dissertation, Edmonton, University of Alberta, 1966.

Lefrancois, G. R. Jean Piaget's developmental model: Equilibration-through-adaptation. *Alberta Journal of Educational Research*, 1967, 13, 161–171.

Lefrancois, G. R. A treatment hierarchy for the acceleration of conservation of substance. *Canadian Journal of Psychology*, 1968, 22, 277–284.

Lefrancois, G. R. *Psychology for teaching: A bear always faces the front*. Belmont, Calif.: Wadsworth Publishing Co., 1972. (a)

Lefrancois, G. R. *Psychological theories and human learning: Kongor's report*. Belmont, Calif.: Brooks/Cole, 1972. (b)

Lenneberg, E. H. *Biological foundations of language*. New York: John Wiley, 1967.

Lenneberg, E. H., Nichols, I. A., and Rosenberger, E. F. Primitive stages of language development in mongolism. In *Disorders of communication, Vol. XLII: Research Publications, A.R.N.M.D.* Baltimore, Maryland: Williams and Wilkins, 1964.

Lenz, W. Malformations caused by drugs in pregnancy. *American Journal of Diseases in Children*, 1966, 112, 99–106.

Lewin, K. *A dynamic theory of personality*. (B. K. Adams and K. E. Zener, Transl.) New York: McGraw-Hill, 1935.

Lewin, K. *Principles of topological psychology*. (F. Heider and G. N. Heider, Transl.) New York: McGraw-Hill, 1936.

Lewin, K. Frontiers in group dynamics. *Human Relations*, 1947, 1, 5–41.

Lewin, K. *Field theory in social science*. New York: Harper, 1951.

Lindsley, O. R. Experimental analysis of social reinforcement: Terms and methods. *American Journal of Orthopsychiatry*, 1963, 33, 624–633.

Lipsitt, L. T., Engen, T., and Kaye, H. Developmental changes in the olfactory threshold of the neonate. *Child Development*, 1963, 34, 371–376.

Lipsitt, L. P., Kaye, H., and Bosack, T. N. Enhancement of neo-natal sucking through reinforcement. *Journal of Experimental Child Psychology*, 1966, 4, 163–168.

Lloyd, R. E. Parent-youth conflicts of college students. *Sociology and Social Research*, 1954, 38, 227–230.

Lorenz, K. *King Solomon's ring*. London: Methuen, 1952.

Louria, D. *Nightmare drugs*. New York: Pocket Books, 1966.

Luckey, E. B. and Nass, G. D. The comparison of sexual attitudes and behavior in an international sample. *Journal of Marriage and the Family*, 1969, 31, 364–378.

Lunneborg, P. W. Birth order, aptitude and achievement. *Journal of Consulting and Clinical Psychology*, 1968, 32, 101.

Luria, A. R. Speech development and the formation of mental processes. In *Psychological Science in the U.S.S.R.*, Vol. 1, Scientific Council of the Institute of Psychology, Academy of Pedagogical Sciences RSFSR, Moscow, B. G. Ananyev et al. (Eds.), 1959, 704–788.

Luria, A. R. The development of the regulatory role of speech. From Luria, A. R., *The role of speech in the regulation of normal and abnormal behavior*. New York: The Liveright Pub. Corp., 1961.

Maccoby, E. E. Effects of the mass media. In Hoffman, M. L. and Hoffman, L. W. (Eds.), *Review of Child Development Research*, Vol. 1., New York: Russell Sage Foundation, 1964, 323–348.

Malzberg, B. Some statistical aspects of mongolism. *American Journal of Mental Deficiency*, 1950, 54, 266–281.

Manosevitz, N., Lindzey, G., and Thiessen, B. D. *Behavioral genetics: Method and research*. New York: Appleton-Century-Crofts, 1969.

Maris, R. W. *Forces in urban suicide*. Homewood, Ill.: Dorsey Press, 1969.

Maslow, A. H. *Motivation and personality*. New York: Harper & Row, 1954.

McCarthy, D. Language development of the preschool child. *Institute of Child Welfare Monograph Series*, No. 4. Minneapolis: University of Minnesota Press, 1930.

McCarthy, D. Language development. In L. Carmichael (Ed.), *Manual of Child Psychology*. (2nd Ed.) New York: John Wiley, 1954, 492–630.

McCarthy, D. Language development. *Monographs of the Society for Research in Child Development*, 1960, 25, 5–14.

McClelland, D. C. *Personality*. New York: William Sloane, 1951.

McClelland, D. C. (Ed.) *Studies in motivation*. New York: Appleton-Century-Crofts, 1955.

McClelland, D. C. The importance of early learning and the formation of motives. In J. W. Atkinson (Ed.), *Motives in fantasy, action and society*. Princeton, N.J.: D. Van Nostrand, 1958, 437–452.

McClelland, D. C. and Winter, D. G. *Motivating economic achievement*. New York: The Free Press, 1969.

McCord, W. and McCord, J. *Psychopathy and delinquency*. New York: Grune & Stratton, 1956.

McCurdy, H. G. The childhood pattern of genius. *Journal of the Elisha Mitchell Scientific Society*, 1957, 73, 448–462.

McDougall, W. *An introduction to social psychology*. London: Methuen, 1908.

McGraw, M. B. *The neuromuscular maturation of the human infant*. New York: Columbia University Press, 1943.

McNeil, E. B. *Human socialization*. Belmont, Calif.: Brooks/Cole, 1969.

Meacham, M. L. and Wiesen, A. E. *Changing classroom behavior: A manual for precision teaching*. Scranton, Penn.: International Textbook Company, 1969.

Mead, M. *Sex and temperament in three primitive societies*. New York: New American Library, 1935.

Meissner, S. J. Parental interaction of the adolescent boy. *Journal of Genetic Psychology*, 1965, 107, 225–233.

Melton, A. W. *Categories of human learning*. New York: Academic Press, 1964.

Milgram, S. Behavioral study of obedience. *Journal of Abnormal and Social Psychology,* 1963, 67, 371–378.

Milgram, S. Some conditions of obedience and disobedience to authority. *Human Relations,* 1965, 18, 67–76.

Miller, N. E. Learnable drives and rewards. In S. S. Stevens (Ed.), *Handbook of experimental psychology.* New York: John Wiley, 1951.

Miller, N. E. and Dollard, J. C. *Social learning and imitation.* New Haven: Yale University Press, 1941.

Moffitt, A. R. Consonant cue perception by 20–24 week old infants. *Child Development,* 1971, 42, 717–731.

Montessori, M. *The Montessori method.* New York: Frederick A. Stokes, 1912.

Montessori, M. *Spontaneous activity in education.* New York: Schocken Books, 1965.

Montessori, M. *The absorbent mind.* New York: Holt, Rinehart & Winston, 1967.

Moody, T. A. *Genetics of man.* New York: W. W. Norton, 1967.

Morgan, C. L. *Introduction to comparative psychology.* London: Scott, 1894.

Morgan, C. L. *Habit and instinct.* London: Arnold, 1896.

Moss, H. A. Early environmental effects: Mother-child relations. In Spencer, T. D. and Kass, N. (Eds.), *Perspectives in child psychology.* New York: McGraw-Hill, 1970, 2–34.

Mowat, Farley. *People of the deer.* New York: Little, Brown & Co., 1952.

Munsinger, H. *Fundamentals of child development.* New York: Holt, Rinehart & Winston, 1971.

Murdock, G. P. *Social structure.* New York: The Macmillan Co., 1949.

Murray, E. J. *Motivation and emotion.* Englewood Cliffs, N.J.: Prentice-Hall, 1964.

Murray, H. A. *Explorations in personality.* New York: Oxford University Press, 1938.

Newman, H. H., Freeman, F. N., and Holzinger, K. J. *Twins: A study of heredity and environment.* Chicago: University of Chicago Press, 1937.

Newsweek, January 6, 1969, p. 37.

Nichols, M. M. Acute alcohol withdrawal syndrome in a newborn. *American Journal of Diseases of Children,* 1967, 113, 714–715.

Noyes, P. B. *My father's house: An Oneida boyhood.* New York: Farrar & Rinehart, 1937.

Osgood, C. E. A behavioristic analysis of perception and language as cognitive phenomena. In *Contemporary approaches of cognition.* Cambridge: Harvard University Press, 1957, 75–118. (a)

Osgood, C. E. Motivational dynamics of language behavior. In M. R. Jones (Ed.), *Nebraska Symposium on Motivation.* Lincoln: University of Nebraska Press, 1957, 348–423. (b)

Parten, M. B. Social participation among pre-school children. *Journal of Abnormal Social Psychology,* 1932, 27, 243–270.

Pavlov, I. P. *Conditioned reflexes.* London: Oxford University Press, 1927.

Peck, M. L. Paper presented at the 3rd annual American Association of Suicidologists Convention, San Francisco, 1970. (Cited in Ruch, F. L. and Zimbardo, P. G., 1971).

Peckham, C. H. and King, R. W. A study of intercurrent conditions observed during pregnancy. *American Journal of Obstetrics and Gynaecology,* 1963, 87, 609–624.

Peel, E. A. *The pupil's thinking.* London: Oldbourne, 1960.

Penrose, L. S. *The biology of mental defect.* London: Sedgwick & Jackson, 1949.

Perkins, H. V. *Human Development and Learning.* Belmont, Calif.: Wadsworth Publishing Co., 1969.

Perline, I. H. and Levinsky, D. Controlling maladaptive classroom behavior in the severely retarded. *American Journal of Mental Deficiency,* 1968, 73, 74–78.

Phillips, J. L. *The origins of intellect*. San Francisco: W. H. Freeman, 1969.

Piaget, J. *The moral judgment of the child*. London: Kegan Paul, 1932.

Piaget, J. and Inhelder, B. *Le développement des quantités chez l'enfant*. Neûchatel: Delachaux et Niestle, 1941.

Piaget, J. *Play, dreams and imitation in childhood*. New York: W. W. Norton, 1951.

Piaget, J. *The origins of intelligence in children*. New York: International Universities Press, 1952.

Piaget, J. *The construction of reality in the child*. New York: Basic Books, 1954.

Piaget, J. *Logic and psychology*. New York: Basic Books, 1957.

Piaget, J. *On the development of memory and identity*. Worcester, Mass.: Clark University Press, 1968.

Piddington, R. *An introduction to social anthropology*. Vol. 2. Edinborough: Oliver and Boyd, 1957.

Pikunas, J. *Human development: A science of growth*. (2nd ed.) New York: McGraw-Hill, 1969.

Pines, M. *Revolution in learning: The years from birth to six*. New York: Harper & Row, 1966.

Potter, E. L. Pregnancy. In M. Fishbein and R. J. R. Kennedy (Eds.), *Modern marriage and family living*. Fair Lawn, N.J.: Oxford University Press, 1957, 378–386.

Prado, W. Appraisal of performance as a function of the relative-ego-involvement of children and adolescents. Unpublished doctoral dissertation, University of Oklahoma, 1958.

Pratt, K. C. The effects of repeated visual stimulation on the activity of newborn infants. *Journal of Genetic Psychology*, 1934, 44, 117–126.

Pratt, K. C. The neonate. In L. Carmichel (Ed.), *Manual of child psychology*. (2nd Ed.) New York: John Wiley, 1954, 215–291.

Premack, D. Reinforcement theory. In Levine, D. (Ed.), *Nebraska symposium on motivation*. University of Nebraska Press, 1965, 123–180.

Pyles, M. K. Verbalization as a factor in learning. *Child Development*, 1932, 3, 108–113.

Railo, W. S. Physical and mental endurance, and physical fitness and intellectual achievement. Unpublished reports, Norwegian College of Physical Education and Sports, Oslo, Norway, 1968. (Cited in Cratty, 1970).

Rambusch, N. M. *Learning how to learn: An American approach to Montessori*. Baltimore: Helicon, 1962.

Rank, O. *The trauma of birth*. New York: Harcourt, Brace & World, 1929.

Raths, L. E. and Burrell, A. P. *Understanding the problem child*. West Orange, New Jersey: The Economics Press, 1963.

Razran, G. The observable unconscious, and the inferrable conscious. In Current Soviet psycho-physiology: Interoceptive conditioning, semantic conditioning, and the orienting reflex. *Psychological Review*, 1961, 68, 99–109.

Read, G. D. *Childbirth without fear*. New York: Harper, 1944 (Revised, 1953).

Read, K. H. *The nursery school: A human relations laboratory*. (4th Ed.) Philadelphia: W. B. Saunders, 1966.

Reese, H. W. and Lipsitt, L. O. *Experimental child psychology*. New York: Academic Press, 1970.

Reidford, P. Recent developments in preschool education. In *Psychology and early education: Papers presented at the OISE conference on preschool education*, edited by D. W. Brison and J. Hill. The Ontario Institute for Studies in Education, Monograph Series No. 4, 1968, 5–16.

Rogers, C. R. *Client-centered therapy: Its current practice, its implications, and theory*. Boston: Houghton Mifflin, 1951.

Rogers, C. R. *Freedom to learn*. Columbus, Ohio: Charles E. Merrill, 1969.

Rogers, D. *Child psychology*. Belmont, Calif.: Brooks/Cole, 1969.

Rosen, B. C. and D'Andrade, R. The psycho-social origins of achievement motivation. *Sociometry*, 1959, 22, 185–195, 215–218.

Rosenthal, R. Experimenter expectancy and the reassuring nature of the null hypothesis decision procedure. *Psychological Bulletin Monographs Supplement,* 1969–70, 30–47.

Rosenthal, R. and Jacobson, L. *Pygmalion in the classroom: Teacher expectations and pupils' intellectual development.* New York: Holt, Rinehart & Winston, 1968. (a)

Rosenthal, R. and Jacobson, L. Teacher expectations for the disadvantaged. *Scientific American,* April, 1968. (b)

Rosenzweig, S. Available methods for studying personality. *Journal of Psychology,* 1949, 28, 345–368.

Ruch, S. L. and Zimbardo, P. G. *Psychology and life.* (8th Ed.) Glenview, Ill.: Scott, Foresman, 1971.

Sampson, E. E. Birth order, need achievement, and conformity. *Journal of Abnormal and Social Psychology,* 1962, 64, 155–159.

Sarason, S. B., Davidson, K. S., Lighthall, F. F., Waite, R. R., and Ruebush, B. K. *Anxiety in elementary school children.* New York: John Wiley, 1960.

Schachter, S. Birth order, eminence, and higher education. *American Sociological Review,* 1963, 28, 757–768.

Schaffer, H. R., and Emerson, P. E. The development of social attachment in infancy. *Monographs of the Society for Research in Child Development,* 1964, 29, No. 94.

Schaller, G. B. *The mountain gorilla.* Chicago: Chicago University Press, 1963.

Scheinfeld, A. *The human heredity handbook.* Philadelphia: Lippincott, 1956.

Schneirla, T. C. and Rosenblatt, J. S. *American Journal of Orthopsychiatry,* 1960, 31, 113.

Schramm, W., Lyle, J., and Parker, E. G. *Television in the lives of our children.* Stanford, Calif.: Stanford University Press, 1961.

Schrier, A. M., Harlow, H. S., and Stollnitz, F. (Eds.) *Behavior of nonhuman primates: Modern research trends.* Vol. 1. New York: Academic Press, 1965.

Schultz, D. P. *Panic behavior.* New York: Random House, 1964.

Scott, J. P. Critical periods in behavioral development. *Science,* 1962, 138, 949–958.

Searle, L. V. The organization of hereditary maze-brightness and maze-dullness. *Genetic Psychology Monographs,* 1949, 39, 279–325.

Sears, R. R., Maccoby, E. P., and Lewin, H. *Patterns of child rearing.* Evanston: Row, Peterson, 1957.

Seiden, R. H. Campus tragedy: A study of students' suicide. *Journal of Abnormal Psychology,* 1966, 71, 389–399.

Sherman, M. *Hollow folk.* New York: Crowell, 1933.

Sherman, M. and Key, C. B. The intelligence of isolated mountain children. *Child Development,* 1932, 3, 279–290.

Sherman, M. and Sherman, I. C. *The process of human behavior.* New York: W. W. Norton, 1929.

Shirley, M. M. The first two years: A study of 25 babies, Vol. I. Postural and locomotor development. *Institute of Child Welfare Monographs,* Series No. 6. Minneapolis: University of Minnesota Press, 1933.

Shuttleworth, F. K. The physical and mental growth of girls and boys age 6 to 19 in relation to age at maximum growth. *Monographs of the Society for Research in Child Development,* 1939, 4, No. 3.

Singh, J. A. and Zingg, R. N. *Wolf-children and feral man.* New York: Harper, 1942.

Siqueland, E. R. Reinforcement patterns and extinction in human newborns. *Journal of Experimental Child Psychology,* 1968, 6, 431–442.

Skeels, H. M., Updgraff, R., Wellman, B. L., and Williams, H. M. A study of environmental stimulation: An orphanage preschool project. *University of Iowa Studies in Child Welfare,* 1938, 15, No. 4.

Skeels, H. M. Adult status of children with contrasting early life experiences.

Monograph of the Society for Research in Child Development, 1966, 31, No. 3.

Skeels, H. M. and Skodak, M. Techniques for a high yield followup study in the field. *Public Health Reports,* 1965, 80, 249–257.

Skinner, B. G. How to teach animals. *Scientific American,* 1951, 185, 26–29.

Skinner, B. F. *Verbal behavior.* New York: Appleton-Century-Crofts, 1957.

Skinner, B. F. *Cumulative record.* (Rev. Ed.) New York: Appleton-Century-Crofts, 1961.

Smart, M. S. and Smart, R. C. *Children: Development and relationships.* New York: The Macmillan Co., 1967.

Smedslund, J. The acquisition of conservation of substance and weight in children, I. Introduction. *Scandinavian Journal of Psychology,* 1961, 2, 11–20. (a)

Smedslund, J. The acquisition of conservation of substance and weight in children, II. External reinforcement of conservation of weight and of operations of addition and subtraction. *Scandinavian Journal of Psychology,* 1961, 2, 71–84. (b)

Smedslund, J. The acquisition of conservation of substance and weight in children, III. Extinction of conservation of weight acquired "normally" and by means of empirical controls on a balance scale. *Scandinavian Journal of Psychology,* 1961, 2, 85–87. (c)

Smedslund, J. The acquisition of conservation of substance and weight in children, IV. An attempt at extinction of visual components of the weight concept. *Scandinavian Journal of Psychology,* 1961, 2, 153–155. (d)

Smedslund, J. The acquisition of conservation of substance and weight in children, V. Practice in conflict situations without external reinforcement. *Scandinavian Journal of Psychology,* 1961, 2, 156–160. (e)

Smith, C. P. *Achievement-related motives in children.* New York: Russell Sage Foundation, 1959.

Smith, G. H. Sociometric study of best-liked and least-liked children. *Elementary School Journal,* 1950, 51, 77–85.

Smith, M. E. An investigation of the development of the sentence and the extent of vocabulary in young children. *University of Iowa Studies in Child Welfare,* 1926, Vol. 3, No. 5.

Smith, M. E. Measurement of vocabularies of young bilingual children in both of the languages used. *Journal of Genetic Psychology,* 1949, 74, 305–310.

Smith, M. E. Word variety as a measure of bilingualism in pre-school children. *Journal of Genetic Psychology,* 1957, 90, 143–150.

Smith, M. K. Measurement of the size of general English vocabulary through the elementary grades and high school. *Genetic Psychology Monographs,* 1941, 24, 311–345.

Sokolov, A. N. Studies on the problem of the speech mechanisms in thinking. *Psychological Science in the U.S.S.R.,* Vol. 1, Scientific Council of the Institute of Psychology, Academy of Pedagogical Sciences, RSFSR, Moscow: B. G. Ananyev et al. (Eds.), 1959, 669–704.

Sontag, L. W. and Richard, T. W. Studies in fetal behavior, I. Fetal heart rate as a behavioral indicator. *Monographs of the Society for Research in Child Development,* 1938, 3, No. 4.

Southwick, C. H. *Primate social behavior.* New York: D. Van Nostrand, 1963.

Spelt, D. K. The conditioning of the human fetus in utero. *Journal of Experimental Psychology,* 1948, 38, 375–376.

Spitz, R. A. Hospitalism: An inquiry into the genesis of psychiatric conditions in early childhood, Part I. *Psychoanalytic Studies of the Child,* 1945, 1, 53–74.

Spitz, R. A. Unhappy and fatal outcomes of emotional deprivation and stress in infancy. In I. Galdston (Ed.), *Beyond the germ theory.* Health Education Council, 1954, 120–131.

Spock, B. *Baby and child care*. Richmond Hill, Ontario: Pocket Books of Canada Ltd., 1957.

Staats, A. W. and Staats, C. K. *Complex human behavior*. New York: Holt, Rinehart & Winston, 1963.

Stearns, G. Nutritional state of the mother prior to conception. *Journal of the American Medical Association,* 1958, 168, 1655–1659.

Stern, C. Hereditary factors affecting adoption. In *A Study of Adoption Practices,* Vol. 2, New York: Child Welfare League of America, 1956.

Stone, L. J. and Church, J. *Childhood and adolescence: A psychology of the growing person*. New York: Random House, 1968.

Strauss, A. *On social psychology: Selected papers*. Chicago: University of Chicago Press, 1964.

Tanner, J. M. *Growth at adolescence*. Springfield, Illinois: Charles C Thomas, 1955.

Taussig, H. B. A study of the German outbreak of phocomelia. The thalidomide syndrome. *Journal of the American Medical Association,* 1962, 180, 1106–1140.

Templin, M. C. *Certain language skills in children*. Minneapolis: University of Minnesota Press, 1957.

Terman, L. M. and Merrill, M. A. *Stanford-Binet intelligence scale*. Boston: Houghton Mifflin Co., 1960.

Thompson, H. Physical growth. In L. Carmichael (Ed.), *Manual of child psychology*. (2nd Ed.) New York: John Wiley, 1954.

Thompson, W. R. The inheritance and development of intelligence. In *Genetics and the inheritance of integrated neurological psychiatric patterns, Vol. XXXIII. Proceedings of the Association of Nervous Mental Diseases.* Baltimore: Williams and Wilkins, 1954.

Thompson, W. R. Influence of pre-natal maternal anxiety on emotionality in young rats. *Science,* 1957, 125, 698–699.

Thorndike, E. L. *Selected writings from a connectionist's psychology*. New York: Appleton-Century-Crofts, 1949.

Todd, V. E. and Heffernan, H. *The years before school: Guiding preschool children*. (2nd ed.) New York: The Macmillan Co., 1970.

Travis, L. D. Conservation acceleration through successive approximations. Unpublished master's thesis, University of Alberta, Edmonton, Alberta, 1969.

Trent, J. W. and Crais, J. L. Commitment and conformity in the American college. *Journal of Social Issues,* 1967, 22, 34–51.

Trent, J. W. and Medsker, L. L. *Beyond high school: A study of 10,000 high school graduates*. Berkeley, Calif.: Center for Research and Development in Higher Education, University of California, 1967.

Tryon, R. C. Genetic differences in maze learning in rats. *Yearbook of the National Society for Studies in Education,* 1940, 39, 111–119.

Tuddenham, R. D. Studies in reputation: III. Correlates of popularity among elementary school children. *Journal of Educational Psychology,* 1951, 42, 257–276.

Vandenberg, S. G. Hereditary factors in normal personality traits (as measured by inventories). In J. Wortis (Ed.), *Recent advances in biological psychiatry,* Vol. 9, New York: Plenum Press, 1967.

Verplanck, W. S. The control of the content of conversation: Reinforcement of statements of opinion. *Journal of Abnormal and Social Psychology,* 1955, 51, 668–676.

Vincent, C. E. Teenage unwed mothers in American society. *Journal of Social Issues,* 1966, 22, 22–23.

Vincow, A. and Hackel, A. Neonatal narcotic addiction. *General Practitioner,* 1960, 22, 90.

Vygotsky, L. S. *Thought and language*. (Ed. and trans. by Eugenia Hanfmann and Gertrude Vakar). New York: John Wiley, 1962.

Walker, E. L. *Conditioning and instrumental learning.* Belmont, Calif.: Brooks/Cole, 1968.

Walsh, M. E. The relation of nursery school training to the development of certain personality traits. *Child Development,* 1931, 2, 72–73.

Walters, R. H. and Llewellyn, T. E. Enhancement of punitiveness by visual and audiovisual displays. *Canadian Journal of Psychology,* 1963, 17, 244–255.

Walters, R. H., Llewellyn, T. E., and Acker, C. W. Enhancement of punitive behavior by audiovisual displays. *Science,* 1962, 136, 872–873.

Warren, J. R. Birth order and social behavior. *Psychological Bulletin,* 1966, 65, 38–49. ·

Watson, E. H. and Lowrey, G. H. *Growth and development of children.* (5th Ed.) Chicago: Yearbook Medical Publishers, 1967.

Watson, J. B. *Behavior: An introduction to comparative psychology.* New York: Holt, Rinehart & Winston, 1914.

Watson, J. B. *Behaviorism.* (2nd Ed.) Chicago: University of Chicago Press, 1930.

Watson, J. B. and Rayner, R. Conditioned emotional reactions. *Journal of Experimental Psychology,* 1920, 3, 1–14.

Watson, J. D. Involvement of RNA in the synthesis of proteins. *Science,* 1963, 140, 17–26.

Watson, J. D. and Crick, F. H. The structure of DNA. *Cold Spring Harbour Symposium on Quantitative Biology,* 1953, 18, 123–131.

Weber, E. *Early childhood education: Perspectives on change.* Belmont, Calif.: Wadsworth Publishing Co., 1970.

Weikart, D. P., Lambie, D. Z., Wozniak, R., Hull, W., Miller, N., and Jeffs, M. Ypsilanti-Carnegie Infant Education Project: Progress Report, Department of Research and Development, Ypsilanti Public Schools, Ypsilanti, Michigan, September, 1969.

Weil, A. T., Zinberg, N. E., and Nelson, J. M. Clinical and psychological effects of marijuana in man. *Science,* 1968, 162, 1234–1242.

Weisberg, P. Social and non-social conditioning of infant vocalizations. *Child Development,* 1963, 34, 377–388.

Wertham, F. *Seduction of the innocent.* New York: Rinehart & Co., 1954.

Wertheimer, M. Psychomotor co-ordination of auditory and visual space at birth. *Science,* 1961, 134, 1692.

West, S. Sibling configurations of scientists. *American Journal of Sociology,* 1960, 66, 268–274.

Whiting, H. T. A. *Acquiring ball skill, a psychological interpretation.* London: G. Bell & Sons, 1969.

Whorf, B. L. *Language, thought and reality.* New York: John Wiley, 1969.

Williams, C. D. and Kuchta, J. C. Exploratory behavior in two mazes with dissimilar alternatives. *Journal of Comparative and Physiological Psychology,* 1957, 50, 509–513.

Wingfield, A. H. *Twins and orphans: The inheritance of intelligence.* London: Dent, 1928.

Winterbottom, M. R. The relation of need for achievement to learning experiences in independence and mastery. In J. W. Atkinson, *Motives in Fantasy, Action and Society.* Princeton, N.J.: D. Van Nostrand, 1958, 453–478.

Wolff, M. and Stein, A. Headstart six months later. *Phi Delta Kappan,* 1967, 48, 349–350.

Woods, P. J. and Jennings, S. Response to environmental change: A further confirmation. *Psychological Reports,* 1959, 5, 560.

Wortis, H. Social class and pre-mature birth. *Social Casework,* 1963, 45, 451–453.

Wozny, J. R. Psychological and sociological correlates of use and nonuse of marijuana. Unpublished masters thesis, University of Alberta, Edmonton, Alberta, 1971.

Wright, H. F. Observational child study. In Mussen, P. H. (Ed.), *Handbook of research methods in child development*. New York: John Wiley, 1960, 71–139.

Wright, J. C. Cited as personal communication, 1969, in Nash, J. *Developmental psychology: A psycho-biological approach*. Englewood Cliffs, N.J.: Prentice-Hall, 1970, 453.

Yarrow, L. J. Research in dimensions of early maternal care. *Merrill-Palmer Quarterly*, 1963, 9, 101–114.

Zingg, R. N. Reply to Professor Dennis. *American Journal of Psychology*, 1941, 54, 432–435.

Zubek, J. P. *Sensory deprivation: Fifteen years of research*. New York: Appleton-Century-Crofts, 1969.

Zuckerman, S. *The social life of monkeys and apes*. London: Routledge & Kegan Paul Ltd., 1932.

Index